KT-221-406

Sophie Grigson's
taste of the times

Sophie Grigson's
taste of

Photographs by Jess Koppel

the times

for Annabel

with love and thanks for all her help, support and friendship

This book is published to accompany the television series entitled *Sophie Grigson's Taste of the Times* which was first broadcast in 1997. The series was produced by Wall to Wall Television for Channel 4.

Executive Producer: Jane Root
Producer: Nicky Spencer
Director: Peter Jamieson

Published by Network Books,
an imprint of BBC Worldwide Publishing.
BBC Worldwide Limited, Woodlands,
80 Wood Lane, London W12 0TT

First published 1997
Reprinted 1997

ISBN 0 563 38325 9

Designed by Harry Green

Photographs © Jess Koppel
Styling by Roisin Nield
Home economist: Lyn Rutherford

The recipe for *Olive Oil and Sauternes Cake* on page 213 is from *Chez Panisse Menu Cookbook* by Alice Waters. Published by Random House. Copyright © 1982 by Alice L. Waters.

Set in Gill and Century Expanded
Printed in Great Britain by Cambus Litho Ltd, East Kilbride
Bound in Great Britain by Hunter and Foulis Ltd, Edinburgh
Colour separations by Radstock Reproductions Ltd, Midsomer Norton
Jacket printed by Lawrence Allen Ltd, Weston-super-Mare

contents

cook's notes

Over the past year, I've successfully managed to train myself to use metric measurements, rather than the old imperial, and I'm a convert – they really are very easy to work with. Having said that, whether you think metric or imperial, the important thing is to stick with one or the other as you weigh and measure ingredients for a recipe.

All spoon measurements in this book are rounded, unless otherwise stated. I use a 15 ml tablespoon and a 5 ml teaspoon.

Treat all timings as approximate guidelines. Ovens vary immensely, and the exact size of a saucepan or frying-pan will affect cooking times in many cases. Judge doneness by eye, by taste and by common sense.

All eggs are the old size 2 which is the new 'large' (and in my kitchen, free range). Pepper and nutmeg should always be freshly ground as needed. Herbs are fresh, unless dried are stipulated in the ingredients list. Seasonings are always a personal matter, and remember that herbs vary in intensity so sometimes you will need to add more to achieve the same result.

acknowledgements

Where to begin? At the beginning, I suppose, and that is with Channel 4 and Wall to Wall Television, who, together, made this book and the television series that it accompanies possible. Channel 4's Sylvia Hines gave the project the go-ahead, and Mark Galloway took it forward with encouraging enthusiasm. Jane Root and Helen Fletcher at Wall to Wall worked with me on the original idea. The entire production team transformed my ramblings into coherent programmes, but I'd especially like to thank director Peter Jamieson for making them look so stylish and guiding me tactfully in the right directions, and the two researchers, Anna Richardson and Susie Worster, for finding such marvellous interviewees.

I'm extraordinarily lucky to have had an editor like Heather Holden-Brown at Network Books, whose surprising confidence that I can deliver readable copy on time somehow makes it achievable. I'd also like to thank Doug Young, for gathering together the bits of book, and creative director, Frank Phillips. Once again, the photography is remarkable and, once again, it is my dear friend Jess Koppel who has made it so, together with home economist Lyn Rutherford and food stylist Roisin Nield.

Back at the ranch, I know I could not have completed this book without the help of Annabel Hartog who has tested most of the recipes, a few of them several times over, and Michele King who keeps me organized and laughing. Everything, but everything, would collapse without Jennine Bierton, who looks after the children with endless patience and love, and has become such an integral part of our lives. My husband, William Black, has been wonderful, particularly as deadlines approached. Thank you, again, for baby-sitting, hoovering, the emergency dash to the stationers, sorting out the printer, staying up half the night to help me print and collate, and delivering the manuscript.

introduction

It happens all the time. The shopper, wheeling his or her trolley around the supermarket fills up on all the usual stuff – bread and potatoes, a few green vegetables, loo paper and washing powder, apples and oranges – but pauses every now and then as the eye catches sight of something a little more intriguing on the shelf. That jar of sun-dried tomatoes perhaps, or a pack of lemon grass hanging around with the more common herbs, or a tub of crème fraiche loitering in the dairy cabinet ... I've watched people as they hesitate, then pass on by. In a split second, they quash curiosity and temptation and move on to the next comfortingly day-to-day product.

To buy or not to buy? That is the question. And hardly surprising – so many new products from all over the world are making their way into our shops and supermarkets, filtering down from the menus of chefs and gastronomes into the common arena. It is all undoubtedly confusing. What on earth does one do with something as strange-looking as star anise or the tangle-rooted celeriac? Why are those bars of plain de luxe chocolate so very expensive? Is it worth splashing out on balsamic vinegar and how do you choose a good one? Lack of knowledge is the stumbling block.

In *Taste of the Times* I hope to redress that lack of knowledge. I've chosen over 70 thoroughly modern ingredients (though most of them have a long and venerable history somewhere in the world) and have tried to give enough information about them to enable anyone interested in eating well the confidence to buy and use them. Some will be familiar, some more unusual, but all are relatively easily available from good supermarkets and delicatessens. It is by no means a comprehensive collection (my original list was twice as long) but it covers many items that I, for one, would hate to be without now that I know they can transform, often very simply, the food we eat at home. Many of the recipes are simple, some are a touch more complicated, but there is nothing tricky. I hope that with this book in hand, cooks of all levels will give in to temptation and try some of those ingredients they've noticed but never bought, or discover new ways to cook with familiar ingredients.

Sophie Grigson

coriander

sage

herbs

kaffir
lime leaves
lemon
grass
basil

lemon grass

I first encountered Thai food when I was about 20, at a time when Thai restaurants were scarce (there were only two, I think, in the whole of London and very few more, I imagine, elsewhere in Britain). That first meal was a startling, overwhelming experience, full of remarkable perfumes and flavours that were quite thrillingly new. We emerged from the restaurant floating on a cloud, delighted and marvelling at something so very special. Later, when I had learned enough about Thai cooking to begin to unravel the complex ingredients, I realized that it was the twin power of lemon grass and coriander, above all others, that had hooked me and sent me into seventh heaven.

Now, of course, Thai restaurants have sprung up left, right and centre. Coriander is as easy to buy as basil and even lemon grass has made its way into supermarkets. For all that, lemon grass still seems a magical substance to me, with its hidden fragrance of lemon oil mixed with a hint of ginger and mint.

Lemon grass is indeed a grass-like plant that grows prolifically in big clumps in warm climates. One single stem planted at the beginning of the growing season will have multiplied up to a battalion of fifty or so by the end. The grassy blades are discarded, in favour of the fleshy, tightly furled lower stems. The plant is native to India, though it doesn't feature strongly in Indian cooking. Sri Lankans have developed more of a taste for it but it is the countries of south-east Asia – Indonesia (where they believe that lemon grass picked by pure young girls has a greater fragrance), Thailand, Vietnam and Malaysia – where it is used with the most aplomb and grace.

Lemon grass has an enormous list of medicinal uses and the oil extracted from the stems is used in perfumery – especially in the manufacture of artificial violet perfume, curiously enough. Next time you smell lemon grass, see if you can catch a fleeting whiff of violet in it. On one of the few occasions that I've been laid low with 'traveller's tummy', some of the pain was soothed away with lemon grass tea; very calming and restorative. Apparently, Queen Victoria was known to sip a glass or two of lemon grass tea every now and then.

Buying and Storing Lemon Grass

Some supermarkets are a little naughty when it comes to selling lemon grass. They cut the useful stem in half and all too often lay two of the upper, less fragrant, portions in a pack, while the fatter lower part seems to be siphoned off elsewhere – it certainly seems far less common to find a matching pack with two of the lower halves snuggling up together but perhaps that is because wise shoppers get there early and spirit them away.

If you can, buy full-length lemon grass from a shop where you can pick out your own stems, still with green hints to them, firm but not dried out, brown or crinkly. If you search around, you may even find one or two with straggles of root and these can be grown on your kitchen windowsill. Pop into water for a few days until the roots multiply and then plant in a large pot. Alternatively, dip straight into rooting powder and plant. If they take, you soon won't have to worry about halved stalks.

Lemon grass, being fairly tough stuff, keeps well in a sealed plastic bag, stashed in the vegetable drawer of the fridge.

Dried lemon grass never has quite the vivacity and enchantment of the fresh stuff but it can play a useful role as emergency back-up, if you like oriental foods but have trouble buying the fresh ingredients near you. It will need to be soaked in warm water for at least an hour before using.

Using Lemon Grass

The fullest flavour lies in the lower, fatter 10 cm (4 inches) or so of the stem and this is what I use for most recipes. The upper length is less effective but has its uses. Sliced up, it can be infused in hot water to make a lemon grass tea or, if you are having a barbecue, make a criss-cross cut at the bottom and then use as a brush to baste foods as they cook, imparting a gentle lemon fragrance. Trendy chefs also use it rather like a skewer, threading pieces of chicken or seafood on to it (you'll need to help by making slits in the food with a knife) before grilling, which is fine if you can lay your hands on a big bundle of lemon grass.

Back to that lower part. There are several ways of preparing it, depending on the dish you are making. First of all, you will need to peel away one or two of the toughest outer layers. For soups and stews, cut it in half and then bash and bruise it flat, with either a wooden rolling pin or the flat of a knife or cleaver. This method releases the juices but means that the chunks of lemon grass can easily be located (think of them rather like bay leaves) and removed when their job is done.

Where the lemon grass is going into a salad or is to be pounded to a paste with other ingredients, you will need to remove another layer or two and then slice what remains very, very thinly, across the tough grain, so that it is not too much of a chewy mouthful.

Butternut Squash with Lemon Grass

A recipe inspired by Vietnamese cooking but made with sweet, orange butternut squash and chunks of red onion. Serve it with rice or naan bread.

SERVES 6

2 medium-sized butternut squash, weighing about 1.5 kg (3 lb) in total

2 red onions

75 g (2½ oz) caster sugar

3 tablespoons sunflower or vegetable oil

5 garlic cloves, sliced

1.5 cm (¾ inch) piece of fresh ginger, finely chopped

45 g (1½ oz) prepared, finely chopped lemon grass

3 tablespoons fish sauce

Salt and cayenne pepper or freshly ground black pepper

4 spring onions, finely chopped, to garnish

Lime wedges, to serve

Cut the butternut squash into rings about 2.5 cm (1 inch) thick, then cut off the rind and remove the seeds. Cut the flesh into cubes. Cut each onion into eight wedges, slicing from stalk to root so that the wedges stay more or less together. Put 60 g (2 oz) of the sugar into a small pan with 3 tablespoons of water. Stir over a moderate heat until the sugar has completely dissolved. Stop stirring, raise the heat and boil hard until the syrup cooks to a rich, hazelnut-brown caramel. At arm's length, pour in 4 tablespoons of water. Swirl the pan to mix in and then stir. If it is lumpy, warm gently, stirring, to melt the lumps.

Heat the oil over a high heat and add the onion wedges. Fry briskly until well browned on both the cut sides. Lift the onion out and reserve. Now add the butternut squash and a pinch of salt. Fry until the squash is patched with brown. Add the garlic and ginger and continue cooking for a minute or so. Add the lemon grass and a scant ¼ teaspoon of cayenne pepper or black pepper. Fry for a minute and then return the onion to the pan, along with the fish sauce, remaining sugar and 1 tablespoon of the caramel mixture. Stir and then add another 300 ml (10 fl oz) of water. Half cover and leave to simmer gently for about 30 minutes, until the butternut squash and onion are tender. Sprinkle over the spring onions and serve with the lime wedges.

Grilled Chicken Thighs with Lemon Grass

A simple recipe from Vietnam, where lemon grass is used extensively and joyfully. Pork chops can be substituted for the chicken thighs.

SERVES 4

8 boneless, skinless chicken thighs

For the marinade:

2 garlic cloves, chopped
2 small shallots, chopped
1 tablespoon caster sugar
3 lemon grass stems, trimmed, bruised and finely chopped
1 tablespoon fish sauce
Salt and pepper

For the dipping sauce:

2 garlic cloves, chopped
1 fresh red chilli, de-seeded and finely chopped
1 cm (½ inch) piece of fresh ginger, roughly chopped
2 tablespoons caster sugar
Juice of 1 lime
4 tablespoons rice vinegar or cider vinegar
4 tablespoons fish sauce

To make the dipping sauce, pound the garlic, chilli, ginger and sugar to a paste in a mortar, with a pestle. Stir in the remaining ingredients, with 3 tablespoons of water.

For the marinade, again pound the garlic with the shallots and the sugar. Add the lemon grass and give that a few poundings as well. Mix in the remaining ingredients and spoon over the chicken thighs. Leave to marinate for at least an hour or, better still, overnight, turning occasionally.

Cook the meat under a thoroughly pre-heated grill (or on the barbecue) for about 5–8 minutes on each side, until cooked through and patched with brown. Serve immediately, with the dipping sauce.

Coconut Ice Cream with Lemon Grass Syrup

This is a great combination of cool, mild ice cream with a perfumed sauce. To make it even more sensational, serve with slices of ripe mango. If you are short of time, replace the coconut ice cream with a scoop of high-quality vanilla ice cream.

The syrup can also be sharpened with lemon juice and then drizzled over a plain cake, such as a pound cake (make a few holes in it with a skewer first), as it comes hot from the oven. Leave to soak up the syrup and serve with crème fraiche or Greek yoghurt or, indeed, with ice cream. It can also be used to make a delicious lemonade (see page 15). Coconut cream is a thick liquid that comes in small 200 ml (7 fl oz) cartons and is *not* the same as the solid blocks of creamed coconut.

SERVES 4

For the syrup:

3 lemon grass stems, trimmed, bruised and thinly sliced

250 g (9 oz) caster sugar

For the coconut ice cream:

400 ml (14 fl oz) tin of coconut milk

1 carton coconut cream

1 vanilla pod, slit open

4 egg yolks

3 tablespoons light muscovado sugar

250 ml (9 fl oz) double cream

To make the lemon grass syrup, put the lemon grass, sugar and 300 ml (10 fl oz) of water in a pan and stir over a medium heat until the sugar has completely dissolved. Bring up to the boil and simmer gently for 5 minutes. Draw off the heat and leave to cool, then strain.

To make the ice cream, put the coconut milk and coconut cream into a pan with the vanilla pod and bring slowly to the boil. Draw off the heat, cover and leave for 10 minutes.

Bring back to the boil. Whisk the egg yolks with the sugar until pale and frothy and then pour on the hot coconut milk, whisking constantly. Set the bowl over a pan of lazily simmering water, making sure that the base of the bowl does not come into contact with the water. Stir until the custard thickens enough to coat the back of the spoon. Take the bowl off the pan and stand it in some cold water, to halt the cooking process. Leave to cool and then remove the vanilla pod.

Whip the cream lightly until it begins to thicken and then stir it into the coconut custard. Freeze in an ice-cream maker, if you have one. If you don't, tip the mixture into a shallow freezer container, cover and place in the freezer, set to its lowest setting. Once the sides have set, break them up and push towards the centre of the container. Return to the freezer and repeat once more. Now leave the ice cream to set until almost, but not quite, solid. Take out and quickly process until smooth or, if you don't have a processor, beat as hard as your arms can manage to crush and smooth out all the ice crystals. Return to the freezer to finish freezing.

Transfer the ice cream to the fridge to soften 45 minutes before eating.

To serve, put two or three scoops of ice cream on each plate or in each bowl and spoon over some of the syrup.

Lemon Grass Lemonade

SERVES 6

4 lemons

120 g (4¼ oz) caster sugar

1 quantity of Lemon Grass Syrup (see page 14)

Fresh mint sprigs and ice cubes, to serve

Slice up the lemons, skin and all, discarding the end slices. Put into a food processor, with any juice. Add 60 g (2 oz) of the sugar and 150 ml (5 fl oz) of water. Process until well chopped and then tip into a sieve and strain, pressing down to extract as much liquid as possible. Scrape the debris back into the processor and repeat with the remaining sugar and another 150 ml (5 fl oz) of water. After you've strained this lot, return it to the processor one last time, add a final 150 ml (5 fl oz) of water but no sugar and process again. Strain out the juice for the last time and then discard the debris.

Stir in about two-thirds of the lemon grass syrup and taste. Add more syrup and water until the lemonade seems about right to you – not too sweet and retaining a pleasant edge but not so sharp that you wouldn't be able to down a whole refreshing glassful. Chill and then serve with lots of ice and a sprig of mint floating in each glass.

coriander

Coriander is a herb that shouts out to be used generously. It needs to be bought in big, verdant bunches that scent the journey home from the shop and tantalize you into cooking up something, anything, that can be strewn with its bright leaves. Unfortunately, few supermarkets (there are exceptions) think it worth stocking coriander in anything other than measly little plastic trays. To buy a sensible, sensuous bunch, you must be lucky enough to live within striking distance of a good Greek, Turkish, Middle Eastern or Asian grocery. There they will understand the addictive nature of this strange herb.

Strange? Yes, I think it is, since at first sniff and taste it has none of the obvious charms of warmly perfumed thyme or peppery scented basil. Even its name, pretty though coriander sounds, has an unprepossessing etymology, coming from the Greek for a bug, *koris*: the leaves are supposed to smell like bed bugs. Thankfully, I have no idea whether this is true, but it is not exactly encouraging.

For all that, coriander is a herb that creeps up on you. At first, it seems merely odd, though not unpleasant, and then it begins to fit certain dishes more than passingly well and, all of a sudden, the cravings begin. There you are, hooked and longing for more and where the recipe says '1 tablespoon chopped fresh coriander' you pile in three or four.

And this brings me to another strange thing about coriander. Why is it that, though the plant is native to southern Europe and conquers the palate so successfully, the only European country to have taken to the leaf in a big way is Portugal? I can't fathom it. Coriander seed, which admittedly is more obviously tempting with its orangey scent, is used in Italy and France, Greece and Turkey, but not a mention of the greenery. Most peculiar.

Portugal aside, coriander seems to have settled most happily into the cuisines of countries that have also embraced the chilli. Add garlic, too, and you have an instant, all-out attack of sensational flavour, which zips up even the most mundane of foods. This trio reappears time and time again, right across the world from Mexico to China, aided and abetted by other pungent additions to mark the exact location.

Primarily, coriander is a herb to throw in enthusiastically at the last minute so that its flavour remains fresh and sprightly. Cooking mutes the flavour and changes it but is not to be avoided altogether. The roots, if you can get them, or stems, pounded pesto-like to a paste, form the basis of Thai marinating pastes and curry bases; the Portuguese boil up a soup of coriander and potato; in the Middle East, whole stems are used like parsley to flavour stews.

In fact, there was a time when food writers suggested that parsley was an adequate substitute for coriander. This is a sin of which I, too, have been guilty in the past, though I've learnt the error of my ways. The two may look similar but, when it comes to cooking, parsley is too tame and too soothing to take the place of coriander. Parsley is an essential member of the supporting cast; coriander is a star.

Buying and Storing Coriander

Try to get it in bunches, if you can. It works out far cheaper, apart from anything else. Look for bright green leaves, perky and lively with crisp, juicy stalks. Avoid coriander that is limp and floppy or that has yellowing or black leaves. Take a closer look at the bunch, to check that it hasn't been padded out with grass and weeds – a rare occurrence but it does happen. When you get home, avoid the temptation to stand the bunch in a glass of water on the windowsill. I know it looks pretty but it won't last at all well (however, if you absolutely must display it, cut off the roots and the lowest inch or so of the stems before you plunge the bunch into water, to give it a marginally longer lifespan).

To store coriander, give the leaves a quick rinse, shake off excess water and then pop it into a plastic bag and keep in the vegetable drawer of the fridge, where it will last for a week or more. Check every few days and, if necessary, remove any yellowing leaves before they turn slimy.

If you can't buy proper bunches of coriander near you, it's worth trying to grow it for yourself. Make sure you have at least four plants and as the wider, flatter leaves appear, harvest and use frequently. The one disadvantage of grow-your-own coriander is that it has a tendency to run to seed as daylight hours lengthen. Some new varieties are being sold which have been bred for maximum leaf production and minimum legginess, and it is worth looking out for these. Otherwise, the best way to delay bolting is to pick over the plants regularly and frequently but, sooner or later, the second-stage feathery leaves will appear and the prettiest white flowers will rise up through them. These lacy little leaves have a good flavour, even if they are fiddly to strip from the stalks, while the flowers look enchanting on salads and floating in soups or anywhere else that seems appropriate. The fresh green seeds are a revelation – a bridge between the flavour of the leaves and the oranginess of the dried seed. Use them while they are around and then let the rest dry for your own supply of dried coriander seeds.

Coriander and Coconut Chutney

As you walk up the stairs of the Wandsworth Workshops you are assailed by waves of heavenly aromas. There is the sweet scent of baking and sugar from the Italian cake-makers (they turn out a very fine lemon cake, amongst others). And then, there are the fabulously fragrant and exotic wafts of spice and vinegar, mangoes and limes, coconuts and chillies, from Unit 133. Here Mrs Bassa and her daughter Niloufer turn out some of the finest, most irresistible Indian chutneys and relishes imaginable. I've always been rather partial to lime pickles but, when I tasted the Bassas', I vowed never to buy the commercial ones again. Luckily, they run a mail-order business, so I won't have to break that vow.

Niloufer also makes a superb, smooth, fresh coriander chutney, which takes her straight back to her childhood in Bombay. The recipe is a closely guarded secret but it begins with marvellous cratefuls of the finest coriander. So impressed was I with this that I decided to make my own version, inspired by their fine example. With a few precious hints and tips from Mrs Bassa's Indian Kitchen, I set to work and this is my version.

Serve the chutney as an accompaniment to curried dishes or stir a spoonful into a dutifully dull soup to give it some verve, or into an average curry to make it top of the class, or spread on bread, or smear over meat or fish before grilling.

It can be kept for up to two weeks in the fridge, in an airtight container, covered with a thin layer of oil (to exclude air) and sealed tightly. I find chutney improves in flavour after a few days. Stir in the oil before serving and cover with a fresh layer of oil, when returning to the fridge.

SERVES 10 MORE OR LESS

3 tablespoons desiccated coconut or 4 tablespoons freshly grated coconut
1 big bunch of fresh coriander
Fresh mint stems
2 tablespoons malt or white wine vinegar
4 tablespoons sunflower oil
1 teaspoon caster sugar
Salt

For the spice mixture:

1 teaspoon coriander seeds
1/2 teaspoon cumin seeds
1/2 teaspoon black peppercorns
1/4 teaspoon aniseed
1/2 teaspoon ground cinnamon

To make the spice mixture, dry-fry the coriander, cumin, pepper and aniseed in a heavy frying-pan over a moderate heat until they give off a heady aroma. Tip into a bowl and leave to cool. Grind to a powder, with the cinnamon.

Place desiccated coconut in a bowl and sprinkle with 3 tablespoons of warm water. Mix and leave for half an hour, to soften. If using fresh coconut, drill or tap holes into the coconut through two of its eyes. Drain out the coconut water (very refreshing). Crack open the coconut and prise out the flesh. Peel away the brown skin and then grate the flesh coarsely. You need 4 tablespoons, so you won't need to attack every last piece of coconut.

Trim off and discard the lower half of the coriander stems. Chop the remaining stems and leaves roughly. Strip a small handful of mint leaves off their stems and chop roughly.

Put the coriander, mint, coconut, two-thirds of the spice mixture and all the remaining ingredients in a food processor. Process to a smooth paste. Taste and adjust the seasoning, adding more spices if you wish, and then scrape into a bowl. Store in the fridge if not using immediately.

Sopa de Coentro

This Portuguese coriander and potato soup maximizes the potential of a bunch of coriander. First, the flavour of the stalks is extracted in the pan as the potatoes cook but the leaves go in right at the end, to preserve their fresh zip. It is a brilliantly simple soup.

SERVES 4–6

I small bunch of fresh coriander
2 onions, chopped
3 garlic cloves, chopped
3 tablespoons olive oil, plus a little extra to serve
900 g (2 lb) potatoes, peeled and cubed
Salt and pepper

Cut the stalks from the coriander and tie them in a bundle with string. Chop the leaves and reserve.

Fry the onions and garlic gently in the oil until tender, without browning. Add the potatoes and coriander stalks, stir and then cover and leave to sweat over a low heat for 5 minutes. Now add 1.2 litres (2 pints) of water, salt and pepper and bring up to the boil. Simmer until the potatoes are very tender. Remove and discard the coriander stalks. Pass the contents of the pan through a *mouli-légumes* (vegetable mill) or rub through a sieve. Only use a food processor if you have time to let the soup rest for a good few hours, otherwise it will be gluey.

Stir in the coriander leaves and re-heat gently, without boiling. Serve immediately, with an extra drizzle of olive oil poured over each bowlful.

Fried Eggs with Coriander, Cumin and Balsamic Vinegar

This dish of fried eggs, Latin-American style (with a dash of Italian vinegar), is totally sublime and very quick to make. It is perfect, reinvigorating supper material.

SERVES I

Olive oil
2 eggs
1/4 fresh red chilli, de-seeded and finely sliced
1/4 teaspoon cumin seeds
1/2 garlic clove, chopped
I or 2 slices of bread, toasted, to serve
1/2 teaspoon balsamic vinegar
Chopped fresh coriander
Coarse salt

Pour enough olive oil into a heavy frying-pan to cover the base. Heat over a moderate heat and then carefully break the eggs into it. Fry as usual, spooning hot oil over the eggs to help them set. When they are about half-cooked, add the chilli, cumin and garlic to the pan and continue cooking until the white is set. Lift the eggs out on to the bread, together with the bits of chilli and garlic and then spoon over a little of the oil. Drizzle over the balsamic vinegar, season with salt and scatter over lots of chopped coriander. Eat immediately.

Roast Cod with a Coriander Crust

This use of coriander in a breadcrumb crust owes little to more exotic locations but it is the kind of thing that has become very fashionable in Britain over recent years. If you can lay your hands on a really fresh bit of cod, this recipe will show it off at its very best.

SERVES 4

675 g (1 1/2 lb) freshest cod fillet

85 g (3 oz) soft or slightly stale white breadcrumbs

3 generous tablespoons chopped fresh coriander

3 garlic cloves, crushed

Finely grated zest of 1/2 lemon

60 g (2 oz) butter, melted

Salt and pepper

Lemon wedges, to serve

Pre-heat the oven to 220°C/425°F/Gas Mark 7. Season the cod with salt and pepper. Mix the breadcrumbs with the coriander, garlic, lemon zest, salt and pepper and then add the butter and mix thoroughly with your fingers. Place the cod in a shallow, ovenproof dish and press the buttered crumbs firmly on to the cod, to form an even crust. Bake for 20–30 minutes, until the crust is browned and the fish just about cooked through. Serve immediately.

sage

Sage is a beguiling but dangerous herb. It can be as seductive as a siren in the right place but wreaks havoc and destruction when it is used with a heavy hand. It's a herb that we know well in this country and that means that we tend to be slapdash, lazy and unimaginative with it.

Sage and onion stuffing is a prime example of our way with sage, potentially both the best

Opposite *Fried Eggs with Coriander, Cumin and Balsamic Vinegar*

and worst of destinations. On those all-too-rare occasions when it is made lovingly with fresh sage, from scratch, it is one of the most delicious foils for any fatty meat, though it goes nicely with a plain roast chicken too. Badly made with too much dusty dried sage, or out of a packet, it doesn't merit a second sniff. In fact, sage might have been made for pork or goose or for a fatty fish like eel, a most successful German combination. It is the Italians, however, who really know how to use sage with style and, over the past few years, good cooks and smart chefs have been picking up tips from them. I love the gentle discovery of its flavour with veal or other pale meats, or its marvellous affinity with hot melted butter puddled over pasta or gnocchi. I've also been surprised by how good deep-fried, batter-coated sage leaves are, as long as the batter is perfectly crisp and dry. Deep-fried naked leaves (they need only a few seconds in hot oil) make a fine embellishment to baked pork chops, calves' liver or a creamy vegetable risotto.

Sage is a native of the northern Mediterranean coasts. It was said that the sage of the islands of Veglia and Cherso and the neighbouring Dalmatian coast, where it grew in abundance (and no doubt still does, despite the ravages of war), was the best wild sage to be had. Hot sun ensures that Mediterranean sage will be more highly flavoured than our own but the essence is the same. Whatever the location, it is a happy, accommodating plant that relishes parched heat as much as it revels in the damp and the cool. It's even hardy enough to struggle through our winters, which makes it well worth growing at home.

The Latin name for garden sage is *Salvia officinalis*, which translates as 'apothecary's sage', emphatically showing its original use as a medicinal herb. *Salvia* (and the word 'sage', too, for that matter) comes from *salvere*, to save or to heal, while *officinalis* is the specific name given to many plants that had a place in the pharmacopoeia. Sage seems to have been considered quite a cure-all, with an endless list of medicinal uses to its credit, from diuretic to migraine soother and even antidote to snake bites. It was also an indicator of the domestic *status quo*; a vigorous sage bush in the garden predicted prosperity and was also a sign that the woman wore the trousers in that house. Get out there right now and nurture that sage plant ... or buy one quickly, if you want to get on in life!

Buying and Storing Sage

When I write 'sage' I mean fresh, not commercially dried, sage. Drying intensifies the flavour of a few herbs to their advantage, but not sage. Compacted, bullying and musty, its camphorous overtones are intensified to an uncomfortable degree. And the final blow is that in this anonymous, almost powdery state, it is all the more easy to overdose.

So, when it comes to sage, make it fresh above all, picked from the garden or begged from friends and neighbours, or bought from the shop. Sage leaves are sturdy things and will last fairly well for a few days out in the open and longer in the fridge, in a plastic bag in the vegetable drawer. The characteristic colour of sage leaves is that beautiful, muted grey-green, though bruised purple is common too and there are many more varieties of variegated sage leaves, which can all be used interchangeably. Special types of scented sage, such as pineapple sage, are rather different, often too different to stand any comparison. Don't attempt to substitute them for ordinary sage.

Using Sage

Strength of flavour varies considerably from batch to batch, from season to season. On some occasions, you may find that you need to boost the number of leaves used in a recipe to get a genuine presence, but don't go overboard. Rely on instincts and frequent tasting where practical.

If you have more sage than you can practically use at one time, you can hang the branches up to dry in a cool, airy, dry place; though home-dried or semi-dried sage seems more approachable than the commercially dried kind, it still needs to be used with discretion. Freezing fresh leaves is perhaps a better alternative, cut into strips and stuffed into ice-trays, covered in water and frozen to give icy sage-cubes. Note that freezing tends to intensify flavour, though leaving it truer to its original.

Saltimbocca alla Romana

A repeat recipe, I'm afraid (it appeared in my *Meat Course*) but it is the quintessential Italian sage recipe, too important to omit. This is a recipe that absolutely has to be made with fresh sage and, if you are partial to the flavour, it can take an extra sage leaf in each roll of meat. It really is best made with veal and, these days, it is easier than ever to buy pink-fleshed meat from calves that have been humanely raised. Turkey breast is a tolerable replacement but has less flavour, can be dry and may well have been raised in less salubrious conditions.

SERVES 4

8 slices of veal or turkey breast steaks
8 slices of air-dried ham (*prosciutto*)
8–16 sage leaves
30 g (1 oz) butter
110 ml (4 fl oz) Marsala
Salt and pepper

Sandwich the slices of veal or turkey between two sheets of greaseproof paper and flatten them out using a rolling pin. Don't be too violent about this, as you don't want to end up with a cobweb of meat, but do try to get each piece as thin as possible.

Lay a piece of ham on each flattened piece of meat, trimming it to fit. Season with pepper and then lay one or two sage leaves in the centre. Flip the sides in over the sage and then roll up neatly and secure with a wooden cocktail stick.

In a frying-pan brown the rolls in the melted butter and then pour in the Marsala and season with salt and pepper. Cover and leave to simmer for about 10 minutes, until cooked through. Serve immediately.

Sage and Sunflower Seed Rolls

These rolls are heaven-sent for a fine slice of Cheddar or other good British hard cheese, though they are also irresistible warm from the oven, with nothing more than a smear of butter. Guard them jealously if you are making them for a special occasion, as they disappeared in a twinkling of an eye in our household.

MAKES 6 ROLLS

15 g (1/2 oz) fresh yeast
1 teaspoon sugar
450 g (1 lb) strong white flour
1 1/2 teaspoons salt
1 tablespoon olive oil
30 g (1 oz) sunflower seeds
2 tablespoons chopped fresh sage
Milk

Cream the yeast with 150 ml (5 fl oz) of warm water and the sugar and leave in a warm place for 5–10 minutes, until it's frothing merrily. Sift the flour with the salt into a large bowl and make a well in the middle. Pour in the yeast mixture and the oil and start mixing, gradually adding more warm water, until you have a soft dough. Knead thoroughly for a good 5 minutes, until the dough is smooth and elastic. Place in a lightly oiled bowl, turn to coat in oil, then cover with a damp tea-towel and leave in a warm place until it has doubled in bulk – about an hour.

Pre-heat the oven to 200°C/400°F/Gas Mark 6. Punch the dough down and gradually knead in the sunflower seeds and sage. Divide into six pieces and roll each one into a ball. Place the balls on a greased baking tray, flattening them slightly to give neat bun shapes. Leave plenty of space between the balls to allow them to expand. Leave in a warm place for about 30 minutes, until they have doubled in size.

Brush lightly with a little milk and bake for 20 minutes, until lightly browned. If they are done, the buns will lift easily off the tray. One final check – tap the underneath of one of the buns. If it sounds hollow, it really is done. Transfer to a wire rack to cool.

Gnocchi alla Romana con Salvia

This has to be my favourite sage recipe of all time. *Gnocchi alla Romana* are made with semolina, not potato, and are verging on the addictive. The gnocchi themselves are enriched with Parmesan and then drenched in sage-scented butter and more Parmesan. A wicked and wonderful main course, best served with simple accompaniments – a tomato and olive salad, perhaps, and/or a rocket-laden green salad.

SERVES 4

For the gnocchi:

570 ml (1 pint) milk
170 g (6 oz) semolina
60 g (2 oz) freshly grated Parmesan
2 eggs, beaten

For the sage butter and to finish:

60 g (2 oz) butter
8 fresh sage leaves
2 garlic cloves, chopped
45 g (1 1/2 oz) freshly grated Parmesan
Salt and pepper

Bring the milk up to the boil and pour in the semolina in a steady stream. Stir constantly with a wooden spoon, until the mixture is so thick that you can stand the spoon up in it. Draw off the heat and beat in the Parmesan and then the eggs and salt and plenty of pepper. Spread the mixture out in a shallow buttered dish to form a layer about 5 mm (1/4 inch) thick. Leave to cool.

Pre-heat the oven to 200°C/400°F/Gas Mark 6. Cut the cooled semolina mixture into diamonds, with sides around 4 cm (1 1/2 inches) long. Arrange in overlapping rows in an ovenproof dish. Melt the butter over a low heat and add the sage and garlic. Let it infuse gently for about 5 minutes and then pour over the gnocchi. Sprinkle with Parmesan and pepper and bake for about 20–30 minutes, until browned and sizzling.

Serve up and warn greedy guts to hold back for a few minutes. I've burnt my tongue many a time on this, so eager have I been to dig in.

basil

When it comes down to it, there are only two types of basil that really matter in the kitchen: Mediterranean basil and Asian basil. All the other variants, cinnamon basil, ginger basil, lemon or purple or ruffle-leaved, are fun to play with from time to time but, in the end, they are just minor diversions.

Mediterranean basil, *Ocimum basilicum,* the one that goes so brilliantly with tomatoes, has now become a relatively common sight in northerly Britain. It may have big, medium or tiddly leaves (in which case it's actually *Ocimum minimum*, sometimes known as Greek basil) but the flavour and scent are much of a muchness, varying only in strength. Mediterranean basil is big, heady, peppery, almost clove-like and wildly evocative of lazy, long, hot summer days in the south of France, or Italy or Greece or wherever your day-dreaming takes you.

From Asia comes holy basil, *Ocimum sanctum*. This bears the characteristic pepperiness of all basils but is distinctly anise-scented and deliciously aromatic. Its long stems are flagged with tapering leaves, a slightly slatier green, often streaked with purple. Presumably this is the 'truer' basil, as India is where the plant is thought to have originated.

On the rare occasions that you do find holy basil here – in Thai or Malaysian grocery stores – it has usually been flown in from south-east Asia, which is all to the good. Basil, any kind of basil, likes strong sunlight. Searingly hot sun fuels the intensity of flavour in the growing plant. Italian basil, grown out in open fields in the belting summer heat, can be quite overwhelmingly marvellous, ten times more aromatic and punchy than basil grown in this country, however proud you may be of your own home-grown plants.

Buying and Storing Basil

Greenhouse basil, carefully shielded from the full glare of the sun, can be disappointing. I well remember gleefully buying an enormous boxful of ravishingly green, healthy and vigorous basil imported from Israel, where it had been grown under glass. The leaves smelled sensational and I determined to make a vat of pesto. My eagerly anticipated evening of pesto-indulgence turned out to be quite an anticlimax. The pesto was as dull as ditch-water and we mourned a great idea and a considerable outlay.

Most of the time there is no way of telling how basil has been grown, unless it is your own. I guess the best you can do is to ignore tempting trays of basil in the supermarket during the winter months, when there's more than a passing chance that the plants have been mutedly grown under glass. Basil is a summer herb, anyway, and is best left that way. Look forward to it during the colder months; then buy four or five plants in pots (there's no point in being niggardly with it) from a good garden centre as the days lengthen and the air warms and grow it on yourself, on the windowsill until summer is getting into gear and then outside while the growing is good. Keep picking leaves and it will last you right through until autumn.

If you do have to buy basil, pick it up on a need-to-use basis and then make sure that all the leaves are in good form, with no shrivelling and wilting and no brown edges. Actual leaf-size makes little difference. Greek basil, with its tiddly leaves, can be very potent. Don't be seduced by the supermarkets' 'growing basil' clumped together too tightly in a plastic flowerpot. It is often very immature and weak in flavour. It does improve if kept for a week or so in full summer sunlight but, if you can't wait that long, the cut stems will probably be a safer bet. Like most tender herbs, they are best stored, wrapped in damp kitchen paper, or in a plastic bag, in the vegetable drawer of the fridge.

Using Basil

Devotees tend to hold strong views over the way basil is handled. I've often heard that the leaves should never be cut with a knife but, like lettuce, only torn up by hand. I am not convinced that it makes a great deal of difference either way. The edges of torn basil are bruised and will darken just as much as those of knife-shredded basil. Do whatever suits you best.

When it comes to making pesto, or the French *pistou*, the debate is pestle and mortar versus processor. Here I am prepared to admit that the pounding of the pestle may have the edge taste-wise, as it presses out the juices, but the difference is not enormous. Pestle and mortar is more sensuous but more arduous. Processor pesto is blissfully quick but this method is useless for small quantities.

Most recipes are written and tested with medium-sized leaves, of course, so, if your basil is particularly small-leaved, or out-sized, you will have to use your common sense and adapt the number of leaves to suit.

Basil, as you could hardly fail to know, goes with anything tomatoey (I've even used it very successfully in a sweet tomato jam!) but that is just the beginning. I happen to love it with lamb and it can be brilliant with seafood. It shouldn't be restricted to savoury dishes, as basil has a natural sweetness that goes rather well with fruit. Add a few torn (or shredded) leaves to a fruit salad, stir in and then leave for an hour or so before serving. They will add a surprisingly exotic edge to a straightforward pudding.

On the whole, I think that basil is best added to hot sauces and other dishes right at the end of the cooking time. Heat seems to destroy some of its mystery. If you are unable to get holy basil for some Asian dish, sweet Mediterranean basil is absolutely fine as a substitute but, to replicate some small measure of the anise-scent, boost it with a small measure of French tarragon.

Tomato and Pesto Terrine

This is a recipe for high summer, when tomatoes are cheap (or fully ripened, if you grow your own) and full of flavour and plentiful. It is very simple and makes a light, fresh-tasting first course for a summer dinner party. Skinning and preparing all those tomatoes takes time, it's true, but you will be glad you did it when you slice through the terrine to reveal bands of red separated with thin lines of pesto. Set aside the evening before your do and then settle down to work in the knowledge that you are creating a tearaway success of a dish.

The bigger the tomatoes, the more you'll need as they contain a higher ratio of seeds and pulp to flesh (so for beef tomatoes, you'll probably need the full 3 kg/6lb.)

SERVES 8
1 quantity of *Pesto* (see page 30)
Olive oil
2–3 kg (4–6 lb) ripe tomatoes
1 tablespoon white wine vinegar
Sugar
Salt and pepper
8 fresh basil sprigs, to garnish

Put 1 tablespoon of the pesto into a small pot, cover with 2 tablespoons of olive oil and then with cling film and reserve for the dressing.

Pour boiling water over the tomatoes, leave for about 30 seconds and then drain and skin. If the skin on some of the tomatoes remains reluctant to part company, bathe the offending tomatoes again in boiling water and then try again. Cut the tomatoes into quarters (or eighths if they are very large) and de-seed. Use a small, sharp knife to slice away the inner ridges and knobs, to leave neat flat sheets of tomato. Lay them out on wire racks (or baking sheets if you're short of racks) and sprinkle lightly with a little salt and sugar. Leave to drain for half an hour.

Line a 500 g (1 lb) loaf tin with cling film allowing some of the film to trail over the sides. Brush the inside lightly with olive oil. Pat the tomato pieces dry and then arrange a layer, tightly snuggled together, over the base. Spread with a little of the pesto. Repeat these layers until the tomato is all used up, finishing with a layer of tomato. Fold the trailing cling film over loosely. Sit another loaf tin of the same size on top and weight it down (use cans of food or bags of rice or whatever is handy and heavy). Stand on a dish and leave overnight in the fridge, draining off the pressed out liquid whenever you dive into the fridge to get something else out (you'll be amazed by how much oozes out but don't let it unnerve you).

To make the dressing, whisk the vinegar with the reserved pesto and oil. Gradually whisk in another 1–2 tablespoons of olive oil and a touch of sugar. Taste and adjust the seasoning and then set aside until needed.

To serve, carefully drain any remaining juice from the tomato terrine and then turn it out onto a chopping board or serving dish, gently peeling away the cling film. Either take it to the table as is or, if you can rely on a really good, sharp-as-a-razor knife, cut into 2.5 cm (1-inch) slices. Lay each one on a plate and drizzle some of the pesto vinaigrette around it. Garnish with basil sprigs. Serve immediately.

Opposite *Tomato and Pesto Terrine*

Pesto

Pesto is the most renowned way of using basil. There's not much nicer than a steaming hot dish of pasta, drenched with pesto made with good basil. If you want to do things properly, as they do in Genoa, throw some diced potato, sliced carrots and maybe some green beans into the pan before you add the pasta, which, if it isn't the Genoese *trenette*, should be spaghetti or at least tagliatelle (jiggle timings to fit). The idea is that vegetables and pasta should be cooked at more or less the same time. Drain together and toss with the pesto and if necessary, a little extra olive oil to lubricate. Serve with more Parmesan or pecorino if you want it.

SERVES 4 ON PASTA
75 g (2½ oz) fresh basil
60 g (2 oz) Parmesan and/or hard pecorino, broken up into chunks
60 g (2 oz) pine nuts
2–3 garlic cloves, roughly chopped
100 ml (3½ fl oz) olive oil
Salt (optional)

Strip the leaves off the basil and place in the food processor. Add the cheese, pine nuts and garlic and process to a paste. Gradually trickle in the olive oil, to give a creamy sauce. Add salt to taste if you wish.

You want to do it properly? OK. Pound the garlic to a paste with a pinch or two of salt in the mortar. Add the basil and nuts and keep pounding until you have a paste. Work in the cheese, constantly grinding and pounding and then enough olive oil to give a creamy sauce. I bet you feel smugly virtuous after all that!

Basil Cremets

The sweet nature of basil is often overlooked but it can work well in puddings, if treated with consideration. Here it is folded into the cream and cheese mixture that will be drained to form *cremets*, so good with soft summer fruit and/or a raspberry coulis (sieved raspberries sweetened with a little icing sugar).

SERVES 6
280 g (10 oz) cream cheese
150 ml (5 fl oz) fromage frais or Greek yoghurt
200 ml (7 fl oz) crème fraiche (or whipping cream, lightly whipped)
2½ tablespoons caster sugar
3 tablespoons chopped fresh basil
1 egg white

If you have them, line six small *coeurs à la crème* moulds with muslin. Failing that, collect together six small yoghurt or cream pots or clean plastic flowerpots and pierce holes in the bottom with a hot skewer. Rinse the pots and line them with muslin.

Beat the cream cheese with the fromage frais or yoghurt, until smooth. Fold in the crème fraiche or whipped whipping cream, caster sugar and basil. Whisk the egg white until stiff and fold that in last of all. Spoon the mixture into the lined moulds. Stand on a wire rack over a shallow dish, cover and leave overnight in the fridge to drain. Turn out just before serving.

lovage

Some things in life are hard to fathom and one of them is the virtual disappearance of lovage from common culinary knowledge. Lovage is a sensational herb, with just about everything going for it. It makes an early appearance in the spring, ready to enliven cold-weather soups and stews, but carries on growing and thriving right into the late autumn. It grows remarkably easily, tolerating considerable neglect and maltreatment without complaint (mountainous heaps of builder's rubble and blankets of dust did nothing to deter a plant of mine from thrusting up vigorously and gloriously above the chaos). It looks majestic and grand at full height, with long, leafy stems and great umbels of yellow flowers stretching as high as your shoulder. And, most importantly of all, it has a superb flavour, underlined by celery tones but more spicy and with a distinct lemon-zest warmth.

Lovage is a powerful herb and perhaps that contributed to its downfall: too strong, too dominant, too daring. The fact is that, where once it was widely grown in this country, now it is confined to knowing cooks who have room enough in their garden for its striking form. The scene is set to change, however. Flat packs of lovage have at last been glimpsed on the market, though complete with a ridiculously high price tag. Try it once, to see if it pleases you (if you hate celery, you'll probably loathe lovage) and then nip round to any good plant nursery, buy a plant at a reasonable rate and grow it yourself. That way, not only can you enjoy the flavour that the leaves impart but, if the fancy takes you, you can try steaming or blanching the young stalks (older ones need peeling, which is a drag) to eat like asparagus or sea-kale, with melted butter or olive oil and shavings of Parmesan; also try drying the seeds, to use with pork or in old-fashioned seed-cake. You could even try digging up the root and eating that, too, boiled like any other root vegetable. I have read that it is excellent, though you won't get much of a meal out of a single plant and, of course, you'll lose all the foliage in the process. Maybe it's worth it, maybe I've been missing out on one of the great forgotten vegetables but my curiosity is not such that I'm willing to sacrifice all those marvellous, spicy leaves.

Using and Storing Lovage

Lovage is an easy herb to become addicted to, especially if you have a soft spot for the more old-fashioned, classic, northern flavours. It has the potential to become the coriander of cooler climates, if only those who guard it as their own little secret would be prepared to shout loud about it. If lovage is new to you, I suggest you start by making a traditional *Lovage Soup* (see page 33), which shows it off simply and to advantage. With that under your belt, let rip.

In spring and early summer, lovage leaves are milder and the stems more delicate. As the year ripens so does the flavour, so you will need less to make an impact. Young, tender leaves make a welcome addition to salads, at a time when interesting saladings are relatively thin on the ground. Later on, when the leaves are too strong, you can still impart their taste to a salad by wiping them firmly around the bowl before mixing the dressing and adding other greenery.

In similar vein, try wrapping lovage leaves round young goats' cheeses, leaving them overnight and then eating the delicately scented cheese on bread, or lightly grilled. Chopped lovage (or, later on, its fresh or dried seeds) go well with cream cheese, either mixed in with other finely chopped herbs or in a marinade – a good way of creating an exciting cheese course when you only have access to a tub of bland cream cheese. In fact, lovage is welcome with practically any mild dairy product – stir it into *tzatziki* (yoghurt and cucumber sauce or dip) instead of mint, or use it to scent simple cream sauces.

Lovage and fish are, by and large, a first-rate partnership (there are exceptions: lovage doesn't do a great deal for fresh tuna or salmon, nor for other oily fish such as herring or mackerel) but special care must be taken not to overwhelm more delicate fish. Shellfish and smoked fish take kindly to lovage, as well. Try adding a few shreds to something like a smoked haddock chowder. The white meats, chicken, veal, turkey and pork, benefit from the celery-spice of lovage, as do milder feathered game, such as pheasant and partridge. And, finally, if you are making stock and you have no celery, or don't want to buy a whole head of it for the sake of one stalk, you'll find that a small sprig of lovage does just as good a job, if not better – you may even want to start adding it to all your *bouquets garnis*.

To store lovage, wrap the cut leaves and stems in a plastic bag and stash in the salad drawer of the fridge. The leaves have a tendency to wilt quite swiftly but they'll hold their scent for a few days.

Lovage Soup

The best showcase for the pure flavour of lovage is this traditional soup that has been reappraised and reappreciated over the past few years. The potato softens the intensity of the herb, without reducing it to pale insignificance.

SERVES 4–6

60 g (2 oz) butter
1 onion, chopped
250–300 g (9–11 oz) floury potatoes, peeled and diced
1 large carrot, diced
A handful of fresh lovage leaves
1–1.2 litres (1¾–2 pints) chicken, light game or vegetable stock
6 tablespoons double cream
Salt and pepper
Cayenne pepper, to serve

Melt the butter in a large pan and add the onion, potatoes, carrot and lovage. Stir and then cover and sweat over a low heat for 10–15 minutes. Add the stock and a little salt and pepper. Bring up to the boil and leave to simmer for 15 minutes, until all the vegetables are very tender. Cool slightly, liquidize and sieve. Taste and adjust the seasoning. Re-heat when needed and stir in the cream. Serve with a dusting of cayenne pepper.

Pineapple, Lovage and Avocado Salsa

This fruity salsa goes particularly well with grilled or roast duck, neatly counterpointing the richness of the meat.

SERVES 6–8

1 lime
1 medium-sized pineapple
1 avocado
5 fresh lovage leaves, finely chopped
1 red onion, finely chopped
1 fresh red chilli, de-seeded and finely chopped
Salt

Pare the zest from the lime in long strips. Blanch in boiling water for a minute. Drain well, dry and chop. Squeeze the lime juice. Peel and core the pineapple and dice the flesh finely. Mix with the lime juice and zest. Peel and dice the avocado finely and add to the pineapple, along with the remaining ingredients. Turn quickly and carefully, to mix without battering the avocado to a pulp. Cover and leave for at least half an hour, for the flavours to blend.

Taste and adjust the seasonings, adding a little more lovage if you think the salsa could take it.

Smoked Salmon with Lovage Cream Cheese, on Bagels

SERVES 3

3 bagels, split open

4 tablespoons cream cheese

1 tablespoon chopped fresh lovage leaves

2 teaspoons creamed horseradish (optional)

Lots of sliced smoked salmon

Freshly ground black pepper

Toast the cut sides of the bagels, if you wish. Mash the cream cheese with the lovage and horseradish, if using, and smear thickly over the cut sides of the bagels. Sandwich as much smoked salmon as is humanly decent (or available) between the two halves of each bagel, seasoning generously with freshly ground black pepper. Eat greedily.

Bruno Loubet's Lovage Sauce

A brilliantly simple sauce for chicken from Bruno Loubet's *Chicken* (Weidenfeld & Nicolson). He serves it with a chicken baked inside a salt crust but it goes perfectly with a plainly roast chicken or grilled chicken breasts or legs. Try it, too, with turkey escalopes, or even veal. Don't season it absentmindedly with salt and pepper – it really doesn't need any.

SERVES 4–6

100 g ($3^1/2$ oz) unsalted butter

4 tablespoons Worcestershire sauce

100 ml ($3^1/2$ fl oz) chicken stock or water

1 tablespoon chopped fresh lovage leaves

Lemon juice

Melt the butter in a saucepan and heat until it turns hazelnut brown. Draw off the heat and stir in the Worcestershire sauce, stock or water and lovage. Add a squeeze of lemon juice and keep warm.

Deep-Fried Lovage and Courgette Salad with Tomato and Parmesan

This salad makes a lovely, bold first course, with the unexpected flavour of deep-fried lovage to bring it to life. If you have no lovage, replace it with sage leaves or curly-leafed parsley and try harder to find lovage next time.

If you want to serve individual platefuls, toss the leaves and tomatoes separately in the dressing at the last minute, arrange on the plate and then top with fried courgettes, lovage and Parmesan. Serve with lemon wedges to squeeze over the fried courgettes.

To turn it into the makings of a light lunch, add to each portion a poached egg and/or slices of *prosciutto* or *jamón serrano*.

SERVES 4

4 small courgettes, or 2 medium-sized ones, weighing about 350 g (12 oz) in total
A hunk of Parmesan
4 cos lettuce leaves, roughly torn up
4 ripe tomatoes, skinned, de-seeded and diced
Sunflower or vegetable oil and/or olive oil for deep-frying
15 fresh lovage leaves
Salt and pepper

For the dressing:
1 tablespoon lemon juice
1 garlic clove, crushed
2 tablespoons lemon olive oil and 1–2 tablespoons olive oil or 4 tablespoons olive oil
Salt and pepper

Slice the courgettes diagonally, to give elongated ovals. Spread out in a colander, sprinkle lightly with salt and leave to drain for 30 minutes.

Rinse the courgettes and dry them thoroughly with kitchen paper or a clean tea-towel. Use a vegetable peeler to shave off a generous handful of paper-thin curls of Parmesan.

To make the dressing, whisk the lemon juice with the garlic and a little salt and pepper in a large salad bowl. Whisk in the oil(s), a tablespoon at a time, to make a dressing that has a slightly sharp edge but is not mouth-puckeringly acidic.

Put the lettuce leaves into the bowl and scatter over the tomato pieces. Shortly before serving, heat the oil to 170°C/325°F. Deep-fry the courgette slices until browned and then drain briefly on kitchen paper and salt lightly, if they need it. Drop in half the lovage leaves and fry for about 30 seconds. Scoop out and drain on kitchen paper while you deep-fry the remaining leaves. When all the frying is done, add the courgettes to the salad and then scatter the fried leaves and Parmesan over the top. Toss at the table.

angelica

This is a herb that you will have to grow yourself. I've never seen it for sale, except in garden centres, and that's a crying shame for a plant that is rightly named after the angels (Latin *Angelica archangelica*). Still, give a plant a tolerable start in life and a sunny spot, and even the least green-fingered and most negligent of gardeners (me) can soon be the proud owner of a magnificent, architectural plant. Angelica is a stately umbellifer that most of us have only ever seen cut to small pieces, candied and dyed a violent green. I've only recently discovered what a cracking fresh herb it is. Angelica has a heavenly, tender fragrance that is quite unlike anything else.

Angelica is definitely a sweet herb, a herb for puddings rather than savoury dishes, a kind of fresh leafy equivalent of vanilla. I like to infuse either the leaves or stems in milk or cream for puddings and tarts. It brings a soft but unmissable scent, though it's hard to pinpoint. I particularly like it in the custard filling for fruit tarts (it goes marvellously well with rhubarb and peaches, for instance) but I've also used it very successfully in ice cream, rice pudding and in straight creamy *crème anglaise*. Use it, too, to flavour a summer fruit salad – just stir in a few torn-up leaves when making and leave for at least an hour before using. A few leaves thrown in with fruit as they stew reduces the need for sugar, as well as imparting fragrance, and it can be sensational in jams (try a few leaves in rhubarb or strawberry jam). It's quite easy to candy your own stems, too.

kaffir lime leaves

These small, dark, glossy leaves look like Siamese-twin bay leaves, joined tip to end in pairs. They are unmistakable when fresh, both for their unique look and their citrus and spice fragrance, sharp and scented and not unlike lemon verbena (which, by the way, is probably the best substitute in terms of flavour; failing that, strips of lime or lemon zest are better than nothing).

Kaffir lime leaves come from a wild citrus tree, *Citrus hystrix*, and are usually imported from south-east Asia, where they are used to magical effect in Thai and Indonesian cooking. Dropped into soups and curries, rather as we might use bay leaves, they impart their particular pure flavour. Try adding a few, roughly torn up, to chicken and fish dishes. The leaves can be fished out at the end if you wish.

The same tree produces beautiful, gnarled-looking limes but it is their zest, rather than the negligible amounts of juice, that is used in cooking.

Kaffir lime leaves are available for the time being from Thai and other oriental food stores and occasionally in packs of Thai spices in supermarkets. Infuriatingly, they are now threatened by an EC plant-health directive, which bans their importation (though it hasn't had an enormous effect yet, except to boost the price of lime leaves). Buy what you can when you can and freeze or dry them just in case.

vanilla pods

fresh chillies

dried chillies

spices

ginger
saffron
black peppercorns
star anise
Szechuan peppercorns

fresh ginger

Root ginger is a funny term. Most of us read it as meaning fresh ginger but, in fact, all ginger, fresh or dried, comes from the root of the ginger plant. Dried ground ginger is one of those 'granny's cupboard' spices, warm and safely prickly, at home in good, honest, old-fashioned baking or at its most exotic sprinkled over a slice of watery melon – an odd habit, but understandable when so many melons are tasteless and flabby. Actually, powdered ginger can enter the realms of the exotic – it is used with more flair in Moroccan cooking, for instance – but it is fresh (or green) ginger that has stolen the show in recent years.

In fact, the difference between fresh and dried ginger is so marked that it is best to think of them as two quite different spices. Fresh ginger has an unmistakable, sprightly freshness and an invigorating smack of heat, which have made it a fundamental element in the cooking of the East. Along with garlic and chilli, it forms the essential holy trinity of basic flavourings that unites the very different cuisines of this vast area.

Ginger is a rhizome, or 'race' or 'hand', in other words a creeping root, closely resembling the iris root though not related in anything but form. I have read that it produces beautiful yellow flowers with a purple lip, given the right conditions. It sounds like quite a sight but, should you discover a forgotten piece of ginger root sprouting green shoots in the smog of your kitchen, I wouldn't hold out for any flowers – it's extremely unlikely to bloom. Instead, chop the shoots roughly and add them to a salad, from which you'll derive assured benefit.

Buying Fresh Ginger

Though fresh ginger is widely sold these days, it is still exotically strange enough for a few unscrupulous purveyors to get away with pushing substandard rhizomes. Fresh ginger should be firm from the first knobble to the very last, with not a bruise or soggy patch in sight. The skin, though not glossy, should be taut and blessed with a sheen of health. Old ginger, well past its sell-by date, will either be bruised or drying and wrinkly. Mould may sometimes make a warning appearance: discard the root and complain loudly.

Ginger is by nature knobbly but I always try to pick out the plumpest and least knobbly piece – it makes peeling much easier and minimizes waste. It is said that the best ginger comes from Jamaica but Kenyan ginger runs a close second best.

Using and Storing Fresh Ginger

Most recipes will call for a specified length of fresh ginger – a rough measurement but quite adequate, leaving you room for interpretation according to your own taste – but more than a couple of inches is rarely needed. Unless you are passing through an obsessive fresh ginger phase, you are unlikely to work through an entire lump of ginger while it is at its prime. The remainder will keep fairly well for several weeks, wrapped in newspaper or a brown paper bag, in the vegetable drawer of the fridge.

An even handier trick is to store ginger in the freezer, where it will keep for months. When recipes call for grated ginger, grate it straight from the freezer. It's a brilliant way to prevent that irritating tangle of fibres. What you end up with is a neat pile of perfectly grated ginger, instead of a hopeless mess and minimal usable returns.

A more old-fashioned way of preserving ginger, dating, I suspect, from a time when it was hard to come by in the West, is to preserve the sliced, peeled ginger in sherry or vinegar. What you end up with is something rather different, but not without merit. The ginger itself can still be used though, obviously, the flavour of the sherry or vinegar will make itself known in any dish to which you add it. More to the point is the liquid itself, which is spicy and delicious. Use the sherry to flavour soups or sauces – it is particularly good with tomatoes, I find, or, used with restraint, with seafood, especially crab. The vinegar will pep up any salad dressing or mayonnaise.

Nuoc Mam Gung

Simple as a recipe can be, this Vietnamese dipping sauce is a real joy if you have even the most minimal liking for the flavours of the Far East. It's gingery, sweet, hot, sharp and salty all at once. Try serving it with plainly grilled prawns or chicken. Once you've had a taste, you will probably come up with a hundred and one other ways to use it.

The recipe comes from *The Simple Art of Vietnamese Cooking* by Binh Duong and Marcia Kiesel (Simon & Schuster).

MAKES ABOUT 110 ML (4 FL OZ)

5 cm (2 inch) piece of fresh ginger, peeled and finely chopped
2 tablespoons caster sugar
2 small, fiery, fresh red chillies, chopped
2 garlic cloves, chopped
1/2 small lime, peeled and sectioned
2 tablespoons fish sauce

Pound the ginger, sugar, chillies and garlic in a mortar with a pestle, to form a syrupy sauce. Add the lime sections and pound again, working them into the mixture. Finally, work in the fish sauce. Serve at room temperature, with rice or as a dipping sauce. The sauce can be kept, in an airtight jar, for up to a week in the fridge.

Butaniku Shoga-yaki

This Japanese recipe for pork uses ginger in quite a different way from the Vietnamese *Nuoc Mam Gung* (see page 41). Here, it is fresh ginger juice that is called for to spice up the marinade and sauce for a quickly fried dish of pork and vegetables. To extract the ginger juice, grate a large knob of ginger (no need to peel first) and then squeeze hard with your fingers. Mirin is a sweet cooking wine; sake or dry sherry and a little sugar makes an acceptable substitute.

SERVES 3–4

450 g (1 lb) tender, boneless, lean pork
2 tablespoons vegetable oil
110 g (4 oz) beansprouts
1 large carrot, cut into fine matchsticks

For the marinade:

3 tablespoons sake or dry sherry
1 1/2 tablespoons mirin, or 1 more tablespoon sake or dry sherry, mixed with 1 teaspoon caster sugar
3 tablespoons dark soy sauce
1 tablespoon fresh ginger juice

Slice the pork as thinly as you can (chilling it in the freezer for 30 minutes will make slicing easier). Mix all the marinade ingredients and pour over the pork. Turn to coat nicely and leave for 30 minutes. Drain off the marinade and reserve.

Heat the oil in a wide frying-pan over a high heat. Add half the pork and sauté for about a minute, until all but cooked through. Scoop out and repeat with the remaining pork. Quickly return the first batch to the pan, along with the marinade. Bring up to the boil, stirring so that the meat is evenly coated. Scoop the meat out on to a plate and keep warm. Throw the beansprouts and carrots into the juices left in the pan and stir for 1–2 minutes, to heat through. Serve with the pork.

vanilla pods

I fulfilled one of my small ambitions a few years ago when I finally got to see a vanilla orchid growing, not as an exhibit in a European hothouse, but in its proper place in a warm steamy climate, all set to produce vanilla pods for human consumption. Vanilla orchids don't often make it to showy orchid exhibitions, except, perhaps, as an illustration of the fact that not all orchids are wildly glamorous. The flowers are small and inconsequential ... or at least, they would be inconsequential if it weren't for the fact that they are poised at the end of the lengthening green vanilla bean.

For all its dowdiness, this is perhaps the most important of orchids, appreciated by millions of people who may not even be aware of its existence. Vanilla is one of those ubiquitous flavourings, slipping into ice cream, cakes, biscuits, puddings and all manner of confectionery with little or no fanfare. In muted form, it makes the perfect unobtrusive background for larger flavours, like that of chocolate, but can happily stand on its own when boosted in intensity. Vanilla's popularity has, to some extent, proved to be its downfall. Synthetic vanilla substitutes (notably vanillin) are harsh, but cheap and hence widely used, giving vanilla if not a bad name, at least an inferior one.

The orchid is native to Mexico, where, with luck, it is pollinated by native bees. In other countries, the flowers must be pollinated painstakingly by hand, a process that was discovered, it is said, by a 12-year-old slave on the island of Réunion in 1841. It would be nice to think that he grew rich on his discovery, but no doubt it was the plantation owner who reaped the rewards.

The pods take as long as a human pregnancy to mature to the state where they are ready to harvest. Then comes the complex curing process, during which time enzymes work to produce the magical flavour. Last, but by no means least, the pods are dried, bundled and packaged.

Buying and Storing Vanilla Pods

Good vanilla should always be plumply pleated, waxy and pliable, never bone-dry, stiff and woody. The dark brown or black pods, with their hint of rust, should bear a strong scent and, in the case of the *crème de la crème*, a shaking of powdery white crystals known in the trade as *givre* (although this can be faked, so don't be conned if the price seems remarkably low). The best vanilla is said to be Bourbon vanilla, or in other words, pods grown and cured on the island of Réunion. However, much of the Bourbon vanilla is sent to France and the United States, leaving little for the rest of us. I'm glad to say, though, that Birgit Erath of The Spice Shop (see the list of suppliers on page 315) confirms my opinion that vanilla from Madagascar (where they weave it into beautiful shapes – pineapples and horses, for instance) is every bit as good, if not superior.

Vanilla pods are inevitably expensive, though a single vanilla pod can be used four or five times if it is treated with respect. Store pods in an airtight container and, if you want to get the most out of them, make that an airtight jar of caster sugar. After a week or two, the sugar will have taken on some of the fragrance of the pods (without diminishing their potency), and – hey, presto! – you are blessed with an ample supply of vanilla sugar.

Using Vanilla Pods

Extracting the pure vanilla flavour from the pods either takes time, as in the making of vanilla sugar, or damp heat. For something like a slow-baked rice pudding, you can just slip the vanilla pod in with the rice, sugar and milk. To infuse milk or cream or a syrup with vanilla, bring them slowly up to the boil together, and either leave over the lowest imaginable heat, half covered, for 20–30 minutes, or, if you can't get the flame low enough, draw off the heat, cover and leave. After use, wash the vanilla pod in warm water, dry thoroughly and then return it to the sugar jar.

For a stronger, more insistent burst of vanilla slit open the pod with the tip of a sharp knife. Inside lie thousands of tiny, sticky, black seeds, true bearers of the vanilla power. Infuse the pod as above, stirring it every now and then to release the seeds; or for cakes or biscuits, scrape the seeds straight out into the batter or dough. Even a de-seeded vanilla pod should be treated lovingly and is still worth returning to its sugar jar. It may have had its heart scraped out but, remarkable thing that it is, it will have the power to waft gentle fragrance into a few more puddings yet.

A fashion for using vanilla with fish or seafood has raised its head once or twice over the past decade or so, but I have yet to be convinced that it works particularly well. I remain firmly of the opinion that vanilla is a sweet spice.

Vanilla'd Fruit Salad

Here, vanilla adds sparkle and a unifying note to an exotic fruit salad. The daring amongst you could try adding a sliced, de-seeded red chilli for extra kick. It is suprisingly good.

SERVES 6

1 small pineapple, peeled, cored and cubed

1 mango, peeled, stoned and diced

1 papaya, peeled, quartered, de-seeded and sliced

2 bananas

Juice of 1 lime

For the syrup:

110 g (4 oz) caster sugar

150 ml (5 fl oz) water

1 vanilla pod, slit open

Make the syrup first. Put all the ingredients into a saucepan and stir over a moderate heat, until the sugar has dissolved. Bring up to the boil and simmer for 5 minutes, stirring once or twice to help dislodge the vanilla seeds. Leave to cool.

Mix the pineapple, mango and papaya. Peel the bananas, slice them and turn the slices in the lime juice. Add to the salad, with the juice. Pour over the syrup. Turn gently, cover tightly and leave for half an hour or so before serving.

Baked Vanilla Custard with Apricots

Baked vanilla custard is marvellous in its own right, but can also form the basis of many other puddings. It is what makes the best *crème caramel*, the best *crème brulée,* but, in this recipe, it covers the tartness of a layer of poached apricots, fresh or dried. Other fruit can be substituted in season – gooseberries, currants or rhubarb, perhaps.

The richness of the custard is something that can be varied at will. For a rather plain custard, use milk instead of cream. Single cream is a nice halfway house *en route* to sheer gluttony; whipping cream takes you a step further along the road and double cream makes baked custards of the most devastatingly indulgent texture in the world. I recommend it.

SERVES 6

6 fresh or 12 dried apricots

140 g (5 oz) caster sugar or vanilla sugar

2 strips of lemon zest

For the custard:

425 ml (15 fl oz) single, whipping or double cream

1 vanilla pod, slit open

4 egg yolks

Pre-heat the oven to 150°C/300°F/Gas Mark 2. Skin, quarter and stone fresh apricots. Chop dried ones roughly. Put the caster or vanilla sugar in a pan with 300 ml (10 fl oz) of water and stir over a moderate heat until dissolved. Add the apricots and the lemon zest, and poach gently until the fruit is tender. Scoop out the fruit and divide it between six medium-sized ramekins. Boil the liquid down until it's syrupy. Reserve about half of it and spoon the rest over the apricots, discarding the lemon zest.

For the custard, put the cream into a pan, with the vanilla pod, and bring very slowly up to the boil, stirring frequently. Draw off the heat, cover and leave to infuse for 20–30 minutes.

Beat the egg yolks with the reserved syrup and gradually beat in the warm cream. Strain over the apricots. Stand the ramekins in a roasting tin and pour in enough hot water to come about halfway up their sides. Bake for about 40–50 minutes, until just set. Serve warm or chilled.

Vanilla and Walnut Ice Cream

This recipe makes an absolutely sensational ice cream but, if you want something a mite plainer, just leave out the walnuts to produce a deep, rich, unmistakably classy straight vanilla ice cream. If what you are after is nothing more than a neutral, vaguely vanilla flavour backdrop for other puddings, leave the pod whole and untampered with.

SERVES 6
300 ml (10 fl oz) full-cream milk
1 vanilla pod, slit open
3 large egg yolks
110 g (4 oz) caster sugar
85 g (3 oz) chopped walnuts
300 ml (10 fl oz) double cream

Put the milk into a pan, with the vanilla pod, and bring slowly up to the boil, stirring every now and then. Draw off the heat, cover and leave to infuse for 20–30 minutes.

Pre-heat the oven to 200°C/400°F/Gas Mark 6. Whisk the egg yolks with the sugar and then whisk in the milk, together with the vanilla pod. Set the bowl over a pan of lazily simmering water, making sure that the base of the bowl does not come into contact with the water. Stir until the custard thickens enough to coat the back of the spoon. Leave to cool and then strain.

Meanwhile, spread the walnuts out on a baking tay and toast in the oven, until they turn a shade or two darker. Allow around 4–7 minutes, checking and shaking them once or twice as they roast. Tip into a metal sieve and shake over a piece of newspaper to dislodge all those flakes of papery skin. Leave to cool.

When the custard is cool, whip the cream lightly and fold in the custard. If you have an ice-cream maker, freeze according to manufacturer's instructions adding the walnut pieces when the mixture is sludgey, but not too thick.

Opposite *Vanilla and Walnut Ice Cream*

If you don't, pour the mixture, without adding the walnut pieces, into a shallow container and pop into the freezer, set to its coldest setting. Leave until the mixture has set around the sides. Break them up and push towards the centre of the container. Return to the freezer and leave until set but not yet solid. Scoop into the bowl of a processor and whizz quickly, to smooth out coarse ice crystals. If you don't have a processor, flex your muscles and beat hard. Finally, fold in the walnut pieces and return to the freezer to set solid.

Transfer from the freezer to the fridge to soften about 45 minutes before eating.

chillies

We are not, by nature, a chilli-using country. Our climate is all wrong for chillies, which need heat to flourish and develop their burn, and our gardeners are probably too indulgent and loving because they grow most fearsome on arid, dry soil. Besides, our traditional foods are too tame, allowing only the occasional excursion to something hotter and spicier. For all that, or maybe precisely because of that, many of us have a tendency to fall, hook, line and sinker for the unbridled heat of chillies when we finally get a chance.

In the days of the Raj, many an otherwise conservative eater discovered that the pain of chilli heat in the mouth became a pleasure on further acquaintance. Indian restaurants abound and thrive on hot curries still. But, of late, there's been a new wave of chilli appreciation and, all of a sudden, the world's chillies are beating a path to our doors.

In the eighties, fresh chillies – mostly the small, conical green Fresno or *jalapeño* varieties grown in Kenya – began to make regular appearances in supermarkets. As for whole dried chillies, the long, slender, brick-red *serrano* was already dominating the scene. Fine chillies these are, but they are only the beginning. There are literally thousands of different types of chilli growing all around the world, wherever there is heat and a desire for their special spice. Now a few more of the most notable varieties are to be had in chilly Britain. The joy of this is that we can, at last, appreciate at first hand not just the fieriness of these little fruit but also their flavours, which differ so widely.

From Mexico, true home of the chilli, we are beginning to get a few extraordinary and fascinating chillies. Dried ones are light as a feather and so easy to import. Look out for the crinkled, brick-red *ancho*, medium-hot with a sweetish, fruity flavour hinting at liquorice and tobacco, or the little round *cascabel*, smooth and shiny, dark red, with a nutty flavour and a moderate heat. A third medium-hot Mexican chilli that you may come across is the long, scrunched, black-brown *pasilla* or 'little raisin', which tastes grassy and fruity.

From Asia come some of the hottest chillies of all. The long, slender, fresh Thai chillies – usually red – breathe fire into any dish, while little dried 'bird' chillies eclipse the fresh ones with their concentrated flavour. A rough rule of thumb has it that the smaller the chilli, the hotter it is, but the Caribbean Scotch Bonnet chilli (practically identical to the South American *habanero*) torches that notion, with an incendiary heat in a medium-sized, squashed, boxy shape.

The delightful thing about cooking with chillies is that, as you become more familiar with their individual quirks, you also realize that you can never be entirely sure what you will end up with. A new variety will bring a new complexity to a dish. One batch will be hotter than the next, though the variety is the same. A red chilli, which, after all, is nothing more than a fully ripened green chilli, will be no less hot, but it will have a sweeter, more rounded flavour that tones down the heat a little. Dried chillies have a totally different, concentrated, spicy flavour. There is endless room for experimenting and discovering new, fabulous combinations as the fancy takes you. Why stick with just one type of chilli? What about using dried and fresh in a dish to gain the benefits of both? The possibilities are endless and it's very easy to develop a mercifully healthy addiction to these little capsules of spice and fire.

Buying and Storing Chillies

Fresh chillies should be firm, glossy and glowing with health. Give them a quick sniff, too, to make sure that they smell as fresh as they look. Avoid chillies that are flabby or wrinkled. Wrapped in kitchen paper or in a paper bag and stashed in the vegetable drawer of the fridge, away from damp, chillies will keep for two or three weeks.

When buying dried chillies, look out for an even, deep, glowing colour. Dusty or fading chillies, which have been hanging around for too long, are best avoided. And, like any spice, they are best bought whole, so that none of their essential oils have evaporated. Store them in an airtight box, in a cool, dark place well away from any humidity. Pretty skeins of chillies look lovely strung up in the kitchen but, unless you use them up fast, they are probably best left as decorations.

When it comes to buying chillies, it is worth scouring around. Supermarkets carry an increasingly wide selection – Fresnos or *jalapeños*, green and red, are common, but red Thai chillies are to be seen more and more frequently. Scotch Bonnets occasionally make their way into the big stores but you are more likely to find them in West Indian groceries. Other types of chilli are also making an appearance, so grab what you can when you can.

Dried chillies lag behind and, for interesting varieties, you may have to find a Spanish shop, or an oriental food store. Better still, buy them by post (see the list of suppliers, page 314). In season, you can also buy some of the most interesting fresh chillies, many of them ideal for stuffing in the Mexican style, by mail order from Devon, of all places, where an enterprising and well-travelled market gardener raises them in poly-tunnels with an impressive view out over the sea (again, see page 314).

Using Chillies

Be careful. The heat-bearing substance, capsaicin, is released as you cut into chillies and it clings furiously to hands and chopping board and knife. If you have sensitive skin, you may even need to pull on rubber gloves before you begin to prepare chillies. Otherwise, make sure you wash your hands and all equipment thoroughly, in soapy water, and rinse well as soon as you have finished dealing with them. It is murder if you forget and rub your eyes with a chilli-tainted finger (and worse if you are male and take a pee, I am reliably informed). And while I'm on the subject of capsaicin, it is worth noting that it is not water-soluble. If your mouth becomes over-inflamed halfway through a curry or some other hot dish, drink something alcoholic to cool it down. Water only provides very temporary relief.

Chillies can be used in a huge number of ways, not only in savoury dishes but also, more surprisingly, in some sweet dishes, too. Fresh chillies have a lovely juicy, grassy flavour, while dried chillies have deeper, spicier notes and are more concentrated. There are few rules to using chillies, except to be a little cautious the first time you use an unfamiliar variety. In most instances, you can boost the heat in one way or another later on in the cooking process but it is harder to dampen it down if you've overdone matters (though yoghurt, stirred in or on the side, can help).

Most recipes printed in English suggest that you de-seed the chillies, to reduce the heat. It may also be worth removing the white ridges of pith that lie inside as these can be ferocious as well. The advantage of doing this is that you can then use more chillies, so boosting their flavour in a dish. However, when I've travelled in hot countries that take chillies for granted, I've often noticed that the whole chilli goes in, seeds and all. In the end, it is the cook who must make the final decision. If you want to leave the seeds in, there's nothing wrong with that.

Thick-fleshed fresh chillies (such as *jalapeños* or Fresnos but not Thai chillies) can be grilled and skinned like sweet peppers. This adds a smoky note to the finished dish, lovely in something like a salsa. Leave the chillies whole and grill them close to a thoroughly pre-heated grill or, better still, over charcoal turning frequently. When the chillies are blackened and blistered all over, drop them into a plastic bag, knot the bag loosely and leave until cool enough to handle. The trapped steam helps to free the skins. Strip off the skins and discard, pull away the stalk, open the chillies and de-seed them. The very daring may like to stuff these lightly cooked little bombs to eat whole. Keep the stuffing mild and soothing: ricotta or cream cheese and crab with mint, for instance, makes an ideal filling.

Thai-style Fried Noodles with Pork

I find a big plateful of noodles totally irresistible and always end up eating more than my fair share. This recipe is based on the Thai noodle dishes that sustained me royally and cheaply when I travelled round the country. All the effort goes into the preparation of the ingredients; the cooking is only a matter of a few minutes. For this dish, I like to use the tiny, slender, fiery red Thai chillies – a singleton will give a fairly mild heat, while two will liven things up rather more. In Thailand, the table would be set with extra bowls of condiments – one of sugar, a bowl of fish sauce with chopped chillies in it (a bottle of Tabasco or other chilli sauce is an easy option for those who crave violent heat), and another bowl with rice vinegar and probably more chillies in it! Assemble and prepare all the ingredients before you start cooking – this is what takes the time.

SERVES 4

280 g (10 oz) Thai *sen lek* noodles or medium Chinese egg noodles
3 tablespoons sunflower oil
4 garlic cloves, chopped
2.5 cm (1 inch) piece of fresh ginger, finely chopped
1–2 small fresh Thai chillies, de-seeded and thinly sliced
280 g (10 oz) minced pork
4 tomatoes, de-seeded and cut into strips
3 eggs, lightly beaten
Juice of 1 lime
2 tablespoons fish sauce
½ tablespoon caster sugar
4 tablespoons chopped roasted peanuts
6 spring onions, sliced
75 g (2½ oz) beansprouts
Salt and pepper
3 tablespoons roughly chopped fresh coriander, to garnish
Lime wedges, to serve

Soak and drain the noodles, or cook them according to the packet instructions.

Heat a large wok over a high heat, until it begins to smoke. Add the oil, warm through for a few seconds and then add the garlic, ginger and chillies. Give them a couple of stirs and then add the pork. Stir-fry for about 2 minutes, breaking up the lumps, and then add the tomatoes and eggs. Fry for a couple of seconds, add the noodles and toss and stir, scraping up egg and bits from the sides of the wok.

Now in go the lime juice, fish sauce and sugar. Mix well and then quickly add the peanuts. Stir-fry for a few seconds and then add the spring onions and beansprouts. Give the whole lot another couple of quick turns and tosses to heat it all through. Draw off the heat. Taste, adjust the seasonings and sprinkle with coriander. Serve with wedges of lime to squeeze over.

Chocolate and Chilli Ice Cream with Orange and Cinnamon Sauce

An absolute humdinger of an ice cream: the first taste reveals a rich chocolatey flavour with just a slight hint of a mysterious tingle. The tingle turns into a mild heat as you eat more, revealing its source and making a brilliant contrast with the cold. The orange sauce is optional but turns it into an even more spicy affair.

SERVES 6

300 ml (10 fl oz) single cream
1 dried red chilli, halved
1 cinnamon stick, halved
4 egg yolks
110 g (4 oz) light muscovado sugar
120 g (4¼ oz) plain chocolate, coarsely grated or finely chopped
250 ml (8 fl oz) double or whipping cream

For the sauce:

2 oranges
1 cinnamon stick
2 cloves
200 g (7 oz) caster sugar

Put the single cream into a pan, with the chilli and cinnamon stick halves. Bring gently up to the boil and then draw off the heat, cover and leave to stand for 20 minutes.

Meanwhile, using a hand-held electric beater, whisk the egg yolks with the sugar until pale (relatively speaking: the colour of the sugar means it will never go white) and fluffy. Bring the cream back to the boil, draw off the heat and stir in the chocolate. As soon as it has melted, pour (and scrape – it makes the mixture quite thick) on to the egg yolks, whisking constantly. Place the bowl over a pan of gently simmering water, making sure that the base does not come into contact with the water. Stir for 5 minutes. Lift the bowl off the pan and stand it in a basin of cold water. Leave to cool until tepid and then pick out the bits of chilli and cinnamon.

Whip the double or whipping cream lightly and fold it into the chocolate custard. Freeze in an ice-cream maker. If you don't have an ice-cream maker, pour the mixture into a shallow freezer container, cover and freeze at your freezer's lowest setting. Once the sides begin to harden, break them up and push into the centre. Return to the freezer. Repeat once more and then leave in the freezer until the ice cream is just set but not yet rock solid. Scrape into a processor or mixer and whizz fast to smooth out ice crystals. If you are totally lacking in machinery, you'll just have to flex your arm muscles and beat hard. Return the ice cream to the freezer.

Transfer from the freezer to the fridge about an hour before serving.

To make the sauce, pare the zest from the oranges in wide strips and then shred the strips (or use a zester, if you prefer). Blanch the shreds in boiling water for a minute, drain and then repeat. Squeeze the juice of the oranges. Put the juice and the blanched zest into a pan, with the cinnamon stick, cloves, sugar and 200 ml (7 fl oz) of water. Stir over a moderate heat until the sugar has dissolved and then bring up to the boil and simmer for about 25 minutes, stirring occasionally. Skim off what scum you can and then leave to cool.

To serve, put two or three small scoops of ice cream on each plate and spoon a little of the orange sauce, with its zest, around them.

Marinated Drumsticks with Salsa Mexicana

Salsa Mexicana, which runs around under a variety of aliases, is the most fundamental of all salsas, the prototype for a hundred and one variations. It is very easy to make – just a matter of chopping really – and can be served with all kinds of foods, from grilled beef steak, to fish and chicken. I usually make up a double batch because we will always use it up in one way or another. I rather like it with bread and cheese, and one or two spoonfuls scattered over a dull soup can work wonders.

SERVES 4

8 chicken drumsticks

For the marinade:

Juice of 1 lime

4 tablespoons olive oil

1 teaspoon ground cumin

1 tablespoon tomato ketchup

1 tablespoon honey

1 medium-hot fresh red chilli, de-seeded and finely chopped

2 thyme sprigs, bruised

Salt and pepper

For the salsa:

500 g (1 lb 2 oz) tomatoes, skinned, de-seeded and cut into 3 mm (1/8 inch) dice

1/2 fresh red Scotch Bonnet or *habanero* chilli or 1 milder red or green chilli, de-seeded and finely chopped

Juice of 1/2–1 lime

Sugar

1/2 red onion, finely chopped

2 garlic cloves, crushed

4–5 tablespoons chopped fresh coriander

Salt

Mix all the ingredients for the marinade and smear them over the chicken drumsticks. Leave to marinate for an hour or two.

Mix together all the salsa ingredients and then taste and adjust the seasoning, adding salt and a pinch of two of sugar, to taste. Cover and set aside until needed.

Pre-heat the oven to 190°C/375°F/Gas Mark 5 or pre-heat the grill to hot. Either roast the drumsticks for 20–30 minutes, turning occasionally, until browned and cooked through, or else grill them gently, turning frequently, until browned and perfectly cooked. Pierce the thickest part with a skewer to make sure the juices run clear and the flesh isn't pink.

Pipian Rojo de Almendras

This is the most sensational, deep brick-red stew, adapted from a Mexican original. It relies absolutely on dried *ancho* chillies and there is no substitute for them. They are not readily available in shops but you can order them by post (see page 314). If you have any small fondness for chillies, I urge you to try them, because they are quite unlike any we get here. Fairly huge, they have a marvellous, nutty, fruity flavour and give a startling colour. Raw, they taste moderately hot but once they have been cooked, as in the recipe, the heat is softened and transformed.

You'll probably end up with more sauce than you need for one sitting; save the rest for the next day. It's lovely spooned over plain rice with a dollop of soured cream or Greek yoghurt on top.

SERVES 4

1 chicken or duck, cut into 8 pieces
2 tablespoons lard or rendered duck fat
1 onion, sliced
2 garlic cloves, chopped
Salt and pepper

For the sauce:
12 *ancho* chillies
250 g (9 oz) whole blanched almonds
1/4 teaspoon ground allspice
Pinch of ground cloves

Pre-heat the oven to 190°C/375°F/Gas Mark 5. To make the sauce, lay the chillies on a baking tray and spread the almonds on another. Roast for about 5 minutes. The almonds should be a good golden brown; if not, return them to the oven for a few minutes more. Discard the stem and seeds of the chillies and soak the flesh for at least 4 hours, preferably overnight.

Drain the chillies. Grind the almonds to a powder in a food processor. Purée the soaked chillies with 300 ml (10 fl oz) of fresh water and mix with the almonds and the ground spices.

Brown the chicken or duck pieces in the fat. Set aside. Fry the onion in the same fat, until golden. Add the garlic and cook for a few minutes longer. Return the chicken to the pan, season with salt and pepper and add enough water to almost cover. Bring up to the boil and leave to simmer for 30 minutes.

Add the chilli and almond mixture and stir. Leave to simmer very gently for another 15 minutes or so, until the chicken is cooked and the sauce has thickened to a pleasing consistency.

black peppercorns

We all know that black pepper is a spice but few of us ever use it as one. At best, we fill our pepper mills with whole black peppercorns, grinding them instinctively over practically every savoury dish we make. At worst, we buy a small tub of ready-ground black pepper, which loses its flavour very quickly, adding nothing but a vestige of weary heat. It is quite a comedown for what was once the most highly valued spice of them all. Pepper was the king of spices, the one we fought wars over, the one that launched explorers across the seas to discover the new worlds and, they hoped, new sources of black pepper. It seems hard to believe now that we all take pepper for granted.

But pepper, high quality black peppercorns, are scheduled for rediscovery. They deserve not just a statutory corner in every kitchen but a place of honour. Black pepper is a spice with a full, pungent aroma, almost, indeed, a perfume; if it is used well, this can be brought out and enjoyed quite dramatically. Think in terms, say, of peppered steaks, one of the few well-known dishes to use pepper boldly. I'm not suggesting for one minute that pepper abandons its companion salt on the dining table, but it's worth giving it a chance to shine in its own right, too.

Peppercorns are the fruit of the vine *Piper nigrum*, native to the humid, steamy forests of Asia but now grown in many parts of the world. The vine stretches up and over its host tree, entwining it and hiding it in a swathe of green. Most of the black peppercorns that we get in this country are actually harvested when green and then left to dry in the sun. As they dry, the outer skin blackens and wrinkles. Green peppercorns are picked at exactly the same stage but then either freeze-dried or pickled in brine, to preserve their colour and fresh taste.

The best, most aromatic, black pepper I've ever tasted came from Kerala, in India: many years ago, I bought a tin labelled 'Tellicherry Pepper' and was struck by the difference. More recently, the king of kings has arrived here – Wynad black pepper, grown on the Wynad plateau in Kerala. This pepper is left on the vine until fully ripened and red, so that the flavour has more time to develop fully. Dried in the same way as ordinary peppercorns, these have a rustier colour and an intensity that is quite remarkable.

Buying and Storing Black Peppercorns

Always buy whole peppercorns and, if you don't already have one, buy a pepper mill to go with them. Ready-ground black pepper is a complete waste of money. The volatile oils that give pepper its aroma are released as soon as the pepper is ground, so, every time you open the tub of pepper, more of them will evaporate into thin air and pretty soon you will be left with nothing but greyish dust, with some heat to it but no pleasure.

Straightforward, everyday black peppercorns are fine but, if you come across anything a little more unusual (you can, for instance, buy light-roast and high-roast black peppercorns from Brazil, which have a distinctly nuttier flavour and heightened aroma), snap it up. Peppercorns keep well, stored in a dark, airtight container on a cool shelf. Some pepper enthusiasts even say that they improve in flavour as they age.

Using Black Peppercorns

Grind them over anything savoury, of course, but don't leave it at that. For a more unusual, highly aromatic flavour that highlights the spiciness of pepper, you can create your own pepper-mill mix. Recently, I've taken to keeping a special mill, filled with a mixture of roughly three parts black peppercorns to one part freeze-dried green peppercorns and one part coriander seeds. White peppercorns can be substituted for the green, or used as well. Some people also include pink peppercorns (which, incidentally, aren't peppercorns at all but the berries of the unrelated shrub *Schinus terebinthifolius*, though they do have a peppery heat to them), which look pretty, though that's not so noticeable once they've been ground.

However, peppercorns have a greater destiny than mere last-minute seasoning. I often dry-fry them, to heighten their flavour, and then crush them roughly in a mortar, to use as a hot spice, rather like chilli in intensity. They are delicious in quick-cooked chutneys, such as the *Lemon, Tomato and Black Pepper Chutney* (see page 57), but they go well, too, in practically any situation where the heat of a chilli might be welcome.

A few twists of black pepper can highlight and bring out the sweetness and subtlety of fruit, too. Pepper on strawberries is the most obvious example, but it does much the same job on pears, or more exotic fruit like mangoes. Be daring and try it.

Peppered Tarragon Peaches

Serve these peach slices, flavoured with the hot aroma of pepper and the aniseed scent of tarragon, with cold meats or even with a curry instead of a chutney. Try to get freestone peaches which come easily away from the stone. Clingstones will be harder to slice neatly and you will end up with a bit of a mush, even though the taste won't be impaired.

MAKES ENOUGH TO FILL THREE 250 ML (9 FL OZ) JARS

1.5 kg (3 lb) just-ripe peaches or nectarines
300 ml (10 fl oz) white wine vinegar
500 g (1 lb 2 oz) caster or granulated sugar
Three 5 cm (2 inch) pieces of cinnamon stick
2 teaspoons black peppercorns, coarsely crushed
3–6 fresh tarragon sprigs

Try skinning the peaches. Sometimes, if they are of the right type and right degree of ripeness, the skin will just pull away with little need for encouragement. If it sticks fast, bring a pan of water up to the boil and, one by one, dip the peaches into it for about 30 seconds and then strip off the skins if they are sufficiently loosened. Pop the peaches back in for another 30 seconds if need be, but don't just leave them idling in hot water – you don't want them half-cooked and mushy. Quarter the skinned peaches, discarding the stones. Cut out and discard any bruised or damaged patches.

Put all the remaining ingredients, except the tarragon, into a saucepan and stir over a moderate heat, until the sugar has completely dissolved. Bring up to the boil and simmer for 3 minutes. Add the peaches and simmer very, very gently over a low heat until they are tender and slightly translucent. Turn them once or twice, if you have to, but don't stir or you'll damage their shape. As soon as they are cooked, lift out with a slotted spoon and pack into sterilized jam jars or Kilner jars (see page 124 for sterilizing method), tucking a sprig or two of tarragon in with them and making sure that a piece of cinnamon and some of the peppercorns make their way into each jar. Reduce the syrup by about half and immediately pour it over the peaches, making sure that they are completely submerged. Seal with non-corrosive lids and label. When cold, store in a cool dark cupboard for at least three weeks before eating.

Grilled Mackerel with Lemon, Tomato and Black Pepper Chutney

This sweet, sharp, peppery and slightly bitter chutney combines cooked and fresh ingredients and goes particularly well with the rich flesh of mackerel, touched with the smokiness that grilling or barbecuing brings.

SERVES 4

4 mackerel
1 lemon, quartered
Olive or sunflower oil
Salt and pepper
For the chutney:
2 lemons
4 tablespoons caster sugar
1/2 tablespoon black mustard seeds
1 teaspoon coriander seeds, coarsely crushed
1/2 teaspoon black peppercorns, coarsely crushed
2 plum tomatoes, de-seeded and finely diced

To make the chutney, slice the lemons thinly with a sharp knife, discarding the ends. Save all the juice that is squeezed out as you cut. Lay the lemon slices in a shallow dish in a single layer. Pour over enough boiling water just to cover. Leave for 3 minutes and then drain and repeat. Drain again. Cut the blanched lemon pieces into quarters. Put the sugar into a saucepan with 6 tablespoons of water. Stir over a medium heat, until the sugar has dissolved. Now add the quartered lemon slices, any juice and the spices. Simmer for about 20 minutes, stirring occasionally, until the liquid is reduced and syrupy, and the lemon is translucent and tender. Draw off the heat and stir in the tomatoes. Leave to cool.

For the mackerel, make two or three deep slashes across the fattest part of the body on each side. Season inside and out with salt and pepper and slip a wedge of lemon inside each fish. Brush with oil and grill, close to the heat, for 4–5 minutes on each side, until just cooked through. Serve with the tomato and lemon chutney.

Steak au Poivre

Retro Cuisine is the latest buzz. In other words, all those dishes that were the height of fashion in the seventies are making a comeback – *Beef Wellington*, *Coq au Vin*, prawn cocktail and the like – far more exciting and appetizing than the renaissance of flared trousers. Let's hope it will be more of a success, too. One dish that has been severely neglected is *Steak au Poivre* (which actually dates from the early years of this century), a luxurious but quickly made dish for a special occasion. If you don't fancy all that cream, just eat the steaks with the pan juices poured over them. And, if you're not a meat-eater, you can use the same method for firm fish steaks.

SERVES 4

3 tablespoons black peppercorns, crushed
4 fillet or rump steaks, about 2.5 cm (1 inch) thick
30 g (1 oz) clarified butter or 2 tablespoons sunflower oil
2 tablespoons brandy
100 ml (3½ fl oz) dry white wine
300 ml (10 fl oz) double cream
Salt

Spread the peppercorns out on a plate. Press the steaks firmly into them, so that each side is evenly coated. Heat the butter or oil in a frying-pan that is large enough to take all four steaks. Fry them over a moderate heat, until they are done to your liking. For a medium-rare steak, allow around 3–4 minutes on each side. Take the steaks out of the pan and keep them warm.

Skim off the fat in the pan, leaving only the juices. Add the brandy, warm through for a minute or so and then, if you have a gas hob, tilt the pan so that the juices ignite; if you have an electric hob, light the juices with a match at arm's length. Once the flames have died down, add the wine and bring up to the boil, scraping in all the residues. Boil until reduced by half and then stir in the cream and boil down for another 3–4 minutes, until reduced to a sauce with a pleasing consistency. Season with salt and then serve with the steaks.

star anise

This veritable star of Eastern cooking has become something of a bright spark in the West over recent years. Not before time. Star anise was first introduced to Europe, reputedly by an English seaman, at the end of the sixteenth century. It found a discrete importance in the manufacture of anise-scented liqueurs, such as anisette – the essential oil anethole is common to both star anise and the commoner Western spice aniseed, though they are quite unrelated – but has remained relatively unknown in kitchens.

This pretty spice is actually composed of a cluster of pointed seed pods (usually eight, although there may be as few as five or as many as ten), radiating out like the petals of a flower. It comes from a small tree, a member of the otherwise poisonous magnolia family, that grows prolifically in northern Vietnam and south-west China and is also cultivated in Japan. Curiously, the spice has occasionally been called 'Siberian cardamom', perhaps because it was brought to Europe along the China–Russia tea route.

You may well have come across it without realizing, since it is one of the spices used to make Chinese five-spice powder. Don't be put off by descriptions of the flavour as 'harsher' or 'more bitter' than ordinary aniseed. It is different, that's all, with an attractive bitterness, and an echo of liquorice which even liquorice-loathers like me find immensely appealing.

Buying and Storing Star Anise

Though it is widely available, I do my best to buy star anise from a specialist spice shop, or from an oriental food store, rather than a supermarket. I like to buy it whole in its proper, charming stars (or at least mostly whole – there are bound to be a few broken pieces in any packet), not squashed into small jars willy-nilly, section by section. Since it keeps for months, and probably years in an airtight jar, I reckon it's worth waiting for the opportunity to buy the best you can get.

Using Star Anise

I usually use it as it is, without grinding it up or tampering with it, except, perhaps, to snap a star in half or into individual sections when I want a gentler hint of aniseed than a whole star might impart. It makes a surprising, aromatic, enticing difference to braised meat and chicken dishes, used in particular in the Chinese way with soy sauce and sugar, though it can work well with fish in moderation. It is also an important ingredient in Vietnam, where it scents their national dish, the beef soup *pho*. I often add star anise to stewed fruit dishes or compotes, or dot a few sections around the filling for a crumble before covering and baking.

Don't be tempted to try to extract the shiny seeds from the individual seed pods. It's not worth the bother, since these are the least aromatic part of the spice. If you want to grind star anise, break up your stars into sections and grind in a sturdy electric coffee grinder or, better, a purpose-made tough spice grinder. If you want to create your own five-spice powder, grind together 4 star anise (broken up), 1 tablespoon of toasted Szechuan peppercorns, 2 teaspoons of cinnamon, 1 tablespoon of fennel seeds and 1 teaspoon of cloves. Dried or ground ginger, liquorice root or cardamom can also be added.

Peking Star Anise Pork

The smell as this cooks is heavenly. It's almost worth cooking for that alone. As it happens, the finished product is every bit as good: subtly scented pork, to be served cold with a little of the cooking juices. It is an ideal dish for a cold summer lunch, or even a Christmas-time buffet, since it can be made a day or two in advance. Try serving it with a watercress salad or with peppery rocket: not very authentic but very good. Left-overs make great sandwiches.

The pork rind gives a gelatinous, smooth quality to the liquid and improves the flavour but I've made this with a rindless joint, too, and it is still very good though the juices are less likely to gel.

SERVES 4–6

1 kg (2¼ lb) boned pork shoulder or leg
2 teaspoons Szechuan peppercorns or black peppercorns
1 cm (½ inch) piece of fresh ginger, sliced
5 star anise
1 cinnamon stick
4 spring onions, roughly chopped
120 g (4¼ oz) demerara sugar
60 ml (4 tablespoons) dry sherry
100 ml (3½ fl oz) dark soy sauce
1 litre (1¾ pints) chicken or pork stock or water

Bring a large pan of water to the boil and lower the pork into it. Bring back to the boil and blanch for 3 minutes. Drain thoroughly and cut off the rind. Cut the rind into postage-stamp sized pieces. Place the pork in a pan that will take it neatly, along with the pieces of rind. Dry-fry the peppercorns in a heavy frying-pan, until they give off a heady scent. Tip into the pan. Tuck the ginger, star anise, cinnamon stick and spring onions around the pork. Add the sugar, sherry and soy sauce. Pour in the stock or water. Bring up to the boil and then reduce the heat, cover the pan and leave to simmer very gently for 2½ hours, until the pork is heart-rendingly tender. Turn the meat every now and then, so that it cooks evenly.

Lift the cooked pork out into a deep bowl. Return the pan to a high heat and boil hard, until the liquid has reduced by about half. Strain the liquid over the meat and leave to cool. Cover and store in the fridge overnight or longer, turning the meat once in a while.

Serve the pork thinly sliced, with a little of the juices, roughly chopped if they have set.

Pear and Blackberry Compote with Star Anise

A twist on that old favourite, stewed apple and blackberry. Here it is pears that make the grade, and the compote is flavoured with star anise. One whole star gives a fairly subtle aniseed flavour; use two if you are rather partial to it and would like a bolder presence. Serve the compote hot or cold, with clotted cream, vanilla ice cream, crème fraiche or Greek yoghurt.

SERVES 6–8

5 pears, peeled, cored and sliced

1–2 star anise

450 g (1 lb) blackberries

250 g (9 oz) caster sugar

1 cinnamon stick

Put all the ingredients in a pan and add about 150 ml (5 fl oz) of water. Cover and cook over a low heat for about 5 minutes, until the blackberry juice begins to flow, stirring once or twice to dissolve the sugar. Simmer until the pear slices are very tender (this may be no more than a few minutes if they were fairly ripe, longer if they were on the hard side). Serve hot or cold.

Winter Squash Soup with Star Anise and Basil and Lime Cream

An excellent autumn or winter soup, with a beautiful, rich orange colour. The sweetness of winter squash carries the scent of star anise, ginger and basil well. For a more everyday supper leave out the finishing swirl of whipped flavoured cream, if you like, but this sharp basil and lime cream melting into the soup is a perfect finish for a smarter occasion.

SERVES 6–8

1.5 kg (3 lb) piece of winter squash, seeds and rind removed, roughly cubed

5 garlic cloves

1 large onion, chopped

3 cm (1 1/2 inch) piece of fresh ginger, chopped

3 tablespoons sunflower oil

2 fresh parsley sprigs

1 fresh thyme sprig

1 bay leaf

3 star anise

340 g (12 oz) tomatoes, skinned, de-seeded and roughly chopped

2 litres (3 1/2 pints) vegetable or chicken stock

Salt and pepper

For the basil and lime cream:

300 ml (10 fl oz) whipping cream

Juice of 1 lime

Fresh basil leaves

After preparation, you should end up with about 1 kg (2 1/4 lb) of cubed squash flesh. Chop two of the garlic cloves but leave the rest whole. Put the chopped and whole garlic into a large pan, with the onion, ginger, oil and squash. Tie the herbs together in a bundle with a length of string and throw those in, too. Cover the pan and leave to sweat over a low heat for 10 minutes, stirring once or twice.

Uncover the pan and add the star anise, tomatoes and stock. Season with salt and pepper and bring up to the boil. Leave to simmer for 20 minutes, until the squash is tender.

Pick out and discard the bundle of herbs and the pieces of star anise. Either pass the soup through a *mouli-légumes* (vegetable mill), or liquidize and sieve it. Taste and adjust the seasoning. Re-heat, if necessary, when needed.

Shortly before serving, make the basil and lime cream. Pour the cream into a bowl and add the lime juice. Whisk until it holds its shape loosely. Chop a small handful of basil leaves and fold in. As you ladle the soup into bowls, top with a floating crown of the cream.

Szechuan pepper

Szechuan pepper, Sichuan pepper, *fagara*, anise pepper, Chinese pepper, flower pepper: all the same thing, but not a true pepper at all. Szechuan pepper is the sun-dried berry of a Chinese wild prickly ash. The tiny berries are rusty brown and it is the husks, rather than the seeds themselves, that form the bulk of the spice, giving it its warm, heady scent of incense and citrus.

Szechuan pepper is a hot spice but its heat is more of a tingle on the tongue than a direct heat. It is widely used in the cooking of the Szechuan province of China, usually with ginger and star anise, and is an essential component of Chinese five-spice powder. It is

Opposite *Winter Squash Soup with Star Anise and Basil and Lime Cream*

excellent with fatty meats, such as duck or pork, even when used as nothing more than a simple table seasoning, like pepper. In fact, the Chinese make a condiment of ground roasted Szechuan pepper and salt (five parts pepper to one part salt) and it's an idea well worth appropriating.

To get the best out of Szechuan pepper, dry-fry over a low to moderate heat in a heavy frying-pan, until it scents the air (this is worth doing for the smell alone). Throw out any blackened husks, which will be bitter. Leave to cool and grind before using.

saffron

I tend to associate saffron with hot places, such as Spain, Iran or India. It is an exotic spice, without any doubt, rich in history and portent, beloved of kings and sultans, an Arabian Nights spice. If you've ever read anything about saffron, you are bound to know that it is the most expensive spice in the world, worth more than its weight in gold; but, for all that, for all its exalted past and honoured present, it is a spice that rewards the user ten fold. A tiny amount, a small fraction of a gram, betrays its presence in any dish with all the grandeur of true nobility, bestowing its pure golden colour streaked sparsely with fiery red and, naturally, its remarkable, incomparable flavour.

Describing the taste of saffron is well-nigh impossible. It's often labelled bitter-sweet. I think it has a suprisingly alluring, metallic edge to it, but the description I like best is 'honey laced with the sea'. This comes not from some romantic Eastern poet but from the one commercial British grower, Caroline Riden, who is quite besotted with the stuff. She says, too, that using it is like cooking with living gold. When she began to grow saffron, back at the beginning of the eighties, it was hard to come by in her corner of north Wales. She planted her first autumn-flowering saffron crocuses for her own pleasure and as a challenge. She had been told that growing saffron here was at best difficult, and probably impossible. Now she has two thriving plots and dries and sells her pure British saffron for exclusive delicatessens.

British saffron is nothing new, of course. It was said to have been brought to this country by Phoenician traders. Saffron Walden in Essex took its name from the once-vigorous saffron business (saffron was used to dye wool as well as to 'endor' – make golden – food) that surrounded the town; and a tradition for saffron buns and cake survives still in Cornwall (and very good they can be too – don't miss out if you are ever down there on holiday). The Industrial Revolution killed off this highly labour-intensive business, leaving it to other countries to produce the world's saffron supplies – some of the best comes from Spain (the

Phoenicians brought it there, too), from the great plains of La Mancha, where Don Quixote tilted at windmills.

Caroline longs to bring back British saffron fields in their full glory. She has a missionary zeal for the promotion of saffron, lecturing when she can, selling crocus bulbs to fellow-enthusiasts. Spurred on by my own fondness for saffron, I travelled to the farm she and her husband John run near Wrexham, on a phenomenally miserable, rain-sodden day, expecting to be cheered by the sight of carpets of purple crocuses as far as the eye could see. The late Indian summer had seen to it that only a sparse speckling of flowers greeted me. The saffron crocus needs a ground temperature of 5°C (41°F) to flower in its full glory and the cold just hadn't struck yet. But at least I have now seen a real saffron crocus in the flesh and I've learnt firsthand why saffron is so very costly. Every flower has to be picked by hand, on a dry day (hah!) and then, again by hand, the fiery red tassel that will become the saffron itself must be nipped or pulled away. It takes 150 flowers, give or take, to make a single gram of dried saffron; if grams and kilograms don't mean much to you, that's an astonishing 70,000 flowers to a pound.

Buying Saffron

Saffron is actually the dried style branches, tipped by the stigma, of the autumnal saffron crocus – not to be confused with the ordinary springtide garden crocus, though they look very similar. These style branches meet at the top of the style, the long yellow thread that dives down to the base of the flower. Traditionally, the highest grade of saffron is called 'nipped', because the branches alone are nipped off to give an unsullied, molten-red spice. When the saffron is 'pulled', the yellow style comes with it. Some think the flavour of pulled saffron is actually warmer and more complex, even if it is reckoned to be only the second grade. I've never been able to detect a difference, but this explains price variations.

The one thing you should always avoid is cheap saffron. In fact, this is a contradiction in terms. Real saffron is never cheap. Bargain-bin saffron is bound to be adulterated (maybe including the tasteless yellow stamen of the flower or inferior wild crocuses or, worse still, the saffron may be cut with marguerite petals or something similar).

Good saffron will have a vivid, deep, powerful colour, long threads and will be crackly and crisp to the touch, though of course you can't test for that until you get home. Dull, dusty, drab, short threads are old and have been badly stored. It is harder to distinguish the quality (and purity) of powdered saffron, which is why I never buy it. Grinding the threads to a powder is a matter of seconds, anyway.

Storing and Using Saffron

Saffron stored in an airtight container, away from the light (ignore the spice rack and opt for the obscurity of the kitchen cupboard), will last for several years, but don't forget it's there.

Saffron and rice go hand in glove together – in paella, in risotto, in pilaffs – but this is just the beginning. Saffron with fish is something of a classic, too, particularly in those great Mediterranean fish soup-stews, such as *bouillabaisse* and *zarzuela*. It marries particularly well with tomato sauces, though the glorious colour is obscured. On the sweet side, it turns quite homely baking into something decidedly sophisticated and transforms milky or creamy puddings such as custards and ice creams.

To use whole threads of saffron, which will leave beautiful tell-tale streaks of red as well as colouring the main body of the dish yellow-gold, take a pinch of saffron – that's about 25 threads if you're new to the stuff, but 30–35 if you love it, as I do – cover with hot water or milk and leave for at least 20 minutes, to develop its full colour and flavour. If you don't want to use it immediately, or have more than you need, the infusion can be kept, covered, in the fridge for up to four or five days if soaked in water; two or three days if in milk. Excess saffron water can also be frozen in ice-cube trays (a tip I picked up from Caroline Riden).

Ground saffron delivers a perfect even gilt, and can be added straight to a dish without any need for soaking. To grind saffron, toast the strands for a few seconds in a dry pan over a moderate heat, to crisp them up and heighten the flavour. Tip into a mortar, cool for a few minutes and then grind with a pestle.

Saffron and Garlic Mash

Olive oil mash may be all the rage but I still love butter in my mashed potatoes. These ones are traditionally buttery but they are togged up with two other stylish ingredients – garlic and golden saffron. Don't be too taken aback by the quantity of garlic: cooked this way, the garlic mellows and softens to something very subtle. Surprisingly, the mere pinch of saffron gives far more definition.

SERVES 4–6

10 garlic cloves, peeled but whole
1 kg (2¼ lb) floury potatoes
300 ml (10 fl oz) milk
A good pinch of saffron strands
60 g (2 oz) butter
Salt

Put the garlic into a small pan, cover with water and bring up to the boil. Drain. Boil the potatoes in their skins, with the blanched garlic. While the potatoes are cooking, bring the milk up to the boil, draw off the heat and sprinkle the saffron strands over it. Drain and peel the potatoes and return them to the pan, along with the garlic and the butter. Mash thoroughly with a potato masher while still hot. Beat over a low heat, gradually adding the saffron milk a splash or two at a time. Season with salt. Taste and adjust the seasoning and serve.

Saffron Tea Bread

Though Caroline Riden's range of saffron recipes spans all the great saffron countries, she particularly likes to use it in baking, an art that still thrives in Wales. This tea bread is lifted instantly out of the ordinary by the addition of saffron. If you want to slice it neatly, you will have to keep it for a day to firm up, but I admit to loving it warm from the oven even if it does crumble hopelessly.

MAKES ONE LOAF

Good pinch of saffron strands
100 g (3½ oz) butter
100 g (3½ oz) caster sugar
100 g (3½ oz) golden sultanas
50 g (1¾ oz) glacé cherries, halved
280 g (10 oz) plain flour
2 teaspoons baking powder
A pinch of salt

Put the saffron in a jar or jug and pour in 230 ml (8 fl oz) of hot water. Leave for 20 minutes (or longer if more convenient).

Put the butter and sugar into a pan large enough to take all the ingredients and stir over a moderate heat, until the butter has melted and mixed evenly with the sugar. Now add the sultanas and cherries, give them a quick stir and then pour in the saffron water, complete with all the threads. Return to the heat and simmer gently for 5 minutes. Leave to cool.

Pre-heat the oven to 180°C/350°F/Gas Mark 4. Prepare a 500 g (1 lb) loaf tin by greasing it and then cutting two wide strips of non-stick baking parchment and laying them at right angles in the tin, pressing down against the inside so that one runs the length of the tin and up the ends, with an overhang at each end, while the other runs across the first, over the narrow base of the tin and up the sides again, with an overhang. The idea is to form a sort of cradle, so that the cooked loaf can just be lifted straight out of the tin when it is done.

Sift the flour with the baking powder and salt. Tip into the saffron mixture and stir to form a batter. Pour into the prepared loaf tin and smooth down. Bake for 1–1¼ hours, or until a skewer inserted into the centre comes out clean. Lift out of the tin on to a wire rack and leave to cool. Serve thickly sliced and plentifully buttered.

Brill with Saffron Sauce

Once you've made and reduced the fish stock (which can be done in advance), this is a brilliantly easy dish to make. The pale fish surrounded by golden sauce, dotted with capers and bright green parsley, looks and tastes magnificent. Lemon sole or plaice make a more everyday substitute for brill.

SERVES 4

2 brill, lemon sole or plaice, weighing about 1.5 kg (3 lb) each, filleted and skinned
3 tablespoons plain flour
1 heaped teaspoon ground cumin
30 g (1 oz) butter
1 tablespoon sunflower oil
1/8 teaspoon ground saffron
Salt and pepper
Lemon juice
For the fish stock:
Bones and trimmings from the fish
100 ml (3 1/2 fl oz) Noilly Prat or dry white wine
1 tablespoon Pernod
1 carrot, quartered
1 leek, thickly sliced, or 1/2 onion, quartered
1 celery stick, thickly sliced
6 peppercorns
1 bay leaf
2 fresh parsley sprigs
1 tablespoon small capers
Chopped fresh parsley
Lemon or lime wedges

Begin by making the fish stock. Put all the ingredients into a pan, with enough water to cover generously. Bring up to the boil and leave to simmer for 20 minutes. Skim any scum off the stock. Strain the stock and discard the debris. Pour it into a wide frying-pan and boil hard, until syrupy and reduced by about three-quarters. Measure out 150 ml (5 fl oz) and reserve (any left-over stock can be frozen). Season the fish fillets lightly with salt and set aside for half an hour.

Pat the fillets dry. Mix the flour with a little salt and pepper and the cumin. Heat half the butter and all the oil until foaming, in a frying-pan that is large enough to take all the fillets. Dust the fish fillets with the seasoned flour, shake off any excess and lay them in the pan. Fry for about 2 minutes on each side, or until just cooked through. Transfer the fish to a warm serving dish and keep warm while you finish the sauce.

Tip excess fat out of the pan and add the reduced fish stock. Sprinkle over the saffron and stir over a moderate heat until very hot. Season with salt and pepper and a dash of lemon juice. Add the remaining butter in small knobs and swirl, tip and tilt the pan until the butter has melted into the sauce, thickening it lightly and giving it a rich gloss. Taste and adjust the seasoning.

Serve the fish surrounded by a pool of saffron sauce, scattered with capers and parsley and accompanied by lemon or lime wedges.

Opposite *Brill with Saffron Sauce*

Saffron and Honey Ice Cream

Saffron and honey, two of nature's golden foods, are well suited to each other. I've loved the combination ever since I tasted Joyce Molyneux's (of the Carved Angel in Dartmouth) baked honey and saffron custards, with gooseberries. Here, they are diluted again by cream but frozen stiff to a rich, ambrosial ice cream.

SERVES 6
5 egg yolks
300 ml (10 fl oz) milk
150 ml (5 fl oz) single cream
A generous pinch of saffron strands
85 g (3 oz) runny honey
230 ml (8 fl oz) double cream

Whisk the egg yolks in a large bowl. Bring the milk and the single cream up to the boil. Draw off the heat and stir in the saffron strands and honey. Quickly pour the hot, milky mixture on to the egg yolks, whisking constantly. Set the bowl over a pan of gently simmering water, making sure the bottom of the bowl doesn't touch the water, and stir until the custard thickens enough to coat the back of the spoon. Lift the bowl off the pan and dunk into a shallow bowl of cold water, to halt cooking. Leave to cool, stirring occasionally to distribute the streaks of colour left by the saffron strands.

Whip the double cream until it is just beginning to hold its shape, but is still floppy. Fold it into the custard and then freeze in an ice-cream maker. If you don't have one, pre-set your freezer to its coldest setting. Pour the mixture into a shallow freezer container, cover and slide into the freezer. Leave until the sides are setting and then take out, break them up and shove into the middle of the container. Repeat once and then leave until the mixture is just set firmly, but not yet solid. Scrape out into a food processor and whizz quickly until smooth, to break down all those jagged ice crystals. If you don't have a processor, take a deep breath, flex your muscles and beat the ice cream hard. Return for the last time to the container, put it back into the freezer and leave it alone to freeze solid.

To serve, transfer from the freezer to the fridge about 40 minutes before serving.

Shrikand

I first tasted Shrikand when I was a student and my tight budget led me inexorably to the doors of a shiny Indian vegetarian restaurant in London's Westbourne Grove. It was love at first mouthfuls as well as profound admiration for the imaginative, almost magical, way that simple ingredients were combined and spiced and turned out in different guises. This scented creamy pudding was the crowning glory and since then I look out for it on Indian menus, though it doesn't surface as often as I might like. Still, it is very easy to make at home, as long as you allow plenty of time for the curds to drain. Cheaper, thinner yoghurts can be used instead of the Greek yoghurt, but you'll need to increase the quantity and increase the draining time, so you save nothing at all – not even calories! Even with Greek yoghurt, you'll be amazed at how much liquid drains off.

SERVES 6–8

1 kg (2¼ lb) Greek or Greek-style yoghurt
Generous pinch of saffron strands
1 tablespoon hot milk
4 green cardamom pods
2 tablespoons skinned pistachio nuts, chopped
½ tablespoon rosewater
1 tablespoon chopped blanched almonds
125g (4 oz) caster sugar

Line a large sieve with damp muslin and spoon the yoghurt into it. Leave to drain for about 5 hours until the curds are fairly firm. Scrape the drained curds into a bowl. Soak the saffron threads in the hot milk for half an hour. Slit open the green cardamom pods and extract the black seeds. Crush to a powder. Beat the saffron milk, cardamom, half the pistachio nuts and the remaining ingredients into the drained yoghurt. The pudding should be very thick and creamy, but if it seems too dry, stir in one or two tablespoons of milk or cream. Divide between 6–8 small ramekins (it may not look much per person, but it is very rich) and serve lightly chilled, scattered with the remaining pistachios.

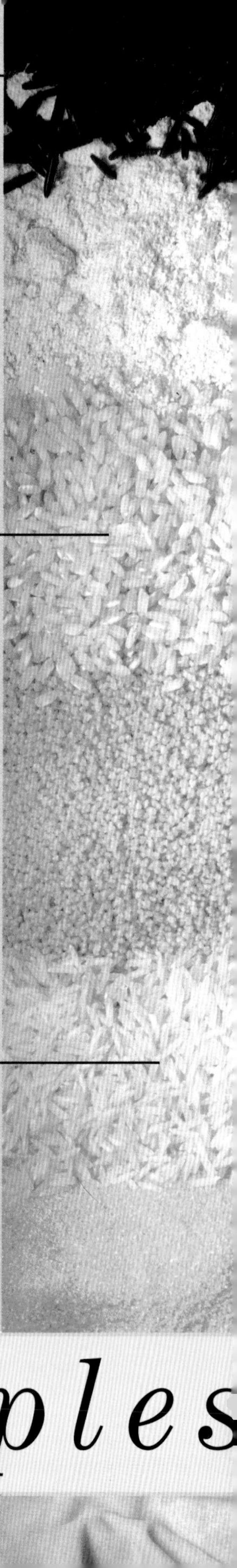

wild rice

risotto rice

basmati rice

starchy staples

spelt
flour
couscous
cornmeal
filo
pastry

couscous

Couscous is a dish that expatriate Moroccans yearn for. They cook it to remind them of their homeland, their family and their friends. It assuages homesickness and fills the stomach, distracting them from the chill of colder climates. A communal dish, it can bring families or like-minded compatriots together. But couscous is also a simple grain, or more technically, the smallest of pastas, which comes rattling and swooshing in boxes emblazoned with pretty pictures of camels or the like. Or it comes in big sacks, rolled down to expose the pale yellow grain, if you can find a Moroccan shop catering to traditional Moroccan cooks or if you head off to Morocco.

Couscous, the grain, forms the starchy filling substance of couscous, the dish. The other part is a big stew, usually of meat and vegetables boiled up in a spicy broth. Together they form what is, I suppose, the national dish of Morocco. When it is well made, it is a superb dish and a brilliant way to feed a crowd of people.

An invitation to lunch at the Moroccan Women's Centre, in the lower floors of the distinctly unexotic Trellick Towers (an almightily ugly, grey concrete tower block that dominates the west London skyline) took me into a new world. I'd never realized that this part of London was home to a large community of Moroccans, but a shopping trip with Karima and Zohra to buy the wherewithal for the weekly lunch party was a real eye-opener. They took me to a nearby Moroccan grocery, where they dismissed the quick-cooking, instant couscous with a disparaging wave of the hand. The fully dried couscous that needs lengthy steaming was what they were after. We bought spices and meat and the requisite seven vegetables, *smen* (aged butter with a most particular aroma) and bulging bags of couscous. If you're in the area, shop at the market stalls and Le Maroc, where you can buy halal meat, several different kinds of couscous, metal *couscoussières*, tagines, beautiful earthenware dishes and teapots, wonderful gaudy clocks depicting the Koran, spices of all kinds displayed in earthenware bowls, teas – mostly green tea and gunpowder tea for making fresh mint tea – nine different kinds of olive (the mixed olives with chilli are fabulous) and beautiful sugar cones wrapped in deep blue tissue paper.

They introduced me to an elderly lady who used to make her own couscous, rolling the tiny grains of semolina in fine semolina flour to make little rounds of couscous no bigger than a pinhead. No one much does that any more. And then they showed me the proper, time-consuming way to cook couscous, each tiny grain steamed and oiled and separated and steamed again and again, and insisted that it was far superior to modern quick-cooking couscous. Next day, at home, I cooked it their way and I tried out four different brands of quick or instant couscous. The traditional method did produce the most perfect, fluffy, silky- smooth grains, but the best of the five-minute versions was so good that I breathed a sigh of relief.

I've always thought of couscous as a brilliant storecupboard stand-by, ready in minutes but patient enough to hang around if supper has to wait. It is an excellent accompaniment to all kinds of stews and damp dishes, since it soaks up juices in a most encouraging way. Moroccans deftly gather up the broth-soaked couscous into a ball with the right hand, to pop straight into the mouth.

Buying and Storing Couscous

If you are ever strolling past a Moroccan grocery, or take a trip to Morocco, it really is worth buying a stock of the fully dried, slow-steaming couscous, since it will keep for months. Then, when time is on your side and you want to make a proper, fully fledged Moroccan couscous for a special party, you can do it all properly and taste couscous at its best.

For normal, everyday cooking, though, you can be more than satisfied with any of the boxed, quick-cooking or instant couscous, sold now in many supermarkets as well as specialist shops including French delicatessens. The only one to avoid is the boil-in-the-bag one-minute couscous which, when cooked to packet instructions, turns out soggy and damp and rather unpleasant.

Loose couscous should be stored in an airtight container.

Using Couscous

The traditional cooking method is given in the recipe on page 78. For quick-cooking couscous, either follow the packet instructions or try my fail-safe method. Tip the grain into a measuring jug and note the volume then pour into a bowl. Add double the volume of very hot water or stock. Leave for 20–30 minutes to absorb the liquid. Drain off any excess. Pile into a shallow ovenproof serving dish (I usually use a gratin dish), dot generously with butter and cover loosely with foil. Slip into a low to warm oven, and leave for at least 20 minutes, and up to 1 hour, while you get on with something else. The couscous steams away contentedly inside its foil tent and, by the time you get it out of the oven to serve, the grains just need to be forked up a little and it is not only ready but also light, fluffy and buttery. If you think it needs minor dressing up, mix in a little very finely chopped parsley.

For a fancier accompaniment, mix chopped apricots, raisins and toasted nuts into the couscous before it goes into the oven. Not too much, or it will end up more like pudding, but enough to liven the grains up nicely.

There are recipes for sweet couscous dishes, where the grain is simmered in milk with sugar and spices (look in Moroccan cookery books) and I've even come across one European recipe for chocolate-flavoured couscous ... I'm not quite sure about that one.

Couscous with Roast Tomatoes, Peppers and Goats' Cheese

This is a distinctly modern, European way of using couscous, topped with an unctuous, deeply flavoured sauce made from roasted tomatoes and peppers and finished with chunks of roasted onion, pepper and tomatoes and salty goats' cheese. I cannot claim the idea as my own, sadly, since I stole it from a press release for an Italian product and then reworked it to do without the poor product in question. Apologies to the public relations company and the producers and thanks for a great idea.

SERVES 4

For the vegetables:

8 plum tomatoes, halved

1 red onion, quartered

2 red peppers, de-seeded and cut into large chunks

1 fresh red chilli

4 whole garlic cloves

2 fresh thyme sprigs

3 tablespoons olive oil

1 tablespoon sherry vinegar

1 tablespoon caster sugar

Salt and pepper

For the couscous:

300 g (11 oz) couscous

600 ml (1 pint) hot chicken or vegetable stock

2 tablespoons olive oil

3 tablespoons chopped fresh parsley

110 g (4 oz) goats' cheese, de-rinded and roughly diced

6 fresh basil leaves, shredded

Pre-heat the oven to 220°C/425°F/Gas Mark 7. Oil a large, shallow, ovenproof dish or roasting tin. Place the plum tomatoes in it in a single layer, cut-side up, along with the onion quarters, the peppers, the whole chilli and the garlic. Tuck the thyme sprigs amongst them. Drizzle over the olive oil and the sherry vinegar. Then sprinkle on the sugar, salt and pepper. Bake, uncovered, for 40–50 minutes, until the onions are beginning to brown and catch at the edges.

Meanwhile, put the couscous into a bowl and pour on the steaming hot stock. Leave for 15 minutes, until all the liquid has been absorbed, stirring once or twice. Drizzle over the olive oil and mix well. Cover with foil and keep warm in a moderately hot oven.

When the vegetables are done, pick out about half the tomatoes, peppers and onions and keep warm. Unless you want a hot sauce, remove the chilli. Tip the rest into a food processor, scraping in any juices and caramelized brown goo. Don't worry about the garlic skins. Process until smooth; then sieve. Thin with a little water or stock if necessary. Taste and adjust the seasoning.

Take the couscous out of the oven, add the parsley and fork up a little to mix in the greenery and separate the grains. Pile up in a serving dish. Pour over the sauce, arrange the reserved vegetables on top and and scatter with goats' cheese and basil shreds. Serve hot.

Opposite *Couscous with Roast Tomatoes, Peppers and Goats' Cheese*

Tabbouleh

This Moroccan salad is a wonderfully fresh, zingy mixture of couscous (it is usually made with left-over couscous but it's worth preparing a batch from scratch) with oodles of chopped fresh herbs and lots of lemon juice. It is a perfect summer salad, lovely as part of a mixed buffet (and handy, since the flavours improve on keeping for 24 hours) or indeed just as a side dish with cold chicken or grilled prawns, or good cheese and pitta bread. For a more Middle Eastern feel, serve with warm pitta bread, hummus, spiced black olives and taramasalata.

SERVES 6

150 g (5 oz) quick couscous or 310 g (11 oz) cooked couscous
6 tablespoons finely chopped fresh parsley
3 tablespoons chopped fresh mint
3 tomatoes, skinned, de-seeded and very finely diced
1/2 red onion, very finely chopped
Juice of 1 1/2–2 lemons
4 tablespoons olive oil
Salt and pepper

Pour 300 ml (10 fl oz) of boiling water over the couscous and leave for 20 minutes, stirring once or twice, until all the water has been absorbed.

Mix with all the remaining ingredients. Taste and adjust the seasonings. Cover and leave overnight.

Stir and taste again. Serve at room temperature.

Traditional Moroccan Couscous with Seven Vegetables

The traditional method of cooking couscous, steamed and massaged with oil and steamed again, and then finished with aged butter (*smen*, which you will only find in Moroccan food stores) or ordinary butter, takes time and patience, but it does produce the finest tasting and textured grain of all.

When you can't spare the time to coddle your couscous into its finest state, use one of the quick-cooking types instead, to serve with this most popular stew of lamb and vegetables.

In this version, based on the one cooked for me at the Moroccan Women's Centre in west London, the seven types of vegetable are onions, carrots, swede, cabbage, courgettes, winter squash and tomatoes, but these can be varied according to what is most readily available, as long as there is a good balance of tastes and textures.

SERVES 8

1 kg (2 1/4 lb) couscous

100 ml (3 1/2 fl oz) sunflower oil

100 g (3 1/2 oz) butter or 1 generous tablespoon *smen*

2 tablespons salt

For the stew:

1/2 shoulder of lamb, weighing about 1.5 kg (3 lb), cut into chunks (a good 7–10 cm/3–4 inches) across, bone and all

2 large onions, chopped

4 garlic cloves, chopped

2 heaped teaspoons ground ginger

2 teaspoons freshly ground black pepper

1 tablespoon ground cumin

A generous pinch of saffron strands

100 ml (3 1/2 fl oz) sunflower oil

4 large carrots, cut in half lengthways and each length halved

1 swede, peeled and cut into 5 cm (2 inch) chunks

1/2 small white cabbage, cut into 6 chunks

700 g–1 kg (1 1/2–2 1/4 lb) orange-fleshed winter squash, e.g. onion squash, or pumpkin, peeled, de-seeded and cut into 5 cm (2 inch) chunks

340 g (12 oz) courgettes, cut into 5 cm (2 inch) chunks

4 tomatoes, halved

Salt

To cook traditional couscous, with grain that has not been pre-cooked and dried, you will either need a proper *couscoussière* or else you will have to rig up an approximation. First of all the *k'dra* or *barma*, in other words the bottom part of the *couscoussière*. For this, you will need a large, deep saucepan or casserole, preferably one that is comparatively narrow and tower-like, rather than wide and squat, so that less of the juice evaporates off as the stew cooks. And for the top part, the *kesskess*, where the grain itself is cooked, you can get away with a capacious colander lined with muslin that will sit comfortably and safely on top of the saucepan. This means that the rightful lid won't fit properly, so you will also need several large sheets of foil, to cover the whole ensemble as the couscous cooks.

Begin with the stew. Put all the meat, the onions, garlic and spices into the saucepan, with the oil. Add a ladle of water and season with salt. Cook over a moderate heat for about 10 minutes, stirring occasionally. Now add the harder, slower-cooking vegetables, that is, carrots, swede and cabbage, and enough water to cover generously. Bring up to the boil and then simmer gently for 40 minutes.

Meanwhile, tip the couscous into a wide, shallow bowl. Measure out about 300 ml (10 fl oz) of water and start sprinkling it over the couscous with your hands. Turn the couscous as you do it and continue until the water is all used up. Once the stew has been simmering for 40 minutes, place the colander or *kesskess* over the saucepan and add a couple of generous handfuls of the moistened couscous. Spread out on the base of the colander. As soon as steam starts to rise through, add another two handfuls of couscous and spread out again. When the steam rises again, add the remaining couscous and flatten it. Cover and leave for about 20 minutes, until steam rises up through all the couscous. Tip the couscous into a wide bowl and leave to cool for a few minutes. Now drizzle over about 100 ml (3½ fl oz) of oil. Measure out about 300 ml (10 fl oz) of water and add the 2 tablespoons of salt. Stir, then dip your hands into the water and scatter over the grains again. Use your fingers to turn the grains and break up any lumps. Keep going until the couscous is more or less lump-free.

Add all the remaining vegetables to the stew. Return the couscous to the colander, in the same way as before, and cover again. Steam for another 20 minutes, until the couscous is tender. Tip it out again into a large serving bowl and dot with butter or *smen*. With a large slotted spoon, lift the meat and vegetables out of the saucepan and arrange them on the couscous. Pour over a few ladles of the cooking juices, to moisten, and then pour the remaining juices into a separate bowl. Place both bowls on the table, so guests can moisten their own couscous to their liking.

basmati rice

If you want perfect, separate, fragrant, fluffy grains of rice, look no further than Indian basmati. This is the undisputed king of the long-grains, with slender, crescent-moon grains and a unique scent (occasionally described as mousy, but forget that) that mark it out from the others. This has to be the best multi-functional savoury rice. I cook it to accompany all sorts of stews and curries and add it to soups. It is the only rice to use for pilaus and birianis.

It is a good idea to rinse basmati rice before you use it. Some cooks like to soak it, to reduce the cooking time a little, but I've never found that it makes a great deal of difference. It takes only 10 minutes or so to cook in salted, boiling water, anyway. To give it colour, add ¼ teaspoon turmeric to the water.

In fact, I usually use the pilau method to cook my basmati, even though it does well enough thrown straight into boiling water. The method goes something like this: measure the volume of rice in a measuring jug. Rinse the rice and drain well. Heat a thin film of oil in the base of a saucepan and add the rice. Stir the rice about for a minute or so, then add twice its volume of cold water, a bay leaf and a cinnamon stick. Season with salt and bring up to the boil. Cover tightly and reduce the heat as low as possible. Cook for 10 minutes without disturbing, by which time the rice will have absorbed all the liquid and will be just about cooked, but not mushy. Transfer the rice to a shallow ovenproof dish, dot with butter and cover with foil. Leave in a low oven for at least 10 minutes, to fluff up in its own steam, though it can stay there for up to 45 minutes. Fork it up lightly before serving.

cornmeal

The thing I like best about cornmeal is its colour. The sunshine-yellow grains are so cheerfully bright and enticing that I'd be tempted to cook with them, even if they tasted of absolutely nothing. Luckily, they don't. I am not going to pretend that they have an enormously powerful presence, but the gentle, pleasing flavour has its own quiet charm.

There was a time when writing about cornmeal was simple and straightforward. A few years ago, the only kind you could get was Italian slow-cook polenta and then only from an Italian delicatessen. Not so now. The word has spread and even supermarkets, the larger ones at any rate, stock polenta, though more often than not it is 'quick-cooking' or even 'instant'. In fact, it is not really polenta at all. The proper Italian name is *grano Turco*, 'the Turkish grain'. Polenta is really the thick mush that is made from this grain, in northern Italy.

Then there is American or West Indian style cornmeal, again stocked by enterprising supermarkets and delicatessens as well as many ethnic stores. A few clever healthfood shops also sell a strange-looking blue cornmeal, actually a purplish slate-grey. America and small regions of Italy share another form of polenta, this one white, though it is hard to tell the difference between white and yellow in terms of taste or performance.

In a small restaurant in the backwaters of Greenwich, I was introduced to yet another form of cornmeal, this time speckled like golden granite with flecks of buckwheat. It comes from one valley high in the cooler, northern hills, that form the cuff of the Italian boot. My guide to his native cornmeals was Domenico Lovecchio, the moustachioed and effervescent proprietor of the excellent Caffe Italia in Greenwich, just the kind of local I'd love to have.

Domenico regaled me with stories of his childhood in Italy: born in the south, where impoverished aunts regularly scrubbed their wide stone doorsteps to virginal cleanliness, so that they could tip the vat of steaming polenta out on to its cool surface to take off its mouth-burning heat; brought up in the north of the country, he remembered trips up to little huts in the balmier climate of the hills, where the cornmeal porridge graced the table rather than the doorstep, and was eaten with marvellous, dark, robust, slow-cooked stews.

Meanwhile, his English wife Sara was down in the kitchens, which she runs like clockwork, cooking up the rustic, delicious dishes that bring in full houses every night. In the autumn and winter, polenta dishes feature strongly on the menu, as they would in any northern Italian household. Fried polenta with stews, a complicated layered *pasticciata,* like a polenta lasagne, polenta porridge enriched with unhealthily good amounts of butter and cheese, and crisp polenta and Parmesan biscuits. For me, this is a sort of heavenly purgatory – what to choose, what to sample, how can I decide? The advantage of being a guest of the *padrone*, of course, is that, if you ask nicely, you get a chance to dip your finger into everything.

Buying and Choosing Cornmeal

All types of cornmeal are ground down from dried maize. Polenta is usually the coarsest. What is sold as 'coarse cornmeal' is marginally smaller grained. Fine cornmeal is soft and silky smooth. The blue cornmeal that I've come across has usually been finely ground. You can swap all of them around freely in most recipes though, naturally, the texture of the finished article will be affected. Mind you, I don't think I much fancy blue cornmeal mush.

Most big supermarkets now sell some kind of polenta and, in areas with a fair sized West Indian community, they may well carry cornmeal as well. Italian delicatessens are a good source of fancier, higher grade polentas. I've usually found blue cornmeal at healthfood and wholefood stores, where you are also quite likely to come across blue corn tortilla crisps. They taste much the same as ordinary tortilla crisps but look impressive. Good delicatessens may also stock a selection of different cornmeals.

The quick and instant polentas, though they are no doubt frowned upon by purists, are excellent stand-bys (Domenico and Sara swear by them). You may lose a teensy bit on taste, but barely enough to notice. There is an Italian vacuum-packed totally cooked, boil-in-the bag polenta that is well worth searching out (from a few Italian delicatessens, again). You can even slice it cold straight from the pack, for grilling or frying. I'm not quite so convinced by a Greek version, flavoured with musty basil, that I came across recently.

Using Cornmeal

Polenta has made a name for itself in modish restaurants, as the backdrop for all kinds of robustly flavoured food. It's usually cooked as a kind of porridge or purée, with water and salt. I sometimes use stock, rather than water, for more flavour. If it is the straight, old-fashioned grain, cooking it requires patience and sturdy arms, as you need to stir the ever-thickening yellow gloop for 40 minutes.

I've tried the traditional stuff a few times and, to be frank, I think it is hard to tell the difference between it and quick-cook polenta, except in terms of how much your arms ache. So my advice is to stick with the almost instant versions – these are now the easiest to find anyway – which take only 5–10 minutes to cook. Follow the packet instructions to begin with, but do feel free to add extra hot liquid if you like your polenta on the runny side, as I do.

Straight-cooked polenta can be pretty boring but beat in a generous knob or two of butter (and I do mean generous) and some freshly grated Parmesan (the more, the merrier) and it is instantly transformed into a purée that is every bit as good as, if not better than, mashed potatoes. If you prefer to do the hard work in advance, pour the hot, cooked polenta straight from the pan into a well-greased loaf tin and leave it to cool and set. Slice it thickly, and either fry or grill, brushed with olive oil, until crusty and brown. This is even nicer than the purée.

Maize or sweetcorn is native to the New World, so the Americas can lay a far greater historical claim to cornmeal than the Italians. They use it with – dare I say it? – more imagination than the Mediterraneans. They've had more time to play with it, so that's not so surprising.

There isn't room here to go into details of the endless recipes using cornmeal from the Deep South, and further down in Central America, nor, for that matter, the delicious dumplings and porridges from the Caribbean or, closer to home, those of Romania and Hungary. But I do just have space for one quick use for cornmeal that you may not have come across, and that's as an alternative to breadcrumbs for coating foods that are to be fried. Coat the pieces of fish, or vegetables or whatever, in flour and then in beaten egg, as usual, and then turn them in seasoned fine cornmeal. The result, when fried to a nutty brown, will be a perfect crisp casing with a nutty sweetness. Try it with thickly sliced green tomatoes in the autumn, for a real, down-home, American treat.

Cornmeal in cakes and puddings gives a startling golden colour and a great, grainy texture.

Polenta Syrup Cake

A beautiful, burnished-gold cake, soaked in a sweet citrus syrup, this is fairly quick to make and perfect for a party, since it needs to be baked a day in advance. It is at its best served with Greek yoghurt, to cut the sweetness, and soft fruit, in season.

SERVES 6–8

For the cake:

3 eggs

110 g (4 oz) caster sugar

110 g (4 oz) butter, melted and cooled until tepid

Juice of 1/2 orange

225 g (8 oz) polenta or fine cornmeal

1/2 tablespoon baking powder

Finely grated zest of 1/2 lemon

Finely grated zest of 1 orange

1 teaspoon vanilla essence

A pinch of salt

Greek yoghurt, to serve

Soft fruit, in season, to serve

For the syrup:

Juice of 2 oranges

Juice of 1/2 lemon

140 g (5 oz) caster sugar

Pre-heat the oven to 190°C/375°F/Gas Mark 5. Line a 20 cm (8 inch) cake tin with non-stick baking parchment. Whisk the eggs with the caster sugar until pale and thick. Beat in the butter and the orange juice. Mix the polenta or cornmeal with the baking powder and salt and gradually beat it into the egg mixture. Stir in the two zests and the vanilla essence. Pour the cake batter into the prepared tin. Place in the oven and immediately reduce the heat to 170°C/325°F/Gas Mark 3. Bake for about 30–40 minutes, until the cake is brown and pulling away from the tin. Test it with a skewer, which should come out clean.

Once the cake is in the oven, make the syrup. Put all the ingredients into a pan and bring up to the boil. Simmer gently for 5 minutes. Leave to cool.

When the cake comes out of the oven, make holes in it with a skewer and pour over the cool syrup. Leave to cool. Turn the cake out and serve with Greek yoghurt and soft fruits.

Grilled or Fried Polenta Diamonds with Chicken Liver Ragout

Often, people who are not over-enthusiastic about hot polenta mush are won over by grilled or fried polenta. Here, the softness of the cooked polenta is encased in a crisp, browned crust – I happen to like the grilled crust best but I'm fairly partial to the fried version, too. These polenta squares, or diamonds, are the perfect accompaniment to meaty stews (at Caffe Italia they serve them with a rich venison stew but they are just as good with, say, a beef, red wine and olive or mushroom casserole). They are also excellent with grilled or roast vegetables, particularly slow-roasted tomatoes, or as the base for a simple canapé of air-dried ham, rocket and Parmesan, perhaps.

One of the best of all toppings for grilled polenta is also one of the cheapest – this ragout of chicken livers (frozen ones are fine) and tomatoes.

SERVES 6 AS A STARTER, 4 AS A MAIN COURSE

For the polenta:

200 g (7 oz) polenta
4 tablespoons freshly grated Parmesan
30 g (1 oz) butter
Olive oil
Salt and pepper

For the ragout:

2 shallots, finely chopped
3 garlic cloves, chopped
2 tablespoons olive oil
250 g (8 oz) chicken livers, cleaned and fairly finely chopped
1 large fresh rosemary sprig
450 g (1 lb) fresh tomatoes, skinned, de-seeded and chopped
1 generous glass (200 ml/7 fl oz) red wine
2 tablespoons sun-dried tomato purée or red pesto
1/2 tablespoon sugar
3 tablespoons chopped fresh parsley
Dash of balsamic vinegar
Salt and pepper

Opposite *Grilled Polenta Diamonds with Chicken Liver Ragout*

Line a Swiss roll tin with non-stick baking parchment or grease it well. Cook the polenta according to the packet instructions, adding, if necessary, a little extra hot water as it cooks to give a fairly runny purée. When it is done, stir in the Parmesan, butter, salt and pepper, making sure that it is adequately seasoned. While the polenta is still very hot, pour it into the tin, spreading it out evenly to make a thin, even layer. Leave to cool completely.

To make the ragout, fry the shallots and garlic gently in the olive oil until tender, without browning. Now add the chicken livers and rosemary and fry for 2 minutes, stirring. Tip the tomatoes into the pan, pour in the red wine, and add the sun-dried tomato purée or pesto, the sugar, half the parsley and salt and pepper. Bring up to the boil and then leave to simmer until you have a thick, sauce-like mixture. When it is done remove the rosemary sprig, stir in a splash or two of balsamic vinegar and the remaining parsley. Re-heat when needed, without boiling.

To finish the polenta, cut it into moderately large diamonds, or squares, or fingers or whatever takes your fancy. Either fry in sizzling hot oil until browned on both sides, or brush with oil and grill close to a thoroughly pre-heated grill, until brown and crusty on both sides.

Place a few diamonds of polenta on each plate and top with the ragout. Serve immediately.

Cracklin' Cornbread

Cracklin' cornbread should be made with real, down-home, pork cracklin', the browned crisp scraps left after rendering down the fat from the family pig. Failing that, fried bacon has to do instead (don't be tempted to try those tough packet cracklings).

For something rather trendier, replace the bacon with sun-dried tomatoes, or add chopped fresh chilli or coriander.

As the American food writer Craig Claiborne says, there are more recipes for cornbread than there are magnolia trees in the South.

SERVES 6

225 g (8 oz) cornmeal
110 g (4 oz) plain flour, sifted
1 teaspoon baking powder
1 teaspoon salt
½ tablespoon caster sugar
300 ml (10 fl oz) buttermilk
120 ml (4 fl oz) milk
2 eggs, beaten
80 g (2¾ oz) unsalted butter, melted and cooled
6–8 bacon rashers, grilled until crisp and roughly chopped
85 g (3 oz) mature Cheddar, diced small (optional)
½ teaspoon coarsely crushed black peppercorns (optional)

Pre-heat the oven to 200°C/400°F/Gas Mark 6. Mix the cornmeal with the sifted flour, baking powder, salt and sugar. Make a well in the centre and add the buttermilk, milk, eggs and melted butter. Mix to a batter and then stir in the bacon, Cheddar and black peppercorns, if using. Pour into a greased 22 × 22 cm (9 × 9 inch) or 25 × 20 cm (10 × 8 inch) baking tin or ovenproof dish and bake for 25–30 minutes, until the edges are browned. Test in the centre of the cornbread with a skewer or the blade of a knife. If it comes out clean, the bread is done. Cut into squares and serve warm as an accompaniment to a main course or on its own, slathered with butter.

Variations:

Add 1 or 2 fresh red or green chillies, de-seeded and finely chopped, as well as, or instead of, the bacon. Cheddar is optional, again. Omit the black peppecorns.

Add 3 tablespoons chopped fresh coriander, together with 1 or 2 fresh red or green chillies, de-seeded and finely chopped, omitting the bacon and black peppercorns. Cheddar is optional.

Add 5 pieces of sun-dried tomato, finely diced, and 2 tablespoons chopped fresh basil or 1 or 2 fresh red or green chillies, de-seeded and finely chopped, omitting the bacon and black peppercorns. Omit the Cheddar but sprinkle freshly grated Parmesan liberally over the surface, before baking.

filo pastry

Watching filo pastry being made by an expert is quite fascinating. The dough is stretched and stretched by hand, pulled expertly this way and that, floured again and again, with never a hole or a rip. The whole room is transformed by a snowstorm of white flour, peopled by white ghosts, every item, down to the telephone, camouflaged in pure white. It is only when you emerge into the real world that you realize that you are as ghostly white from hat and hair to shoes as the spectres you watched.

The results are sheets of impossibly thin, pliable pastry – you should be able to read newsprint through good filo – which harden if exposed to air for any length of time. Used layer upon layer, generously buttered, they bake (or fry) to a perfect, flaking crispness, firm enough to hold a filling safely. They are Greece, Turkey and the Middle East's answer to puff pastry but, in many ways, a great deal more versatile since they can be wrapped and twisted into an infinite number of shapes and swirls.

It's hard to distinguish between filo pastry and Austria's *strudel* pastry or south-west

France's *croustade* pastry. No doubt, regional experts could argue their differences but, in practice, they are all remarkably similar. I suppose the basic technique is just a refined treatment of a rather elementary dough, in which skill and deftness are more important than expensive ingredients. What is interesting is the diverse ways in which these paper-thin pastries are used in their native lands. A *croustade* is indisputably French, a magnificent, beautiful, crumpled joy of an apple and brandy tart. The solidity of a *strudel*, savoury or sweet, has an undeniably Germanic air to it. And the syrup-soaked, scented, nut-laden pastries of the Middle East have the instantly indulgent, exotic appeal of the Orient.

Buying and Storing Filo Pastry

You can get it frozen or fresh, nicely packaged, from most supermarkets and any Greek or Turkish food store. Some of the best filo pastry I've ever bought came from a Greek baker's in London, where they made it themselves. Small filo factories are often hidden away in areas of cities with large Greek, Turkish or Middle Eastern communities. Keep an eye out for them and you may be able to buy direct, or from a nearby shop. Quality really amounts to thinness, and the thinner the better. Try various different brands and make a note of the one that is easiest to handle and gives the crispest results.

Unopened rolls of filo pastry should be stored in the fridge, or frozen. Once the plastic wrapping has been opened, any unused pastry can be frozen. Freezing tends to dry the pastry a little, making it more brittle, so handle it carefully when it has been defrosted.

Using Filo Pastry

It is impossible to be precise about the number of sheets of filo you will need for any recipe, as the measurements vary from one brand to another. One packet is usually sufficient for most purposes, unless you are creating canapés for the masses.

Once you've opened the plastic packet inside the box, take out as many sheets as you think you will need, wrap the rest and return them to the fridge or freezer. Lay the sheets out on your work surface, cover with a sheet of greaseproof paper and then cover that with a damp tea-towel (a tea-towel alone can make the edges so gluey that they stick together). Take the sheets from their covering one by one, and use one sheet up before starting on the next, so that none of them dry out and become too brittle to use.

Filo pastry needs some form of fat to make it crisp and to keep the layers separate. Melted unsalted butter gets top marks, both for colour and flavour. Oil, olive or not, can be substituted, but it doesn't work quite so well.

Before each sheet is used, it should first be brushed with butter. Cut into long strips, filo can be rolled around a filling to make cigar-shaped pastries (a *strudel* is the giant form of this) or folded to form triangles. For little money bags, the edges of squares of filo are gathered up around the filling and twisted together at the top. With a bit of imagination, other small shapes can be conjured up. The filling should be moist but never damp or runny, which would prevent the filo crisping up, if it didn't actually dissolve it first! Don't overfill small filo pastries as the filling will expand in the heat and spill out.

Layered up in whole sheets in a baking tray, filled with nuts and then covered with more sheets, filo can be baked like a huge cake, doused in syrup and then cut into squares, to create sweetmeats like *baklava*.

Goats' Cheese and Sun-Dried Tomato Pesto Money Bags

Hot from the oven, these goats' cheese purses make an irresistible first course (serve three or four each), or go down a treat at parties. You can make them several hours in advance and leave them in the fridge until needed. You may then need to give them an extra minute or so in the oven.

MAKES 10–12

6–12 sheets of filo pastry, depending on size

85–100 g (3–3½ oz) unsalted butter, melted

For the filling:

110 g (4 oz) goats' cheese, de-rinded and mashed

2 tomatoes, skinned, de-seeded and cut into small pieces

4 teaspoons *Sun-Dried Tomato and Toasted Walnut Pesto* (see page 250), bought red pesto or sun-dried tomato purée

Cut the filo pastry into 12 cm (5 inch) squares. Keep them covered with a sheet of grease-proof paper and a tea-towel wrung out in cold water. Take a square at a time, brush with melted butter and lay a second square on that, twisted round to look like an eight-pointed star. Brush with butter. Place a scant teaspoon of goats' cheese in the centre, top with a piece or two of tomato and finish the whole lot with ⅓ teaspoon of pesto or sun-dried tomato purée. Gather all the points and edges of the star up and twist them together, to enclose the filling. On your first attempt, you will probably discover that you have overfilled your money bag. Backtrack and remove a little filling. Place the filled money bags on a buttered baking tray. Continue until filling and filo are all used up. Brush any extra butter over the bags. Chill until needed.

To cook, pre-heat the oven to 200°C/400°F/Gas Mark 6. Bake the money bags for about 7–10 minutes, until they are browned and crisp. Serve hot or warm.

Filo Cigars Filled with Crab and Coriander

Here, the crisp filo pastry encloses a blissfully oozy filling of crab, coriander and cream cheese. Shaped like a cigar, this is probably the easiest of ways to use filo pastry. Serve as a first course, allowing three or four cigars per person (add a little mixed green salad to the plates) or just as something to savour with drinks. Use fresh crab meat, not frozen, which isn't worth its price. One fairly large dressed crab will contain about the right amount.

MAKES ABOUT 18

220 g (8 oz) mixed white and brown crab meat
110 g (4 oz) cream cheese
1 tablespoon chopped fresh coriander
1 tablespoon chopped fresh parsley
1 tablespoon lemon juice
6–10 sheets of filo pastry, depending on size
60 g (2 oz) unsalted butter, melted
Salt and pepper

Flake the large pieces of white crab meat, if necessary. Beat the cream cheese with the herbs, lemon juice, salt and pepper. Mix in all the crab meat.

Cut each sheet of filo pastry into long strips about 13–15 cm (5–6 inches) wide. Cover with a sheet of greaseproof paper and cover that with a tea-towel wrung out in cold water.

Pre-heat the oven to 200°C/400°F/Gas Mark 6. One at a time, take a strip of filo, brush with melted butter and place a teaspoon of the crab mixture at one end, shaping it into a neat sausage but leaving a good 2 cm (3/4 inch) border. Roll the strip of filo up, to form a neat cylinder, flipping over the edges as you go, to prevent the filling from falling out. Place on a greased baking sheet. Repeat until filling and filo are all used up. Brush the cigars with any remaining butter. Chill until needed.

Bake for 10 minutes, until golden brown. Eat as soon as they've cooled enough not to burn your mouth.

risotto rice

Risotto rice is grown in the north of Italy and is the only rice that is suitable for making Italian risotto. Nothing else will do. Although Italians usually describe it as a long-grain rice, it is actually medium-grain, verging on short grain, if you compare it with truly long-grained rices from elsewhere in the world. The stubby, plump grains are almost square in cross-section and what makes them unique is their ability to absorb very large quantities of liquid without collapsing to a mush, allied with a generous ration of starch. This is part of the secret of making a creamy risotto (the other parts are copious amounts of butter and Parmesan).

Tradition has it that the Venetians introduced the art of growing rice to the inhabitants of the Po valley in the fifteenth century, though it seems more likely that the Spanish brought rice with them to the south of Italy and that it spread from there to the north, where water was in more plentiful supply. Whoever it was, they certainly endowed the northern Italians with a great gift. Though the practice of opening meals with a bowl of pasta has kept rice-eating in check, it still forms an important staple in this part of the country.

Buying and Storing Risotto Rice

There are two grades of risotto rice. The supreme rice is the aptly named *superfino*, with relatively long, firm grains. The most widely available *superfino* is arborio rice, which has made its way into most good supermarkets. Other famous examples are carnaroli, Roma and baldo, which you may be able to track down in smart delicatessens and Italian food stores.

One of my favourite risotto rices actually belongs to the lower grade, the *fino* rice with slightly shorter grains. Vialone nano has an excellent flavour, even if it isn't reckoned to be quite so classy by the Italians. It is the only *fino* rice that I've been able to buy over here, though you may come across others in Italy.

Once a packet of rice has been opened, store it in an airtight container in a dry cupboard.

Using Risotto Rice

You can use risotto rice for many dishes other than risotto but, since that is what it is best known for, we might as well start there. Risotto itself is a relatively late invention, dating from the nineteenth century, and is quite unlike any other rice dish. It is undoubtedly worth mastering. Once you are familiar with the technique, you will be able to conjure up a risotto out of practically anything, within reason. Within half an hour or so, you can have a marvellous, filling supper, more than suitable for company, on the table. Just make sure you keep a bag of risotto rice in the larder, butter and Parmesan in the fridge and some chicken stock in the freezer (and, yes, in a dire emergency a weakly diluted stock cube will do). Remember never to rinse or wash the rice or you'll send half the starch spiralling down the plug hole.

Proper risotto rice, as I've said, is essential, but the method is every bit as crucial. It's no good tipping in all the liquid in one fell swoop and leaving it to bubble away – you'll end up with a substandard gluey parody of an Indian pilau. The slow addition of liquid, ladle by ladle, and the constant stirring both work to create the proper consistency. The rice is done when it is tender but still with substance and a little bite left in it – barely *al dente*, in other words. Quite how wet a risotto should be is largely a matter of taste. I like mine on the runny side but others prefer to keep their risotto thicker. The last finishing touch to any risotto is a very generous endowment of fresh butter and lots of grated Parmesan, stirred in just before serving, to bind and thicken the sauce and, of course, to complete the balance of richness and flavours. For risotto recipes, turn to the recipes for *Rocket, Saffron and Fresh Tomato Risotto* and *Mushroom Risotto* (see pages 166 and 171).

The starchiness of risotto rice makes it a marvellous addition to soups, imparting a quiet and digestible creaminess that doesn't interfere with other ingredients. It also makes it work well in timbales or other moulded rice dishes, gluing the grains together without making them sticky.

For quick, effortless eating, risotto rice can be baked in the oven (see the recipe for *Saffron and Tomato Rice* on page 93), leaving you free to deal with other matters, and, although what you end up with doesn't have the unique charms of a risotto, it still makes most enjoyable eating. Risotto rice can be used very successfully to make puddings, much as you would use pudding rice, though the grains will not soften to the same extent.

The one thing I wouldn't bother doing with risotto rice is boiling it plainly. This doesn't do it any justice and you would be far better off with a good long-grain rice, such as basmati.

Minestra di Riso e Castagne

This rice and chestnut soup comes from the mountains of northern Italy and has long been a favourite of mine. This is a quick version, made with pre-cooked, vacuum-packed chestnuts that dispense with the tedium of peeling chestnuts (and the pain of catching a splinter of chestnut husk under a fingernail), without sacrificing too much of the flavour. If you prefer to use fresh chestnuts (and you will gain a little in flavour), peel about 450 g (1 lb) and cook for an extra half an hour in the stock.

SERVES 6

340 g (12 oz) vacuum-packed chestnuts, halved or quartered roughly
1 fresh thyme sprig
1 fresh rosemary sprig
1 bay leaf
1.5 litres (2½ pints) chicken or vegetable stock
100 g (3½ oz) risotto rice
30 g (1 oz) butter
300 ml (10 fl oz) creamy milk
Salt and pepper

Put the chestnuts in a pan with the herbs tied together with a length of string. Add the stock, salt and pepper and bring up to the boil. Leave to simmer gently, uncovered, for 40 minutes.

Now add the rice and continue simmering for another 10 minutes. Next, add the butter and milk and simmer away until the rice is just cooked but still *al dente* (another 10 minutes or so). Taste and adjust seasoning and serve.

Saffron and Tomato Rice

Not a risotto, nor a paella or a pilaff for that matter, this is a simpler affair altogether, since it is baked in the oven and requires little attention, other than the occasional stir. I love it on its own but it is really meant as an accompaniment, best served with fairly plain food: perhaps some prawns, sizzling hot from the barbecue, or grilled lamb chops and a green salad, or lightly cooked courgettes or spinach. It can be made with ordinary long-grain rice, though I prefer the taste and texture of risotto rice. Either way, the rice re-heats fairly well, if necessary, as long as you sprinkle over a couple of extra tablespoons of water or stock before you put it into the oven.

SERVES 6–8

1 red onion, chopped
2 tablespoons olive oil
3 garlic cloves, chopped
310 g (11 oz) risotto rice, e.g. arborio or carnaroli
A good pinch of saffron strands
2 tablespoons sun-dried tomato purée or ordinary tomato purée
1 teaspoon sugar
2 tablespoons chopped fresh parsley
520 ml (18 fl oz) vegetable or chicken stock or water
Salt and pepper

Pre-heat the oven to 150°C/300°F/Gas Mark 2. Fry the onion in the oil in a roasting tin, or flameproof and ovenproof shallow dish, until beginning to colour. Add the garlic and fry for another 2 minutes. Add the rice and stir for 1 minute. Now add the saffron strands and all the rest of the ingredients and bring up to the boil, stirring to mix. Cover with foil and bake for 30 minutes, stirring once as it cooks, until the rice is tender and the liquid has all been absorbed.

Sweet Rice Fritters

An alternative way to serve up your rice pudding, these fritters are crisp on the outside and creamy and tender inside. The starch in the risotto rice gives them extra richness and helps them to hold together, without being too heavy and doughy. Lovely as they are with no more than a sprinkling of sugar, they are even better with spoonfuls of home-made jam.

SERVES 4–6
110 g (4 oz) risotto rice
500 ml (17 fl oz) creamy milk
30 g (1 oz) caster sugar
30 g (1 oz) butter
Finely grated zest of 1 lemon
3 eggs, separated
60 g (2 oz) plain flour, sifted
2 tablespoons Cointreau or Grand Marnier
A pinch of salt
Sunflower or olive oil, for frying
Sugar or blackcurrant or raspberry jam, to serve

Put the rice, milk and salt in a large pan and simmer gently for 15 minutes.

Now add the sugar, butter and lemon zest. Continue cooking until the rice is very tender and has absorbed the milk. Draw off the heat and leave to cool. Beat in the egg yolks and then the sifted flour and liqueur. Shortly before frying, whisk the egg whites stiffly and fold them in.

Pour 1 cm (1/2 inch) of oil into a frying-pan and heat up over a medium heat. Drop in tablespoonfuls of the mixture, flatten slightly and fry on both sides, until golden brown. Drain briefly on kitchen paper and serve piping hot, dusted with extra sugar, or with a spoonful of blackcurrant or raspberry jam.

wild rice

One of the great trips of my life began with a seven hour journey in a tiny Twin Otter plane across Ontario, to the heart of a maze of lakes that straddles the border with Wisconsin. That amazing autumn day, we sped over the blue waters, under deep blue skies, surrounded by blazing trees, gold-, red- and orange-leaved, to a quieter spot where we abandoned the motor boats for peaceful Indian canoes and paddled off to find the wild rice lakes.

That wild rice really was wild, growing as it has done for centuries in the endless lakes.

There, Native Americans have the right to harvest all wild wild rice (where it has been deliberately sown into new waters, the owner of the lake reaps the yields). They paddle through the rice stalks, hitting the ripe ears of dark rice with their paddles and shaking some into the boat, while the rest falls back into the water to re-seed itself for the following year. No chemicals are used and the one concession to modern times is an occasional outboard motor.

In fact, wild rice isn't a true rice at all but a water grass, with svelte, elongated glossy grains that bear only a passing resemblance to true rice. Once harvested, the rice is cleaned and toasted, to remove the chaff and heighten the flavour. Then it is ready to cook. It has a nutty flavour and a pleasingly chewy texture but is far more elegantly styled than heavy, worthy brown rice. I've seen it described as 'the caviar of grains', which is perhaps overstating the case, but it is still something quite special. It takes about 35–40 minutes to cook in salted, boiling water. When it is done, the grains butterfly open to reveal a pale tan interior. You can play around with it in stuffings or salads but I reckon that the best way to serve it is still the simplest: dressed with plenty of butter and finely chopped parsley and perhaps a squeeze or two of orange juice.

spelt flour

Spelt flour is sold in fetching blue packets sporting a rather jaunty pair of toga-clad Romans. He manfully clutches a golden sickle, while she, obliviously exposing one bare breast, snatches three stalks of wheat out of his range. There is a relevance to all this. Spelt grain is a precursor of our modern wheat, once grown right across Europe and into Asia. The Romans seem to have been especially fond of it, turning it into bread and dumplings (or it may just have been that they were more inclined to note what they ate, or that these references survive while others disappeared).

After a long spell in obscurity, spelt grain is back and is being grown organically in this country, as it was in the dim and distant past, if only by default. The promotional literature tells me that spelt is richer in minerals than modern wheat and that, although it is high in gluten, some people who are allergic to wheat can tolerate spelt flour. That doesn't seem terribly logical to me but, if you or someone you know is allergic to wheat, it may be worth exploring further.

My interest in spelt flour is purely based on its flavour. Though it is a stoneground wholemeal flour, it is lighter than wholemeal wheat flour and has a nutty, sweetish flavour that is immensely appealing.

Buying and Storing Spelt Flour

There's not a lot of choice about this. As far as I know, only one company, Doves Farm, mills it on any scale and they are the ones that wrap it up in the blue packets I describe above. Larger branches of a few of the top supermarkets do sell it but you are more likely to come across spelt flour in a wholefood or health-food store or in a good general delicatessen.

Once opened, store it, like any other flour, in an airtight container well away from the damp.

Using Spelt Flour

Use it just as you would wholemeal wheat flour. To me, that means in bread and spelt does make marvellous bread. To be frank, there's not much else that I cook with wholemeal flour, except, perhaps, digestive biscuits once in a very long while. I'm no great fan of wholemeal pastry but I suspect that, if you were to make it with spelt, it might turn out lighter and more palatable. All three recipes (one for biscuits, one for bread and one for a tart) on the sides of the packet of spelt flour are sweetened with honey. No doubt honey does go well with spelt but I suspect it is here purely on the basis that this is the only sweetener that would have been available to Roman cooks.

Quick Spelt Flour Bread

This is the bread that we make for ourselves most days (it is hard to find decent bread in our area), either from spelt flour or wholemeal flour. It takes 5 minutes to put together (including getting all the ingredients out of the larder), an hour or so to rise, and less than half that to cook. If you have an Aga or Raeburn, cook the bread in the hot oven for the best results of all.

MAKES 1 LOAF

450 g (1 lb) spelt flour
1 teaspoon brown sugar
2 teaspoons salt
1 sachet easy-blend or easy-bake yeast
1 tablespoon olive oil
360–400 ml (12–14 fl oz) cold water
Sesame, nigella (black onion), pumpkin or sunflower seeds (optional)

Pre-heat the oven to 220°C/425°F/Gas Mark 7. Mix the flour with the sugar, salt and yeast. Make a well in the centre and add the oil, and then stir in enough water to make a damp, sticky dough, far too loose to be kneaded.

Turn the dough into an oiled 500 g (1 lb) loaf tin and sprinkle evenly with seeds of one sort or another, if using. Cover with a damp tea-towel and leave in a warm place until the dough has just risen above the rim of the tin. Bake for about 27–30 minutes, turning the loaf once so that it browns evenly.

When it is done, the loaf should slide freely out of the tin or should, at least, need no more than a quick loosening with the blade of a knife. Tap the bottom. It should sound hollow; if it is soft and makes a dull thud, return the loaf to the oven, without its tin, for another 3–4 minutes. Leave to cool on a wire rack.

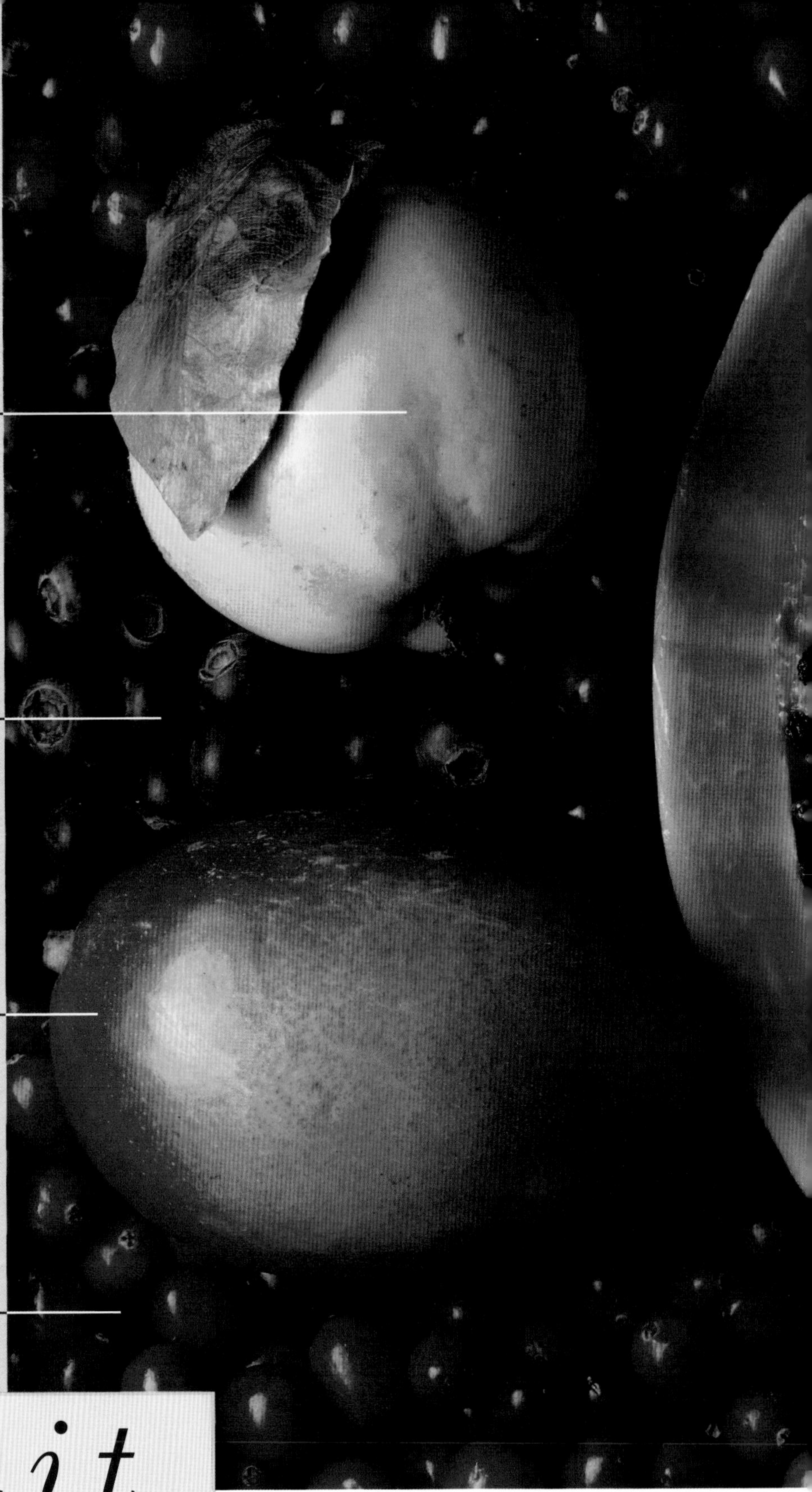

quince

blueberries

mango

cranberries

fruit

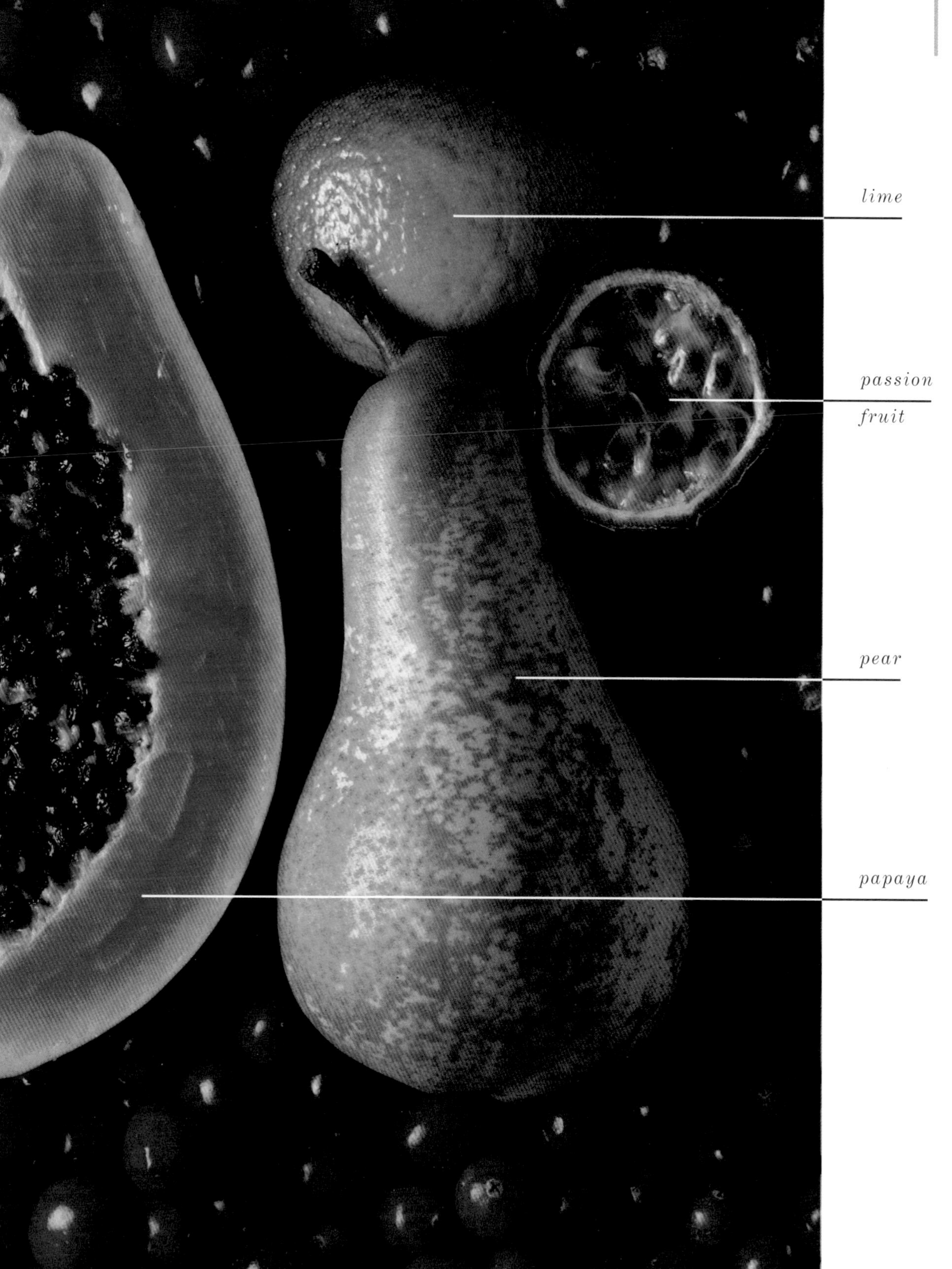
lime
passion fruit
pear
papaya

blueberries

Shortly after the war a discreet advertisement was placed in an English market gardener's trade journal by the University of British Colombia. It was offering 100 blueberry bushes, entirely free and with no strings attached, to anyone in Britain who had the right kind of land to grow them. Six people took up the offer but only one of them saw the commercial potential and started to grow blueberries seriously. He was David Trehane, whose New Forest heathland was as acid as any American blueberry bush could desire. By the time he handed the business on to his son Jeremy, 20 years later, it was a thriving concern with fields full of blueberry bushes next door to his renowned camellia nursery. Now the Trehanes are this country's biggest producers of blueberries, dominating the market throughout the British season. Between July and September, they supply shops and supermarkets with up to 30 tons of fruit.

It was bliss to wander through the high bushes of blueberries, popping them straight from the branch into my mouth, comparing varieties and savouring their sweet, perfumed, slightly spicy flavour and grape-like texture. Jeremy guided me through the alleys, explaining why this variety worked best for supermarkets but that variety (the Idaho) was a personal favourite, with an outstanding flavour, but hard to sell because of its thin skin. On the bush, each berry is coated with a beautiful blue-frosted bloom, a kind of natural wax, which protects the fruit, extending its shelf-life off the plant. The moment you touch the fruit, the wax begins to rub off, so pickers are trained to handle the berries as little as possible.

Once picked, the blueberries are sorted and picked over by hand in a ridiculously pretty thatched packing-shed, in a clearing in the forest, near the Trehane's chocolate-box thatched cottage. In the height of the season, cousins, siblings and friends are hauled in to help and the lights burn through the night as the family works. Within hours, the blueberries are off on their journey to supermarkets and shops around the country, ready to take their place beside more traditional British summer fruit.

Buying and Storing Blueberries

In the summer months, you will have no problems buying British blueberries. At other times of the year, blueberries are imported from Poland, Australia, America and Germany amongst other places. Blueberries have a naturally long shelf-life – they will stay sound for two or three weeks after they have been picked. The shelf-life can be reduced if the blueberries were harvested damp and swollen, after heavy rainfall, so don't expect them to last quite so well during a rainy summer.

Look carefully at the blueberries in their plastic punnet before you buy. They should be firm and well rounded, still tolerably well coated in their beautiful blue bloom, though inevitably some of it will have rubbed off. Avoid blueberries that are cracked or wrinkled, or with traces of juice on the bottom of the punnet.

Until such time as varieties are labelled, you must expect considerable variation in flavour. Some varieties are sweet and rather bland but beloved by supermarkets for their thick, sturdy skins, while others will have a welcome trace of acidity and stronger perfume. Varieties may well be mixed within punnets.

Store the blueberries in the vegetable drawer of the fridge, where they can last as long as a week or more. They freeze excellently. Just pop the punnet straight into the freezer set to its lowest setting. No need for any greater effort than that!

Using Blueberries

I'm delighted to see blueberries shoulder to shoulder with raspberries and strawberries in the summer. There can be few nicer summer desserts than a huge bowl heaped high with mixed fruits, the dark blue hue of the blueberries emphasizing the dusky pink of raspberries and the pillar-box red of strawberries. Such a beautiful sight, too. Serve them with crème fraiche, or crème Chantilly – lightly sweetened whipped cream, flavoured with a few drops of vanilla essence.

On their own, the flavour of blueberries is greatly enhanced by a squeeze or two of lime juice. The mild acidity of crème fraiche or Greek yoghurt also works well with them. A more unusual, but lovely, way of serving them is with goat's cheese, a singularly good partnership. If they need sweetening, try a drizzle of maple syrup instead of ordinary sugar.

To get the best out of blueberries, you will need to cook them. Somehow, heat intensifies and enhances their flavour, turning them into a truly delicious fruit. Use them in pies, of course, simply piled into the dish, tossed with a little cornflour and some sugar, and perhaps a few pinches of ground cinnamon, and then covered with pastry and baked. For a simple blueberry sauce, which can be spooned hot or cold over ice cream, follow the method in the first part of the recipe for *Blueberry and Cornmeal Grunt* (see page 102) simmering the sauce for about 10 minutes. Vanilla, cinnamon and orange all go well with cooked blueberries. Mixing them with apple is a good way of stretching a few precious blueberries, either in a compote (i.e., nicely stewed blueberry and apple) or in a pie.

Blueberry and Cornmeal Grunt

Also known as 'blueberry slump', this is a speciality of Nova Scotia, though it is made in many parts of Canada and America, particularly in blueberry country. It can be cooked on top of the stove or in the oven (my favourite) and I give both methods. Cornmeal is a fancy innovation – the dumplings are usually made of plain flour but cornmeal makes them look and taste even nicer.

SERVES 4–6

For the blueberry sauce:

450 g (1 lb) blueberries
1 cinnamon stick
1/4 teaspoon freshly grated nutmeg
150 g (5 oz) caster sugar
2 tablespoons lemon juice
100 ml (3 1/2 fl oz) water

For the dumplings:

75 g (2 1/2 oz) fine cornmeal
85 g (3 oz) plain flour
1 teaspoon baking powder
1 tablespoon caster sugar
Finely grated zest of 1/2 lemon
30 g (1/2 oz) butter
Milk
A pinch of salt
Cream, to serve

To make this on the hob, put all the sauce ingredients into a wide pan and bring gently up to the boil, stirring until the sugar has dissolved. Simmer gently for about 4 minutes.

To make the dumplings, sift the cornmeal with the flour, baking powder and salt. Stir in the sugar and the lemon zest. Rub in the butter and then add enough milk to make a soft dough that will just drop off the spoon. Drop spoonfuls of the dough into the blueberry sauce, cover tightly and simmer for a further 10–15 minutes, without raising the lid. The dumplings should have puffed up nicely and be cooked through. Serve immediately, with cream – double or whipped or crème fraiche, as the fancy takes you.

To make this in the oven, pre-heat the oven to 190°C/375°F/Gas Mark 5. Spread the berries out in a wide ovenproof dish and tuck the cinnamon stick in amongst them. Sprinkle over the nutmeg and sugar and then pour on the lemon juice and water. Bake, uncovered, for 5–10 minutes, until the juices begin to run.

Make the dough for the dumplings as above. Take the dish out of the oven and raise the oven heat to 220°C/425°F/Gas Mark 7. Drop spoonfuls of the dough into the berries and then return to the oven for 20 minutes, until the dumplings are puffed and patched with brown. Serve immediately, with cream as above.

Opposite *Blueberry and Cornmeal Grunt*

Wild Duck with Blueberry and Port Sauce

The perfume and sweetness of blueberries is a lovely foil for the darker meat of a wild duck (and it goes well with venison or grouse, for that matter). Here, they are cooked with the bird and then fresh berries are added to the sauce, as well. If you prefer domesticated duck, use the same method for the sauce but adapt cooking times to suit.

SERVES 2–3

30 g (1 oz) butter
1 mallard
2 fresh thyme sprigs
150 g (5 oz) blueberries
1 shallot, sliced
1 bay leaf
150 ml (5 fl oz) port
1 tablespoon red wine vinegar
Salt and pepper

Pre-heat the oven to 220°C/425°F/Gas Mark 7. Rub about half the butter over the mallard, paying particular attention to the breast. Season the bird inside and out with salt and pepper. Slip the rest of the butter inside it, along with one of the sprigs of thyme and about one-third of the blueberries. Cover the breast of the bird with cooking foil and place in a fairly closely fitting roasting tin. Scatter the shallot around the bird and add the remaining thyme and the bay leaf. Moisten with about 4 tablespoons of water, more if the dish is rather large. Roast for about 30–35 minutes. After 20 minutes, remove the foil and baste the bird. Baste again once in the remaining cooking time.

When done to your liking, lift the bird and tip it carefully downwards, to let any juices in the interior drip out into the roasting tin. Transfer the mallard to a warm serving dish and leave it to rest in a warm place. Spoon off any fat from the roasting tin. Put the roasting tin on the hob, add the port and vinegar and bring up to the boil, scraping in any residues and roasting juices. Boil until reduced by about one-third and then strain into a clean pan. Add the remaining blueberries and simmer gently for a few minutes, to warm through. Taste and adjust seasoning. Serve with the duck.

Mrs Trehane's Blueberry and Apple Cake

All the Trehanes love their blueberries and eat them enthusiastically, both fresh and cooked. When I visited them, Mrs Trehane placed a superb blueberry and apple cake before us on the kitchen table. Who could resist? Her recipe is based on one she noted down from the radio – she replaces the original sultanas with blueberries and adds a little ground cinnamon or mixed spice for good measure.

SERVES 8

330 g (12 oz) self-raising flour
1 teaspoon ground cinnamon or ground mixed spice
220 g (8 oz) butter
160 g (6 oz) caster sugar
220 g (8 oz) blueberries
450 g (1 lb) cooking apples, peeled, cored and diced
3 eggs, lightly beaten
Pinch of salt

Line a 20 cm (8 inch), loose-bottomed cake tin with non-stick baking parchment, or grease and flour it. Pre-heat the oven to 180°C/350°F/Gas Mark 4.

Sift the flour with the cinnamon or mixed spice and salt. Rub in the butter until the mixture resembles fine breadcrumbs. Stir in the sugar, blueberries and apples. Add the eggs and mix evenly. Spoon into the prepared cake tin and bake for 1½–2 hours. Test with a skewer, by plunging it into the centre of the cake tin. If it comes out dry (bar a smear of blueberry juice, of course), the cake is ready. If not, return it to the oven for a little longer. Turn out of the tin and leave to cool on a wire rack.

cranberries

For years, I have longed to see an American cranberry harvest. By all accounts, it is a spectacular sight. The boggy fields of low, heather-like bushes are artificially flooded, the cranberries knocked off into the water and then drained off in an enormous scarlet wave, jostling together as they are swept away. Imagine what it must look like on a perfect day, with blue, blue skies and blazing gold- and orange-leaved trees.

Once harvested, cranberries will keep literally for months under the right conditions. They must have been one of the greatest blessings for Native Americans and early settlers in North America, a source of plentiful vitamin C and a fresh flavour that would last through the snow-bound winter months. Sailors were saved by them, too; barrels of cranberries in water were stashed away in the hold on long sea voyages, to stave off the threat of scurvy.

Domestic cultivation began in the early nineteenth century at Cape Cod, still one of the main centres for commercial cultivation. Tons of cranberries are harvested every year, for Thanksgiving, for Christmas, and now for sending overseas to us. Cranberry sauce, without which any self-respecting American roast turkey would feel singularly naked, has made considerable inroads here. No surprise there as cranberry sauce slots neatly into our already extensive repertoire of sweet-sour, fruity accompaniments to hot and cold meats.

Buying and Storing Cranberries

Fresh cranberries arrive in our shops a few weeks before Thanksgiving at the end of November, and remain prominently in evidence until Christmas, lingering perhaps until the New Year. Then they disappear, really quite suddenly. So if you have a taste for them, make the most of it while the going is good and lay down stocks for leaner times.

Cranberries are tough things but it is still worth casting a lingering glance over the plastic punnet before you buy. The individual berries should be firm and glossy, a beautiful ripe, bright, rich pinky-red. Soft berries or, worse still, wrinkled berries or, horror of horrors, mouldy berries, are an abysmal sign of neglect somewhere along the line, since cranberries have remarkable staying power. Never accept anything but the best – you really don't need to. Once you have the perfect little rubies in your grasp, they will keep for at least two or three weeks in the fridge, and probably a great deal longer if you pick over them regularly and chuck out any bruised, soft or otherwise dubious fruits. Cranberries freeze easily – just pop the punnet straight into the freezer – with virtually no deterioration in quality, so take advantage of them while you can.

Using Cranberries

Though cranberries are undoubtedly ideal for making quick, chutney-like sauces, it is a shame to limit them to just this one use. I am the proud owner of an American booklet that is jam-packed with some hundred or more cranberry recipes. It's a brilliantly amateurish production but the recipes are inspirational and I love it. Inside its cranberry-red covers are recipes for sauces and relishes, of course, but also for jams and jellies, cakes and tarts, muffins, stuffings, savoury bakes and sweet pies.

However you use cranberries, they will always demand a considerable load of sugar, even in savoury dishes, since they are naturally tart and bitter. They have an instant affinity with orange and lemon, with warm spices such as cinnamon, cloves and ginger and with port or red wine. Their special flavour makes them just as at home with chocolate (try stirring a generous handful into a chocolate cake batter before baking), as it does with poultry and, even better, in my opinion, with game.

Cranberry and Orange Sauce

There are endless variations on this basic theme – some tempered with orange juice or port, or with this spice or that. This is one version I happen to like, though I tamper with it practically every time. As the sauce keeps well in the fridge, it's worth making a fairly large quantity. Serve it with the turkey, of course, but try it also with ham, or in sandwiches, or with cheese. I love it with roast game – the best partnership of all.

SERVES 8–10

450 g (1 lb) cranberries
Finely grated zest and juice of 2 oranges
225 g (8 oz) caster sugar
1 cinnamon stick
3 cloves
1 teaspoon ground allspice

Put all the ingredients into a pan and stir over a medium–low heat, until the juices begin to run and the sugar has dissolved. Bring to the boil and simmer for about 5–8 minutes, until the berries have popped. Spoon into a bowl, leave to cool and store, covered, in the fridge.

Cranberry Butter Tart

This is an old favourite of mine, which I come back to time and again. The butter in the filling gives the tart a rich translucence, balanced by the tartness of the cranberries.

SERVES 6–8

For the pastry:
220 g (8 oz) plain flour
110 g (4 oz) butter
1 tablespoon caster sugar
Finely grated zest of 1 orange
1 egg
A pinch of salt

For the filling:
220 g (8 oz) cranberries
220 g (8 oz) caster sugar
110 g (4 oz) unsalted butter, cut into small pieces
2 eggs, beaten
30 g (1 oz) flaked almonds

To make the pastry, stir the flour with the salt and then rub in the butter. Stir in the sugar and orange zest. Make a well in the centre and break in the egg. Mix, adding just enough cold water to form a dough. Knead briefly to smooth out and then wrap in cling film and chill for 30 minutes.

Line a 25 cm (10 inch) tart tin with the pastry, prick the base with a fork and leave to rest again in the fridge for half an hour.

Pre-heat the oven to 200°C/400°F/Gas Mark 6. Line the pastry case with greaseproof paper or foil, weight it down with baking beans and bake blind for 10 minutes. Remove the beans and paper and return to the oven for about 5 minutes, to dry out without browning.

To make the filling, put the cranberries into a pan, with a quarter of the sugar and 2 tablespoons of water. Stir over a low heat until juices begin to run and the sugar has dissolved.

Bring up to the boil and boil rapidly until the cranberries have all burst. Off the heat, beat in the remaining sugar and the butter. Leave to cool until tepid.

Beat the eggs into the cranberry mixture. Pour the filling into the pastry case, scatter with almonds and return to the oven for about 30 minutes, until just set. Serve warm.

Cranberry and Ginger Relish

If I have a little time on my hands before Christmas, I make this whole cranberry relish baked slowly in the oven. Stored in sterilized jars, it will keep for a month or more in a cool, dark place. A good stand-by for unexpected guests, and a great present.

MAKES ABOUT 650 G (1 LB 6 OZ)
450 g (1 lb) cranberries
225 g (8 oz) caster sugar
Finely grated zest and juice of ½ orange
3 pieces of preserved stem ginger in syrup, drained and finely chopped

Pre-heat the oven to 180°C/350°F/Gas Mark 4. Spread the cranberries in a single layer in an ovenproof dish or roasting tin. Sprinkle evenly with the remaining ingredients and cover with foil. Bake for about 45 minutes, stirring twice. Spoon into hot sterilized jars (see page 124 for sterilizing method).

forced rhubarb

My mother inculcated an edgy distrust of rhubarb in me. She had never recovered from being forced to eat sour, teeth-furring, stringy rhubarb as a child. Re-reading what she wrote about rhubarb, I can see now that she realized, reluctantly, that she would never really be able to embrace even the choicest rhubarb, most perfectly cooked, with anything approaching enthusiasm, despite the fact that she could see that young, pink, tender stems might well offer some sort of edible pleasure to the unprejudiced.

Luckily, my distrust was not so strong that it couldn't be overcome. I suffered occasionally from enforced school rhubarb but, once I started to cater for myself, I had enough curiosity left intact to risk cooking it. In fact, what fired me was probably not so much curiosity as the startling colour scheme of the first forced rhubarb of the year.

Vivid pink stems, long and slender, topped by a froth of bromide-yellow leaf. What a sight ... it's hard to believe that this isn't a man-made creation. In part, I suppose, it is. Forced rhubarb, as the name suggests, is coerced into an early appearance by human trickery.

The art of forcing rhubarb belongs to the Leeds area, where rhubarb is grown in great, dark hangars. All light is excluded, and the young shoots thrust up and out in search of illumination. Light-deprivation is what gives them their psychedelic appearance. It also tempers the harshness of flavour that so often characterizes outdoor rhubarb.

Forced rhubarb is delicate and delicious and a pleasure to cook with. It arrives in January or early February, like a beacon amongst the duller fruit of that time. Though rhubarb is not technically a fruit at all, it has all the attributes of fruit and is welcome as the first home-grown dessert-maker of the year. Like snowdrops, it promises that winter will not last forever.

Buying and Storing Forced Rhubarb

Choose firm, relatively unblemished, shocking pink stems that are long and slender. Always buy it with the leaves, even though you can't eat them. They should be bright yellow and crisply furled. Floppy leaves, like floppy stems, are a sign that the rhubarb is well past its best. Leaves that are tinged with green tell you that, somewhere along the way, the rhubarb has been exposed to too much light. Try to choose stems that are all much the same thickness, so that they will cook evenly.

Don't store forced rhubarb for more than a day or two, in a cool, dark place. Use it up quickly – what you can't eat straight away is best cooked with a little sugar and stashed in the fridge, where it will keep for three or four days, or frozen.

Using Forced Rhubarb

Forcing transforms rhubarb without removing the fresh invigorating acidity that makes it seem healthy fare, despite the amount of sugar it soaks up. Preparation is easy. Just trim off the leaves (*never* eat them: they are toxic) and the base of the stem. There is no need to peel forced rhubarb. Cut it up into manageable lengths and it is ready. These young tender stems take precious little time to cook, though they exude enormous amounts of liquid. Unless you actually want juice rather than substance, never add more water or other liquid than absolutely necessary. None at all is often best.

The high acidity means that you will have to be generous with the sweetening. Count on adding at least a quarter of the weight of trimmed rhubarb in sugar. However sweet you make it, don't cook rhubarb in an aluminium or unlined iron pan or both rhubarb and pan will end up discoloured.

Good things to enhance rhubarb are orange – so common a partner it's almost a cliché, but justifiably so; ginger – either ground or, better still, preserved stem ginger, finely chopped; star anise and almonds. If you have a sweet cicely plant that is already bravely putting out a few tentative shoots, throw them in with the rhubarb. They will flavour it beautifully and reduce the acidity.

Forced rhubarb cooks well in a microwave. To 250 g (9 oz) trimmed stalks, cut into 2.5 cm (1 inch) lengths, add the juice of 1/2 orange and 60–85g (2–3 oz) vanilla or caster sugar, cover tightly with cling film and then cook on full power for 2 1/2–3 minutes, stirring once or twice. Failing that, the oven is a good bet, using the same proportions of rhubarb and sugar and the method outlined in the recipe for *Rhubarb and Honey Compote* (see page 111).

Rhubarb Meringue Tart

One of the best of all rhubarb puddings, with a thick almondy base that soaks up some of the rhubarb juice without becoming unpleasantly soggy, and a finishing swirl of meringue. Looks good, tastes even better.

For the pastry:

110 g (4 oz) ground almonds
110 g (4 oz) plain flour, sifted
170 g (6 oz) unsalted butter
85 g (3 oz) light muscovado sugar
2 egg yolks, beaten
Pinch of salt

For the filling:

450 g (1 lb) forced rhubarb, trimmed and cut into 2.5 cm (1 inch) lengths
60 g (2 oz) raisins
1 1/2 tablespoons cornflour
170 g (6 oz) caster sugar
2 egg whites

To make the pastry, mix the ground almonds, flour and salt and rub in the butter. Stir in the sugar and then add the egg yolks and, if necessary, just enough cold water to make a soft dough. Using your hands, press it into a 20 cm (8 inch), loose-bottomed tart tin, to form a fairly thick crust, rising up the sides. Leave to rest for half an hour in the fridge. Pre-heat the oven to 200°C/400°F/Gas Mark 6.

Prick the pastry case with a fork and line it with cooking foil or greaseproof paper, weight down with baking beans and bake blind for 10 minutes. Remove the beans and foil and return to the oven to dry out, without browning, for about 5 minutes. Leave to cool until tepid.

To make the filling, toss the rhubarb with the raisins, cornflour and 60 g (2 oz) of sugar and then spread the mixture over the tart base and bake for 10 minutes. Meanwhile, whisk the egg whites until they form stiff peaks. Add half the remaining sugar and whisk again, until glossy and smooth. Fold in the last of the sugar and whisk as before. Pile up on top of the rhubarb, making nice swirls with a fork. Return to the oven for 10 minutes, until the meringue is beginning to catch and brown on the crests. Serve warm or cold.

Rhubarb and Honey Compote

If you don't have a microwave, this is probably the simplest way to cook rhubarb without ending up with a collapsing mush. Baked in the oven, sweetened with honey and sugar (or all sugar if you prefer), scented mildly with orange, it just needs an occasional glance to make sure it is not overcooking. Cooking time depends largely on the girth of the stems.

SERVES 6–8

900 g (2 lb) rhubarb, trimmed and cut into 2.5 cm (1 inch) lengths
5 tablespoons honey
85 g (3 oz) caster sugar
4 strips of orange zest
Juice of 1 orange
Cream or Greek yoghurt, to serve

Pre-heat the oven to 170°C/325°F/Gas Mark 3. Place the rhubarb in a shallow, ovenproof dish. Drizzle over the honey and then sprinkle with sugar. Add the orange zest and juice. Cover with foil. Bake for 25-30 minutes, stirring every now and then, until the rhubarb is tender but not disintegrating. Serve hot, warm or cold, with cream or yoghurt.

Forced Rhubarb Jellies

A spring tonic, in the best of senses. These jellies slip down like a dream – cool and fresh and scented.

SERVES 6

4 green cardamom pods
675 g (1 lb 7 oz) trimmed weight forced rhubarb, cut into 2.5 cm (1 inch) lengths
Juice of 2 oranges
140 g (5 oz) caster sugar
11 g (0.4 oz) sachet of powdered gelatine
150 ml (5 fl oz) single cream, to serve

Split open the cardamom pods and extract the black seeds. Crush them finely. Place the rhubarb and cardamom seeds in a pan, with the orange juice and sugar. Cook over a low heat until the juices begin to run and then raise the heat a little and leave to simmer for 5 minutes, or until the rhubarb is collapsing. Tip the contents of the pan into a jelly bag or non-metallic sieve lined with muslin, set over a bowl, and allow to drip without pressing down on the debris. Leave for an hour.

Measure the liquid – you should have about 600 ml (1 pint). If necessary, top up with a little water. Then taste it. It should be sweet enough but retain a mild tartness. This is largely a matter of personal taste so, if you think it needs more sugar, warm it gently with a little extra sugar until you get the right balance.

Put 3 tablespoons of hot water into a small pan and sprinkle the gelatine evenly over. Stir until dissolved. If there are a few stubborn globs that refuse to disappear, warm gently, stirring, without boiling, until they dissolve.

Stir a tablespoon of rhubarb juice into the gelatine and then another and then a third. Finally, pour the whole lot into the remaining rhubarb juice and stir until nicely mixed. Again, if there are blobs of gelatine, warm gently, stirring, until they have dissolved. Pour the jelly into six glasses or small bowls and chill until set.

Just before serving, pour a little single cream over the surface of each jelly if you like.

limes

The glowing, dark green skin of the lime has become a familiar sight, nestling alongside the lemons and oranges. It originated in tropical Asia, but has spread its way around the world, making new homes for itself wherever the climate suits it, from India through to Israel and into the New World. It is used with joyous abandon in the cooking of Latin America, the West Indies and south-east Asia, where it replaces lemons as the all-important bearer of a fruity acidity.

The juice of the lime is as sharp as the lemon's and possibly even sharper, but the flavour is far more aromatic and spicy. Although they are interchangeable in many recipes, they are not identical and each will change the nature of the dish. Lime brings a tropical feel, while lemons speak of the Mediterranean.

To extract the maximum amount of juice from a lime, warm it gently, by dunking it in hot water, by a very quick blast in the microwave or a few minutes in a warm oven, then roll it firmly on the table to loosen the flesh. Cut it in half and squeeze. A trick that works just as well with lemons, incidentally. As with the lemon, the zest of the lime has its own highly scented presence, free of acidity, and can be pared off in strips or finely grated.

I don't much care for lime juice in European-style vinaigrettes – lemon works far better – but, when used in Asian fashion, with chilli, sugar, and fish sauce, it is magic. From the other side of the world come salsas, such as *Salsa Mexicana* (see page 53), and, here again, lime juice comes into its own.

One of my favourite uses for lime is as a marinade for fish. It quickly 'cooks' the raw flesh to an opaque white, to form the basis of a *ceviche* which can be fleshed out with avocado, chilli and tomato and finished with fresh coriander leaves. Lime can replace lemon to make lime cakes and icings and is superb mixed with sugar syrup and frozen to a sorbet, but there are few things nicer than home-made lime curd. Simply replace the lemon juice and zest with lime in a rich lemon curd recipe and then thrill to the pale green-yellow ambrosia that emerges.

mangoes

The mango is a majestic tree, reaching as high as 30 metres (100 feet) in maturity. Its ample, evergreen branches stretch out to give welcome shade from the shimmering midday heat – the bus stop in many a tropical village is placed conveniently near a mango tree, so that patient travellers are shielded from the sun as they wait and wait for a bus. The fruit drip down between the heavy foliage, strung along long green stems like fairy lights that have come adrift at one end. They are plump, inviting and profuse.

The mango is native to Malaysia though it is grown most prolifically in India, from which it takes the second part of its Latin name, *Mangifera indica*. It belongs to the same family as the cashew nut and shares one irksome characteristic – a clever natural defence mechanism. The sap of both trees is an unpleasant irritant. Since the sap of the mango is inclined to squirt out viciously from the stalk of the fruit as it is picked, harvesters are wise to protect both hands and eyes. Woe betide any young rustlers.

From the East, the mango has spread around the tropical and subtropical world, finding a home wherever it will grow. This proliferation has ensured that there are countless varieties. In India alone there are at least 500 named varieties, and that's before you start to count those from Africa, Australia, South America and Florida.

An early morning trip to Birmingham's wholesale market brought me face to face with a mere half dozen or so of this multitude of mangoes and with a true mango connoisseur. Leon Edwards and his brother Lesley run a small Afro-Caribbean grocery in the Handsworth district of the city but they began as teenage mango dealers. The young brothers clubbed together to buy a box of the best Jamaican Julie mangoes and sold them from the back of a van to revellers leaving pubs and clubs late at night. A stroke of genius! Soon they could afford to fill the back of the van to the brim with mangoes and business was booming.

As spring changed to summer, summer to autumn and then winter and round again, Leon began to know the pattern of mango varieties and sources. Now he knows exactly what he will find when, and reels off a list of seasonal varieties without hesitation – he showed me Tommy's and Tommy Atkins (some of the most widely grown mangoes); the last of the year's Julies (every Jamaican's favourite mango); peach mangoes, fibrous and sweet; Grahams; and Honey mangoes – the Pakistani favourites – which drip syrupy sweetness.

The perfect mango is obviously a very personal matter, as much to do with what you are used to as anything else. There's no doubting, however, that a ripe, high quality mango is a thing of great joy. The flesh will be perfumed and sweet with a balancing trace of acidity and that unique, strangely beguiling hint of turpentine. Mangoes do actually contain a trace of kerosene! The other essential for the perfect mango is a smooth, slippery texture. In all varieties there are fibres that radiate out from the large flattish seed in the centre but, in the choicer fruit, they are short enough to be negligible. In the less good ones they can be so long, tough and omnipresent that the only way to tackle them is to suck the juices out and then throw away the dry fibrous mass that is left.

Buying Mangoes

A ripe mango is firm but gives very slightly when squeezed gently (don't bruise the poor fruit in an excess of enthusiasm). It also has a beautiful, perfumed scent. Usually, the skin has turned from green to a clear straw yellow, flushed with orange or rosy pink. The odd brown freckle indicates full ripeness but this mango needs to be eaten straight away, before it begins to slide down into an overblown state. Mind you, one or two excellent varieties remain semi-green when ripe – the awkward exceptions that prove the rule. Shape is neither here nor there. Mangoes can be elongated and slender with a pronounced tip-tilted beak at one end, or so fat and rounded that the beak barely shows. Ungainly great hunks of mango can be every bit as good as petite cuties.

Variety plays a huge part, too, so when you come across a brilliant mango that sends your taste buds spiralling heavenward, make a note of its name (most mangoes are labelled these days) so that you can track it down again. Tommy Atkins is a reliable, very common variety developed in Florida. Not sensational, but easy to find and rarely disappointing. Tommy's are similar but smaller. It is often said that the Indian Alphonso mango is the most exquisite of them all, but it has a very short season, around April, so keep an eye out for rare imports at that time.

Although you will have no trouble locating mangoes in any decent supermarket, you may well find more interesting varieties in smaller ethnic food stores where the buyers, like Leon Edwards, are really passionate about their favourite fruit.

Under-ripe mangoes will ripen naturally in the fruit bowl, or on a plate in a warm kitchen. Eat them up when they begin to soften, and before they start to wrinkle or develop patches of brown rot.

Using Mangoes

In countries where mangoes are plentiful, unripe green ones are often cooked almost like a cross between a fruit and a vegetable, and their sharpness can be exploited to good effect. In India they even use ground, dried green mango, *amchoor* powder, as a tart spice.

Here, most of the mangoes that we buy are already too ripe for cooking, though they may still be too under-ripe to bring out their full scent. For slicing, cubing or chopping in general, you will want a barely ripe mango, with flesh soft and sweet enough for pleasure but not so soft that it collapses under pressure.

Understanding the anatomy of the mango is a help when it comes to cutting. Inside is a long, thin, oval stone that runs from stalk end to tip, with two fat cheeks of mango clinging on either side. To cube a mango, or to cut it for easy, relatively mess-free eating (and this looks pretty on a mixed plate of fruit, too), slice the two cheeks off as close as possible to the stone. If you bring a sliver of the stone with you, just cut it out. Now make criss-cross cuts in the cut surface of each cheek, penetrating almost down to the skin, but without piercing it. Hold the cheek with both hands and, with a twist of the wrists, turn inside-out, so that the cubes of flesh stand out hedgehog-fashion. For separate cubes, just pull them away from the skin, or slice off with a sharp knife. The flesh left clinging to the stone can either be hacked off as best you can, or nibbled off – I always reckon that this is the cook's perk.

For long, thin, elegant slices, leave the mango unpeeled (peeled ripe mango is far too slippery to get a grip on), and make a cut from stem to tip, down at right angles to the stone, in the centre. Make another cut close by and ease the slice away from the stone. Repeat, working your way out to the edges of the stone and then turn over and slice the other side in the same way. Lastly, trim off the peel. For slightly less elegant but quite functional slices, peel the mango and then slice off the cheeks. Lay them flat on the work surface and slice.

Slices of fresh mango just as they are make a brilliantly exotic dessert and look as pretty as a picture fanned out on a plate. To jazz them up, serve with a scoop of vanilla or nut ice cream, or a lighter fruit sorbet. Cubes of orange mango can enliven a fruit salad, especially in winter, when the commonplace fruit begin to lack lustre – keep the combinations simple. Just mango and orange is lovely, or mango and hothouse black grapes which looks dramatic. Pineapple, mango and papaya dressed with the juices and seeds of a few passion fruit and a shake of sugar is about as good as you can get.

But mango doesn't have to be kept for the end of the meal. It fits surprisingly well in the earlier stages. Try it right at the start. Simply arranged on a plate, paper-thin slices of air-dried ham – Parma, *jamón serrano*, or our own Cumbrian air-dried ham (see page 188) – are just as good as melon. Finely diced and mixed with chilli, fresh coriander and lime juice, it is transformed into a fashionable salsa, which goes so well with barbecued chicken, lamb or even prawns. In south-east Asian curries, particularly those made with coconut milk, its sweetness can bring a most appetizing note to the dish. Wherever the mango is to be added to a hot dish, it is best to stir it in right at the end of the cooking time so that it retains its fresh, sweet vivacity.

You could try making your own mango tea. Save mango skins, cut them into strips and spread them out on a rack. Leave to dry in the airing cupboard for several days. Chop roughly and then process until finely chopped. Mix with best Chinese tea and store in an airtight container.

Pan-Fried Lamb with Fresh Mango Chutney

One step on from a straight salsa, this chutney combines the depth of cooked spices and fruit with the freshness of uncooked mango. I love it with lamb but it goes well, too, with chicken or prawns.

SERVES 4

4 lamb leg steaks
Juice of 1/2 orange
1/2 teaspoon ground coriander
2 tablespoons oil
Salt and pepper
For the chutney:
1 orange
2 tablespoons white wine vinegar
4 tablespoons caster sugar
1 teaspoon cumin seeds, coarsely crushed
1 teaspoon coriander seeds, coarsely crushed
1/2 tablespoon black mustard seeds
1 medium-sized mango, peeled, stoned and finely diced
1 fresh red chilli, de-seeded and finely chopped

Marinate the lamb chops with the orange juice, ground coriander, oil, salt and pepper for at least an hour.

For the chutney, slice the orange thinly, discarding the ends. Quarter the slices and put them in a pan, with the vinegar, sugar and spices. Add 300 ml (10 fl oz) of water. Bring to the boil, stirring once or twice, and then simmer for about 25 minutes, until the peel on the orange slices is translucent and most of the liquid has boiled away, leaving just a moist mixture.

Peel, stone and dice the mango finely, tipping any juice over the lamb steaks and then stir the flesh into the orange, together with the chilli. Leave to cool and, if not using immediately, cover and store in the fridge for no longer than 24 hours.

Pre-heat the grill to hot. Grill the lamb steaks for about 4 minutes on each side, until just cooked through but still tender inside. Serve with the mango and orange chutney.

Mango, Lime and Cardamom Fool

A very easy, but glamorous, pudding, scented with fragrant cardamom. Evaporated milk, rather than cream, gives it richness though you couldn't tell when eating it. Though this can be eaten as soon as it is made, it will thicken a little if left overnight in the fridge. Serve with crisp biscuits, such as *Pecan Tuiles* (see page 280).

SERVES 6

3 fresh mangoes, weighing about 300 g (11 oz) each, peeled, stoned and diced (see page 115)
2 limes
4 cardamom pods
4–5 tablespoons light muscovado sugar, to taste
180 ml (6 fl oz) evaporated milk
1 large mango, to serve

Put the mango dice in a food processor. With a zester or a vegetable peeler, take the green zest off one of the limes and shred it finely. Blanch for a minute in boiling water, drain and reserve. Squeeze the juice of the limes and add to the mango. Slit open the cardamom pods, extract the black seeds and crush to a fine powder in a mortar with a pestle. Tip into the processor. Add 3 tablespoons of light muscovado sugar. Process until smooth and then add the evaporated milk and process again, to mix. Taste and add a little more sugar, if you think it needs it. Divide between six glasses, ramekins or custard cups, cover and leave in the fridge for at least an hour and up to 24 hours, to thicken.

Shortly before serving, sprinkle a little more light muscovado sugar over the top of each fool and finish with a few strands of the reserved lime zest. Take the last mango and slice it, by cutting at right angles to the central stone, to release long, new-moon-shaped slices of flesh. Trim the peel from the slices and serve them alongside the fool.

Mango Tatin

The poor old Tatin sisters are probably turning in their grave, if not whirling. Their original upside-down, caramelized apple tart has been twisted and played with, adapted and misused endlessly by cooks and chefs. The original, made with a short, not puff, pastry remains one of the all-time most glorious puddings, one that is impossible to beat. So, I make no claim that this is better – it is just a delicious way of using mangoes and I freely admit to appropriating the name, the caramel and the upside-downness, all for the sake of the exotic mango.

The trick to this pudding is timing and knowing your pan. I make it in a heavy cast-iron frying-pan that holds the heat very efficiently, so I need to draw the pan off the heat as soon as the juices begin to colour, as they will continue to cook and caramelize in the heat of the pan. If you are using a thinner pan, you may have to cook the mango over the heat for a little longer, until the juices are light brown. In short, I would advise that you make it once for the family, before you attempt to dish it up for a smart dinner party.

SERVES 6
250 g (8 oz) puff pastry
100 g (4 oz) butter, cut into thin slivers
200 g (8 oz) vanilla sugar
Juice of 1/2 lime
3–4 mangoes, depending on size, peeled
Crème fraiche, mascarpone or Greek yoghurt, to serve

Pre-heat the oven to 220°C/425°F/Gas Mark 7. Find a heavy-based frying-pan with an oven-proof handle or a handle that can be removed, or a sturdy flameproof and ovenproof tart tin. It will need to be around 25 cm (10 inches) in diameter or very slightly larger. Roll out the pastry thinly and, using your frying-pan as a template, cut out a circle of the same size. Prick all over with a fork and then chill in the fridge for at least half an hour.

Lay slivers of butter all over the base of your frying-pan, and then strew the sugar more or less evenly over the butter. Drizzle about a tablespoon of lime juice over the sugar.

Slice the cheeks off both sides of two (or three if they are small) of the mangoes and then cut into long curved slices, about 6 mm (1/4 inch) thick, keeping each cheek together (see page 115). Slide a palette knife or a wide-bladed knife underneath, lift up carefully and then turn over on to your hand and lay, curved side down, in the pan. Press down gently, flattening slightly to fan the pieces out. You should be able to fit four cheeks into the pan quite comfortably if the mangoes are large. If they are small, put five cheeks around the edge of the pan and lay the sixth in the centre. Cut up the remaining mango in the same way and use the slices to fill in gaps around the edges and anywhere else. The slices should be quite densely packed.

Place the pan over a moderate heat, raising it to high as the butter melts and the juice begins to run. Continue to cook, letting the juice bubble and boil around the mango slices until it just begins to colour (see introduction), turning the pan so that it is heated through evenly. Don't stir or you'll ruin all your artistry with the slices!

Draw off the heat. Cover with the pastry. Bake for 12–15 minutes, until the pastry is puffed and nicely browned. Let the tart sit for a minute or two in its pan and then place a large serving plate on top, and quickly invert on to the plate. If any bits of mango are left sticking to the pan, carefully dislodge them and arrange them back in place on the tart – no one will ever know.

Serve the tart hot or warm, with crème fraiche, mascarpone or Greek yoghurt.

Opposite *Mango Tatin*

papayas

The papaya or pawpaw started out in Central America and worked its way in the opposite direction to the lime, courtesy of the Spanish and Portuguese, all the way over to Asia. It is shaped like a hefty cross between a pear and a melon, with green skin that ripens to yellow, orange, pink and/or red in varying combinations. When the papaya is at its best it is a sensational fruit, with pink-orange flesh that melts sweetly and seductively in the mouth. Unfortunately, it is often disappointing, at least in this country where ripening is less even and assured. On balance though, I've been lucky enough to meet more good papayas than bad.

To prepare a papaya, simply cut it in half and scoop out the grey seeds. They are edible and some people even use them ground up in dressings, but I can't say that I've ever found their taste very appealing. To eat papaya fresh, just squeeze a little lime juice over the flesh and dig in with a teaspoon. For fruit salads, peel, cut up and mix with other fruit, again adding a dash of lime juice to compensate for the papaya's lack of acidity. Liquidized with fizzy water, lime juice and sugar, the flesh can be transformed into refreshing fruit drinks. Green papaya can be cooked as a vegetable, steamed or roasted and dressed with butter and coriander or spices.

Never try to use papaya in a jelly. The flesh contains an enzyme which chomps gleefully on protein and will reduce any jelly to a pool of liquid. The plus side of this is that papaya works remarkably well as a tenderizer for meats. Try marinating chicken overnight with sliced or puréed papaya, or even just wrapped in the skin, and you will see how effective it is when the chicken is cooked.

quinces

The measure of a quince is its perfume. At its ripest, it should scent the room more exquisitely than any Dior or Chanel creation. This is one of those heart-stopping fragrances that only nature can create, leaving the most lauded of perfumes lagging miserably behind.

That's the theory, anyway, but I have to admit that, every now and then, it has crossed my mind that quinces might be overrated. I remembered the scent from my childhood but I sniffed for it in vain when I bought quinces from my local Cypriot greengrocer. Left in a warm spot to ripen, they did develop some vestige of perfume but hardly enough to qualify. Still, I've always been grateful to lay my hand on any quinces at all. Heady fragrance or no, those Cypriot quinces made a pleasing change from cooked apples or pears.

My faith in quinces has been restored by fruit of three very different origins. The first came all the way from the Lebanon and were of a more truly golden hue than most. They were beautifully scented and, looking at them, I could believe that they might well have been the golden apple that Paris gave to Aphrodite. The second batch was French and the quinces were smaller and lighter in colour but no less perfumed. So pleased was I to smell that scent again that I stupidly left them in the fruit bowl until they began to rot. I finally lost the perfume without ever tasting the flesh. The third batch of quinces was English, from a neighbour's garden (our tree is still too young to bear fruit) and these were the smallest but the best of all.

We used to be rather partial to quinces in this country but, like so many choice vegetables and fruits, they've fallen out of favour. I imagine this is due to laziness. You can't eat a raw quince. It is hard as rock and too astringent for enjoyment. Quinces must be cooked and they need time to soften, to tame their astringency and transform their scent into taste, and their pale gold and cream tones to remarkable rich, glowing rust red.

Choosing and Storing Quinces

If you don't have a quince tree in your garden, beg or buy the fruit when you can. They are an autumnal fruit in the northern hemisphere, though some South African quinces are imported out of season in the early summer. Quite wrong for the time of year, of course, since they clash with the best of the strawberries. They vary enormously in quality though, with odd exceptions, they do seem to improve the further north they are grown, within their own natural limits. Until recently, Greek and Turkish shops have had the most reliable supplies, though at last quinces are beginning to creep into the displays of ordinary greengrocers and even the supermarkets.

They are a shopkeeper's dream, since they have a naturally long shelf-life and are slow to bruise or rot. When buying, make sure that they are firm all over, without wrinkles or severe damage. The downy coat rubs off easily, so it is bound to be patchy.

If you intend to use your quinces within a few days, leave them in the fruit bowl so that everyone can enjoy their scent. For longer storage, arrange on slatted trays, without touching, in a cool place where they will keep for a month and possibly longer.

Using Quinces

In many ways, quinces can be treated rather like apples or pears with an extra-long cooking time. Cutting them up is harder work and demands a sharp knife and patience. If they are not to be peeled, you should remember to wipe the light grey down from the skin before use. The ivory flesh discolours quickly when cut but, in most cases, this doesn't matter at all, as it helps the natural cooked quince-red to develop.

Their flavour is strong enough to penetrate and spread right through a dish, so a single quince can add a generous dose of quinciness to, say, an apple pie (cut the quince up into tiny pieces or paper-thin slices, so that it cooks about as quickly as the larger chunks of apple). I often blanch sliced, peeled and cored quinces for 10 minutes in water and then add enough sugar to make a light syrup, enhancing it with strips of lemon or orange zest, or a vanilla pod. I keep the quince slices simmering gently until they are very tender and beginning to turn translucent. They always take much longer than I expect (an hour is not unusual, and maybe even longer) but it is worth persevering until quinces and syrup cook to the famous deep brown-red. The liquid level must never drop too low as the quinces cook (they should always remain covered), though the liquid may need to be reduced to a syrupy consistency once they are done.

Quinces are a surprisingly astringent fruit, so you need to add quite a lot of sugar to them when making puddings. For savoury dishes (poached quince slices go famously with game, duck and other rich meats), a modicum of sugar will pay dividends, too.

Quinces have a high pectin level and are perfectly suited to jelly-making, either on their own or bulked out with cooking apples. They produce a superb, garnet jelly that is as good on toast as it is with a roast leg of lamb.

Baked Quinces

This is the easiest way to cook quinces and probably the best. They look pretty and they taste elegantly and purely of quince and a hint of caramel. Serve with single or double cream.

SERVES 4
4 small quinces
30 g (1 oz) butter
4 tablespoons caster sugar
Cream, to serve

Pre-heat the oven to 200°C/400°F/Gas Mark 6. Cut each quince in half horizontally (not from stalk to stem). Trim a thin slice from the stem end and from the top, so that you can sit the two halves flat, without too much wobbling around. Use about two-thirds of the butter to grease an ovenproof dish generously and arrange the halved quinces in it, trimmed-side down, central cut upwards. Dredge with caster sugar and dot with the remaining butter. Spoon about 3 tablespoons of water around the quinces.

Bake for about 45–60 minutes, until tender. Check occasionally and baste with their own juices once or twice. If the dish threatens to burn dry, add a little more water. Serve the quinces with their syrup and some cream.

Opposite: *Baked Quinces*

Spiced Quinces

These sweet, sharp, spiced quinces are lovely served with cold meats or even cheeses. Make them in the autumn months and save at least one jar for Christmas, to go with thick slices of cold cooked ham on Boxing Day.

FILLS ABOUT FIVE 1 LB JAM JARS (220 ML/8 FI OZ CAPACITY)

4 large quinces or 8 smaller ones
240 ml (8½ fl oz) white wine vinegar
500 g (1 lb 2 oz) granulated or caster sugar
1 cinnamon stick
1 teaspoon coriander seeds
8 cloves
1 teaspoon black peppercorns
1 mace blade
60 ml (4 tablespoons) sherry vinegar

Peel and core the quinces and cut into 12 slices each, if large, or eight, if small. Cook in plain water until almost tender. Strain and measure out 600 ml (1 pint) of their cooking liquid.

Put the liquid into a pan with the white wine vinegar, sugar and spices and stir over a moderate heat, until the sugar has dissolved. Carefully return the fruit to the pan and simmer quietly until the fruit is translucent – another 20 minutes or so. Lift the fruit and whatever spices come with it, out with a slotted spoon and transfer to warm, sterilized jars. If necessary, boil the cooking liquid down a little to make it syrupy and then stir in the sherry vinegar and pour over the fruit, making sure that it is entirely covered. Seal with non-corrosive lids and store in a cool, dark place for least a month before opening.

To Sterilize Jars:

Pre-heat the oven to 110°C/225°F/Gas Mark ½. Wash the jars in warm, soapy water and then rinse in hot water. Without touching the insides, set them upside-down on a wire rack in the oven. Leave for at least half an hour and use hot from the oven.

pears

We are a divided family. My children and I adore pears. My husband loathes them. How can he? I really can't fathom how anybody could dislike pears. Even a rather dull, under-ripe pear is still pleasantly crisp and juicy, but a perfectly ripe, honeyed, fragrant pear melts in the mouth like nothing else. In its prime, the pear has a place amongst the great fruits of all time, every bit as startling and sensational as the best pineapple or the most elegant of mangoes. I reckon that it can hold its own against the fanciest of puddings. It is certainly one of the temperate countries' triumphs.

The pear is a fruit that has swung in and out of fashion but has long been recognized as a fruit worthy of interest. Horticulturalists and gentleman gardeners of the past have all sought to improve and develop pears, recognizing their potential. One of the pitfalls of the pear has always been that the moment of perfect ripeness is notably short. A day or so and it has gone, the flesh descending swiftly into overblown blowsiness. Newer varieties seem to be addressing that problem. The fabulously huge, tawny-skinned Taylor's Gold ripens readily and holds its perfect sweetness and texture for several days or more, as does the smaller, prettier, golden-skinned Rochas pear from Portugal. This does not mean that you should despise older varieties, just that the enjoyment of pears is no longer limited to the rare, heavenly splurge.

Buying and Storing Pears

Enjoy them. There's no need to stick religiously to one variety any more. Try new ones, compare and make the most of the best of them. A fully ripe pear will give very slightly but anything more than light pressure may bruise it. Unless you are going to eat them immediately, there's no point in buying seriously ripe pears. By the time you get home they will be bruised and battered beyond redemption. Choose pears that are still on the firm side, so that they can finish ripening in the safety of your fruit bowl. Avoid any that are already damaged, or have broken skins. Extra fine pears appear every now and then, with stems capped with red sealing wax, cradled in a bed of soft tissue, and complete with an arty producer's seal. They can be extraordinarily good and, if you are going to pay the price, continue treating them with kid gloves until the moment they reach your mouth.

Once pears have ripened, there's nothing for it but to eat them or cook them. Don't try stashing them in the fridge – it won't prolong their lives at all.

Using Pears

There is little nicer than a beautifully ripe, fragrant pear eaten just as it is, perhaps with the skin peeled away but no more artifice than that. For a change, or when you are not sure that the pear is going to live up to high expectations, serve it with cheese. Pears are excellent with slices of Parmesan, Stilton, or goats' cheese – the pungency of these cheeses heightens the sweet succulence of the pear.

If you are going to add pears to a fruit salad, leave them until the last moment or they will soften and become slimy. Whenever you are cutting up pears for salads, or for other dishes, turn the pieces in lemon juice as you work, to prevent them browning. Dressed with a vinaigrette and partnered with smoked chicken, they make a good first course or main-course salad for an early autumn meal. I like them, too, mixed with watercress and cubes of goats' cheese, again, dressed with a light vinaigrette.

If you are faced with a haul of infuriatingly hard pears that refuse to ripen in time for a special meal, the best way to deal with them is to poach them, peeled and sliced, in a sugar syrup flavoured with a vanilla pod, orange or lemon zest or a cinnamon stick, until very tender and glassily translucent.

Pear *tarte Tatins* have become rather fashionable, made in a similar fashion to the proper apple *tarte Tatin*, though they will need a shot or two of lemon juice somewhere along the line, to make up for their low acidity. Sweet and sour pear compotes or spiced pears are excellent accompaniments to all kinds of meat, feathered or furred.

Tarte de Cambrai

The recipe for this moist, buttery, pear pudding-cake was given to my mother many years ago, by the woman who ran the *droguerie* in the small French town we visit every year. It quickly became a family favourite and I still love it.

SERVES 6–8

4–5 large, ripe pears
Juice of 1/2 lemon
60 g (2 oz) butter
Sugar

For the batter:

110 g (4 oz) self-raising flour
A pinch of salt
80 g (3 oz) vanilla sugar or caster sugar
4 tablespoons sunflower oil
120 ml (4 fl oz) milk
2 eggs, lightly beaten
Cream, to serve

Pre-heat the oven to 200°C/400°F/Gas Mark 6. Grease a 25 cm (10 inch) shallow cake tin.

Peel, core and slice the pears then turn them in the lemon juice. To make the batter, sift the flour and salt. Stir in the sugar. Make a well in the centre and add the oil, milk and eggs. Beat together, gradually drawing in the flour and sugar to make a smooth batter. Pour the batter into the prepared tin. Arrange the pear slices on top, and then dot with butter and sprinkle evenly with sugar (around 2 tablespoons should do it). Bake for 50–60 minutes, until golden brown and puffed. Eat warm to get it at its best, with cream.

Roast Pears with Ginger

Roasting halved pears with butter and ginger concentrates their flavour and cooks them to a tender buttery state. The ginger steers them away from any hint of blandness. This is a pretty pudding, which tastes superb.

SERVES 4

4 pears
Juice of 1 lemon
60 g (2 oz) butter
3–4 pieces of preserved stem ginger in syrup, drained and chopped
3 tablespoons vanilla sugar or caster sugar
Single cream, to serve

Pre-heat the oven to 220°C/425°F/Gas Mark 7. Peel the pears and cut them in half. Turn in the lemon juice, to prevent from browning. Carefully scoop out the core, without breaking each pear half. Slice the pears lengthways, cutting up towards the stem but not quite cutting right through, so that the halves hold together. Lay them in a buttered ovenproof dish, flattening them slightly to fan out the slices. Scatter over the ginger and then the sugar and dot with the remaining butter. Spoon 4 tablespoons of water around the pears (or a little more if the dish is on the large side). Roast for about 30 minutes, basting occasionally, until the pears are very tender and translucent, with the odd hint of brown. Serve piping hot, with single cream.

Pear, Stilton and Walnut Strudel

A savoury twist on a fruity pudding. Adding Stilton, salt and pepper to this *strudel* turns it into a substantial main course for a vegetarian meal.

Try to get large sheets of filo pastry – the exact dimensions vary considerably but they should be around 45 x 30 cm (18 x 12 inches).

SERVES 6–8

6 sheets of filo pastry
90 g (3 oz) butter, melted and cooled until tepid
2 tablespoons dry breadcrumbs or semolina
1–2 teaspoons poppy seeds
A bunch of watercress, to serve

For the filling:

700 g (1 1/2 lb) ripe pears, peeled, cored and diced
Juice of 1/2 lemon
140 g (5 oz) Stilton, de-rinded and crumbled
75 g (2 1/2 oz) walnuts, toasted and roughly chopped
Salt and pepper

Pre-heat the oven to 190°C/375°F/Gas Mark 5. As you prepare the pears for the filling, turn them in the lemon juice, to prevent them from browning. Mix with all the remaining filling ingredients.

To prevent the filo pastry from drying out, cover it with a sheet of greaseproof paper and cover that with a tea-towel wrung out in cold water. Lay a large sheet of greaseproof paper on the work surface. Take the first sheet of filo and lay it out flat in front of you on the greaseproof paper. Brush with melted butter. Take the next sheet and lay it out flat, overlapping the first along one of the long edges by about 7.5 cm (3 inches). Brush with butter. Lay the third sheet exactly over the first and then brush it with butter, the fourth over the second and so on until all the pastry is used up. You should end up with a large rectangle, about 45 x 52 cm (18 x 21 inches).

Sprinkle the dry breadcrumbs or semolina over the top half of the filo pastry, in a band that runs parallel to the central overlap, leaving a 5 cm (2 inch) border around the edges. Pile the filling evenly over the semolina. Flip the bare edge over the filling. Now, starting at the top, roll up the pastry round the filling, using the greaseproof paper to help you and making sure that the edges stay neatly tucked in. Carefully lift on to a greased baking tray and curve round gently to fit. Brush the top with the remaining butter and sprinkle with poppy seeds.

Bake for 40–50 minutes, until browned and crisp. Poke a skewer into the centre of the *strdel*, to make sure the pear is tender. Loosen with a knife and then slide carefully on to a serving dish. Serve hot, with the watercress tucked in around it.

passion fruit

I was ticked off recently for using the word passion in its colloquial sense. I meant passion in the sense of enthusiasm, rather than in any sexual context, but I was firmly reminded that the original meaning of the word was suffering. It is that meaning that has given passion fruit its name. Spanish missionaries in South America used the beautiful flower of the *Passiflora edulis* to explain Christ's Passion on the Cross. The nails were symbolized by the three styles, the crown of thorns by the filaments, Christ's wounds by the stamen and the apostles by the petals.

There are several different types of edible passion fruit, all of them native to South America, though they are now grown wherever there is heat enough to ripen the fruit. Even in this country, passion fruit vines will flower prolifically and produce orange fruit. Unfortunately, these fruit are of no culinary value whatsoever. The two edible types of passion fruit that are commonly imported for sale here are the small, dark purplish-green skinned passion fruit and the grenadilla, like a large, smooth, orange lollipop.

The purple passion fruit has a hard shell, which is smooth when the fruit is under-ripe, and wrinkles up most discouragingly as it ripens. Inside is a frog spawn of little black seeds, coated in the most heavenly scented, tart pulp. Don't let the look put you off. The seeds are quite edible and rather pleasantly crunchy. This type of passion fruit is the one that people and chefs in particular get quite ... well, passionate about, in the colloquial sense.

The grenadilla looks pretty and remains smooth-skinned when ripe. There is a greater mass of pippy pulp but the flavour is less intense. Save this one for eating neat, with a spoon. It doesn't have the intensity needed for cooking.

Buying and Storing Passion Fruit

A dream of easiness. I don't think I've ever seen a rotten passion fruit. A cracked one very occasionally, but that is about it. As long as they are firm all over, without any splits, they should be fine. Smooth-skinned, purple passion fruit will ripen away quietly in a fruit bowl and, once ripe, they last for several weeks with no great deterioration. Grenadillas remain smooth-skinned but they always seem to eat well.

Synthetic bottled passion fruit juice is no substitute for the real McCoy.

Using Passion Fruit

To eat passion fruit as they are, slice them open and scoop out the pulp, seeds and all, with a teaspoon. You'll taste an explosion of heady, incredible tart-sweet juice.

The flavour of the dark-skinned passion fruit is by far the stronger so always use this type for flavouring dishes. Try mixing the pulp into a fruit salad, together with a little sugar for an instant sharp boost. Or go for Australian-style passion fruit Pavlova: just top your Pavlova with whipped cream and spoon over the yellow pulp of several passion fruit. Spooned haphazardly around slices of creamy cold tarts, ice creams and puddings, it makes an instant uplifting sauce.

If you want to loosen the juice from the pips, scoop the pulp into a small saucepan, add a little sugar and, if it is a very small amount, a dash of water or orange juice. Warm gently, stirring, without boiling, for a couple of minutes and then sieve. Save some of the seeds to use as a decoration on the finished dessert. Passion fruit juice can be used to make cooling summer drinks, or to scent sorbets or ice creams. Add it to mousses, and fools, orange puddings, or fruit tarts. Anything made with orange juice will be vastly improved by a shot of passion fruit juice.

Passion Fruit and Orange Jellies

I love proper fruit jellies. Light and refreshing, they make a great finale to a rich meal. These orange jellies are boosted with the scent of passion fruit and there is nothing childish about them at all. If you set them in narrow wine or champagne glasses, there will be enough for six small servings. Larger glasses look mean if they are only half-filled so, if that is what you've got, you'll only end up with four servings.

SERVES 4–6
4 passion fruit
3 tablespoons caster sugar
550 ml (1 pint) freshly squeezed orange juice
11 g (0.4 oz) sachet of powdered gelatine
Single cream, to serve

Halve the passion fruit and scrape their innards into a small saucepan. Add the caster sugar and stir over a low heat for a few minutes, until the sugar has dissolved and the fruit is warmed through. Scrape fruit into a sieve set over the bowl of orange juice and press all the juices through, leaving behind little but the black seeds. Save a few of them for decoration.

Heat 3 tablespoons of water in a small pan, until very hot. Draw off the heat and sprinkle the gelatine over. Stir until dissolved. If a few stubborn specks of gelatine remain, warm through gently, stirring constantly, without letting it boil, until they disappear. Cool the gelatine until tepid and then stir in a tablespoon of the orange and passion fruit juice. Then stir in another, and then a third, and then tip the whole lot back into the bowl of juice. Stir to mix well. Pour into stemmed wine glasses, and leave to set in the fridge. To serve, pour a small slick of single cream over the surface and scatter with a few passion fruit seeds.

Tropical Sorbet

Mix passion fruit juice with tropical fruits to make an unusually fragrant sorbet.

SERVES 4–6

4 passion fruit

2 tablespoons plus 200 g (7 oz) caster sugar

1/2 medium-sized pineapple, peeled, cored and roughly chopped

2 large bananas, peeled and sliced

Juice of 1 lime

Extract the passion fruit juice with the 2 tablespoons of sugar (see page 130), then strain to remove pips. Heat the remaining sugar in a pan with 200 ml (7 fl oz) water until it has completely dissolved. Bring to the boil, then draw off the heat and leave to cool.

Process the passion fruit juice and remaining ingredients to a smooth mush. Gradually add enough sugar syrup to sweeten to taste, bearing in mind that freezing dampens down the sweetness.

Freeze the mixture in an ice-cream machine, according to the manufacturer's instructions. If you don't have an ice-cream maker, pour the mixture into a shallow freezer container, cover and freeze at your freezer's lowest setting. Once the sides begin to harden, break them up and push into the centre. Return to the freezer. Repeat once more and then leave in the freezer until the sorbet is just set but not yet rock solid. Scrape into a processor or mixer and whizz fast to smooth out ice crystals. If you are totally lacking in machinery, you'll just have to flex your arm muscles and beat hard. Return the sorbet to the freezer.

Passion Fruit Syllabub

This is an incredibly rich pudding that can be made very quickly, and tastes divine.

SERVES 4

4 passion fruit

3 tablespoons caster sugar

300 ml (10 fl oz) double cream

Juice of 1 lime

Icing sugar

Extract the passion fruit juice by heating the flesh with the sugar (see page 130). Strain and cool. Reserve some of the seeds.

Put the cream into a bowl, and whisk, gradually adding the passion fruit then the lime juice. When it holds its shape softly, taste and stir in a little icing sugar if it is too tart – syllabubs shouldn't be too sweet. Divide between four glasses, or small bowls, and serve instantly or lightly chilled, scattered with the reserved seeds.

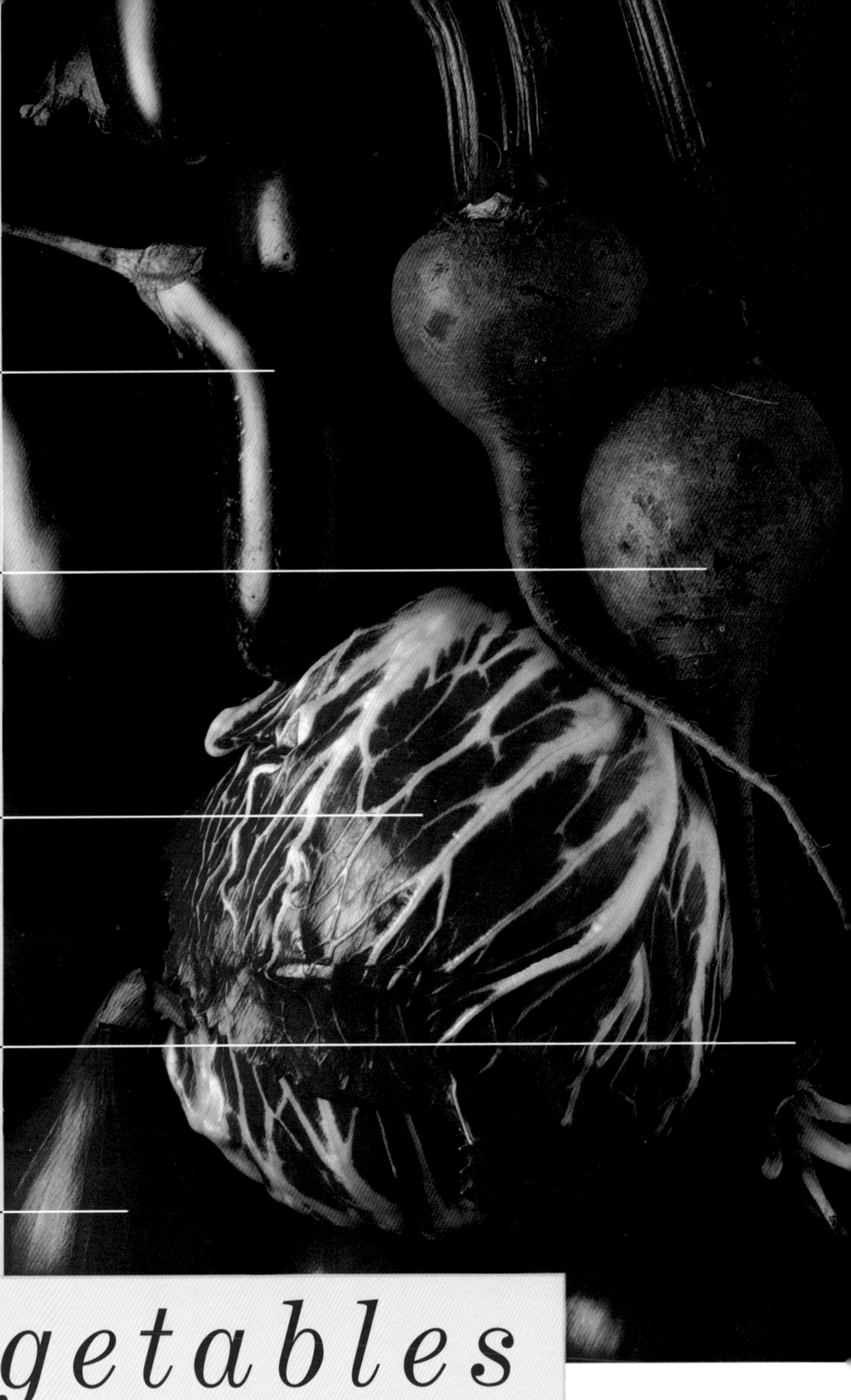

aubergines

beetroot

radicchio

black salsify

red onions

vegetables

sorrel
sweet potato
fennel
shallots
rocket
celeriac

aubergines

Aubergines, peppers, tomatoes and courgettes – the essential quartet of Mediterranean vegetables that have become so beloved of cooks in the nineties. In fact, none of them is a true vegetable (botanically, they are fruits) and none of them is native to the Mediterranean. Interlopers, the whole lot of them. Peppers, tomatoes and courgettes all hail from the Americas but the aubergine travelled a different route to its adopted homelands. The aubergine is probably native to China – it was certainly being grown in gardens there some two and a half thousand years ago. It has a long history in India, too, where it is known as *brinjal.* It arrived in Europe, as did so many other good things, via Persia, ready clothed with the magic of Eastern spices and other exotic travelling companions.

The aubergine needs warmth to swell and mature, so the balmy sunshine of the Mediterranean did it proud. Quite unlike any other vegetable, it has a distinct flavour and texture that allow it to take on the mantle of any number of different cuisines, integrating easily, without ever losing its identity.

Of course, there are aubergines and aubergines. They come in a multitude of sizes, shapes and colours, almost as diverse as the dishes they are used in. The fairly tubby, fairly long, purple-black version that we know is one amongst many. In Sicily, for instance, they have 'Turkish' aubergines (squatter, large, purple, streaked with white) and *nostrano*, their own, which are club-shaped, longer and darker skinned. From Japan come elegant, elongated, striped aubergines. Beautiful pure creamy white aubergines, sometimes streaked with purple, are grown in the Middle East. Perfect egg-shaped aubergines, white and yellow, are common in Jamaica, where they may be known as 'garden eggs' (was this the type that gave rise to the old English name 'egg plant', which still survives in America?). Miniature purple aubergines are used to make pickles and jams in Arabic countries, while in Thailand it is easy to mistake the tiny green round aubergines for peas in a green curry – until you bite into one, and then there's no mistaking its nature.

In short, the aubergine is uniquely adaptable, even promiscuous. It has spawned recipes by the dozen. No, probably by the hundred. Every country that has fallen prey to its charms has developed an amazing repertoire of aubergine dishes. It is a truly cosmopolitan character.

Buying and Storing Aubergines

Any aubergine, and it doesn't matter what size or shape or colour it is, should be firm and plump-looking, with taut, glossy or pearly skin. Anything that is flabby, wrinkled, dull or tired is not worth buying. Make a beeline for aubergines that look a little out of the ordinary, as they may well have a better, smoother and creamier texture than the common, highly commercial, purple-skinned aubergines.

Use aubergines fairly swiftly, though they will keep happily enough for a couple of days in the vegetable drawer of the fridge. When handling, avoid picking them up by the stem end, which is often rather prickly.

Using Aubergines

The aubergine is so remarkably versatile that it's hard to know where to begin. I suppose the best place is with the initial preparation, and the big question ... do they really need salting? Yes and no is about the best answer I can come up with. These days, it is rare to come across an aubergine that is truly bitter, so you don't *have* to salt them before use, if you are short of time. However, I do think that salting aubergines improves the flavour, by drawing out the tinny juices that can otherwise linger, slightly uncomfortably, in the mouth. Salted aubergines will also absorb less oil when fried, which is an undoubted plus.

The salting process is simple. Just slice or dice the aubergine, spread the pieces out on baking trays or in a colander, whichever is more appropriate, and sprinkle lightly with salt. Leave for at least half an hour, longer if possible, and then wipe clean of all the brown juice (or rinse under the tap). If aubergines are to be cooked whole and then mashed or cut up, drain the cooked aubergine flesh thoroughly in a colander, pressing out as much liquid as possible. It will look a bit mangled but in most recipes this won't matter at all.

Slice off the prickly stem end but never peel an aubergine, unless the recipe specifically directs you to do that. The skin looks pretty, adds texture and flavour, and often helps to hold the pieces of aubergine together. Aubergine seeds and flesh oxidize and brown quite quickly. There is not much point worrying about this, because it is unlikely to show in the finished dish.

One of the commonest ways to cook aubergine is to fry it, in slices or cubes. It should be cooked over a moderately hot heat and will sop up a heart-stoppingly large amount of oil, some of which will be thrown back out when the aubergine is almost done. This process completely obliterates the aubergine's healthy pretensions – it has a mere 27 calories per 100 g (3½ oz) when raw – but frying does make it taste very good, as long as it is drained on kitchen paper for a few minutes before eating or using. The alternative is to brush aubergine slices with oil and then bake them in a moderate oven, until brown. Or you could grill them, again brushing them first with oil – lovely not only for something like moussaka, but as a salad dressed with lemon, mint, garlic and a little more oil. A fourth option is to cook them on a heavy, cast-iron griddle, which you should heat up thoroughly over a high heat, before you lay the oiled aubergine on it.

Whole aubergines can be roasted or, better still, grilled, skin and all, until they are charred and tender. Then drain the flesh, chop it for salads or stuffings or process to a purée for dips. It's even quicker to microwave them but, of course, you don't get any of the smokiness from the grill.

Grilled Aubergine and Red Pepper Tart with Goats' Cheese

A very trendy type of quiche, if that is still possible, and very, very good, even if it isn't. Grilling the vegetables imbues this tart with an unusual smoky flavour, while Greek yoghurt is rich enough to give a silky-soft texture to the filling.

SERVES 6–8

340 g (12 oz) shortcrust pastry

For the filling:

3 large garlic cloves

1 large aubergine

2 large red peppers

240 ml (8½ fl oz) Greek yoghurt

2 egg yolks

1 egg

85 g (3 oz) goats' cheese, de-rinded and thinly sliced

1 teaspoon finely chopped fresh rosemary leaves

Salt and pepper

Line a 28 cm (11½ inch) tart tin with the pastry and prick it all over with a fork. Rest in the fridge for at least half an hour. Pre-heat the oven to 190°C/375°F/Gas Mark 5.

Line the pastry case with greaseproof paper or foil, weight the paper or foil down with baking beans and bake blind for 10 minutes. Remove the beans and paper or foil and return the pastry case to the oven for 5–10 minutes, to dry out without browning. Leave the pastry case to cool and turn the oven down to 180°C/350°F/Gas Mark 4.

Pre-heat the grill to hot. Thread the unpeeled cloves of garlic on to a skewer, to prevent them from falling through the bars. Grill the garlic, the whole aubergine and whole red peppers close to the heat, turning occasionally, until all are thoroughly charred. The garlic will be ready first and should feel soft to the touch. Remove from the skewer, leave to cool for a few minutes and then peel. The aubergine, too, will feel soft and squishy when it's ready. Drop into a plastic bag and leave until cool enough to handle. Then strip off the skin, cut the flesh up roughly and leave it to drain in a colander. Drop the peppers into a plastic bag and leave until cool enough to handle. Strip off the skins and cut the flesh into strips.

Press the aubergine gently, to expel excess moisture, and then drop into a food processor, with the peeled garlic and a couple of spoonfuls of the yoghurt. Whizz until smooth and then add the remaining yoghurt, egg yolks and egg and salt and pepper. Process again briefly, to mix. Spread half the mixture on the base of the pastry case. Cover with the strips of red pepper and then smooth over the rest of the aubergine mixture. Arrange the cheese on top and scatter with rosemary. Bake for 25–30 minutes, until just set. Serve warm or cold.

Amalfitana Aubergine and Chocolate Pudding

Yes, honestly! ... and it really is amazingly delicious. I was introduced to the pudding by the owner of the Al San Vincenzo Restaurant in Bayswater, London, and recently came across this recipe for it in a book of Neapolitan desserts. It's best made 24 hours in advance. Try to find good quality candied peel, in whole pieces. It's worth chopping it yourself, as the taste is so much better than the ready-prepared stuff.

SERVES 6–8

3 medium-sized aubergines, sliced lengthways
Salt
Olive oil and sunflower oil, for frying
Plain flour
Cocoa powder, to decorate

For the crème patissière:

300 ml (10 fl oz) full-cream milk
1 vanilla pod, slit lengthways
3 egg yolks
150 g (5 oz) caster sugar
45 g (1½ oz) plain flour
A pinch of salt
85 g (3 oz) finely chopped mixed candied peel

For the chocolate cream:

30 g (1 oz) cocoa powder, sifted
45 g (1½ oz) plain flour, sifted
60 g (2 oz) caster sugar
300 ml (10 fl oz) full-cream milk
A knob of butter

Sprinkle the aubergine slices lightly with salt and set aside for an hour.

Rinse the slices clean and pat dry. Heat 2.5 cm (1 inch) of oil (I use half olive oil and half sunflower oil) in a wide frying-pan. One by one, dust each aubergine slice with flour and fry until golden brown. Drain on kitchen paper.

While the aubergine is being salted, make the *crème patissière* and the chocolate cream. For the *crème patissière*, heat the milk slowly with the vanilla pod, until it starts to boil. Cover, draw off the heat and leave to infuse for 20 minutes. Beat the egg yolks with the sugar, flour and a pinch of salt. Gradually tip in the milk, whisking constantly. Pour back into the pan and stir over a medium heat. Bring up to the boil, stirring constantly, and then let it bubble and heave for 3 minutes. Draw off the heat, stir in the candied peel and leave to cool. Remove the vanilla pod.

For the chocolate cream, mix the cocoa, flour and caster sugar in a pan and gradually whisk in the milk. Bring gently up to the boil, stirring constantly. Simmer for 2–3 minutes, until the taste of raw flour has gone. Draw off the heat and beat in the butter.

Cover the base of a deep dish (around 22 cm – 9 inches – square or slightly smaller) with a layer of aubergine. Cover with a layer of *crème patissière* (warmed slightly, if necessary, to make it runnier) and then spoon over a layer of chocolate cream. Repeat the layers once or twice, depending on the size of your dish, finishing off with a layer of chocolate cream. Chill for at least 4 hours, or longer if possible.

Dust with cocoa just before serving. Cut into squares with a large knife, and ask your guests to guess what the mystery ingredient is.

Baba Ganoush

There's many a form of aubergine purée to be found around the Mediterranean but this Middle Eastern one is, perhaps, the king of them all. Tahina (sesame seed paste) and cumin are the distinguishing factors. Serve it with warm pitta bread, or other good bread, and/or batons of raw vegetables.

SERVES 6

2 medium-sized aubergines, weighing about 450 g (1 lb) in total
1–2 garlic cloves, roughly chopped
4 tablespoons tahina
Juice of 1 lemon
1–1 1/2 teaspoons ground cumin
6 tablespoons olive oil
10 fresh mint leaves (optional)
Salt and cayenne pepper

Grill the aubergines close to the heat, turning them fairly frequently, until the skin is charred all over and they feel squishy and soft. Drop into a plastic bag, knot loosely and leave until cool enough to handle. Quarter lengthways, strip off the skin and leave the pulp to drain in a colander for 15 minutes or so. Press to squeeze out the last juice.

Process the aubergine flesh with the garlic, tahina, lemon juice, cumin and salt. Trickle in 5 tablespoons of oil. Taste and adjust the seasonings, adding more cumin, lemon or salt as the will takes you (the purée shouldn't actually taste sharp but there should be enough lemon juice to prevent it seeming insipid). Shred all but two of the mint leaves and stir the shreds into the mixture. Pile into a bowl. Just before serving, drizzle over the last tablespoon of olive oil, dust lightly with cayenne and decorate with the last two mint leaves. Serve at room temperature.

beetroot

I'm beginning to think that there is a highly organized, efficiently run conspiracy to discredit the beetroot. It operates from a small room tucked away discreetly, perhaps in some dusty corner of a pickling factory, or down a forgotten corridor of some major food distributor's offices, or even in the bowels of the headquarters of one of our major food retailers. Access is strictly controlled and no one but the conspirators themselves knows what goes on behind that anonymous locked door. And who are they? We can only guess at their profile but some, at least, must be getting on a bit or second generation, because the beetroot has had a rough time of it for a considerable number of decades. I'm not sure whether they are monumentally selfish beetroot-lovers, who don't want others to know what a marvellous vegetable beetroot really is, or whether they have a deep-seated loathing that stems from being beaten with a beetroot when they were babies, or some other such psychological trauma.

Whatever their motives, this gang of conspirators has been very successful so far but they are beginning to lose their grip. Where once you could only buy ready-cooked beetroot drowned in malt vinegar, thus killing off all their charms stone-dead, now I notice an increasing flow of raw beetroot making it through to our supermarkets and greengrocers. Hurrah! At last ordinary cooks and their families can discover what beetroot should really taste like.

Buying and Storing Beetroot

Choose firm, raw spheres, still rather dusty or earthy, complete, if possible, with roots and a headdress of stalks and green leaves (which, incidentally, are very nice cooked, or even raw, if they are young, small and tender). The leaves should still be rather perky, indicating that your beetroot haven't been languishing out of the ground for too long. Go for the smallest beetroot you can find. If you are very lucky indeed, you may come across bouquets of tiny golf-ball sized beetroot in chi-chi greengrocers and, occasionally, even in supermarkets. Buy them and celebrate, for they will have a sweet, delicate flavour that can only be bettered by beetroot that have travelled straight from the ground to the pan.

Of course, if you grow your own, you will have no doubt that beetroot are amongst the aristocracy of vegetables. You will probably also know that they don't necessarily have to be that majestic deep purple-red colour but also come in very fetching shades of golden yellow, with a correspondingly fine flavour, and even in white.

Though beetroot do keep tolerably well, they are at their best when they are at their freshest. Store them in a vegetable rack, or the cool of the vegetable drawer if you must but it's better to cook them as quickly as possible.

Using Beetroot

Some people like to grate raw beetroot into salads. I don't and, besides, this is a messy business. Steer clear. You'll get far more pleasure out of your beetroot if you cook them.

When it comes to cooking, the first priority is to prevent the bleeding away of juices, because a) the red dye stains horribly and even golden beetroot leave tell-tale marks and

b) the flavour is diminished. Don't trim off the roots. Cut the stems off (if they are there at all) a good inch above the beetroot themselves. Wash the roots gently but don't scrub them, as this may pierce the skin.

The best way to cook them is to wrap them individually in foil and bake in a slow oven (150°C/300°F/Gas Mark 2) for 1–3 hours, depending on their size. Joint second-best is to wrap in cling film and microwave on full power for about 6–8 minutes for a brace of beetroot. Alternatively, boil them whole, a matter of 20–60 minutes. The beetroot are done when the skin scrapes easily away from the stem end.

Beetroot do like some sharpness but it should not be aggressive. A vinaigrette flavoured with a little horseradish and plenty of parsley or chervil is perfect for a salad. Soured cream, crème fraiche or yoghurt are delicious with beetroot, as are fried slices of apple, or puréed, cooked cooking apples. Malt and spirit vinegars are murderous.

Torshi Lift

The Middle Eastern *torshi lift* is really a turnip pickle but beetroot is an essential element, colouring the dull chunks of turnip a brilliant, beautiful pink, as well as imparting something of a beetrooty sweetness. The final pickle is remarkably delicious. It is so good that you might well just want to serve the pieces of pink turnip and beetroot as pre-dinner nibbles, which is how we worked our way through most of the first jar we made. Not subtle, I'll grant you that, but extremely moreish, and excellent, too, served with decent bread and butter and a traditional hard British cheese.

FILLS 1 LITRE (1¾ PINT) JAR

1 kg (2¼ lb) small turnips
1 large raw beetroot, weighing about 200 g (7 oz)
4 garlic cloves, thinly sliced
A small bunch of celery leaves
4 tablespoons sea salt
350 ml (12–13 fl oz) white wine vinegar

Peel the turnips and cut them in halves or quarters, depending on their size. Peel the beetroot, cut it in half and slice. Pack in sterilized jar(s) (see page 124 for sterilizing method), alternating layers of turnip and beetroot, adding the garlic slices and celery leaves every now and then. Put the salt into a pan with 1 litre (1¾ pints) of water and bring up to the boil, stirring until the salt has dissolved. Add the vinegar and then pour over the vegetables, making sure that they are completely covered. Seal with a non-corrosive lid(s).

Store the jar(s) in a warm but not hot place. On a shelf in a warm kitchen will do. The pickles will be ready to eat in 10–12 days. Once they are suitably softened and pickled, and suffused with pink, transfer to a cool place, where they will keep for another month or so.

Opposite *Torshi Lift*

Beetroot Gratin

This gratin brings out the very best in beetroot, with its mild hint of horseradish, smooth sauce and crisp crumbs. Serve it with ham, gammon or lamb, or maybe just on its own, which is how we ate it because it was too good to wait for anything else.

SERVES 4–6

4 medium-sized beetroot, weighing about 650 g (1 lb 6 oz) in total, cooked, peeled and sliced (see page 140)
4 tablespoons fine, stale breadcrumbs
1 tablespoon freshly grated Parmesan
20 g (3/4 oz) butter

For the sauce:
30 g (1 oz) butter
30 g (1 oz) plain flour
300 ml (10 fl oz) milk
4 tablespoons crème fraiche
1 1/2 tablespoons creamed horseradish
lemon juice
salt and pepper

Pre-heat the oven to 200°C/400°F/Gas Mark 6. To make the sauce, melt the butter in a pan and stir in the flour. Stir over a low heat for a minute. Draw off the heat and gradually stir in the milk. Bring back to the boil, stirring constantly, and then leave to simmer for 5 minutes, until fairly thick. Stir in the crème fraiche and the horseradish, followed by a squeeze or two of lemon juice. Season to taste with salt and pepper.

Arrange one-third of the beetroot in a layer in a 30 cm (12 inch), lightly greased gratin dish. Spoon over about one-quarter of the sauce. Repeat the layers twice more, using up all the sauce on the last one. Mix the breadcrumbs and Parmesan together and scatter them evenly over the top. Dot with butter. Bake for 25–30 minutes, until golden brown. Serve immediately, or at least while still warm.

Beetroot and Apple Mash

This mash turns out the most sensational, unbelievable colour and tastes wonderful too. Serve with browned, sizzling sausages.

SERVES 4

2 medium-sized beetroot, weighing about 325 g (12 oz) in total
600 g (1 1/4 lb) floury potatoes
1 large cooking apple, peeled, cored and diced
60 g (2 oz) butter
Milk
2 tablespoons chopped fresh parsley

Cook the beetroot (see page 140). When cool enough to handle, peel and grate them.

Peel the potatoes and cut them into large chunks. Put them into a pan with salt and enough water to cover by about 2 cm (3/4 inch). Bring up to the boil and leave to simmer, uncovered, for 5 minutes. Add the apple and continue cooking until both apple and potato are very tender.

Drain off the water carefully. Mash the potatoes and apple with the butter. Over a low heat, beat in enough milk to give a soft, light mash. Stir in the beetroot and the parsley and then season well and give it all a final stir. Serve immediately.

Hildegard's Potato and Beetroot Salad

This salad disappeared in the twinkling of an eye in our kitchen. In fact, it produced a scene of unabashed and embarrassing gluttony, forks flailing, all of us jostling to regain our positions near the bowl. The recipe comes from the mother of my friend Michele. Hildegard serves it at Christmas alongside the cold turkey and ham, but don't wait until then to try it out.

SERVES 4–6

675 g (1 lb 8 oz) waxy potatoes
1 medium–large beetroot
250 g (9 oz) *matjes* or dill-pickled herrings
1/2 onion, finely chopped
4 *cornichons* (baby gherkins), finely chopped, or 2 tablespoons capers, roughly chopped
2 hard-boiled eggs, shelled and chopped (optional)
2–3 generous tablespoons mayonnaise
Salt and pepper

Cook the potatoes and beetroot (see page 140) separately. When cool enough to handle, peel both of them.

Cut the potatoes and beetroot into 1.5–2 cm (5/8–3/4 inch) cubes. Cut the herrings into strips about 2 cm (3/4 inch) long by 5 mm (1/4 inch) wide. Put them all into a bowl, with the onion, *cornichons* or capers and eggs, if using. Add enough mayonnaise to coat everything lightly and season with salt and pepper.

celeriac

There's a tendency to lump celeriac in with celery, almost as an afterthought. Botanically, this is fair enough, since both are forms of the same plant, *Apium graveolens*, but, when it comes to culinary application, it makes no sense whatsoever. The hefty, gnarled spheres of celeriac may hint at the flavour of slender-stemmed celery but there ends the similarity. Cultivated celery was a relative latecomer to our shores, arriving in the late seventeenth century, but celeriac was even tardier, taking another 40 or so years to make its way across the Channel. With its head start, celery stole the scene, and poor old celeriac has lagged behind in the popularity stakes ever since. This is most unfair; though I like celery well enough, celeriac is really a far more interesting vegetable.

Celeriac is not a root vegetable, as you might well imagine, but a corm, or in other words the base of the stem section (rather like kohlrabi, for instance). Its grizzled exterior bears the scars of old leaf shoots on the upper portion, while the other end is no more than a mess of tapering roots. It is not elegant, this ungainly sibling of willowy celery but, as we all know, appearance is not everything and what's hidden inside this exterior is definitely high calibre.

Buying and Storing Celeriac

Buying celeriac is simply a matter of choosing firm spheres with no obvious bruising. If some of the green stalks have been left *in situ*, check that they are in good condition – wilting stalks mean that the celeriac has been out of the ground for too long. Larger celeriac have the advantage of a marginally reduced ratio of waste to usable matter but, if they've been left too long in the ground, the centres may begin to turn spongy. Medium-sized celeriac are often a safer bet but, if your only choice is large or large, pick out the spheres that are heaviest, that is, with least air hidden inside. Store celeriac in a plastic bag in the vegetable drawer of the fridge, where it will keep for a week or more.

Using Celeriac

To prepare, I usually slice the unpeeled celeriac and then trim off the skin with all its ins and outs and convolutions. At first I work in a pernickety, precise fashion, soon becoming more slapdash, slicing off larger chunks as my patience dwindles.

The pure white of the interior discolours quite quickly when exposed to air. In some recipes this may not matter but, where it does, drop the prepared celeriac into a bowl of water acidulated with the juice of half a lemon or a tablespoon or two of cider vinegar or white wine vinegar as you work. Add a shot of lemon juice or vinegar to the cooking water, too.

Some people like salads made with raw, grated celeriac but I find that the flavour is immeasurably improved by a quick dunk in boiling water, to cook it lightly. For the classic French salad, *céleri-rave rémoulade*, it is best cut into narrow matchsticks (use a food processor if you can, since this is as tedious as peeling the celeriac in the first place, though worth it in the long run) then blanched for a couple of minutes. Drain the celeriac well and let it cool, then dress it with mustardy mayonnaise and a shake or two of chopped fresh parsley and enjoy it as part of an hors d'oeuvre.

Celeriac Purée

Probably my all-time favourite celeriac dish is a straight celeriac purée, one of autumn and winter's highlights. Serve it in place of potato mash – it is lovely with game and a blissful partner for rich, meaty winter stews. It isn't at all bad with fish, either. Celeriac purée is so easy to make that it needs no real recipe – the method alone will suffice.

Mash roughly equal quantities of cooked celeriac and potato together, over a moderate heat, with a generous knob of butter (or two) and hot milk or, for a really luxurious version, milk and cream, beating vigorously until fluffy and light. Season with salt, pepper and lots of freshly grated nutmeg.

Roast Celeriac

These caramel-brown wedges of celeriac, baked slowly in the oven, are quite irresistible. They would make a marvellous accompaniment to a dish of roast game, though I found myself eating them all on their own, just because they were there and too good to ignore. They can be cooked in advance and re-heated, when needed, in the oven. There is no need to fiddle around with acidulated water as you're peeling as the wedges of celeriac will brown as they cook.

SERVES 4

1 medium-large celeriac
Sunflower oil
A knob of butter
75 ml (5 tablespoons) Madeira or Marsala
Salt and pepper

Pre-heat the oven to 180°C/350°F/Gas Mark 4. Cut the celeriac into eight wedges and then trim off the skin as neatly and economically as you can. Toss the wedges in just enough oil to coat. Smear butter thickly around an ovenproof dish, just large enough to take the celeriac wedges lying down flat (well, flattish, anyway). Lay the celeriac in the dish, season with salt and pepper and pour over the Marsala or Madeira. Roast for about an hour, turning the wedges and basting every now and then, until they are richly browned all over and very tender. You may find that you have to add a tablespoon or two of water towards the end, to prevent the celeriac from burning.

Celeriac Gratin

Celeriac makes a first-rate gratin, rather in the mould of a *gratin dauphinois*. A scattering of Parmesan accentuates its particular flavour, as does a small measure of mustard. This goes very well with fish, being neither too strong nor yet too insipid, but it is excellent, too, with roast chicken – a great combination, in fact, for a family Sunday lunch.

SERVES 6–8

2 medium-sized celeriac, peeled and thinly sliced
Lemon juice or white wine vinegar
300 ml (10 fl oz) single cream
1 tablespoon plain flour
1 tablespoon Dijon mustard
45 g (1 1/2 oz) butter
2 tablespoons freshly grated Parmesan
Salt and pepper

Pre-heat the oven to 180°C/350°F/Gas Mark 4. Drop the slices of celeriac into water acidulated with lemon juice or vinegar as you work and then drain and blanch them in acidulated boiling water for 2 minutes. Drain and run under the cold tap. Drain thoroughly.

Butter a 25–30 cm (10–12 inch) gratin dish. Mix a spoonful of the cream into the flour, to give a smooth paste, and then gradually work in the rest. Stir in the mustard and season with salt and pepper. Spread about one-third of the celeriac in the dish, dot with a little butter and pour over one-third of the cream mixture. Repeat twice more, until the celeriac, butter and cream are all used up. Sprinkle the Parmesan over the top. Bake for about an hour, until the celeriac is completely tender and the top browned. Serve hot.

sweet potatoes

The first potatoes to be planted in Britain were probably sweet potatoes. In other words, not real potatoes at all but *Ipomoea batatas*, a relation of that garden pest, the wild convolvulus (bindweed) and of the morning glory. The crop failed miserably; the climate here is not conducive to a tuber that hails from tropical America. Potatoes, real potatoes, from the chillier heights of the Andes, eventually fared far better once we got used to the idea of them, but that is another story.

To this day, our sweet potatoes have to be imported and they wing their way here not only from their native Americas but from all around the hotter parts of the world. The most remarkable display of sweet potatoes I've ever seen was on a distinctly chilly morning in the East End of London. We arrived just as the sun was rising. There was something distinctly surreal about the soulless modernity of New Spitalfields market, half-hidden in the mists rising from Hackney Marshes. Inside the hangars, there was constant bustle and clangs, shouts and calls as fruit and vegetables arrived, changed hands and were whisked away. Dave Dayes and his brother specialize in importing Caribbean foods. They are one firm of many but what distinguishes them is their expertise and knowledge. There, amongst the other exotics, were some half-dozen different varieties of sweet potato, some long and thin, others chunky and hefty, some verging on spherical. The sweet potatoes from Uganda (not highly rated) had an almost fluorescent purple skin; others, from Egypt, were more uniform in shape. From Jamaica came crates of sweet potatoes nestling in coconut fibres.

What you can't tell from the outer appearance, though, is the colour of the flesh inside. There are two quite distinct types of sweet potato – orange-fleshed, which seems to be the easier to find at the moment, and white-fleshed. Orange-fleshed sweet potatoes have a smoother, denser, waxier texture and a chestnut-like flavour. White-fleshed sweet potatoes are mealier, more like a mature King Edward in texture, still sweet but not quite as sugary as the orange ones.

Buying and Storing Sweet Potatoes

My sweet potato mentor, Dave Dayes, gave me a quick rundown on what to look for. Shape doesn't affect flavour or quality but it does matter. Long, thin sweet potatoes are not suitable for baking, as they dry out too quickly. They are also rather more fiddly to peel, with a greater ratio of skin to flesh so, if your recipe calls for peeled sweet potatoes, you'll get better value from fatter ones.

The potato should be firm and, though the odd minor blemish may not matter too much, watch out for soft spots and extensive bruising. Until the time comes when retailers are sensible enough to inform us on the price label of the colour of the flesh inside, the only way to tell is either to snap off the tip at one end, or discreetly scratch away a little of the skin.

Sweet potatoes should be stored in a cool, dry place, where they will keep well for several weeks. They don't need to be stored in the dark as do ordinary potatoes.

Using Sweet Potatoes

Despite their lack of true kinship, sweet potatoes can be treated in much the same way as ordinary potatoes: they can be baked, fried, mashed, chipped and sautéd. I'm not so keen on boiling them (some of the sweetness leaches out), unless they remain whole and in their skins. In most recipes, white- and orange-fleshed sweet potatoes can be used interchangeably but not all. Beware. The orange-fleshed type holds its shape rather better than the white-fleshed one, which has a tendency to collapse like a floury ordinary potato. Where it matters, therefore, I've specified the type.

I love roast sweet potatoes. Split open, steaming hot and slathered with butter or Greek yoghurt, they liven up a simple supper of grilled sausages, chicken or chops, or perhaps best of all, gammon or warm ham, with which they have a particular affinity (a million times better than a tired bit of pineapple and a Maraschino cherry, though the principle is much the same).

In countries where sweet potatoes are common fare, they are used with the same abandon with which we use real potatoes, added to soups and stews and even served up as puddings. In Mexico, candied sweet potato is sold from street stalls but in the Southern states of America, where they are often known, rather confusingly, as yams (which they definitely are not), candied sweet potatoes are more like our glazed vegetables, sweetened with sugar and spices but still served as an accompaniment to the main course, particularly at Thanksgiving.

Sautéed Sweet Potatoes with Lamb and Mint

A lip-smacking, finger-licking good dish. With the bright colour of orange-fleshed sweet potatoes, it looks as pretty as it tastes.

SERVES 4

Olive oil
1 large red onion, cut into 8 wedges
1 large orange-fleshed sweet potato, peeled and cut into 1.5 cm (1/2-inch) cubes
1 fresh red chilli, de-seeded and shredded
Juice of 1/2 lime
Salt and pepper
A handful of fresh coriander leaves, to garnish
Lime wedges, to serve

For the meatballs:
450 g (1 lb) minced lamb
1 onion, grated
2 garlic cloves, crushed
2 tablespoons chopped fresh mint
Finely grated zest of 1 lime
1 teaspoon crushed coriander seeds
Salt and pepper
A dash of lime juice

Make the meatballs by mixing all the ingredients together, kneading thoroughly with your hands. Dampen your hands with cold water. Now break off walnut-sized pieces and roll into

Opposite *Sautéed Sweet Potatoes with Lamb and Mint*

balls. Heat a little olive oil in a wide, heavy frying-pan and brown the meatballs all over. Lift out and drain on kitchen paper.

Now pour out all the fat and raise the heat under the frying-pan. Let it heat through for a couple of minutes, then add the onion wedges. Cook over a high heat, turning them once or twice, until they are browned on the cut sides. Take out and put with the meatballs. Add a little more oil to the pan and sauté the sweet potato cubes for a few minutes, until they begin to brown. Now return the meatballs and the onions to the pan, along with the chilli, lime juice, 300 ml (10 fl oz) of water, salt and pepper. Stir carefully and simmer, half-covered, for 10–15 minutes, until most of the water has evaporated. Taste and adjust the seasonings, scatter over the coriander and serve with the wedges of lime.

Dave Dayes' Sweet Potato Pudding

A Jamaican pudding that sweet-potato importer Dave Dayes makes to remind him of home, this turns out rather like an exotic version of our bread pudding. It only works with white-fleshed sweet potatoes, as I know all too well, having tried it three times with orange-fleshed ones!

It can be eaten hot from the oven but is nicer chilled overnight in the fridge and eaten cold the next day.

SERVES 6

2 fairly large white-fleshed sweet potatoes, weighing about 800 g (1 3/4 lb) in total
170 g (6 oz) light muscovado sugar
1/4 teaspoon freshly grated nutmeg
60 g (2 oz) raisins
1 teaspoon vanilla essence
600 ml (1 pint) coconut milk (see page 204)
Butter for greasing

Pre-heat the oven to 180°C/350°F/Gas Mark 4. Generously butter a shallow, 24 x 19 cm (9 1/2 x 8 inch) ovenproof dish. If you don't have such a dish, follow Dave's example and use a round Pyrex dish but a gratin dish or a china quiche dish will do just as well. Peel the sweet potatoes and chop roughly into chunks (you should end up with about 675 g/1 lb 7 oz). Put into a processor with the sugar, nutmeg, raisins, vanilla essence and the coconut milk. Process to a purée. Add more coconut milk, if necessary, to give a mixture that will only just pour from the processor bowl with a light, helpful nudge of the spatula. Pour and nudge and splodge the purée into the greased dish and then smooth down. The pudding mixture should be no more than 2.5–3 cm (1–1 1/2 inches) deep. Bake for 1 1/2 hours, or until set firm.

Sweet Potato and Broccoli Soup

Broccoli and sweet potato are an unexpected but well-matched pair. Though the colour given by orange-fleshed potatoes is jazzier, white ones will work extremely well.

SERVES 6

1 medium-sized onion, chopped
45 g (1 1/2 oz) butter
350 g (12 1/2 oz) broccoli, trimmed and sliced
3 whole garlic cloves, peeled
675 g (1 lb 8 oz) orange- or white-fleshed sweet potatoes, peeled and cubed
2 fresh marjoram sprigs or 1/2 teaspoon dried marjoram
Salt and pepper

For the pastry croutons (optional):

Small amount of left-over puff or shortcrust pastry
1 egg, beaten
Poppy, caraway or sesame seeds or finely grated Gruyère cheese or coarse salt

To serve:

Buttermilk or soured cream
Chopped fresh chives or parsley

Sweat the onion in the butter, covered, over a low heat, for 5 minutes. Add the broccoli, garlic, sweet potatoes and marjoram, stir and then leave to sweat for another 10 minutes. Add 1.2 litres (2 pints) of water, salt and pepper and bring to the boil. Simmer gently for 20–30 minutes, until all the vegetables are tender.

Liquidize and sieve the soup, or pass it through the fine blade of a vegetable mill. Add extra water, if it is on the thick side, taste and adjust the seasonings.

If making the croutons, pre-heat the oven to 230°C/450°F/Gas Mark 8. Roll the pastry out thinly. Cut into small diamonds or other shapes, arrange on a baking tray and leave to rest for 15 minutes in the fridge. Brush with beaten egg. Scatter the seeds, Gruyère or coarse salt lightly over the top. Bake for 5–10 minutes, until golden brown.

When you are nearly ready to eat, re-heat the soup and quickly crisp up the croutons in the oven. Ladle the soup into bowls and add a spoonful of buttermilk or soured cream and a scattering of chopped chives or parsley. Serve the pastry croutons in a separate bowl, so your guests can help themselves.

Sweet Potato Fritters

Lime, sweet potato and chilli are a magic combination, so I make no excuses for repeating it, though in a very different guise from the recipe for *Sautéed Sweet Potatoes with Lamb and Mint* (see page 148). Here, sweet and rich sweet potato fritters beg those other vibrant flavours to save them from being overwhelming. Together, they make a great first course.

SERVES 6–8

3 sweet potatoes, preferably orange-fleshed
85 g (3 oz) plain flour
1 teaspoon ground coriander
2 eggs, lightly beaten
Sunflower oil, for deep-frying
4 spring onions, finely chopped
1–2 fresh red chillies, de-seeded and finely shredded or chopped
Salt and pepper
1 lime, cut into wedges, to serve

Boil the sweet potatoes in salted water until barely tender. Drain and leave until cool enough to handle. Do not peel. Slice into discs about 5 mm (1/4 inch) thick. Season the flour generously with salt, pepper and the ground coriander, then spread out on a plate. Pour the eggs into a shallow bowl or plate.

Heat the oil to 180°C/350°F. One by one, using a fork, dip the sweet potato slices into the flour and then into the beaten egg, and then back into the flour to coat them evenly. At each stage, make sure they are completely coated – excess is better than parsimony here. Fry in small batches until golden brown – about 5 minutes, turning occasionally. Drain briefly on kitchen paper. Serve hot, scattered with spring onions and chillies and with a wedge of lime to squeeze over.

fennel

Florence fennel is the vegetable form of the fennel plant, which also gives us the feathery fennel herb and fennel seeds. In the plant that forms the vegetable, it is the swollen bases of the stems that interleave, to make a bulb-like sheaf of icy green-white. It was probably developed in Italy, which explains the name that is used to distinguish the vegetable from the herb. It remains enormously popular there and in the south of France.

It was introduced to England in the eighteenth century, where it settled in happily in Hitchin in Hertfordshire. Why that should seem so curious to me, I don't know, but it is a fact that always makes me smile. It has been grown here and there in this country ever since, though it is only in this century that it has become more widely known. It entered America via the vegetable gardens of Thomas Jefferson at Montecello, sent to him by the American consul at Livorno.

Unique amongst vegetables, it has a distinct aniseed taste that is most pronounced when raw and mellows down discreetly when cooked. Many people who find raw fennel too overpowering, love it cooked.

Buying and Storing Fennel

Fennel bulbs are usually sold with an inch or two (or a few centimetres if you think metrically) of the stems left *in situ*, together with the odd feathery tuft of leaves. If the fennel is fresh, these leaves will be perky, with a bright, youthful, green colour. The fennel bulb itself will be ivory coloured, with a hint of green. Choose bulbs that are firm and fresh looking, with as little damage as possible to the outer layer.

In very upmarket greengroceries, you may be able to find the slender baby fennel bulbs that have become so fashionable on the plates of stylish restaurants. They are expensive, but interesting to try once in a very occasional while. Most of the time, the ordinary, fully swollen fennel bulb is actually far more useful.

Store fennel in the salad drawer of the fridge, where it will keep for several days or even longer. Even though it takes some little while to deteriorate drastically, it is still a good idea to use it up swiftly, so that you eat it at its peak.

Using Fennel

Basic preparation requires you to slice off the stalks (they are tough and stringy) taking the fronds with them. Save the fronds to use as a herb, or to garnish your finished dish. Trim a fine slice from the base and discard and remove the outer layer, if it is browned or damaged. The way you treat the fennel from then on will be dictated by the recipe.

For salads, I usually quarter the bulbs from stem to stalk end and then slice them paper-thin. On its own, dress fennel with lemon juice, olive oil and salt and pepper and serve in small portions. It is also excellent added to mixed green salads, again sliced paper-thin, adding not only a hint of aniseed but also its crisp, juicy texture.

Cooking changes the flavour radically, muting the insistent aniseed without losing sight of it altogether but tempering it with sweetness and a soft, tender flesh. Fennel is marvellous in fish dishes – roast fish on a bed of blanched fennel, for instance, anointed with plenty of olive oil, some olives and lemon juice – and almost as good with pale meats, such as chicken or veal. Fennel soup is very good, too. Fennel can be braised, blanched, steamed, or even grilled. For grilling, cut each bulb into six or eight wedges, slicing from stem to stalk end so that the slices hold together. Secure each wedge with a wooden cocktail stick, brush with olive oil and grill, moderately close to the heat, turning until touched with black and softened.

Baked Fennel with Parmesan

To my mind, there is no better way to cook fennel than this. It is simple; it is Italian; it is a classic; it is unbeatable. The recipe appears in my book on vegetables, *Eat Your Greens*, but I feel that it would have been a serious sin of omission to leave it out of this section. Serve this sizzling dish of fennel on its own, as a first course, with good bread, or as a side dish with game, poultry or fish.

SERVES 4–6

3 large or 4 medium-sized fennel bulbs
45 g (1 ½ oz) butter
60 g (2 oz) Parmesan, freshly grated
Salt and pepper

Pre-heat the oven to 200°C/400°F/Gas Mark 6. Trim the tough stalks off each fennel bulb, slice off a thin disc from each base and remove the outer layer, if it is damaged. Quarter the bulbs from top to base. Steam or simmer the fennel in salted water until just tender. Drain thoroughly (all those curved and interleaved layers can trap a fair amount of water).

Butter a shallow, ovenproof dish that is large enough to take the fennel in a single, densely packed layer. Pack in the fennel and season with pepper. Dot with butter and scatter evenly with Parmesan. Bake, in the oven for 20–30 minutes, until the cheese is browned and the butter is sizzling. Serve hot or warm.

Roast Red Mullet with Fennel and Olives

Red mullet and fennel are often cooked together in the south of France, although it is usually the wild herb fennel from the hills, rather than Florence fennel. The soft anise flavour of the vegetable is milder but works just as well.

SERVES 4

2 large or 3 medium-sized fennel bulbs
4 medium-sized red mullet, scaled and cleaned
2 lemons
4 tablespoons olive oil
12–16 black olives
Salt and pepper

Pre-heat the oven to 180°C/350°F/Gas Mark 4. Trim the stalks from each fennel bulb, saving all the feathery green fronds. Trim each base and discard the outer layer, if damaged. Halve and slice thinly and then blanch the slices in salted, boiling water for 2 minutes. Drain well.

Season the red mullet inside and out with salt and pepper. Tuck the feathery fennel leaves inside the mullet. Make a bed of fennel slices in an oiled, shallow ovenproof dish that is large enough to take the four mullet. Season the fennel. Lay the mullet on top, snuggling them down into the fennel. Squeeze the juice of one of the lemons over them and then drizzle over the olive oil, making sure that the fennel gets bathed in oil as well. Roast for about 20 minutes, until the mullet are almost cooked, basting them with the juices every now and then.

Add the olives to the dish, dotting them around amongst the fennel, and return the dish to the oven for a final 5 minutes or so, to finish cooking. Serve hot from the oven, with the remaining lemon cut into wedges.

Candied Fennel with Nuts and Clotted Cream

Fennel for pudding? Yes, and it is sensational. It is, I believe, one of the happening ideas in chic restaurants in Paris and Provence, if that helps to allay your fears. In fact, if you think about it, aniseed and liquorice flavours have long been used in sweet concoctions, so there's really nothing untoward about cooking fennel with sugar.

The thin crescents of fennel are cooked in a spiced syrup until translucent and then their powerful presence is softened with toasted nuts, a bed of brioche and a topping of mollifying cream.

SERVES 4

500 g (1 lb 2 oz) fennel
450 g (1 lb) caster or granulated sugar
1 cinnamon stick
1 vanilla pod
2 cloves
30 g (1 oz) walnuts, lightly toasted
30 g (1 oz) hazelnuts, lightly toasted
30 g (1 oz) pine kernels, lightly toasted
4 slices of brioche
Butter for frying
Clotted or whipped cream, to serve

Trim the fennel and remove the outer layer. Quarter it from stem end to stalk end and then slice across into crescents more or less 3 mm (1/8 inch) thick. Put the sugar into a pan, with 450 ml (15 fl oz) water and the spices. Stir over a moderate heat, until the sugar has dissolved. Bring to the boil, add the fennel and then simmer lazily until the fennel is translucent, 25–30 minutes.

Lift the fennel out of its syrup with a slotted spoon and mix it with the nuts. Boil the syrup down until reduced by about half. Mix a little into the fennel and nut mixture, to moisten it.

Fry the slices of brioche lightly in butter, until golden and crisp. Place each one on a plate. Top with fennel and nuts (warm or cold) and finish with a scoop of cream.

radicchio

Radicchio arrived in purple-red pomp with the bevy of designer salads that found their way to our tables in the eighties. Some of those arty lettuces have settled into everyday familiarity, some have disappeared. Radicchio remains and retains more standing than any mere lettuce. Why? Two reasons that I can come up with. The first is that distinctive bitter flavour and firmness of leaf, which bring substance to any mixed salad they join (the flash of colour is attractive, too, but I don't think it is so important). The second is that radicchio can be cooked without collapsing to nothing. These days, it is hot radicchio that graces smart tables.

Trimmed of ragged outer leaves, whole heads of radicchio are being cut into wedges, quarters or eighths depending on size and then blanched, or fried, or brushed with oil and grilled, or even pickled. The results are surprisingly delicious. Heat changes the nature of radicchio's bitterness and brings out an innate sweetness. The perky colour changes to a murky brown (I told you it wasn't important) but you can't have everything. Cooked radicchio is served in small portions – one or two wedges per person are usually sufficient – and goes well with all kinds of foods, from fish to chicken to steak or even feathered game.

Store radicchio in the fridge salad drawer, without the plastic wrap. It keeps better than many lettuces: up to four days in tip-top condition. Store fresh separated leaves in a plastic bag in the fridge for three days or so.

salsify and scorzonera

At first glance, salsify and its unidentical twin scorzonera do not look too promising. Foot-long, thin tap-roots, covered in earth, you might well be forgiven for passing them by with no more than a cursory glance. The old name for salsify, oyster vegetable, may give you a clue that there is something well worth investigating under the grime.

Both are members of the daisy family, as are lettuce, chicory and dandelions. Salsify is distinguished by a pale, tan skin, while scorzonera is covered in a black skin, and so is sometimes known as 'black salsify'. It is usually sold as plain salsify, and is more widely available than true salsify . There is, I am told, a difference in flavour, but it is not marked. Inside the skin, the flesh of both is pale white, turning a touch translucent as it cooks. The taste is quite delicate and sweet, with hints of artichoke and asparagus. Some people insist that there is a touch of oyster in there, too, but I reckon the oyster connection is more to do with the look of the root when cooked. Store in a paper, not plastic, bag in the vegetable drawer of the fridge.

It is a great shame that these two are not better known, for they are the aristocrats of winter vegetables, with more finesse than parsnips, carrots or cabbage could ever acquire. To prepare, they should be scrubbed clean and rinsed well. There's no need to peel them while raw – if you do you lose an awful lot of the flesh – just cut them up into sensible lengths and drop into salted, boiling water, acidulated with lemon juice. The cut surfaces will bleed a white sticky juice; ignore this, as it disappears on cooking. 20–30 minutes should be quite enough time to render the pieces tender. Drain thoroughly, run under the cold tap and then pull off the thick skins, which will now come away easily.

The pieces can then be re-heated at your convenience, in sizzling butter, letting them brown here or there if you wish (I do, usually). Serve with pale meats such as chicken, or with fish. They also make a very good salad – dress the hot, peeled, cooked roots with a vinaigrette, leave to cool and then sprinkle with chopped fresh parsley. My mother used to make a stunning chicken and salsify pie, the filling moistened with a cream sauce. It was a pie fit for kings.

red onions

Onions come and onions go and nobody pays them very much attention but it is hard to ignore a red onion. With that dark purple skin (odd, in a way, that they are called red), they are the showiest of onions, onions with glamour, with a stand-up-and-take-notice-of-me look, and, as it happens, onions with a distinct flavour to match. OK, so the flavour isn't quite so dramatically different as the colour but red onions do tend to be sweeter, easier on the mouth when raw and somehow more substantial when cooked. Store in a rack, in an airy, dry place.

When I come to think of it, that substantial quality may actually be caused by their high-profile visibility in any dish – you can tell the onion is red at a glance, but who remarks on the presence of the ubiquitous white-fleshed onion? It may also be brought about by the way that they are used. I know that I tend to cut them into rings, or wedges for cooked dishes, to make the most of their fine colour, signalling their presence in no uncertain way. Quartered, turned in olive oil and sprinkled with salt, they are lovely roasted in a hot oven. Cut into eighths, they can be fried in chunky wedges in a very hot pan, either to serve on their own, the pan de-glazed with a little sherry vinegar, or to make the beginnings of a stew, where they will hold their own as a vegetable as well as providing the essential background onion savouriness. Cut into thick slices, secured with cocktail sticks, brushed with oil, they can be grilled, too, until well browned and tinged here and there with black. Serve on their own, tossed in vinaigrette for an onion salad, or mixed with other grilled vegetables, or mixed with chunks of ripe tomato and rocket leaves for a flashy, bright, lively summer salad.

The relative mildness of red onions makes them the perfect onion for salads and salsas, decorative as well as functional. They will still need to be chopped fairly finely, or sliced very thinly, but they mix in with ease and without too much aggression. Other components survive the onslaught unscathed.

Some of the sweetest, most superb red onions I've ever tasted came from a town in the south of Italy, where they celebrate every summer with a red-onion festival. As with so many fruits and vegetables, sunshine makes all the difference. Check the boxes for the southernmost producers.

shallots

Shallots are the babies of the onion family. Like full-sized onions, they come clad in a papery skin that is usually brown, sometimes greyish, sometimes tinged with pink. Like larger onions, they are made up of layer upon layer of juicy flesh, with a sharp oniony whiff. Unlike larger onions, they are mild in nature, with little of the aggression of the big bruisers. They won't induce tears with quite such alacrity. Chefs love shallots because they bring all the benefits of onion to a dish, that essential background depth and fullness, without any coarseness. They are also very handy when you just want a small amount of onion and don't want to waste half or more of a full-sized one.

Babies they may be, but shallots come in a confusing array of sizes and shapes. Commonest are the small, golf ball-sized shallots. They are roundish, with a flat or concave side where the clusters of shallots have grown together from one root. In recipes that stipulate an exact number of shallots, they probably mean shallots of this type. Banana shallots are long and more torpedo-shaped than banana-shaped. Once chopped, a single banana shallot comes in at about twice the size of smaller, round shallots, so you won't need as many. *Echalotes grises*, grey-skinned shallots, are highly favoured in France and lie somewhere between the round and the banana shallot in size.

After shallots are harvested they are 'cured' or, in other words, semi-dried, as are onions and they keep very well in a cool, dark, airy spot away from humidity. Look out for pretty bunched or plaited shallots, particularly in French markets around July and August, when the new season's shallots have come in.

sorrel

Though sorrel has a long history in Britain, I always associate it with France, where every garden seems to have a few plants tucked away within easy reach of the kitchen door. Indeed, the commonest form of sorrel is more correctly known as French sorrel. That's the one with big, green leaves, which flourishes with very little attention. It's part and parcel of ordinary French country cooking but just as at home on the menus of the grandest three-star restaurants.

In the part of France I visit every year, they've served creamy sorrel sauce with fish for as long as I can remember (over 30 years) and no doubt long before that. Then, suddenly, in the eighties, the brilliant pairing of salmon with sorrel sauce shot to fame. Chef Troisgros, one of France's biggest names on the cookery scene, refined the dish, giving it new life, and claimed it as his own. Sorrel knows no social barriers.

What makes sorrel so beloved of cooks is its tart, lemony, green flavour and the way it collapses down to a purée when heated. Technically speaking, I suppose sorrel is a herb, in that it is used as a flavouring, but it is too substantial an item to fit the herbal profile. I always think of it as more akin to salad leaves, or to spinach. Indeed, it is occasionally suggested that you can replace sorrel with spinach and liberal splashes of lemon juice but don't believe it. Spinach just doesn't work in the same way.

French sorrel is the commonest and most useful form of sorrel, but keep a look-out for the pretty, small-leaved buckler sorrel, slightly milder in acidity and ideal for salads. Last year, we also grew two fancy sorrels, one with long, dramatic dark brown tongues of leaves and the other with pale green leaves, webbed with fine red veins. These were lovely to look at but hopelessly tough and fibrous in cooking.

Buying and Storing Sorrel

You can now buy sorrel in plastic packs from the herb section of some supermarkets. This is encouraging, but not good enough, unless you only want it for a salad. In cooking, sorrel needs to be used by the handful, and usually several of them, and it works out costly if you have to buy it.

The answer, of course, is to grow your own if you don't already. Sorrel plants are available from most good garden centres and you don't need green fingers to grow them. You don't even need a garden – a moderately capacious pot on the balcony, or even the windowsill, will do fine. Sorrel flourishes with minimal attention, popping up year in year out, a herald of spring; it grows more abundantly as you pick it and as the summer wears on.

Picked from your own plant, or bought, sorrel should be used up swiftly while it is still perky and fresh. If you have to store the leaves for a few days, pop them into a plastic bag and stash in the vegetable drawer of the fridge.

Using Sorrel

Shredded leaves of French sorrel, or little shield-shaped buckler sorrel leaves, bring a lively note of sharpness to green salads but it is important not to be carried away by them. Too much is not a good thing.

Sorrel really comes into its own when cooked, though it needs only brief heating to bring out its strengths. If you grow your own, make the first sorrel dish of the year soup. It is smooth and invigorating and guaranteed to slough off the lethargy of winter foods. With the plant replenishing its leaves at breakneck speed, you can then move on to other ways of using it.

Sorrel and fish were made for each other, a natural partnership if ever there was one. Eggs are another perfect match – poached eggs with sorrel sauce, baked eggs, or an omelette (either fill the finished omelette with a little sorrel purée and a dollop of crème fraiche or fold raw, shredded sorrel in with the eggs). White meats, such as chicken or veal, also benefit from the zest of fresh green sorrel.

The usual way to prepare sorrel for cooking is to wash the leaves, dry them roughly and then make a *chiffonade*. In other words, shred them very finely. Snip off thicker stalks, pile up five or six leaves at a time and roll them tightly into a cigar shape, then slice thinly to make fine ribbons of sorrel.

Basic Sorrel Purée

This purée is the basis for the simplest sorrel sauce – just add about 150 ml (5 fl oz) of double cream, off the heat, and bring back to the boil, adding a few tablespoons of cooking juices from fish or chicken, if you have them. The purée can also be frozen, a good way to save sorrel for the winter. The proportion of sorrel to butter can be varied.

60 g (2 oz) sorrel

30 g (1 oz) butter

Make a *chiffonade* (fine shreds) of the sorrel (see above).

Melt the butter in a small saucepan and add the sorrel. Stir over a medium heat for around 3–5 minutes, until the shreds have collapsed to a dark khaki sludge.

A More Elegant Sorrel Sauce

The sorrel is added right at the end in this sauce, to preserve its purest, lively flavour. Serve with fish, chicken or poached eggs.

SERVES 4

30–60 g (1–2 oz) sorrel

2 shallots, finely chopped

120 ml (4 fl oz) fish or chicken stock

60 ml (2 fl oz) Noilly Prat or dry white wine

150 ml (5 fl oz) double cream

Salt and pepper

Make a *chiffonade* (fine shreds) of the sorrel (see page 160) and set aside. Put the shallots into a pan with the chicken stock and the vermouth. Boil until reduced to about 4 tablespoons. Now stir in the cream and sorrel and bring back to the boil again. Taste and adjust the seasoning and serve.

Spring Soup

The next best spring tonic to a strong sorrel soup is this sorrel and watercress soup, which is ideal if you have to buy your sorrel. The flavour still comes through, backed up by the pepperiness of watercress. If you grow sorrel and have plenty to spare, abandon the watercress and add 100 g (3½ oz) sorrel to the pan with the stock, then stir some fresh sorrel in at the end of the cooking time, as well.

SERVES 6

60 g (2 oz) sorrel

1 bunch of watercress

2 tablespoons olive oil

1 bunch of spring onions, white and green trimmed and chopped

340 g (12 oz) potatoes, peeled and diced

1 bouquet garni (a bay leaf and a sprig each of parsley and thyme, tied together with string)

1 tablespoon plain flour

Generous 1.5 litres (2½ pints) light chicken or vegetable stock

6 tablespoons double cream (optional)

Salt and pepper

Cut out and discard the tough stems from the sorrel and then shred the leaves roughly. Discard any damaged watercress leaves and cut the leaves away from the stalks. Set both leaves aside. Chop the watercress stalks roughly.

Warm the oil in a large pan and add the spring onions, watercress stalks, potatoes and bouquet garni. Stir to coat in oil and then cover and leave to sweat over a low heat for 10 minutes or so.

Sprinkle over the flour, stir in and cook for a minute. Gradually add the stock, stirring until smooth. Season with salt and pepper and bring up to the boil. Simmer for 10–15 minutes, until the potato is soft. Leave to cool for a few minutes, remove the bouquet garni and then stir in the watercress leaves and sorrel. Liquidize in batches and return to the pan. Taste and adjust the seasoning, adding the cream, if using. Re-heat, without boiling, and serve straight away.

Salmon and Sorrel Parcels

The earthiness and richness of salmon are blessed by the acidity of sorrel. Make a quick sorrel sauce to go with grilled or baked salmon but if you have a little more time, try these parcels of salmon and sorrel wrapped in pastry. Get the upper portion of salmon, if possible, as it will be thicker and chunkier.

SERVES 4

450 g (1 lb) salmon fillet, cut into four portions
60 g (2 oz) sorrel
1 egg yolk
340 g (12 oz) shortcrust pastry
45 g (1 ½ oz) butter, softened
Salt and pepper

Season the salmon with salt and pepper. Make a *chiffonade* (fine shreds) of the sorrel, (see page 160). Beat the egg yolk with a tablespoon of water.

Divide the pastry into four and roll each piece out thinly into a rectangle. Smear a quarter of the butter over the centre of each rectangle, covering a square roughly the same size as the salmon portion. Pile a quarter of the sorrel over the butter and lay a portion of salmon, cut-side down, on the sorrel. Wrap up neatly, to form a parcel, trimming off excess pastry and pressing the edges together to seal. Set the parcels on a greased baking tray, turning them the right way up, with the joins neatly tucked away underneath. If you wish, cut little shapes out of the trimmings of the pastry – leaves, fish or whatever – and arrange them artfully on each parcel, gluing them in place with a little of the egg-yolk glaze. Leave to rest in the fridge for half an hour (or longer, if necessary). Pre-heat the oven to 220°C/425°F/Gas Mark 7.

Brush the parcels generously with the egg-yolk glaze and bake for about 20 minutes.

Sorrel Fritters

This is another recipe that makes the most of a few leaves of sorrel. The crisp casing of flour and egg ensures that the leaves do not collapse in the heat of the oil. The fritters are excellent with grilled fish, but must be made right at the last moment.

SERVES 4
8–12 sorrel leaves
Plain flour, seasoned
2 eggs, lightly beaten
60 g (2 oz) butter
2 tablespoons sunflower oil
Salt and pepper

Leave the stalks on the sorrel leaves, to act as handles. Wash the leaves well and dry. Coat them first in flour and then in egg and then in flour again, making sure that they are evenly coated each time. Err on the side of excess.

Heat the butter, with the oil, in a frying-pan, over a brisk heat. Fry the coated leaves until golden brown on both sides. Drain briefly on kitchen paper, season with salt and pepper and eat immediately.

Baked Eggs with Sorrel

The mildness of baked eggs is lifted by the hidden layer of sorrel at the bottom of each ramekin. This is a lovely first course for a simple May dinner.

SERVES 4 AS A FIRST COURSE
60 g (2 oz) sorrel
15 g (½ oz) butter
4 eggs
4 dessertspoons double cream
Salt and pepper

Make a purée with the sorrel and butter (see page 160). Pre-heat the oven to 190°C/375°F/Gas Mark 5. Set four ramekins in a roasting tin and heat them through in the oven for 5 minutes. Meanwhile, boil a kettle of water.

Take out the ramekins and quickly divide the sorrel purée amongst them. Break an egg gently into each one and spoon over a dessertspoon of cream. Season with pepper only (salt hardens the white in the oven). Pour about 2 cm (1 inch) of hot water around the ramekins, cover loosely with foil and rush back into the oven. They should be cooked within 7–10 minutes: the whites just set but the yolks tender and runny. Season with salt and serve at once.

rocket

Rocket. Not roquette, not arugula, just plain rocket, thank you all the same. Why use a fancy foreign word, when a perfectly good, long-standing, time-honoured English noun exists already? We've been growing rocket in this country for centuries and I mean that quite literally. It was introduced to Britain in the late sixteenth century and, in 1664, John Evelyn listed it amongst the many herbs and leaves that went to make up his salad calendar. So it has a history here going back some four hundred years. It isn't some funny, new-fangled, foody designer leaf at all, though you might be forgiven for thinking so.

By the mid-nineteenth century, rocket had dropped out of fashion: 'its qualities are too biting' says one encyclopaedia of 1849. The Victorians seem to have fought shy of any number of foods with a bit of oomph to them. Rocket just wasn't genteel enough, I guess.

It is true that 'genteel' is about the last word I'd use to describe the taste of rocket. It has a spirited verve to it, a peppery kick that increases as the leaves mature. Rocket is a member of the crucifer family, in other words a relative of cabbage, of Brussels sprouts, and of mustard. As the leaves grow in size, they coarsen and develop an undertone and then an overtone of that characteristic cruciferous flavour. Take small, young tender leaves, no more than the length of your index finger at most, and the flavour, though distinct, remains unbelligerent. Medium-sized leaves announce their presence in no uncertain terms, which rocket devotees will appreciate. Over-sized rocket is strident stuff and there's no doubt whatsoever about *its* lowly family connections, but it is still worth using in cooking even if it is too loud to eat raw.

Buying and Storing Rocket

The tiny, tender, little leaves of rocket that are often sold as roquette are, inevitably, the most expensive. The use of the French name is, presumably, intended to confer some distinction and justify the cost. For all that, this is the most refined and subtle form of rocket, eminently suitable for pure rocket salads. This is the stuff for beginners, too, who wonder at the wisdom of taking mouthfuls of pungent greenery.

Once you get a taste for rocket, you may like to move on to medium-sized leaves. They are just the thing for cooking since not only do they make a more noticeable contribution to the dish in question, but it is also possible to buy them at a perfectly reasonable rate in generous bunches if you happen to live near a Greek or Cypriot greengrocer. They will be sold as *rokka* and, for once, the foreign name seems justifiable.

Of course, the wise amongst you will grow your own rocket. It springs up willingly, I know, because even I have managed to raise a decent crop on occasion. The one pitfall is that, as the

Opposite *Rocket, Saffron and Fresh Tomato Risotto*

days lengthen rocket's tendency to bolt increases. The answer is to pick the crop, lock stock and barrel, as the leaves offer themselves, with no thought to the plants' longevity, and to re-sow every week or two.

Store your rocket in a plastic bag in the vegetable drawer of the fridge, where it will remain lively for two or three days.

Using Rocket

I happen to like rocket a great deal, I admit, and can eat it in unladylike quantity. Reserve the tiddly stuff for salads composed mainly of rocket and little else, or for elegant garnishes and composed, plated salads.

Not only are middling-sized leaves ideal for cooking but they sit well in mixed salads, are lovely in sandwiches (say with slivers of Parmesan and Parma ham or salami) and prove a keen accompaniment to those more vigorous Mediterranean dishes that are all the rage these days.

Rocket, Saffron and Fresh Tomato Risotto

A beautiful risotto, with its fresh reds and greens and soft yellow, creamy sauce. It tastes lovely, too, with the barely cooked tomato and rocket balancing the richness of the rice.

SERVES 4–6

1.2 litres (2 pints) vegetable or chicken stock
A generous pinch of saffron strands
1 fresh thyme sprig
1 fresh rosemary sprig
1 bay leaf
3 shallots, finely chopped
3 garlic cloves, finely chopped
85 g (3 oz) butter
300 g (10 oz) risotto rice, e.g. arborio, carnaroli or vialone nano
675 g (1 lb 7 oz) fresh tomatoes, skinned, de-seeded and diced
1 good glass (about 200ml/7 fl oz) dry white wine
60 g (2 oz) rocket, roughly shredded
60 g (2 oz) freshly grated Parmesan, plus extra to serve
Salt and pepper

Bring the stock up to the boil and then reduce the heat to very low, so that it stays hot but doesn't boil away. Put the saffron in a small bowl and spoon in 2 tablespoons of the hot stock. Set aside until needed. Tie the herbs together in a small bundle with string.

Cook the shallots and garlic gently in half the butter in a wide, deep pan, without letting it brown. When they are translucent, add the rice and the herbs to the pan and stir for about a minute, until the rice becomes translucent. Add one-third of the tomatoes, salt and pepper and the glass of wine. Simmer, stirring constantly, until the liquid has all been absorbed. Add a generous ladleful of the hot stock. Stir again until the liquid has all been absorbed. Continue in this way until the rice is just tender but still has a slight resistance and is moistened with a creamy sauce. Now stir in the saffron and continue stirring for about a minute. Stir in the rocket and remaining tomatoes, stir again and then draw off the heat. Stir in the remaining butter and the Parmesan. Taste and adjust the seasoning and serve immediately.

Penne with Rocket and Tomato Sauce

This pasta dish is based on one I ate years ago in the medieval town of Orvieto, in Umbria. On several occasions we lunched in a restaurant deep under the town, in the cellars that were once part of a Medici palace. This dish of pasta, dressed with a simple tomato sauce (all the better for being made with the juicy, sun-ripened tomatoes of July – here, tinned tomatoes are the best substitute) and a handful of roughly torn-up rocket, featured high on the menu.

The heat of the sauce and the pasta is enough to wilt the rocket a little, releasing and modifying the taste. The tomato sauce can be made in advance and re-heated when needed.

SERVES 3–4

340 g (12 oz) penne
Salt
A generous handful of rocket
Olive oil
For the tomato sauce:
1 onion, finely chopped
2 garlic cloves, finely chopped
1 large fresh thyme sprig
2 tablespoons olive oil
14 oz (400 g) tin of chopped tomatoes
1 tablespoon tomato purée
2 tablespoons chopped fresh parsley
110 ml (4 fl oz) red wine
1 teaspoon sugar
Salt and pepper

To make the sauce, cook the onion, garlic and thyme gently in the olive oil, in a wide pan, without browning, until tender. Add all the remaining ingredients and cook hard over a high heat until reduced to a thick sauce. Taste and adjust the seasoning.

Bring a large pan of lightly salted water to the boil. Drop the penne into the water and cook until *al dente*. Meanwhile, tear up or chop (I don't think it makes much difference either way) the rocket roughly and then re-heat the tomato sauce. Drain the penne, pile into a serving dish, toss with a quick slug of olive oil and pour over the sauce. Scatter the rocket over the top and serve immediately.

wild mushrooms

I never thought I'd see the day when wild mushrooms – really wild mushrooms, that is – were being sold in supermarkets. There they are, though, in the autumn and early winter, as large as life, handsomely set out alongside the cultivated mushrooms. Cultivated mushrooms themselves have come a long way. Not so long ago, the choice was limited to button mushrooms or more mature, flat-cap mushrooms. Now there are chestnut cap mushrooms, which taste pretty similar to button mushrooms and, more interesting still, a handful of varieties of fungi that are still found in the wild, but that mushroom growers have learnt to reproduce and crop at their own convenience. Many people still think of oyster mushrooms, shiitake and the beautiful *pied bleu* or blewitt (that's the one on the cover of the book) as wild fungi, but they are all now cultivated for commerce.

Chanterelles, *trompettes de la mort*, girolles and *pieds de mouton* (the English 'hedgehog mushroom', for its spiny undercarriage) all of which now find their way on to supermarket shelves as well as into good greengrocers, are truly wild, gathered from the woods and often complete with blades of grass to prove it.

What makes these wild mushrooms so special is their full, earthy flavour, which puts the traditional cultivated mushrooms firmly in the shade. Go to one of the new small companies that are marketing carefully checked, safe-to-eat wild mushrooms in the height of the mushrooming season and you will be amazed at the range of wild mushrooms that come in every morning from woods all around the country. Wild Harvest has grown from a tiny back-room (well, garage, actually) operation, to a thriving business housed under the railway arches in south London. As the morning progresses, expert pickers roll up, proudly bearing their haul. A Polish couple had collected an impressive array of boletus mushrooms, distinguished by their spongy gills. Next came Nick, touting some of the most beautiful, most perfect wild mushrooms I've ever seen. There were ceps (also known as penny buns for their plump, brown heads) the best of all boletus mushrooms, but that was just the start. There were orange-peel mushrooms, saffron milk caps, chanterelles and many, many more; a veritable feast for the eyes and for the mouth.

The carefully trained staff at Wild Harvest sort through their woodland bounty, mushroom by mushroom, discarding any that are remotely suspicious and others that are damaged or worm-eaten. Their enthusiasm and their expertise, and that of the owners and staff of other similar companies here and abroad, are what has made it possible for the rest of us to buy wild mushrooms easily, secure in the knowledge that they are perfectly safe to eat.

trompettes de mort
dried shiitake
dried porcini
fresh oyster mushrooms
fresh shiitake

Buying and Storing Fresh and Dried Wild Mushrooms

A certain amount depends on the type of mushrooms but general rules are that they should be firm, not soft or slimy, and should look fresh and lively. Supermarket mushrooms nearly always start off in good condition, so you don't need to worry about unwelcome livestock (it is worth checking for tell-tale signs of gourmet insects when you buy the bigger wild mushrooms, like ceps, from smaller shops, but don't let this put you off). Wilting, drying, wrinkling are all signs of old age, and are not to be recommended.

Fresh mushrooms of all types are best stored in a brown paper bag in the fridge or a cool cellar. They should be eaten as soon as possible (or dried or frozen), certainly within three or four days.

Out of season, you can always get the taste of wild mushrooms from dried mushrooms. Dried porcini are actually dried ceps. They are often labelled with this Italian name, a hangover from the days when the only dried ceps you could get were from Italy. They seem very expensive but a very little goes a long way. Other dried wild mushrooms are becoming increasingly available such as *trompettes de la mort*, honeycomb capped morels, and even *mousserons*, the fairy-ring mushroom. The best quality dried mushrooms come in large pieces, with little or no powdery residue lingering at the bottom of the pack. Once the packet is opened, or if you buy them loose from a delicatessen, store them in an airtight container in a dark, dry cupboard.

Using Fresh Mushrooms

Mushrooms and water should be kept apart as much as possible. Chunkier mushrooms should be wiped clean with a damp cloth and never peeled. The more delicate ones may have to be given a quick rinse in cold water, but pick them out quickly and dry thoroughly on kitchen paper before they become too waterlogged.

All mushrooms exude a certain amount of liquid as they are cooked but wild mushrooms seem to be especially productive. When frying, make sure that you choose a wide frying-pan and get it really hot before adding the mushrooms. That way, a good amount of liquid will evaporate as it oozes out. Don't overcrowd the pan either. You may still end up with so much liquid that the mushrooms threaten to stew rather than fry. Either pour it off, or let them stew (add a splash of white wine or vermouth, if you like, at this stage), boiling off the liquid and then adding more butter or oil to the pan to brown them.

Cook mushrooms, sliced or quartered if appropriate, quickly, turning them carefully so that they cook evenly. Butter and mushrooms were made for each other. Garlic, added towards the end of the cooking time, and a final sprinkling of parsley, finishes off a simple dish of fried mushrooms most successfully.

Wild mushrooms are always expensive but you can mix them with cultivated mushrooms, to stretch them further without sacrificing too much flavour.

Using Dried Mushrooms

Dried mushrooms are a real boon. Cook them with cultivated mushrooms and you can conjure up an unseasonal taste of the woods for a reasonable outlay. Drying condenses and boosts the flavour of mushrooms, so they pack quite a punch. I use them in stuffings for chicken, in soups, in risottos and anywhere that the flavour of woodland mushrooms sits well.

For most recipes, they will need rehydrating. Tip the mushrooms into a bowl, cover with hot water and leave to soak for 20–30 minutes. You can use wine or, better still, sweet sherry, Marsala or Madeira, but pour on the alcohol cold and allow at least 45–60 minutes for the mushrooms to soften.

Pick out the pieces of mushroom and and dry and chop them as required. Save that soaking water – it is prime mushroom stock. Even if you don't want it for the recipe you are cooking, save it for soups or sauces. It will freeze nicely, too. Before you use it, leave it to settle for 10 minutes. The earthy grit and soil from the mushrooms will drop to the bottom and the liquid can be carefully poured off, leaving the sediment behind.

Mushroom Risotto

This mushroom risotto made with dried wild mushrooms and cultivated mushrooms is as good as any, and better than most. If you happen to have a small cache of fresh wild mushrooms, but not enough to flavour a risotto in their own right, make this one and then serve the wild mushrooms, sautéd briefly in butter, as a garnish on top.

SERVES 4–6

30 g (1 oz) dried porcini (or more if you are feeling generous)
5 tablespoons sweet sherry, Marsala or Madeira
1.2 litres (2 pints) vegetable or chicken stock
1 onion, finely chopped
2 garlic cloves, finely chopped
85 g (3 oz) butter
450 g (1 lb) open-cap flat mushrooms, or other cultivated mushrooms, e.g. shiitake or chestnut mushrooms, trimmed and sliced thickly
300 g (10 oz) risotto rice, e.g. arborio, carnaroli or vialone nano
4 tablespoons chopped fresh parsley
1 small glass (150 ml/5 fl oz) dry white wine
60 g (2 oz) Parmesan, freshly grated, plus extra to serve
Salt and pepper

Soak the dried porcini in the alcohol for at least an hour, until softened.

Put the stock into a pan, bring gently up to the boil and then turn the heat down to a mere thread, to keep the stock hot.

Cook the onion and garlic gently in half the butter in a wide, deep pan, without letting it burn. Meanwhile, pick out the porcini and chop them finely. Leave what little remains of the soaking liquid to settle. Add the soaked porcini and the fresh mushrooms to the pan and cook for a further 5 minutes or so, until the water thrown off by the mushrooms has evaporated. Stir in the rice and half the parsley and season lightly with salt and pepper. Stir for about a minute. Pour in the white wine and the soaking liquid, taking care to stop short of the gritty sediment left in the bowl. Stir the risotto until the liquid is all absorbed and then add a generous ladleful of the hot stock. Continue in this way, stirring until one batch of liquid has gone and then adding another, until the rice is just tender and bathed in a rich creamy sauce.

Draw off the heat and stir in the grated Parmesan and the remaining butter and parsley. Taste and adjust the seasoning and serve immediately with extra Parmesan to hand round separately.

Pasta with Wild Mushrooms

Alastair Lomax helps run Taste of the Wild, Wild Harvest's sister company. He came into the business via his passion for wild mushrooms. These days, he is so busy that he hardly ever has time to head off on his own mushroom hunts, but he does make time to cook wild mushrooms for himself and his friends and colleagues. He will rustle up a mean dish of pasta with wild mushrooms and cream at a moment's notice, and I was lucky enough to visit the company just as he was donning his apron. This recipe is one of the easiest ways to use wild mushrooms well, and ideal for using up a mixed basketful of fungi, though it is best of all made with plentiful, copious, generous quantities of cep. If you have only a poor little haul of wild mushrooms, stretch them further by mixing them with cultivated mushrooms – shiitake are particularly good but flat caps will do a more than decent job.

When Alastair cooked this for me and his colleagues, he used a mixture of *pieds de mouton*, saffron milk-caps, *trompettes de la mort* and ceps. He says that the dried porcini are not absolutely necessary but they do give an extra lift against the blandness of pasta.

In Italy, it is often considered a bit of a *faux pas* to sprinkle Parmesan over wild mushroom pasta, but I like it and, luckily, so does Alastair!

SERVES 4

8 g (1/4 oz) dried mushrooms
400 g (14 oz) tagliatelle
30 g (1 oz) butter
1 tablespoon olive oil
1 red onion, chopped
2–3 garlic cloves, chopped
At least 110–220 g (4–8 oz) wild mushrooms, cleaned, trimmed and thickly sliced where necessary
100 ml (3 1/2 fl oz) dry white wine
300 ml (10 fl oz) double cream
3 tablespoons chopped fresh parsley
Salt and pepper
Freshly grated Parmesan, to serve (optional)

Soak the dried mushrooms in hot water for half an hour.

Pick out and roughly chop the mushrooms. Leave the soaking water to settle. Put a large pan of salted water on to heat up for the pasta. Start on the sauce while you are waiting for the water to come to the boil. Once it is boiling, throw the pasta in to cook according to packet instructions. When *al dente*, drain well. The theory is that this moment should coincide, more or less, with the final turn of the sauce.

Alastair uses a wok to make his sauce in which works very well, but a roomy frying-pan is a rather more standard implement for this kind of thing. Either way, heat the butter with the oil and add the onion and garlic. Cook gently until they are just tender. Add the soaked dried mushrooms, fry for a few seconds and then add the fresh wild mushrooms. Fry until tender and until most of the liquid thrown out by the mushrooms has evaporated. Now season with salt and pepper and then add the soaking liquid, taking care to stop short of the earthy grit at the bottom of the bowl. Next pour in the white wine. Simmer for a few minutes, until the liquid is reduced by about two-thirds. Stir in the cream and boil down for another 3–4 minutes, until reduced by about half. Stir in the chopped parsley.

Tip the drained pasta into a large serving bowl. Spoon the mushroom sauce over it and serve, with Parmesan for those who want it.

Deep-Fried Mushrooms in Cider Batter with a Coriander Vinaigrette

Deep-fried mushrooms with garlic has become something of a cliché on pub and restaurant menus, but when the mushrooms include wild ones and the batter is light and airy, *and* they are served with either a coriander vinaigrette like this one or a garlicky, spring oniony mayonnaise like the one on page 180, they are transformed into a sophisticated starter that is hard to beat.

Of course, it can only be cooked at the last minute, as the mushrooms must be eaten post-haste, before their juices seep out into the batter. When choosing the mushrooms, buy at least three different kinds – a few button mushrooms to save your sanity and purse, maybe some shiitake or oyster mushrooms and then, if possible, one or two truly wild mushrooms, such as chanterelles, *trompettes de la mort*, ceps (which will have to be sliced thickly) and so on.

SERVES 4

450 g (1 lb) assorted mushrooms (see above)
Plain flour (see recipe)
Sunflower oil
For the batter:
200 g (7 oz) plain flour
1 level teaspoon baking powder
1/2 teaspoon salt
2 tablespoons olive oil
230–300 ml (8–10 fl oz) dry cider
2 egg whites
For the coriander vinaigrette:
6 tablespoons chopped fresh coriander
1 1/2 tablespoons cider vinegar
1/2 tablespoon caster sugar
2 garlic cloves, roughly chopped
6 tablespoons groundnut or sunflower oil
1 1/2 tablespoons water
Salt and pepper

Trim the mushrooms: remove any very thick, chunky stalks and slice large mushrooms in half. Wipe clean but make sure that they are thoroughly dry before you start cooking. Lay them out on a dish.

To make the coriander vinaigrette, put all the ingredients into a food processor and process until smooth. Spoon into a serving bowl.

The batter can be made an hour in advance, though the egg whites should only be added just before using. Sift the flour with the baking powder and salt. Make a well in the centre and add the oil and cider. Mix to a smooth batter. Just before using, stir the batter. It should have the consistency of double cream so, if it seems on the thick side, dilute it with a little more cider. Whisk the egg whites and fold them into the batter.

Heat the oil to 190°C/375°F. Put the flour on a plate. One at a time, coat the mushrooms in flour, shake off any excess and then dip them into the batter, making sure that they are *completely* covered. Lift them out on a fork and slide into the hot oil. Deep-fry until the batter is puffed, golden brown and crisp, turning once or twice. Drain briefly on kitchen paper and then serve with the coriander vinaigrette.

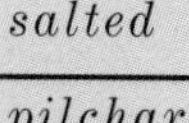

salted pilchard fillets

anchovies in oil

salted anchovies

salt cod

salted pilchards

preserved fish

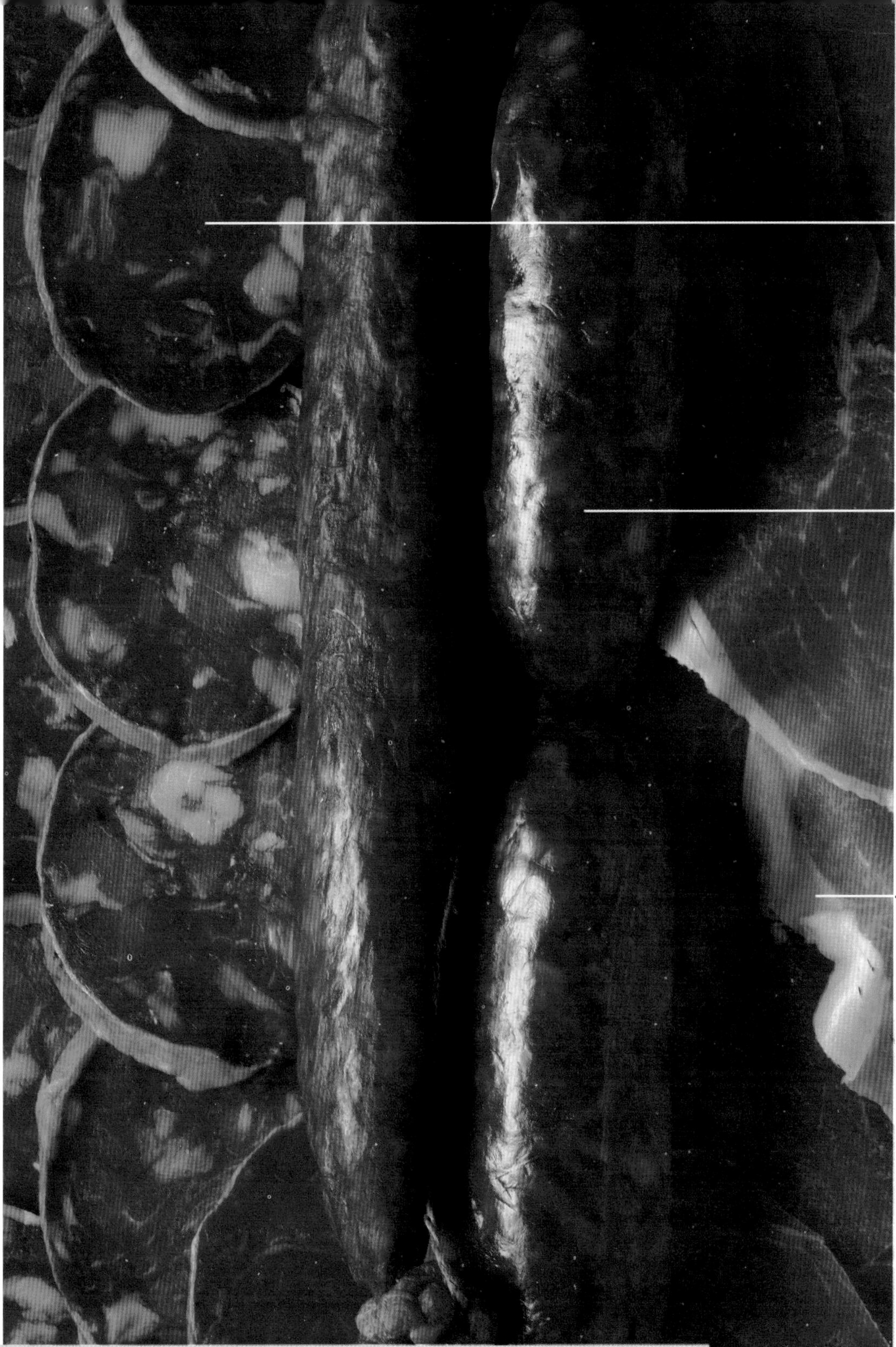

salami-style chorizo

chorizo for cooking

air-dried ham

and meat

salt cod

They love it in Portugal and Spain, in the south of France and in Italy, and in the Caribbean. Here in Britain, we have only just begun to tangle with salt cod. Actually, that's not entirely true. Ethnic communities in large cities have been quietly using it for years, while in Cornwall, where it used to be known as 'toe rag', it was eaten quite widely until barely a generation ago. Generally speaking, however, I think it is fair to say that salt cod is something of a novelty, a baffling unknown.

My first experiences of salt cod generated lukewarm enthusiasm but now I'm a confirmed salt-cod lover and I find myself selling its virtues to others time and again. My sales pitch is simple. When it is good it can be very, very good, and when it is bad it is perfectly horrid. Good, in this case, means two things. Firstly the salt cod itself must be of high quality, and an awful lot of it isn't and secondly, it must be cooked well, which an awful lot of it isn't. It's not difficult to choose well, or to cook well, but you do have to have some idea of what you are doing.

The Portuguese are particularly fond of salt cod; they claim to have 365 ways of cooking it, one for every day of the year. There's a marvellously whiffy street in Lisbon where virtually every other shop specializes in salted fish and other dried foods. Enter any one of them and you are confronted by an impressive array of salt cod, graded according to provenance and quality. The best of it will swell up to a thickness of 5–8 cm (2–3 inches) when soaked and cooked, and will be as succulent as fresh cod, though with a very different texture.

The best salt cod I've come across in this country is made in Cornwall, home of toe rag. Nick Howell owns the last working salted pilchards factory in the county and, since salt was plentiful on the premises and the freshest cod was being landed a few yards away in Newlyn harbour, it made sense to try his hand at salting cod, too. Most salt cod is salted bone-in but Nick begins with fat, pearly fillets of cod, which he salts down in huge white bins. He takes a modern approach to this traditional product. These days we have fridges and freezers, so there's really no need to dry the cod fully after it has been salted (which draws out a fair amount of moisture anyway). He sells his wet-cured salt cod fillets as they come out of the salt, still springy to the touch. They have a long fridge life – months rather than the days of fresh cod – no waste, and a superb texture and taste, which is making them a hot favourite with chefs who have a taste for salt cod.

Buying Salt Cod

Nick Howell will sell his salt cod by mail order (see suppliers, page 314) but otherwise it is very difficult to find wet-cured salt cod. Fully dried salt cod is easier to lay your hands on, though you may have to shop around for it. Your best bet is in the residential areas of a largish city, where local shops cater to a mixed ethnic population. The best quality is to be found in Italian, Spanish and Portuguese delicatessens. West Indian shops and some supermarkets will also stock salt cod.

Good dried salt cod is creamy-white and fairly thick in the centre. Try to buy it from a shop where they stock the whole flat, salty triangle of cod and will slice it for you with a purpose-made salt cod guillotine. The best cut is from the upper, wider part of the beast, where the flesh is thickest, though the 'shoulder', right at the very top, can be highly cartilagenous and sticky, which has its uses for some dishes but on the whole is not to be recommended.

Remember that cheap salt cod is likely to be bad salt cod. The triangles will probably be small, mean and scrawny, the flesh yellowing (a particularly bad sign) and thin, with a high ratio of waste to flesh and often over-salty. No bargain there. In fact, you'll be hard put to turn out anything edible at all.

Wet-cured salt cod, like Nick Howell's, should be stored in the fridge or can be dried fully if you have a dry, airy place to hang it up in.

Dried salt cod lasts almost indefinitely as long as it is not damp. Well wrapped, it can be stored in a larder or dry cupboard, though you may well prefer to keep it in a dry outhouse if the smell begins to seep through the wrapper.

Soaking and Cooking Salt Cod

Most dried salt cod will require 24 hours' soaking to rehydrate it and draw out the salt, but every now and then you hit on a piece that will take a bit more time, so always allow 36 hours to be on the safe side. After all, it doesn't matter if it is soaked for longer than necessary but over salty cod can ruin an entire dish and a terrible waste that would be, too.

Fully dry or wet, begin by rinsing the piece of cod thoroughly under the tap, to remove surface salt. Lay in a shallow dish in a single layer, cut up into chunks with scissors or a saw if necessary, and cover with cold water. Soak for 24–36 hours, changing the water as frequently as practicable. It must be at least three times but more is better. After 24 hours, nibble a small corner of the cod to get some idea of its remaining saltiness. Change the water again and give it more time if it still seems overpowering.

To cook wet-cured salt cod, put the cod into a shallow pan and cover with water or milk. Bring gently up to a rolling boil and then draw off the heat, cover and leave to stand for 15–20 minutes, by which time the cod will be beautifully cooked through. Dried salt cod will need longer cooking – poach it, either in water or milk, for about 10–15 minutes, until it flakes easily. Check regularly, as timing can vary considerably from one batch to another. Poorer-quality salt cod can take as much as 20 minutes. Take care to keep the heat gentle: boiling makes the cod stringy and tough. Once cooked, drain the cod and flake and skin it as necessary, discarding any bones.

Most salt cod dishes begin with soaking and poaching the cod. With basic preparation under your belt, the possibilities are enormous. Salt cod loves big flavours – it begs for olive oil, garlic, tomatoes, olives, herbs, chillies and the like but it also benefits from softer, blander accompaniments that temper its salty nature. Many traditional salt-cod dishes include potatoes in one form or another, or boiled eggs. Whatever way you are finishing it, take great care not to add any salt (it's very easy to do this automatically without thinking), until you've tasted the finished dish and are sure that it really needs it.

Salt Cod Fritters with Spring Onion Aïoli

They fry up fabulous salt cod fritters in Spain and Jamaica, but the best in the world are the ones made by my friend Martin Lam, chef-patron of Ransome's Dock Restaurant in Battersea. This is his recipe, though the spring onions in the aïoli are my idea. Crisp on the outside, tender inside, these fritters are good enough to convert the dubious and even those who profess to dislike salt cod.

SERVES 6 AS A FIRST COURSE

500 g (1 lb 2 oz) floury potatoes
400 g (14 oz) salt cod, soaked (see page 179)
Milk
2 tablespoons double cream
1 teaspoon paprika
1/2 tablespoon lemon juice
Pepper
1–2 eggs
Sunflower or vegetable oil for deep-frying
Lemon wedges, to serve

For the aïoli:

2 garlic cloves, crushed
2 egg yolks
1 tablespoon Dijon mustard
1 tablespoon white wine vinegar
200 ml (6 fl oz) sunflower oil
100 ml (4 fl oz) olive oil
5 spring onions, very finely chopped
Salt and pepper

Bake the potatoes in their skins.

Place the salt cod in a shallow pan in a single layer and pour over just enough milk to cover. Poach in exactly the same way as you would with water (see page 179).

To make the aïoli, mix the garlic, egg yolks, mustard and white wine vinegar. Mix the two oils in a jug. Whisking continuously, trickle the oils very slowly into the egg yolk mixture. When about half has been incorporated, increase the flow to a steady stream, still whisking away non-stop. When all the oil has gone, you will have a wonderful golden, creamy mass of garlicky mayonnaise. Stir in the spring onion and then taste and adjust the seasonings.

Opposite *Salt Cod Fritters with Spring Onion Aïoli*

Drain and flake the salt cod, discarding skin and bones. Weigh the prepared cod.

Scrape out the potato flesh and weigh out an equal quantity to the salt cod. Put into a bowl together, and add the cream, paprika, lemon juice, pepper and one of the beaten eggs. Beat together with a wooden spoon and plenty of elbow grease (if you have a Kenwood Chef or a Kitchenaid, or similar piece of equipment, use that. You can use a food processor, but it will make the mixture gluey and too smooth). Beat the remaining egg lightly and, if necessary, add it gradually until you have a mixture that is soft and holds together well but is not too sloppy to roll into balls. You may not need it at all. Flour your hands and roll into balls about 2.5 cm (1 inch) across.

Heat the oil to 170°C/325°F and deep-fry the balls, a few at a time, until they are a rich, even brown. Drain briefly on kitchen paper and serve with wedges of lemon and the aïoli.

Esqueixada

If you can't stomach the thought of raw fish, this is probably not the recipe for you. But if you tuck into smoked salmon with gay abandon, relish sushi, or have been delighted by ceviches of one kind or another, be bold and try it. *Esqueixada* is a dish that I first ate in Barcelona, sitting on the beach one warm Easter Monday, a few hours before I was due to take the plane back to London, work and grey, rainy weather. It formed the first course of one of the most memorable meals of my life, eaten alone and enthralled by the hubbub around me. The *esqueixada* was followed by a gargantuan feast of grilled fish and shellfish, dipped into golden garlic mayonnaise.

For *esqueixada*, you absolutely must have top-notch salt cod. Second-best will not do and will be quite vile, more so than in any other salt cod dish I can think of. With classy salt cod, however, *esqueixada* is something unusually superb. Serve with lots of good bread and sunshine, if you can get it.

SERVES 4–6

500 g (1 lb 2 oz) best salt cod
500 g (1 lb 2 oz) ripe tomatoes, skinned, de-seeded and chopped
2 garlic cloves, finely chopped
2 dessertspoons sherry vinegar or red wine vinegar
5 tablespoons olive oil
Pepper
Chopped fresh parsley
8–12 black olives

Soak the salt cod for 36 hours minimum, changing the water as frequently as possible – at least four times, as it is particularly important to free the cod of salt for this recipe. Drain well and pat dry. Pull off the skin and any sinews. Using your fingers, tear the flesh into chunks, discarding bones, fins and cartilage.

Mix with the tomatoes, garlic, vinegar, oil and pepper, turning delicately with your fingers. Spoon into a serving dish and set aside to marinate at room temperature (unless your room is on the warm side, in which case it had better be covered and go into the fridge). Leave for 1–4 hours and bring back to room temperature, if necessary, before serving.

Taste and adjust the seasoning. Scatter with parsley, dot with olives and then serve.

Morue à la Crème

From Marie-Therese, Nick Howell's Breton wife, comes this northern French way of serving salt cod. It is essential that the cod has been thoroughly soaked, as some of the cooking water is used in the sauce.

SERVES 4

450 g (1 lb) dried salt cod, soaked and rinsed (see page 179)
1 bay leaf
1 fresh thyme sprig
1 kg (2¼ lb) potatoes
Roughly chopped fresh parsley, to garnish

For the sauce:
60 g (2 oz) butter
1 large onion, chopped
45 g (1½ oz) plain flour
6 tablespoons crème fraiche
2 *cornichons* (baby gherkins), finely chopped (optional)
Pepper

Poach the salt cod (see pages 179–80), adding the bay leaf and thyme to the water. Lift out the cod and flake, discarding bones and skin. Reserve the cooking water.

Boil the potatoes in their skins and then skin and slice them. Once ready, keep the potatoes hot.

To make the sauce, melt the butter in a wide pan and add the onion. Cook gently until the onion is tender, without letting it brown. Sprinkle over the flour and stir in. Stir for a minute. Gradually add 200 ml (7 fl oz) of the water from cooking the cod, stirring it in a little at a time. Bring up to the boil and simmer for 2 minutes. Stir in the crème fraiche. Simmer for another 3 minutes or so, to form a very thick sauce. Stir in the flaked salt cod and the *cornichons*, if using, and season with pepper. Taste to see if it might need a little salt.

To serve, pile the salt cod mixture in the centre of a warm serving dish and arrange the sliced potatoes around the edge. Sprinkle with a little parsley and serve.

anchovies and salted pilchards

Until early this century, almost every port along the Cornish coast had at least one salting yard where the enormous catches of pilchards were salted down to preserve them. They smelled to high heaven on a hot summer's day, as the liquid drained off from the walls of pilchards and oozed across the yards. Women and children sat for hours gutting and cleaning and salting and stacking the fish, day after day.

Today only one pilchards works remains, in Newlyn, a stone's throw from the harbour. The haul of pilchards has shrunk to a fraction of what it once was and the demand for salted pilchards has dwindled with it. A shame, for they are our own, home-grown anchovy, our answer to the Mediterranean delicacy that we now import eagerly in tins and jars. Ironically, Italians and Spanish can't get enough of our meagre supply of salted pilchards. Some 70 per cent of the output goes across the Channel, pressed into neat, old-fashioned, stylish wooden boxes. In Naples, they use salted pilchards or sardines in preference to anchovies and in many southern Italian recipes it is the pilchard that gives the more genuine (and delicious) flavour.

Anchovies and pilchards, which are just grown-up sardines, are both oily fish but they are not otherwise related. Their relative abundance in times past has meant that they have a long history of preservation, usually under salt, though marinated fresh anchovy fillets are a hot favourite in Italy and Spain, and make an excellent hors d'oeuvre (you can sometimes buy them here in vacuum packs). Tinned or salted anchovies are to be used sparingly and should be considered an item quite apart from their fresh counterparts. The extraordinary, salty flavour, not fishy at all by the time the anchovies have lain under salt for around a year, is one of the magic seasonings, and can be hidden away discreetly in a dish so that those poor souls who imagine that they don't like anchovies are never any the wiser. I once had a boyfriend who insisted that he loathed anchovies but merrily and unwittingly chomped his way through his fair share while we were together.

Buying and Storing Anchovies

Anchovies are definitely amongst my top ten tinned products. I don't think I've ever come across a truly duff brand, though some, inevitably, are better than others. The anchovies from Collioure in the south of France, for instance, are reckoned to be the best in the world. If the choice is to be had, buy anchovies that are doused in olive oil rather than cheaper oils. I admit to being swayed hopelessly by pretty packaging – in chic delicatessens, you will often find beautifully designed tins of anchovies, some of them so attractive that it seems a shame to open them. I've ended up with half a dozen displayed on a shelf in the kitchen, to be used only in dire emergency.

Once a tin of anchovies has been opened, the best way to store the contents is to decant them into a small glass jar, cover with extra oil if need be, and seal tightly. Stand the jar in a cool, dark cupboard. They will keep for ages.

In Mediterranean and Portuguese markets there is nearly always a stall laden with opened wooden barrels of salted anchovies and sardines, whole fish, not the safe little fillets we're used to, alongside the olives and pickles. They prefer them to oil-soaked anchovies, and it is true that the flavour is even better. Here, you may find them in Italian or Greek grocery stores, occasionally sold loose but more likely in tins which seem enormous compared to the tiny matchboxes of oil-preserved anchovies. Still, they are worth buying, since they will keep well, even when opened (add a little extra coarse salt then cover tightly with cling film and keep in a cool place, where the smell will disturb no one); they can be filleted and preserved in oil with your own selection of aromatics.

Using Anchovies and Salted Pilchards

Tinned anchovies can be used straight from the tin but salted fish will usually need to be filleted. This is not a problem, as the fillets lift easily and cleanly away from the bone and any tiny, fiddly bones that come with them will dissolve away as they cook. Once filleted the fish may benefit from being soaked in water or milk for 15 minutes to diminsh the saltiness, then they can be used just as tinned anchovies. If you want to preserve them in oil, put the dried fillets into clean jars along with a few sprigs of thyme, maybe a dried chilli, a clove of garlic and a few fennel seeds. Pour in enough olive oil to cover and seal tightly.

Tinned or salted, anchovies add a marvellous though often elusive flavour to all kinds of savouries. As they are cooked they soften and dissolve (unless they are simply laid on top of something like the *Gratin of Cauliflower*, see page 186). Next time you roast a leg of lamb, try studding it with strips of anchovy as well as garlic, or basting it with anchovies that have been melted down in a little olive oil over a moderate heat. One of the nicest, quick, luxurious pasta dishes is tagliatelle dressed with an anchovy sauce: chop the anchovies and melt them in butter over a low to moderate heat; then add a generous slurp of double cream, simmer briefly and finish with pepper and a dash of lemon juice. A few strips of raw tomato and a poached egg on top raise it to heavenly heights.

Gratin of Cauliflower with Anchovies

Cauliflower has a special affinity with anchovies and here, both as fillets and as essence, they come into play to upgrade cauliflower cheese to a much more stylish dish than usual, more than good enough to eat all on its own.

SERVES 4

1 small cauliflower, trimmed and broken into florets (about 370 g/ 13 oz prepared weight)
4 tablespoons fine breadcrumbs
2 tablespoons very finely chopped fresh parsley
2 tablespoons freshly grated Parmesan
6 tinned anchovy fillets, halved lengthways
15 g (1/2 oz) butter
Salt

For the sauce:

1 small shallot, chopped
2 tablespoons oil from the tin of anchovies, or olive oil
30 g (1 oz) plain flour
450 ml (15 fl oz) milk
1 1/2 tablespoons freshly grated Parmesan
1–2 teaspoons anchovy essence or purée
Salt and pepper

Pre-heat the oven to 200°C/400°F/Gas Mark 6. Cook the cauliflower florets in salted, boiling water until just *al dente*. Take great care not to overcook the cauliflower to a grey grimness. Drain thoroughly and place in a shallow, greased baking dish, in as even a layer as you can manage.

To make the sauce,cook the shallot gently in the oil, until tender. Sprinkle over the flour and stir in. Cook for a minute, stirring, and then draw the pan off the heat and gradually mix in the milk, a little at a time. Bring up to the boil, then reduce the heat and leave to simmer very gently for 5–10 minutes, until the sauce is good and thick. Stir in the Parmesan and anchovy essence or purée. Season with pepper and then taste and add salt if needed.

Pour the sauce evenly over the cauliflower. Mix the breadcrumbs, parsley and Parmesan and sprinkle evenly over the surface. Arrange the anchovy fillets in a lattice pattern over the surface and then dot with butter. Bake for 25–30 minutes, until browned and sizzling. Serve immediately.

Spaghetti alla Puttanesca

This is amongst the most vivid of Italian pasta sauces, full of vim and vigour and salty, sharp and spicy notes, which is presumably how it got its name: *puttana* is the Italian for prostitute. It is said to come from the old, picturesque but shabby Trastevere district of Rome, which is home to a number of fine unpretentious restaurants and a fair number of ladies of the night. This version of the recipe comes from Nick Howell, master of the last thriving pilchard works in this country. From him I discovered that it is salted pilchards, rather than the more usually specified anchovies, which should really flavour the sauce.

SERVES 3–4

400 g (14 oz) dried spaghetti
4 tablespoons olive oil
500 g (1 lb 2 oz) tomatoes, skinned, de-seeded and roughly chopped, or a 400 g (14 oz) tin of plum tomatoes, roughly chopped
60 g (2 oz) butter
1 fresh red chilli, de-seeded and finely chopped
4 salted pilchard fillets, chopped, or 8 tinned anchovy fillets, chopped
2 garlic cloves, chopped
100 g (4 oz) large black olives, stoned and sliced
1 tablespoon capers
2 tablespoons chopped fresh parsley
Salt

Bring a large pan of salted water up to the boil and add the spaghetti.

While it is cooking, heat 1 tablespoon of oil in a frying-pan and add the tomatoes. If using fresh ones, cook down hard for about 6 minutes. Tinned ones will probably need only 4 minutes; stir and crush them up as they cook. Set aside until needed.

In a separate large frying-pan, heat the remaining oil with the butter, chilli, pilchards or anchovies and garlic and fry over a moderate heat for about 1–2 minutes, mashing down the pilchards or anchovies with a fork until they dissolve, more or less. Add the tomato sauce, the olives and the capers and cook over a high heat for a further 2–3 minutes, stirring frequently to prevent the sauce catching on the bottom of the pan.

Drain the spaghetti, and tip it into the frying-pan of sauce. Add the parsley and stir for about a minute, so that the sauce coats the strands of spaghetti as they absorb all those piquant flavours. Serve immediately, from the pan!

air-dried ham

When I think of air-dried ham, or *prosciutto*, to give it its Italian name, I think of rosy Parma ham or San Daniele, or the choicest of Spanish *jamón serrano*, mountain ham. Cut paper-thin (across the grain for Italian but often with the grain for Spanish), salty, sweet, subtle and supple, each one of those translucent, almost negligible, slices of meat clasps a phenomenal store of flavour that escapes wildly in the mouth.

These are warm-climate hams. They are made where the winter and early spring air is just warm enough but not too warm, and is free of humidity, so that the hams dry safely as they swing from the rafters of farmhouses and small factories. No risk of mould or unwelcome putrefaction threatens in this climate and there is nothing to taint the tender meat of pigs fed on carefully controlled, healthy diets, or even the meat of humbler pigs that have lived on household slops as they rootled around a sty.

Further north, in damper, drizzlier regions such as ours, this method of preserving pork has not been an option. Not until recently, that is. Oh, we've salted down our meat along with the best of them but our choice was either to opt for a heavy, heavy salt, which made the meat unpalatable when raw, or to go with the short-term option – light salting on a ham that was to be cooked. With the twenty-first century looming ahead of us, technology and human desire have coincided and now we can produce our own British air-dried hams, which stand up well against those Mediterranean hams and their long history.

In Cumbria, or Cumberland as many still prefer to call it, not far from the sea-shore, in the rain-swept, chilly (relatively speaking) village of Waberthwaite, the Woodall family have been making hams since 1828. Cooked hams, of course, until Colin Woodall, seventh generation ham-maker, came along and decided to innovate. He studied his warm-weather rivals' techniques, worked on trial and many errors, until he developed not one but two air-dried hams of his own. The first, Cumbria Air Dried Ham, is distinctly in the style of Parma, dry-salted and matured for at least 12 months in the carefully controlled cool air of his drying sheds. The second has a more Anglophile stamp on it. Cumbria Mature Royal Ham is salted but it also gets a month-long bath in a blend of vinegar, molasses and spice, as many of our traditional cooked hams once did, before it is hung up to dry and mature. This is air-dried ham with attitude. It is stronger, sweeter, more demonstrative still. Not a ham to be taken lightly but one to be served with discretion. It is, by the way, excellent in sandwiches. The Brits may be relatively new at this game but we are catching on fast.

Buying and Storing Air-Dried Ham

I happen to have a soft spot for Spanish *jamón serrano*, particularly that made from the black-footed Iberian pigs who gorge themselves on acorns in the autumn. It is sterling stuff and brings back happy memories of holidays in the south-west of Spain. Even so, I am not partisan when it comes to air-dried ham. I love the Italian *prosciutto* and I was very impressed by the Woodall's Cumberland equivalent (though I've also tasted one lousy British-made air-dried ham, so beware).

Air-dried hams are best cut straight from the ham itself, by a skilled professional who wields a sharp knife. Since they are hardly ten a penny in this country, you'll probably have to settle for getting it straight from the electric slicing machine. Vacuum-packed air-dried ham is, inevitably, a poor cousin to newly cut ham, lacking its fresh zip and finesse. Still, we're not talking bankruptcy, here. Vacuum-packing preserves moistness and flavour fairly well and is a godsend if you can't get to any fancy delicatessens.

Once cut (or once the packet has been opened) the ham should be kept loosely covered, interleaved (but not enclosed) with plastic film, slipped into a paper bag. Eat it up swiftly before it loses too much of its flavour and starts to dry out.

Using Air-Dried Ham

The obvious ways remain some of the best. There is little nicer, or easier on a warm summer's day, than a wedge or two of honey-ripe orange-fleshed melon, draped generously with a curtain of salty *prosciutto*. As autumn approaches, swap the melons for voluptuous, plump figs and then, when winter sets in, go tropical with mango or papaya. Colin Woodall likes to serve his hams, particularly the stronger Cumbria Mature Royal Ham, with ripe pears.

If good fruit is in short supply, serve the ham as part of an Italian *antipasto* – laid out on a plate with, perhaps, some slices of salami or chorizo, slices of good cheese, bowls of sun-dried tomatoes, *cornichons* (baby gherkins) and olives and plenty of crusty bread.

Italian and Spanish cooks have long known how to get the best out of air-dried hams. They add their names to the waiting list for the bones at their local store (you can do this in some delicatessens in Britain, too) and then use them to flavour stocks and soups. Off-cuts – and even thick chunks – of air-dried ham are diced and used to enhance pasta dishes, stews and vegetable dishes, often fried in olive oil with finely diced vegetables and garlic.

I sometimes grill thin slices of *prosciutto* until crisp, to balance them on top of first-course salads as a finishing touch, or crumble them into soups instead of croutons. Wrapped around chicken breasts or fish, air-dried ham imparts a lighter, less overbearing flavour, and provides a crisper wrapping, than sturdy bacon.

Last, but not least, comes one of my favourite sandwiches – plenty of air-dried ham, a handful of rocket, shavings of Parmesan, balsamic vinegar and olive oil and lots of black pepper, clamped between two slices of buttered bread. What a dream!

Tuoni e Lampo

'Thunder and Lightning' or, in other words, chickpeas and pasta. A filling stew from the *cucina della povera*, the poor man's repertoire, it is comforting, cheap and delicious, and highly fashionable these days. It is flavoured with a *soffritto* of finely diced vegetables, herbs and *prosciutto*.

SERVES 4–6

400 g (14 oz) dried chickpeas, soaked overnight
1 onion, quartered
3 garlic cloves, peeled but left whole
1 bay leaf
400 g (14 oz) tin of chopped tomatoes
Bouquet garni of 1 bay leaf, 1 fresh thyme sprig, 1 fresh rosemary sprig and 1 fresh parsley sprig, tied together with string
250 g (9 oz) *ditalini* (small pasta rings)
Salt and pepper
Grated Parmesan, to serve

For the soffritto:

2 carrots, finely diced
1 large onion, finely diced
2 celery sticks, finely diced
3 garlic cloves, chopped
120 g (4½ oz) piece of air-dried ham, diced
3 tablespoons olive oil

To finish:

3 garlic cloves, chopped
1 dried red chilli, snapped in two
1 fresh rosemary sprig
5 tablespoons olive oil

Drain the chickpeas and put them into a large saucepan, with the onion, whole cloves of garlic, bay leaf and enough water to cover generously. Do not add any salt. Bring up to the boil, and simmer for 2–3 hours, until the chickpeas are tender. Skim off any scum and then drain, reserving the cooking water.

For the *soffritto*, put all the ingredients in a large, heavy-based pan (big enough to eventually take the pasta and chickpeas as well, with a bit of room to spare). Warm over a moderate heat and sauté gently for about 10 minutes, stirring occasionally, until the vegetables are lightly coloured. Now add the chickpeas to the pan, stir for a few minutes, then add the tomatoes, bouquet garni, salt and pepper and enough of the reserved cooking water to cover generously. Bring up to the boil, then reduce the heat and leave to simmer for 30 minutes.

Add the pasta and simmer for a further 10 minutes. Draw off the heat, cover and leave in a warm place while you prepare the finishing touch. Put all the finishing ingredients – garlic, chilli, rosemary and oil – in a medium-sized pan and stir over a moderate heat, until the garlic is beginning to colour. Draw off the heat until needed. Remove the chilli and rosemary twig. Ladle the soup into warm bowls, then drizzle over some of the flavoured oil and sprinkle generously with Parmesan. Eat immediately.

Spanish-Style Broad Beans with Air-Dried Ham

Ham and beans get on together famously and this is a perfect sampler. It is best made with garden-fresh, tiny broad beans but that is the counsel of perfection. If you are willing to take the time to skin the individual beans, it works like magic on frozen broad beans as well. Similar Italian recipes replace the air-dried ham with *pancetta*, the Italian equivalent of bacon.

SERVES 4

400 g (14 oz) shelled broad beans, fresh or frozen

2 tablespoons olive oil

2 garlic cloves, finely chopped

100 g (3½ oz) air-dried ham, sliced thickly and diced, or if thinly sliced, cut into narrow strips

2 tablespoons chopped fresh parsley

Salt and pepper

If using fresh broad beans, simmer in lightly salted water for about 5 minutes or until nearly cooked. Drain, run under the cold tap and then drain again. If using frozen beans, simmer in lightly salted water for about a minute and then drain, run under the cold tap and drain again. Unless you happen to have idyllically teensy broad beans fresh from the garden, your dish will be infinitely improved by peeling the beans, although this is a rather tedious process. Slit the tough skin of each bean open and squeeze out the perfect, bright-green inner beanlet.

Shortly before sitting down to eat, warm the olive oil in a frying-pan. Add the garlic and ham and fry for a minute or so. Now in with the beans. Fry the whole lot together for a further 3–4 minutes, until the beans are tender. Stir in the parsley, season and serve immediately.

chorizo

Chorizo is Spain's most remarkable sausage and, believe me, there are plenty of sausages to choose from there, though the rest of them rarely brave the sea to travel to this country. Chorizo, though, is different and it's beginning to get a taste for travel, as we get a taste for its spicy, cheery presence.

Chorizo is not just one specific sausage. It's more of a collective name, a broad encompassing term that gathers in a whole family of Iberian *charcuterie* in one lively embrace. Every region of Spain has its own special chorizo, varying in detail from place to place and butcher to butcher. All members of the family are pork sausages, coarsely chopped to a greater or lesser degree, some semi-dried, some fully dried, some lightly smoked, some plain. What distinguishes them from other sausages is their glorious orange-red colour, painted in with paprika and hot chilli powder, underscored with garlic, maybe some wine and with a handful of aromatics to smooth out the edges. This is no shy, retiring little family of sausages. Chorizos of all types are full-flavoured, invigorating, power-packed charmers.

Broadly speaking, chorizo falls into two categories. There are the dried, salami-type chorizos, usually (but not always) ample in girth (4 cm/1 ½ inches or more) and long. They may be *dulce,* mild or *piccante*, hot and spicy with chilli. These are for eating raw, thinly sliced like the tamer salami, as part of a Spanish-style *antipasto*, as a nibble with drinks (very good with a chilled beer) or in sandwiches – try them with grilled, skinned red pepper in buttered bread.

The second category covers the softer, semi-dried chorizos used for cooking. The cut of the meat tends to be finer; the chunks of fat smaller. The sausages themselves are shorter (usually) and more slender, in other words, similar in shape and size to our fresh pork sausages, though rather firmer. Like the salami-type chorizos, these ones can be *dulce* or *piccante*.

Buying and Storing Chorizo

First things first. Make sure that you are buying genuine Spanish chorizo (or Portuguese *chourico*, which is similar) and not so-called 'Spanish-style' chorizo. I was once inveigled into buying the latter but never again. It was positively disgusting, fit for dogs alone (if even they'd deign to eat it). All Spanish and Portuguese and most Italian delicatessens now stock chorizo. So do a few supermarkets, and a fair number of go-ahead delis.

Secondly, make sure you are buying the right kind of chorizo – hard for slicing and eating

Opposite *Spanish-style Broad Beans with Air-Dried Ham*

raw; semi-dried, slightly squidgy stuff for cooking with. Like salami, get the hard stuff sliced thinly for you if you intend to eat it within 48 hours; otherwise buy it in a chunk and slice it yourself when and as you need it.

Hard chorizo can be hung up in a cool, dry place and will keep for several weeks. If it's already sliced, store as for air-dried ham (see page 189) and gobble it up quickly. Soft, cooking chorizo will last for a couple of weeks wrapped in a paper bag and kept in the fridge.

Using Chorizo

I have a strange, rectangular earthenware dish with earthenware bars across the top that I brought back with me from Spain. This is purpose-made to carry whole fried or grilled chorizo, allowing excess fat to drip away from the hot sausage. Whole grilled chorizo is lovely stuff and you don't need a special dish to enjoy it. Sliced thickly (without peeling), chorizo can be fried to release more of its fat, and served simply on toasted bread to soak up the juices.

Even more interesting, I think, is its use as a flavouring for more complex dishes. I love it in warm salads, its orange fat forming part of the dressing, but it also makes a fine addition to a dish of cooked pulses, or a big stew of meats and vegetables. Sautéed with peppers, perhaps with chicken, it brings an instant Iberian touch to a meal. A favourite picnic dish from Spain is a *hornazo*, a big loaf of bread with a whole hoop of chorizo baked in its centre, to stain and flavour the dough.

I love chorizo in stuffings, too, skinned before cooking so that it crumbles in the pan. And there we have the one important thing to remember about chorizo. If you want to keep slices whole, make them thick (at least 1 cm/½ inch) and don't remove the skin. Whether you use *piccante* or *dulce* chorizo is entirely up to you. I happen to prefer the light heat of *piccante*, especially where it is used in composite dishes, but then I always fall for the pushier flavours of this world.

Roast Chicken with Potato and Chorizo Stuffing

Turn a quiet chicken into a flamenco bird with a stuffing made of *piccante* chorizo and potato, and sherry gravy. It will need to be a sturdier, free-range bird to live up to its dancing partners but what wonders it will learn to perform.

If your bird is bereft of its giblets, as most seem to be these days, it is worth buying a pack of chicken livers for the stuffing as they add an extra richness to it.

SERVES 4

1.5 kg (3 lb) free-range chicken, with livers if possible
Olive oil
½ lemon
1 medium-sized glass of sweet sherry
Salt and pepper
For the stuffing:
250 g (9 oz) potatoes
2 tablespoons olive oil
½ onion, chopped
2 garlic cloves, chopped
2 chicken livers, chopped
110 g (4 oz) piccante cooking chorizo, peeled and sliced
1 level teaspoon fennel seeds or cumin seeds
Salt and pepper

Pre-heat the oven to 200°C/400°F/Gas Mark 6. To make the stuffing, first boil the potatoes in their skins, until just tender. Peel and roughly dice the potatoes. Heat the olive oil in a wide frying-pan and add the onion. Fry over a moderately high heat, until beginning to brown. Now add the garlic, chicken livers, chorizo and fennel or cumin seeds. Fry for another 4 minutes, allowing the bits of chorizo to crumble. Draw off the heat, tip the potatoes into the pan and mix up, mashing them down slightly to give a lumpy stuffing mixture. Season if you wish. Fill the cavity of the chicken about two-thirds full with the mixture.

Place the bird in a roasting tin and rub with olive oil and lemon juice. Season with salt and pepper. Roast for 1–1½ hours, until the chicken is done. About halfway through the cooking time, pour the sherry over the bird, and add an equal quantity of water to the tin. To test if the chicken is done, insert a skewer into the thickest part of the thigh, snug against the body. If the juices run clear, it is ready to eat. While you're at it, give the leg a little wiggle – it should wobble freely in its joint. Serve the chicken immediately, with its own pan-juices, suitably seasoned, for a gravy.

Warm Dandelion and Chorizo Salad

Warm dandelion and bacon salad is a favourite springtime dish in the Touraine, the part of France that I know best. This variation on the theme is spiced up with sizzling hot chorizo and crisp crutons. Pick the young small dandelion leaves in the spring months before they become too bitter. Those of you who really have no access to dandelions, or no time to pick them, will be the poorer, but you could try the salad with a mixture of rocket, radicchio and watercress leaves instead.

To turn the salad into a more substantial main course, perch a whole poached or fried egg on top of each serving.

SERVES 4

A generous salad bowl of young dandelion leaves, well rinsed and dried
2 slices of good bread, cut about 1 cm (1/2 inch) thick
4 tablespoons olive oil
150 g (5 oz) cooking chorizo, thickly sliced
2 garlic cloves, chopped
1 tablespoon red wine vinegar
Salt and pepper

Pile the dandelion leaves into a large salad bowl. Cut the crusts off the bread and then cut the slices into cubes. Heat half the olive oil in a frying-pan and fry the croutons over a moderate heat, turning frequently, until they are more or less evenly browned. Drain on kitchen paper.

Wipe out the pan and add the remaining oil. Fry the chorizo over a high heat, until browned. Add the garlic and fry for a minute or so more and then draw off the heat and tip the entire contents of the pan over the salad. Spoon the vinegar into the pan, swill it around for a couple of seconds and then pour that over the salad, too. Add the croutons, salt and pepper and toss. Eat immediately.

Tuna with Onions and Chorizo

The sweetness of slowly fried onions is lovely with meaty tuna. Here a third element comes into play: spicy chorizo. The tuna itself picks up a hint of the chorizo flavour from the fat that it is cooked in.

SERVES 2

2 portions of tuna steak, cut 2 cm (1 inch) thick, weighing about 170–200 g (6–7 oz) each
1 garlic clove, cut into slivers
1 small fresh rosemary sprig
Olive oil
1 large onion, sliced
½ tablespoon sugar
½ tablespoon sherry vinegar
80 g (3 oz) cooking chorizo, sliced (but not peeled)
Salt and pepper
Lemon wedges, to serve

Make slits all over the tuna and push in slivers of garlic and a few leaves of rosemary. Season and set aside until needed.

Heat 2 tablespoons of olive oil in a frying-pan and add the onion. Cook gently, stirring frequently, for about 10 minutes, until very tender and golden brown. Now add the sugar and vinegar and cook for a further 2–3 minutes, until the onions are nicely caramelized, tender and sweet and sour. Season lightly with salt and pepper. Re-heat, if necessary, when needed.

When you are almost ready to eat, wipe a heavy cast-iron frying-pan or griddle with a little olive oil. Set over a high heat and leave to heat through for 5 minutes. Add the sliced chorizo and cook, turning once or twice, until browned and sizzling. Lift out, leaving its fat in the pan or griddle. Keep the chorizo warm. Lay the tuna steaks in the pan. Cook for about 1–1½ minutes on each side, so that they are browned on the outside but still pink inside. Serve immediately, with a mound of onions and a few pieces of browned chorizo and, of course, a wedge of lemon on each plate.

lemon

olive oil

olive oil

balsamic

vinegar

oils, vinegars, etcetera

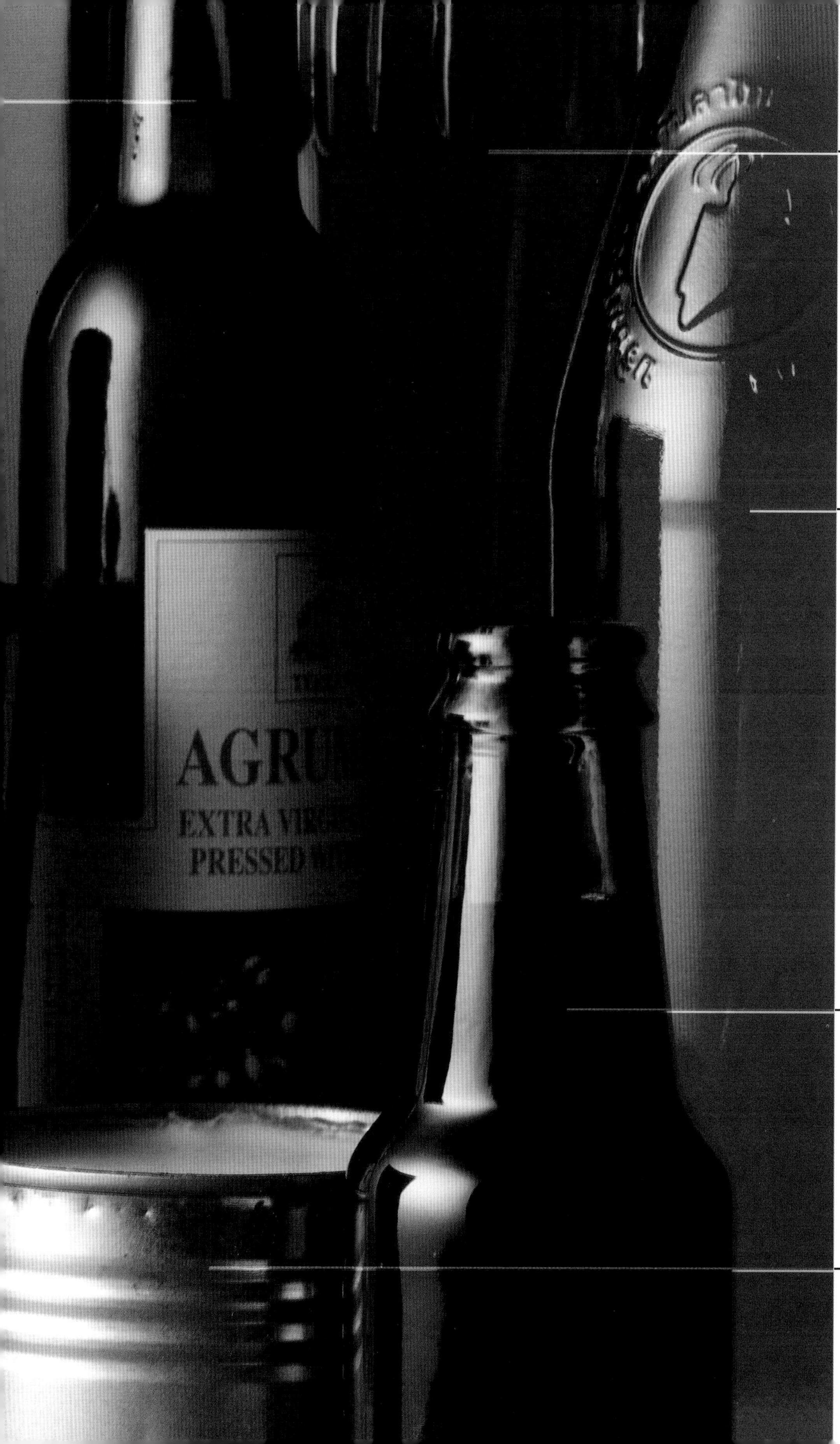

sherry vinegar

Thai fish sauce

kecap manis

coconut milk

balsamic vinegar

First of all, let me say that there is no such thing as bad balsamic vinegar, or at least not in my experience. Even the cheapest balsamic vinegars taste pretty good. Some are better, more skilfully made than others, that is true but, fundamentally, the quality is dictated by age.

There is young, immature balsamic vinegar (three or four years old) with a pleasing taste that can hold its own against most average wine vinegars (balsamic vinegar is made from grape juice, not wine). Cheap stuff, comparatively speaking, but nothing to turn your nose up at. Then there is adolescent balsamic vinegar, older (some eight to twelve years), a little wiser, a lot more depth to it, more polished with, at last, a clear promise of what a delight balsamic vinegar can be. Next comes middle-age, from 20 to 40 perhaps, and the complexity, the consistency, the aromas become indescribably rich and smooth and beguiling. And so the process wiles its way on, time working its magic on the ever darkening, ever reducing, ever more syrupy liquid, taking it patiently to unimaginably ambrosial heights. Imagine is just what most of us will have to do. The really ancient balsamic vinegar, a hundred years or more in the making, is worth a king's ransom.

Go back to the early years of its life, when it was as green and rough-edged as any youngster: balsamic vinegar starts out as the freshly pressed juice (known as 'must') of the white Trebbiano grape, which grows prolifically around the town of Modena in northern Italy. The filtered juice is simmered in vast vats, traditionally copper but more likely stainless steel in this day and age, until reduced by around two-thirds. That is the fast and easy bit, but from now on it is time and the skill of individual vinegar-makers – in some instances, two or even three successive generations will hold sway over a single batch – that collaborate to create the most notable, most valued balsamic vinegars.

The concentrated, darkened must is aged in wooden barrels, left open so that the reduction process can continue slowly. The wood of the barrels is crucial, adding its own particular notes and scents to the vinegar, rather as wine takes on an oaky quality when stored in oak barrels. In Modena they do use oak barrels at some stages, but ash, juniper, mulberry, chestnut and other woods are just as important and, year by year, the vinegar is moved from one to another.

Traditionally, the vinegars are matured and stored in large attics, windows left open to the elements but safe from thieving hands. A small barrel of centennial vinegar might have been treasured for years, to become an important part of a daughter's dowry, and no wise parents would care to run the risk of losing such a precious and rare commodity.

Buying Balsamic Vinegar

With balsamic vinegar, you get exactly what you pay for. The cheap stuff is sharper, less subtle, rougher, though not without charm. You can throw it around with gay abandon, slugging it into salad dressings, stews and roast dishes, without worrying about wanton extravagance. Most of what we get in this country is juvenile and although it is likeable enough, you may well be forgiven for wondering what all the fuss is about.

It really is worth splashing out, just once, on a flask of more mature vinegar, twelve years old or more, to find out why people get so excited about the stuff. The odd smart top-grade supermarket sells aged balsamic vinegar but you will find a better selection at a good delicatessen and, in this case, it is often the more general, but smart, delicatessens rather than small Italian delis that come out trumps. It is fashionable stuff, after all. I suspect that once you have tasted the finer vinegar, you will want more. Try different brands – there's a surprising amount of variation – to find one that shoots you straight to gastronomic heaven.

Twice in my life I have sipped 40-year-old balsamic vinegar, dripped first on to the back of my hand so that the warmth of the skin releases the full fragrance. It is extraordinary nectar, but so costly that I balked at buying the tiny phial of it. Just wait until I win the lottery . . .

Storage is no hassle. Ideally, I suppose, it should be kept away from light and many of the more expensive balsamic vinegars are sold in dark green glass bottles, which do just that. Otherwise, it is an accommodating, uncomplaining product, which sits happily on the kitchen shelf.

Using Balsamic Vinegar

The older it is, the more reverently it should be treated. Heat destroys some of the finer nuances. This doesn't matter so much with the immature vinegar but, the classier it gets, the more care you need to take. Luckily, you will also find that the better vinegars are far more intense and a few drops will stretch a long way.

Cheap balsamic vinegar is fine for cooking – you might slug a little into a tomato sauce as it simmers, or add it to a beef stew or de-glaze a frying-pan with it. But be careful nonetheless, since you don't want to end up with an over-sharpened dish. Balsamic vinegar is much softer than most vinegars but the heat emphasizes its acidity. A neat trick is to cook in a little vinegar and then stir in a fresh, aromatizing slurp at the end of the cooking time, so that you get the best of both worlds.

Of course, any balsamic vinegar makes a superb salad dressing, mixed with olive oil, salt and pepper. More unusual, though, is the way it enhances fruit, in particular strawberries. If you are landed with a punnet of less than exciting berries, bring them to life with a sprinkling of sugar and a few drops of balsamic vinegar. Restraint, naturally, is important, but bear that in mind and you'll be amazed at how effective the vinegar is.

Older balsamic vinegars bring out the best in plainly grilled meats and even steamed or lightly boiled vegetables. Sprinkle over a few drops, turn carefully and enjoy. No need for butter . . .

Grilled Tuna Salade Niçoise

Usually made with tinned tuna, *Salade Niçoise* is even nicer with fresh, dressed with balsamic or sherry vinegar instead of ordinary wine vinegar. All the elements can be prepared in advance (unless you want to serve the tuna hot from the grill), but don't put the salad together until the last possible moment. If you can get them, use the tiny, wrinkled olives from Nice.

SERVES 4 AS A MAIN COURSE

450 g (1 lb) tuna steaks, cut 2–3 cm (3/4–1 inch) thick
Olive oil
340 g (12 oz) small new potatoes, boiled
110 g (4 oz) green beans, topped and tailed and cut in half
8 leaves cos lettuce, torn up
3 hard-boiled eggs, quartered
220 g (8 oz) cherry tomatoes, halved
8 tinned or marinated anchovy fillets, cut in half lengthways
12–16 black olives

For the vinaigrette:

1–2 garlic cloves, crushed
1 tablespoon balsamic or sherry vinegar
4–5 tablespoons olive oil
2 tablespoons chopped fresh chives
Salt and pepper

Grill or griddle the tuna steaks, brushed first with a little oil, for about 1–1 1/2 minutes on each side. They should still be clearly pink in the middle.

Make the vinaigrette in the usual way.

If necessary, skin and bone the tuna and then cut it into large chunks. Toss in a little of the dressing and leave to cool.

Slice the potatoes thickly while still hot, removing stray wisps of skin – if they are very small, leave them whole – and then toss in a little more of the dressing and leave to cool.

Boil the green beans for about 4 minutes, until they are just on the soft side of *al dente*. Drain, run under the cold tap and then drain again thoroughly and mix with the potatoes.

Place the remaining dressing in the bottom of a large salad bowl and cross the servers over it. Just before serving, compile the salad, starting with the lettuce and adding all the other ingredients, mixing lightly with your fingers as you do. Toss at the table.

Roast Chicory with Balsamic Vinegar

Here, a modicum of balsamic vinegar goes in at the start of the cooking time, so that the chicory can absorb some of its flavour then, when the chicory is tender, a little more is added to restore the scent that has been sacrificed to heat. The end result is a lovely, sweet, scented dish of tender chicory which goes beautifully with hot ham or gammon.

SERVES 4
4 chicory heads
30 g (1 oz) butter
3 tablespoons balsamic vinegar
2 tablespoons caster sugar
Salt and pepper

Pre-heat the oven to 200°C/400°F/Gas Mark 6. Trim the base of the chicory heads and remove the outer layer of leaves, if they are damaged or bruised. Smear half the butter over a shallow ovenproof dish that will just take the chicory snugly, without too much room to spare. Drizzle over half the balsamic vinegar, scatter with sugar and add 2 tablespoons of water. Season with salt and pepper and then dot with the remaining butter. Cover with foil.

Roast for 20 minutes. Remove the foil, and turn the chicory. Return to the oven for another 20–30 minutes, depending on the size of the chicory heads, turning them once or twice and basting them with their own juices. When the chicory is very tender, take it out of the oven and drizzle over the remaining vinegar. Turn to mix it in and serve.

coconut milk

Coconut milk is one of the essential cooking liquids of south-east Asia and the Caribbean and other parts of the world where coconuts grow easily. In a hot-weather country, where fridges are not necessarily the commonplace items that we take for granted, coconut milk is a brilliant concept. It is made from a commodity that is plentiful and cheap or, better still, growing in your back yard and can be kept easily for days, without spoiling. The juice of the coconut, in other words the watery liquid inside it, is refreshing if you like it (which I do), but expendable. A quick, practised swipe with a cleaver makes short work of opening a coconut, as long it is done outside and you don't need to worry about the mess. With that accomplished, making the milk itself is moderately quick work – a bit of grating, a bit of squeezing, and again one more time and there you are: a bowl of fresh coconut milk ready for the pan. Exactly what you need, when you need it.

Coconut milk doesn't have a strong flavour but it does have a pleasant one, and a smooth, velvety consistency. Its thickness and richness depend entirely on the maker, not on the milkman. Another rather handy bonus.

Buying, Making and Storing Coconut Milk

Time was when the big question about coconut milk was 'What is it?', never mind 'Where do I get it?' or 'How do I make it?'. These days, the question is 'What kind should I use?' Stroll through a few big food stores and you are likely to come across tins of coconut milk, blocks of creamed coconut, little cartons of coconut cream, powdered coconut milk, desiccated coconut and, yes, even some fresh coconuts on a good day. Phew!

The best option of all, in terms of taste and authenticity, is inevitably that heavy, tough, seemingly impregnable coconut. To make coconut milk from a ***fresh coconut*** without creating a damp mess, it helps to have access to a tool kit, or a willing helpmate. Clamp the coconut in a vice or upright on the floor, with the three eyes facing upwards. Pierce a hole through two of the eyes, using a drill or a bradawl or a strong skewer and a meat mallet. Empty out the coconut juice and chill to drink after all your exertion. Tap the coconut all over firmly with a hammer, to loosen the flesh inside. Then, holding the coconut on its side, bash it down very hard on a concrete floor. Or hit it hard and repeatedly with a hammer or a heavy instrument at the centre of one of the 'ribs' that runs from top to bottom. Or hack at it with an axe or a heavy cleaver. Or saw it open. Prise the flesh from the shell and don't worry about the brown skin. Grate the flesh coarsely and then pour on about 600 ml (1 pint) of hot water. When cool enough to handle, knead the flesh with your hands, squeezing it firmly, and then strain, pressing out every last drop of milk. This will give thick coconut milk. Repeat the operation once more for thin coconut milk, or mix the two to give a medium milk.

To make milk from ***desiccated coconut***, first of all make sure that you have *unsweetened* desiccated coconut. Put 450 g (1 lb) of desiccated coconut into a food processor or liquidiser and pour on 600 ml (1 pint) of hot water. Process for about a minute and then strain through a sieve, squeezing out the thick milk. Repeat for a thinner milk.

Tinned coconut milk is an excellent store cupboard standby and is what I use when I don't want to go to the bother of making milk either from fresh coconut (most of the time) or desiccated coconut (or when I can't face the extra washing-up, which is also a frequent occurrence). It is not the same as fresh by any stretch of the imagination, and develops a somewhat mucilaginous quality when boiled down but, for all that, it is still a real boon when you are in a hurry and want to throw together something spicy and satisfying. Or, indeed, when you want to create a pudding with a hint of coconut in it.

To make milk from ***coconut milk powder***, dilute it according to packet instructions. This is another good stand-by, though I reckon that if it's time you want to save – you might as well opt for the tin-opener and a can of milk. The one advantage the powder has is that it can be made thicker or thinner as you prefer, simply by increasing or decreasing the amount of water.

Creamed coconut comes in a hard block, rather like hardened lard. It can be grated and stirred into hot water to make a form of coconut milk, or stirred into dishes towards the end of the cooking time to thicken the dish and intensify the coconut richness. It is handy to keep in the fridge but isn't the best substitute for fresh coconut milk. It works well stirred into milky puddings at the end of the cooking time.

Liquid ***coconut cream*** comes in weenie cartons and has a worryingly long ingredients list, but is very thick and creamy. Much richer than coconut milk, it makes an almost instant sauce. Fry chicken or prawns and vegetables with a ready-made Thai curry paste and then add the coconut cream and within minutes you have a presentable Thai-style curry. I particularly like it for making coconut ice cream, or to enrich other puddings.

Once made up, or once the tin is opened, coconut milk should be stored in the fridge and used up within 48 hours.

Using Coconut Milk

Thick or thin? If the recipe is not specific, you'll have to use your own judgement. Usually, I go for a mixture of the two, a sort of medium milk, or else I just use it straight from the can as it is. If you need to separate the thick cream from thinner milk and you are using canned milk, pop the can into the fridge for 20–30 minutes. Quickly turn it upside-down, open and pour off the liquid milk, which will be thin. What's left at the bottom is very thick cream.

There are many recipes that use coconut milk, and these usually include spices and herbs and other full, vibrant flavours. Coconut milk is the bland soothing base that carries the rest in its wake, bringing them all together. Most Thai coconut milk curries are meant to end up with loads of liquid, verging on the soupy: it's the sauce-soaked rice that is the best bit.

Coconut milk also plays an important part in Caribbean cooking – one of the most unusual coconut milk dishes I've ever eaten was on a tiny Caribbean island – iguana cooked in coconut milk. The sauce was excellent, but I wasn't so sure about the iguana. Coconut milk is also used in Caribbean puddings, and boiled up with rice or cornmeal. I use it in place of milk in traditional British milky puddings, slipping in a few spices, such as a cinnamon stick or cardamom pods, for a double helping of exotica without losing sight of the original. It does wonders for tapioca and makes a very stylish rice pudding. Made with coconut milk, a whole host of puddings become accessible to people with dairy product allergies, without having to sacrifice flavour on the altar of soya milk.

Prawn, Chicken, Lemon Grass and Coconut Soup

A marvellously aromatic soup which can be made in a matter of minutes if you use tinned coconut milk and have chicken stock in the freezer. It is filling enough to constitute lunch in itself but could also form the first course of a more substantial meal.

SERVES 4

Two 400 ml (14 fl oz) tins of coconut milk, or 800 ml (30 fl oz) medium coconut milk (see page 204)
300 ml (10 fl oz) chicken stock
350 g (12 oz) boneless, skinless chicken, cut into thin slivers
3 lemon grass stems, trimmed and heavily bruised
1.5 cm (1/2 inch) piece of galangal or fresh ginger, cut into thin matchsticks
225g (8 oz) shelled prawns
1 fresh red chilli, de-seeded and thinly sliced
5 spring onions, sliced
Juice of 1–2 limes
3 tablespoons roughly chopped fresh coriander
3 tablespoons fish sauce

Put the coconut milk and stock into a pan and bring to the boil. Add the chicken, lemon grass and galangal or ginger and reduce the heat to a gentle simmer. Cook for 10 minutes, uncovered.

Add the prawns and cook for a further 2 minutes. Finally, add all the remaining ingredients. Taste and add more lime juice, if needed, then serve.

Coconut Crème Caramel

My local Thai restaurant serves a crème caramel made with coconut milk instead of cows' milk – an East-meets-West pudding, if ever there was one. I have taken the idea one step further, flavouring the coconut milk with cardamom and cinnamon as well as the more usual vanilla.

SERVES 6–8

For the caramel:
140 g (5 oz) granulated or caster sugar
For the custard:
600 ml (1 pint) medium coconut milk (see page 204)
1 vanilla pod
1 cinnamon stick
2 cardamom pods
4 eggs
30 g (1 oz) caster sugar

Opposite *Prawn, Chicken, Lemon Grass and Coconut Soup*

Stand either eight 120 ml (4 fl oz) capacity ramekins or six 180 ml (6 fl oz) capacity ramekins in a roasting tin in the oven. Heat the oven to 150°C/300°F/Gas Mark 2.

While the ramekins are heating through, make the caramel. Put the granulated or caster sugar into a saucepan with 5 tablespoons of water. Stir over a moderate heat, until the sugar has completely dissolved, brushing down any sugar crystals stuck to the side of the pan with a brush dipped into cold water. When the syrup is clear, bring up to the boil and boil hard until it caramelizes to a nice hazelnut brown. Don't stir it, but do tilt and swirl the syrup in the pan as it cooks, to even out hot spots. As soon as it is done, whip the ramekins out of the oven. Pour a little of the caramel into each hot ramekin and then quickly tip and tilt them, so that their bottoms and sides are coated in caramel. Once coated, leave the ramekins to cool and then return them to the roasting tin.

To make the custard, put the coconut milk into a pan, with the vanilla pod and cinnamon stick. Slit open the cardamom pods, extract the black seeds and crush coarsely. Add them to the milk, too. Bring gently up to the boil and then draw off the heat. Cover and leave to infuse for 15 minutes in a warm place. Whisk the eggs with the caster sugar. Bring the coconut milk back up to the boil and then pour on to the eggs, stirring constantly. Strain the mixture into the ramekins. Pour enough hot water into the roasting tin to come about halfway up the ramekins. Carefully transfer to the oven and leave to cook gently for an hour or so, until the coconut custard has just set. Leave the ramekins to cool and then store in the fridge, loosely covered with cling film, until needed.

To serve, invert into shallow bowls and pass around a bowl of cream for those who like to go the whole hog.

fish sauce

Fish sauce is the south-east Asian equivalent of soy sauce and absolutely essential in the cooking of the region. A thin, clear, mid-brown liquid, it is the salt of Thai or Vietnamese food, but also more than that. It imparts a remarkable, subtle taste that brings out other flavours like magic. Though it is made from fermented fish and salt, it doesn't taste particularly fishy and it doesn't clash with chicken, eggs or vegetables or whatever else forms the principle ingredient of the dish it seasons. Rather the opposite, in fact; it enhances and gives depth. It is used in all sorts of south-east Asian curries, marinades and dipping sauces. One of Thailand's ubiquitous condiments, found on tables from the humblest roadside food stall right up to smart restaurants, is nothing more than a mixture of fish sauce and finely sliced Thai chillies, sometimes sharpened with lime juice. Marginally more complex dipping sauces may be softened with sugar and flavoured with garlic, ginger and coriander, as well.

Fish sauce is sold in many supermarkets these days, but you'll get it at a better price and in far prettier bottles in oriental food stores, particularly Thai or Malaysian ones. Look out for bottles labelled *nam pla* (from Thailand), *nuoc mam* (from Vietnam), or *ngan-pya-ye* (from Burma). The strength may vary a little from one brand to another – Vietnamese *nuoc mam* tends to be more fishy, with a darker colour – so, when it comes to cooking with fish sauce, always use recipe quantities as a rough guide. Taste and add more fish sauce if you think the finished dish needs it.

A bottle of fish sauce at the back of your cupboard can also earn its keep when used in Western cooking. Add a shake or three to soups or stews that just need a little something to boost them from the mundane to the delicious (a dash of sherry, balsamic vinegar, lemon or lime juice can help, as well). Try it, too, in salad dressings, replacing salt and some of the oil.

lemon olive oil

An old family tradition (aren't they all?) persisted in parts of Italy where olive oil was made in small back-yard presses. As the olives, from the family's own orchard, were loaded into nets and stacked between the boards, lemons, also home-grown, were thrown in with the smaller fruit. The great screw was twisted down and down, increasing the pressure, crushing both olives and lemons, and their juices and oils flowed out in a single stream. The juice was allowed to flow away, but the perfectly blended oils were decanted into enormous bottles and stored in the cellar, for the family to use over the coming year.

Then some bright spark realized that other people, who didn't have their own olive orchards and lemon groves, might like to get a look in on this fabulous, lemon-scented olive oil. Quite right, too. The first lemon olive oil to make its way to our shores was Granverde Colonna, from the Molise region of Italy, and it remains one of the best (it doesn't have an enormous amount of competition, though it doesn't stand alone). Open the bottle and take one whiff and you are transported straight to the Mediterranean. Bottled sunshine, that's what it is ... though it is actually pressed in late autumn or winter. Since it is the essential oil of the lemons, and not the juice, that perfumes the extra virgin olive oil, there is no sharpness, just a marvellous aroma and taste.

I use it primarily in salad dressings and find that it is usually enough to use half to two-thirds lemon olive oil, mixed with ordinary extra virgin olive oil. Perhaps even nicer is lemon olive oil drizzled over freshly steamed or fried or grilled fish – excellent, in particular, with skate. It can be used on vegetables or chicken too, but always treat it as a condiment, for adding last-minute zip. This is not an oil for frying!

kecap manis

Kecap manis is Indonesian sweet soy sauce. For years I read about it in Indonesian cookery books and had to fall back on soy sauce mixed with brown sugar when I tried out recipes. A passable substitute but no match for the real thing. Then I found a bottle in a delicatessen in Aberdeen which at the time seemed rather surprising. Now I can even buy it in my small local town and that is quite an achievement, too.

Kecap manis is like a viscous version of dark soy sauce, with a sweet, salt flavour that enhances no end of Western dishes as well as its own Indonesian cuisine. I use it in salad dressings and in home-made beefburgers or meatballs and drizzle it over pan-fried salmon fillet. It can become something of a sophisticated Asian substitute for tomato ketchup – once you get a taste for it, there's little that it doesn't enhance and, in a trice, it seems, the bottle is empty.

olive oil

So much has been written about olive oil, and there is so much to write about this liquid gold of the Mediterranean that I am going to restrict myself to the basics, in order not to ramble on endlessly. These days, no kitchen seems to be complete without it and for good reason. Olive oil brings a wonderful underlying flavour to any dish. It is also an undisputably healthy oil, high in mono- and polyunsaturated fats it is readily available at a relatively reasonable price. The better virgin oils are all produced without the aid of chemicals: a pure, honest product, with no tampering or unwanted interference.

The exact flavour of olive oil depends on many factors and is often compared to wine. The first and most obvious influence is the variety of olive used. Frantoio, for instance, an olive grown in Italy, tends to give a peppery kick to the oil, while something like the Greek Kalamata yields an oil with a grassy flavour. The Picual olive from Spain produces a fruity but slightly bitter oil. Terrain and climate also affect the outcome but perhaps one of the most easily recognizable traits is a direct result of the age of the olive. Oil pressed from young, green olives tends to have a fresh, yellow, fruity taste, while oil pressed from more mature olives is richer, greener, deeper and stronger. Naturally, there are many exceptions to these generalities but they give some idea of the complexities of olive oil.

Most olive oil now comes from the first, cold pressing, since modern methods mean that a huge amount of oil can be extracted without recourse to damaging heat processes.

The grading of olive oil is strictly regulated. First of all, oils are tested for acidity. Virgin olive oil must have less than 2 per cent acidity, with a good aroma, flavour and colour to boot. The best is extra virgin olive oil, with perfect flavour, aroma and colour and an acidity of, at most, 1 per cent. Within these definitions you will find oils that are, at one extreme, light and golden in colour, with a fresh taste of new-mown hay and, at the other, dark, cloudy, green, heavy and thick, with a raunchy, peppery powerful perfume. Cloudiness, by the way, is nothing to be worried about. It means that the oil is unfiltered and so even truer to its natural state.

Oil that does not make the virgin grade will usually be refined chemically and stripped of flavour and will then have some vestige of character returned by mixing with a few slugs of virgin olive oil. This will be labelled simply 'olive oil' and has a maximum acidity level of 1.5 per cent.

Buying and Storing Olive Oil

If you are new to olive oil, it is probably best to start with the kind of oil that is simply labelled 'olive oil', with not a hint of virginity to it. It will have a light flavour that makes a good introduction. However, once you develop a taste for olive oil, you are faced with a blissfully wide choice. Most supermarkets now sell their own brands of extra virgin olive oil as well as a selection of other big-brand-name, blended oils. All the major blended oils will have a flavour that never changes from bottle to bottle. That is the point of the blending. If you find one you particularly like, you can rely on it time and again. I always have a bottle of blended extra virgin oil on my kitchen shelves, and use it day in, day out.

Fancier, single-estate extra virgin olive oils are a different matter. The price can rocket sky-high, but the scent, the perfume and the consistency . . . aah, they can knock you for six and send you reeling with pleasure. Not always, mind you. and that is part of the fun. These oils will vary from year to year, depending on weather and harvest, but it is those small changes that makes them so special. Buy a special single-estate oil as a treat and use it lovingly and with appreciation.

Olive oil should be stored in a dark cupboard, well away from the ravages of light. Good advice for fancy oils, but I ignore it totally with my blended extra virgin olive oil. Because I use it almost every day and work my way through bottles at a speedy rate, I leave it out on the work surface, right beside the stove. This is totally against the rules but it makes sense when you are cooking with it.

Using Olive Oil

Use it for frying, use it for dressings, trickle it over toasted bread instead of butter, use it for preserving, in cakes and pastries and biscuits, in breads, as a condiment in soups and stews, and practically any place where an oil of quality seems appropriate. The list is endless and I imagine that some 50 per cent or more of the savoury recipes in this book include olive oil, and one or two of the sweet ones, too.

For most purposes, I use a blended extra virgin olive oil. I love the stuff, and I always find light olive oil too bland for my tastes. However, where I've simply stated olive oil in a list of ingredients the choice is yours, according to your preference. Here and there I've been more emphatic and listed extra virgin olive oil, because the bigger oomph it gives is essential to the recipe. In these circumstances, I'd probably bring out a single-estate olive oil, with the full, rich gifts it gives to any food.

Salsa de Mojo

S*alsa de mojo,* or simply *mojo*, is a powerful dressing that surfaces in the Canaries and again in Cuba. There are red mojos and green mojos and many other variations. Though the forms may differ, the essentials stay the same – garlic, olive oil, and warmth. In the Cuban version, it is the oil itself that is heated before being poured on to the other ingredients. In this version, from the Canaries, which I have adapted very slightly from the recipe in Anne Dolamore's *Essential Olive Oil Companion* (Grub Street), hot water brings in the warmth. The salsa is drizzled over hot vegetables in Cuba or salty boiled potatoes in the Canaries. It also goes very well with fish.

SERVES 5–6

3 large garlic cloves, roughly chopped
1 teaspoon cumin seeds
1/4 teaspoon fresh thyme leaves
1/2 teaspoon coarse salt
1 teaspoon paprika
60 ml (2 fl oz) extra virgin olive oil
1 tablespoon lemon juice
60 ml (2 fl oz) hot water

Pound the garlic with the cumin, thyme and salt in a mortar with a pestle, until you have a paste. Work in the paprika and then work in the oil, a few drops at a time. Stir in the lemon juice and then the hot water. Use warm or cold.

Sweet-Sour Garlic and Oil Preserve

The thing about pickled garlic is that it mellows with age without losing its intrinsic garlicky foundation. You'll need to wait at least two weeks before trying this one. If you can leave it even longer, it will get better and better as it matures.

FILLS A 500 ML (16 FL OZ) JAR

4 large or 8 small heads of garlic
300 ml (10 fl oz) white wine vinegar
140 g (5 oz) caster sugar
2 teaspoons cumin seeds
2 teaspoons coriander seeds
2 whole star anise
2 dried red chillies
Extra virgin olive oil
Sunflower oil (optional)

Separate the cloves of garlic and peel the whole lot of them. Put the vinegar, sugar and spices into a pan with 300 ml (10 fl oz) of water and bring up to the boil, stirring until the sugar has dissolved. Simmer for 5 minutes and then add the garlic cloves and reduce the heat. Simmer for 10–15 minutes, until barely tender. Lift the cloves out with a slotted spoon, bringing as many of the spices with them as you can. Leave to drain in a sieve.

Pack into sterilized, but cold, jars (see page 124). Pour in enough olive oil, or olive oil mixed with sunflower oil, to cover completely. Leave to stand for an hour or so to settle and then top up with oil, if necessary. Seal tightly, label and store in a cool, dark cupboard for at least two weeks before using.

Olive Oil and Sauternes Cake

This recipe, from Alice Waters' renowned restaurant Chez Panisse in California, has become something of a classic. No wonder, for the moist, scented cake is a marvel. It is definitely a pudding cake, rather than a tea-time cake, lovely served with sliced fresh peaches or raspberries, or strawberries marinated in Sauternes and some crème fraiche for those who want it.

If you can't get Sauternes, you can substitute another good quality, sweet dessert wine.

SERVES 6

5 eggs, separated
170 g (6 oz) caster sugar
Finely grated zest of 1 orange
Finely grated zest of 1 lemon
140 g (5 oz) plain flour
1/4 teaspoon salt
110 ml (4 fl oz) Sauternes or other good quality sweet dessert wine
260 ml (9 fl oz) extra virgin olive oil
2 egg whites

Pre-heat the oven to 190°C/375°F/Gas Mark 5. Line a 20 cm (8 inch) cake tin with non-stick baking parchment. Whisk the egg yolks with the sugar, until pale and fluffy. Fold in the two zests.

Sift the flour with the salt and beat it, a little at a time, into the egg yolk mixture. Now gradually beat in the wine and the olive oil. Whisk all seven egg whites until they form stiff peaks and fold them into the batter. Pour into the cake tin. Bake for 20 minutes, turning the cake once or twice if necessary so that it cooks evenly.

After 20 minutes, reduce the heat to 170°C/325°F/Gas Mark 3 and continue baking for a further 20 minutes, or until a skewer inserted in the centre comes out clean. Turn off the oven, cover the cake with a round of buttered baking parchment or greaseproof paper (butter-side down!) and leave the cake in the closed oven for 10 minutes more, while the cake deflates like a fallen soufflé.

Run a knife round the edge of the cake tin and invert the cake on to a flat surface. Remove the cake tin and leave the cake to cool completely. The cake can be stored in an airtight container or wrapped in cling film in the fridge for three or four days.

sherry vinegar

From the south-western corner of Spain come two of the Iberian peninsula's most remarkable twinned products. The fortunes of the prosperous town of Jeréz and the surrounding region are built upon the making of fine sherry, a fortified wine of such phenomenal fame that people have almost forgotten where it comes from. Its quieter sidekick is sherry vinegar, for years a well-kept secret that only a wily Andalusian might know about.

The vinegar is made from young sherry that is set aside because of its naturally high acidity and then aged in old sherry casks, in a similar manner to the wine itself. This is achieved under the *solera* system, which involves a great number of barrels, and a lot of toing and froing of small amounts of vinegar (or wine) which can be accomplished only by highly skilled practitioners. It has clear parallels with the creation of Italian balsamic vinegar, though the Spanish barrels will usually be made of oak. The results, however, are very different in character. Good sherry vinegar can be as viscous as balsamic vinegar but it tends to be sharper, with a clear scent of sherry and an underlying oak flavour. It varies considerably in quality, as you might expect, but the best sherry vinegar is probably the finest of all wine vinegars.

Buying Sherry Vinegar

You get what you pay for. The cheaper sherry vinegars are fine for everyday use but the more expensive ones bring real pleasure to the simplest of foods. For starters try the ordinary supermarket versions, to see if you like the general idea, and then look in good delicatessens for something a little bit more stylish. If the vinegar comes in a dark glass bottle, it is absolutely fine to keep it on a shelf in the kitchen. The acidity of vinegar makes it a preservative and there's nothing it will preserve so well as itself.

Using Sherry Vinegar

Sherry vinegar is one of the most powerfully flavoured vinegars you can get, so a little will go a long way. Strength will vary from one brand to another, so go cautiously at first – in most instances, you can add a little extra if you want to liven things up a bit more. Sherry vinegar makes the basis of a very fine salad dressing, blended with olive oil and perhaps a hint of sugar, but try adding a few shakes to a tomato sauce or soup, or to a beef stew, during cooking or right at the very end. I've found that sherry vinegar holds its flavour well under the onslaught of heat, which makes it a good bet for cooking and particularly for marinades.

In Spain, they use sherry vinegar for marinating game, which is an excellent idea, to marinate raw anchovies (delicious) and to heighten the fresh flavours of gazpacho – the last is especially welcome when the tomatoes are not quite as vibrant as they might be in an ideal world.

Our Favourite Salad Dressing

This is the dressing that we use time and again on our salads, and we never tire of it. Friends often ask for the recipe, but there is really nothing much to it, as long as you have either good sherry vinegar or balsamic vinegar and a bottle of *kecap manis*, Indonesian sweet soy sauce (see page 210). This recipe makes enough dressing for a bowl of green leaves for three to four people.

SERVES 3–4

1/2 tablespoon sherry or balsamic vinegar
1/2 tablespoon *kecap manis*
2–3 tablespoons olive oil or 1–1 1/2 tablespoons each of olive oil and lemon olive oil (see page 209)
Salt and pepper

Mix the vinegar and *kecap manis* and season with a teensy bit of salt and a good grinding of pepper. Whisk in the oil(s)and then taste and adjust the balance of flavours.

Three Suns Sandwich

Here we have Italy meets France meets Spain all in one sandwich, and a big, picnic-worthy one at that. We start with an idea from the south of France – the *pan bagna*, a stuffed loaf of a sandwich, compressed overnight so that dressing and juices ooze invitingly into the crumb of the bread. For the bread, I've chosen the lovely, chewy, open-crumbed Italian ciabatta and, for the filling, I've headed to Spain with Manchego cheese and sherry vinegar. And there's more – olives and olive oil from whichever hot weather country you fancy, and air-dried ham from Italy, Spain or Portugal or, indeed, Britain, if you want to anchor your flights of fantasy on home territory.

SERVES 3–4

1 ciabatta loaf, split in half lengthways
4–6 slices of air-dried ham, e.g. Parma, San Daniele, *jamón serrano*, or Cumberland (see page 188)
85 g (3 oz) Manchego, thinly sliced
2 ripe tomatoes, thinly sliced
A handful of frisée lettuce leaves
Freshly ground pepper

For the dressing:

1 tablespoon sherry vinegar
7 tablespoons olive oil
60 g (2 oz) black or green olives, pitted
1 fresh red chilli, de-seeded and roughly chopped
1 level teaspoon chopped fresh oregano
2 tablespoons chopped fresh parsley
1 tablespoon capers
2 *cornichons* (baby gherkins) or 1 small pickled gherkin, roughly chopped
1–2 garlic cloves, chopped
Salt and pepper

Begin with the dressing. Put all the ingredients into a food processor and process until finely mixed and chopped, adding a little more oil or vinegar, if necessary. If you don't have a processor, chop all the solid ingredients together very, very finely and then mix them with the oil and vinegar and season with salt and pepper.

Drizzle a few spoonfuls of the dressing over both the cut sides of the ciabatta. Now build up layers of ham, cheese, tomato and frisée on one half, anointing each layer with a little more of the dressing and seasoning with pepper. Finally, clamp on the second half of the loaf and press down firmly. Wrap tightly in cling film and then lay on a board or plate and weight down with heavy weights (bags of dried beans, tins of tomatoes or whatever else is to hand). Leave overnight in the fridge. Unwrap and cut into chunks just before eating.

Scallops with Sherry Vinegar and Fresh Tomato Sauce

This dish of scallops makes a very quick, very chic starter. Ask for scallops that have not been soaked in water to make them look plumper and weigh more!

SERVES 3–4

8 medium-large scallops, cleaned
2 tablespoons olive oil
3 tablespoons sherry vinegar
4 tablespoons fish or light chicken stock
1 tablespoon caster sugar
350 g (12 oz) firm tomatoes, skinned, de-seeded and cut into 3 mm (1/8 inch) dice
1 1/2 tablespoons finely shredded fresh basil
Salt and pepper

Separate the corals from the whites of the scallops. Depending on the size of the scallops, cut each white into two or three discs horizontally. Season with salt and pepper.

Shortly before you sit down to eat, put a heavy-based pan on to heat through thoroughly. Let it get good and hot and then add the oil. Leave for a few seconds and then lay the scallop discs and the corals in the oil, one by one. If the oil is hot enough, they will be cooked through within seconds. Lift out and keep warm. Tip excess fat from the pan, reduce the heat to moderate and then spoon in the sherry vinegar and stock. Tip and tilt the pan about, scraping up the residues from frying. Stir in the sugar and the tomatoes, give the whole lot a few seconds to heat and then taste and adjust the seasoning. Stir in all but a few shreds of the basil and serve with the scallops, draping the reserved basil over the top.

crème fraiche

mozzarella

Parmesan

goats' cheese

dairy products

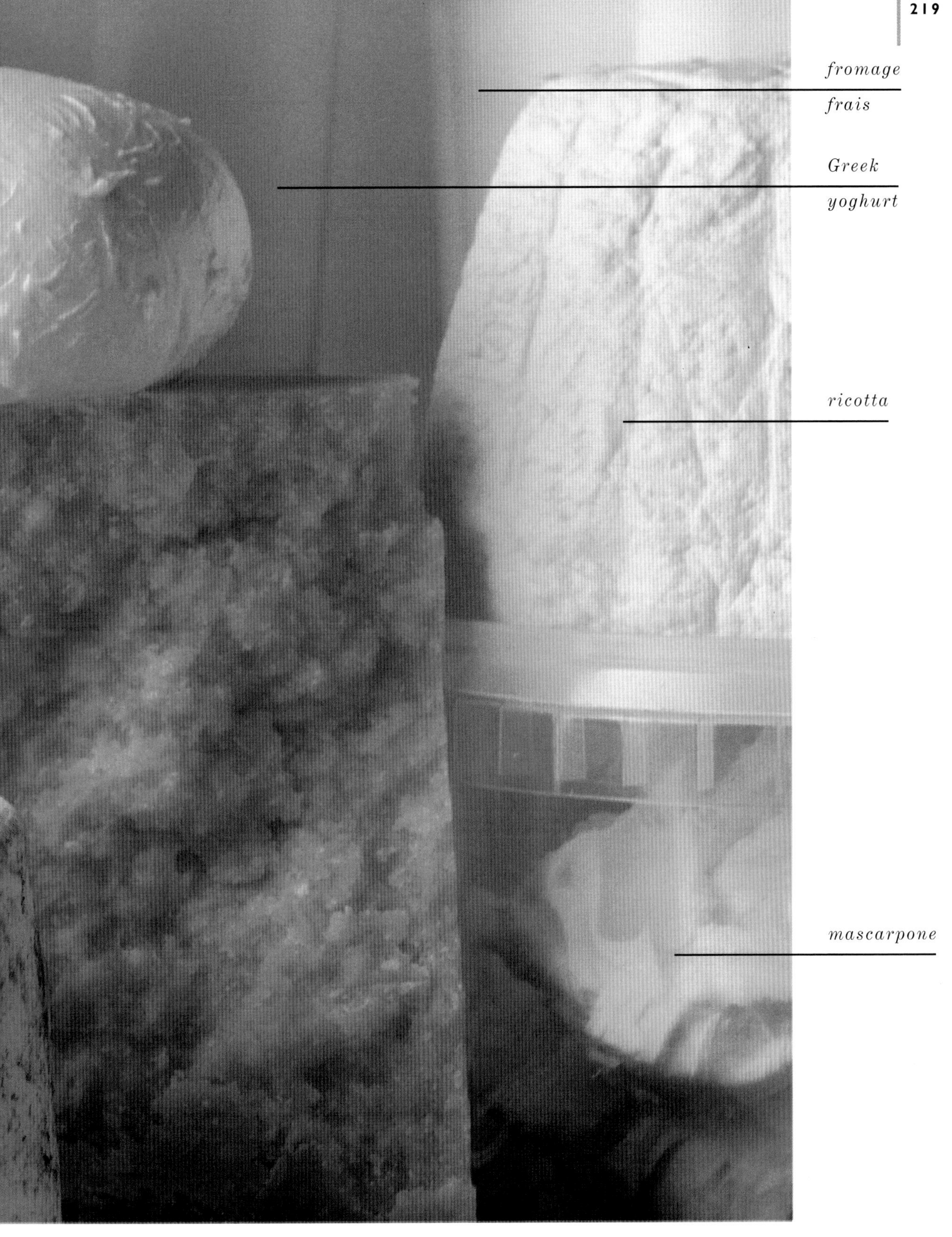
fromage frais
Greek yoghurt
ricotta
mascarpone

goats' cheese

Goats' cheese has always been the province of the French and there can be little doubt that they make the finest in the world. They've been at it for centuries and there are plenty to choose from, so that is quite as it should be. Nevertheless, the French should guard against complacency (unlikely, I admit – the French rarely admit any possibility that they might be beaten at their own favourite game). Enthusiastic foreigners who have travelled the Gallic cheese trail are hard at work developing their own goats' cheeses – here in Britain, in America, Canada and, no doubt, elsewhere. Fired with enthusiasm, a fair number of smallholders, who once seemed cranky and foolhardy, are now churning and cutting their own, home-grown goats' cheeses, with increasing success.

I've tasted a fair number of British goats' cheeses and they are constantly improving. None of them quite come up to a fine French Sainte Maure but, for all that, there are splendid British goats' cheeses to be tasted and enjoyed. One of the pioneers of goats' cheese in this country is Piers Fielden, who set up his own dairy in the early eighties. He could see no earthly reason why good goats' cheese could not be made on this side of the Channel, and resented only being able to buy expensive imports from fancy cheese shops. He left the City and returned to his native Somerset, where his first task was to persuade local dairy farmers to keep goats. They must have thought he was mad ... but not for long.

Working from scratch, Piers gradually developed a cheese that satisfied him, and then satisfied cautious cheesemongers, and eventally conquered the even more cautious supermarket buyers. As he says, 'Good cheese-making is a blend of having a clear view of the product you want, a good understanding of the technology you are grappling with, and an ability to learn from what goes wrong.' He was also blessed with a dogged determination. He needed it, too, for when he started out the majority of us were, at best, suspicious of goats' cheese. Those in the know wanted 'real' French cheese and wouldn't countenance anything less.

His cleverest ploy, if you ask me, was the size and shape of his Capricorn cheeses. Small round drums, they are sold whole, not too big to be daunting, nor too small to seem mean. Sliced in half, they are perfect for grilling which is exactly, I suspect, how goats' cheese gained its first foothold in restaurants and cafés. He also abandoned any notion of emulating the French practice of rolling the cheeses in ash – far too weird for conservative Anglo-Saxons. A clean, white, soft, Brie-like rind was what was called for. Now Capricorn cheese is everywhere – widely distributed and easily recognisable. It's mild fresh flavour and velvety, semi-soft texture have made it popular. While it lacks the verve of so many French goats' cheeses, it was an ideal stepping stone for consumers who were wary of of this unfamiliar substance.

Buying Goats' Cheese

There are, broadly speaking, three kinds of goats' cheese. Hard cheeses are often British, more like Cheddar, and not so common, but well worth looking out for. At the other end of the scale are the young, very fresh, soft goats' cheeses, mild and milky, like cream cheese, that can be scooped up with a spoon. And in the middle sit what most people think of as goats' cheese: semi-soft, with a rind or coating of some sort, in other words, cheeses that are firm enough to slice and crumble but too soft to grate. With the rind removed, they can be mashed up with a fork. Their curd is snowy-white and moist, with a lovely richness and fine texture. Any recipe that lists goats' cheese amongst its ingredients will require this sort of semi-soft cheese, unless otherwise specified.

Goats' cheeses come in all kinds of shapes: small drums, some very small like the famous French *crottin*; logs some 10 cm (4 inches) in diameter, give or take (handy for grilling); and pyramids with the top shorn off. They are never enormous and are usually, with the exception of the log-type, sold whole. In a cheese shop or market in France you will usually be asked how firm and mature you like your cheese. A gentle squeeze will reveal its age: the harder it is, the more mature and the stronger its flavour. You may get this option in a cheese shop in Britain but it is unlikely.

Buying goats' cheese is all about personal preference. One thing to avoid is any cheese that smells actively 'goaty' (just as fish that smells 'fishy' is not to be recommended), which may suggest that the milk was badly handled in the first place. The black-grey coating on some cheeses is ash and not meant to be eaten, while others may have been rolled in herbs or wrapped in leaves. Each method imparts its own stamp on the taste.

The best place to store goats' cheese is in a cool, dark larder. Failing that, the cooler part of the fridge will do, where it will last for several weeks if it has not been cut.

Using Goats' Cheese

The soft, young, rindless goats' cheese can be used like cream cheese. Spread it on bread, or beat it lightly, perhaps with a little cream to slacken it and a dusting of sugar, and then dollop it on soft summer fruit or fruit compotes. It is quite mild enough to form the basis of a cheesecake and can be used to make fillings for savoury tarts.

Semi-soft, rinded cheeses are the real joy. Naturally, they are to be eaten with bread or biscuits just as they are. For a dinner party, you might consider concocting a cheese board of goats' cheeses alone – include a French-style pyramid, an English goats' cheese and maybe a bowl of *Chèvre Tourangelle*, as well (see page 222). Offer the cheeses alongside a mixed green-leaf salad. Goats' cheese and dressed greenery go terrifically well together. So for that matter, do goats' cheese and cherries or figs.

When it comes to cooking, there are endless uses for goats' cheeses. Grilled or baked, on toast or slipped on to a salad, they make a perfect, quick first course. Crumbled, they can be used to flavour a cheese sauce, or a soufflé. Or use them in a filling for a quiche or a savoury roulade. I love goats' cheese in omelettes and it can be mashed and spread in sandwiches, or diced finely to go in a stuffing for vegetables. When heated, it holds its shape quite well. I like to come across little nuggets of hot, softened goats' cheese but, if you want a more even distribution, chop it very finely or sieve it before mixing in.

Chèvre Tourangelle

In the Saturday market in the little French town that I have known since I was a child, the cheesemonger always has a big vat of *chèvre frais à l'ail*: young, milky curds of goats' cheese flavoured with garlic and fresh herbs. We always buy some and wolf it down at supper with big hunks of *pain bâtard*, the equally excellent sturdy bread made by the baker on the corner. Our friends there eat it either as a cheese course or, occasionally, as a simple first course, putting it on the table with some slices of salami.

The soft goats' cheese that we can buy here is not the same as the less processed, local French cheese but it still makes an excellent creamy version of *Chèvre Tourangelle*, to give it its fancy name.

SERVES 4

200 g (7 oz) young, fresh goats' cheese
4 tablespoons creamy milk or single cream
1 tablespoon chopped fresh chives
1 teaspoon chopped fresh tarragon
1 tablespoon chopped fresh parsley
2 teaspoons chopped fresh chervil, if available
2 garlic cloves, crushed

Mix the whole lot together. Eat.

Fromageon Gascon

From the south-west of France comes this superbly boozy cream to serve with summer fruits, or maybe just on its own in small bowls with crisp almondy biscuits to dip into it.

SERVES 4–6

60 g (2 oz) caster sugar
85 ml (3 fl oz) armagnac or brandy
280 g (10 oz) young fresh goats' cheese

Beat first the sugar and then the Armagnac or brandy into the cheese. Chill for at least an hour before serving and beat once more before you put it on the table.

Meatballs in Tomato Sauce with Goats' Cheese

My whole family, from the one-year-old right up to granny and grandpa, loves these meatballs, sizzling in tomato sauce and finished with browned goats' cheese.

Adding bread soaked in a little milk makes tender, delicate meatballs that melt in the mouth. Sometimes I will use basil instead of the oregano, or even coriander. *Kecap manis* (see page 210) is Indonesian sweet soy sauce, sold now in some larger supermarkets. If you can't get it, substitute dark soy sauce and a pinch of light muscovado sugar.

SERVES 4

For the meatballs:

25 g (1 oz) fresh or slightly stale breadcrumbs
Milk
340 g (12 oz) minced pork or lamb
1 tablespoon chopped fresh oregano or marjoram
2 tablespoons chopped fresh parsley
2 teaspoons *kecap manis* (optional)
Salt and pepper
Olive oil, for frying

For the tomato sauce:

1 onion, chopped
2 garlic cloves, chopped
2 tablespoons olive oil
2 × 400 g (14 oz) tins chopped tomatoes
1 tablespoon tomato purée
1–2 teaspoons sugar
8–10 fresh basil leaves, shredded
100 g (3½ oz) goats' cheese, diced
Salt and pepper

Pre-heat the oven to 200°C/400°F/Gas Mark 6. Soak the breadcrumbs in milk for 10 minutes, then squeeze dry. Mix with the pork, herbs, *kecap manis,* if using, salt and pepper. Roll into walnut-sized balls. Pour enough oil to cover the base into a heavy frying-pan. Heat the oil and then fry the balls in it over a medium heat, until nicely browned and cooked through. Drain briefly on kitchen paper.

To make the tomato sauce, fry the onion and garlic gently in the olive oil. Add all the remaining ingredients, except the basil and goats' cheese, and cook hard until reduced to a very thick sauce. Stir in the basil.

Place the meatballs in a shallow ovenproof serving dish and spoon over the sauce. Scatter the goats' cheese over the top (don't worry that it doesn't cover completely: it's not meant to!). Bake for about 30 minutes, until sizzling and bubbling. Serve hot, with good bread and a green salad.

Piers' Baked Goats' Cheese

Piers Fielden uses his own cheeses to grill or bake in a hot oven. He likes to serve them with home-made gooseberry jam, whose sweet tartness brings out the full flavour of the warm cheese. If he runs out of jam, he may smear a little pesto over the bread instead. Instead of gooseberry jam, you could try redcurrant jelly or a fruity chutney. For a more substantial first course, serve on a bed of dressed, mixed green leaves.

Cut the rounds of cheese from a drum-shaped cheese, slicing off the rind at either end but leaving it on around the circumference. If you prefer, use slices cut from a longer log of goats' cheese.

PER PERSON

1 slice of French bread or half a slice of sturdy sour-dough bread or *pain de campagne*

Butter (optional)

Pesto (bought or home-made, see **page 30****) optional**

1 disc of goats' cheese, around 2 cm (3/4 inch) thick

Gooseberry jam, redcurrant jelly or chutney, to serve

Pre-heat the oven to 220°C/425°F/Gas Mark 7 or pre-heat the grill thoroughly. Toast the bread lightly and then lay it on a baking sheet. Butter lightly if you wish, or spread with a little pesto. Lay the cheese on top and either bake or grill until nicely browned. Serve immediately, with gooseberry jam, redcurrant jelly or chutney.

mascarpone

Mascarpone is a cream cheese. True enough, but it bears no comparison with our cream cheeses, except that they are all white, soft dairy products. Mascarpone is a phenomenally rich cream cheese, more like impossibly over-the-top cream than any recognizable cheese. This is definitely not a product for the cholesterol-conscious, though it may be comforting to note that it is not as sinful as clotted cream, weighing in with a mere 40 per cent butterfat as opposed to 55 per cent for its Cornish cousin.

Cheese though it may be, mascarpone is actually used more like cream. It is just soft enough to dollop on top of puddings, like the very best clotted cream. Its taste is sweetish but basically neutral, making it a ready vehicle for other ingredients and an easy way to impart a generous slurp of luxury to all kinds of sweet and savoury dishes. It has become something of an essential in the fashionable world of cooking. No smart menu is complete without at least one item seduced by the velvet touch of mascarpone.

My first encounter with it was when I spent a month studying in Perugia in Italy. Halfway down one of the wide stairways that scaled the heights of the town was what I remember as an unusually fine delicatessen, stocking the best of local products and oddities from abroad. The strangest of all were tins of ants in soy sauce from Japan, something I have never seen anywhere else and a decidedly bizarre find. The mascarpone – a far safer culinary novelty – sat wrapped in muslin in the cool cabinet, well protected from the ravages of the August heat. Not quite sure what to do with it, and bereft of any kitchen paraphernalia, we spread it in the sandwiches we made for our lunch. No doubt the idea was not remotely original (very little is when it comes to food), but it is interesting to see it surfacing again in this country.

Buying Mascarpone

In Italy, the farmhouse mascarpone is the stuff to search out but, in this country, you will have to make do with commercial mascarpone packed into small plastic tubs. Most big supermarkets now sell it – they had to lay in stocks once we discovered *tiramisù*, that lovely, boozy pudding that has become the Italian restaurant equivalent of Black Forest gateau. Once you have the mascarpone, it is a doddle to put together (for recipes, look in any general Italian cookery book).

Store the mascarpone in the fridge and consume by the use-by date.

Using Mascarpone

Mascarpone is lovely just as it is with warm puddings, particularly dark fruit pies (it half-melts and oozes down over them), or spooned straight on to fruit compotes, cold fruit tarts and the like. It is solid enough to shape into quenelles (in other words, small rugby ball-shaped dollops made with a pair of warmed dessertspoons). If you have the time and patience, these can make very pretty additions to plated desserts.

You can make mascarpone airier by folding in some whipped cream, or sweeten it slightly if that suits. In Italy, it is often used to make a *crema di mascarpone*, almost a mousse made of mascarpone sweetened with sugar (or you could use honey), perked up with a dash of rum, scented with a drop of vanilla essence and softened with egg yolks. The whisked egg whites are folded in to give a moussey texture and then the whole lot is spooned into wine glasses and dusted with cocoa before serving.

Similar ingredients form the basis of *tiramisù* and it was while making this pudding in front of an audience on a hot summer's day that I discovered that mascarpone can curdle when beaten with other ingredients. Very embarrassing it was, too. Now I make sure that the mascarpone stays cool in the fridge until the moment it is needed.

When heated, mascarpone melts rather pleasantly which means it can make a brilliant quick, creamy sauce for pasta, stirred straight into the hot cooked pasta along with freshly grated Parmesan and perhaps some fine strips of ham, or sautéed mushrooms (or both).

Grilled Aubergine Sandwich with Mascarpone and Sun-Dried Tomatoes

We filmed the titles for the television series one chilly November day, popping in and out of shops and calling at food stalls the length of London's Portobello Road and the adjoining Goldborne Road (a Mecca for anyone who likes Moroccan or Portuguese food). At lunchtime, we found ourselves under the flyover where the best of the market ends and dived into the Portobello Café for a quick lunch. The grilled aubergine sandwich with mascarpone and sun-dried tomatoes, sluiced down by a big mug of very British tea, was exactly what I needed to get me through the rest of the day.

SERVES 1

2 slices of aubergine, cut about 2 cm (3/4 inch) thick, from stalk to stem end
Olive oil
2 generous tablespoons mascarpone
1/3–1/2 ciabatta loaf, split in half and warmed through in the oven, or 2 large slices of sturdy *pain de campagne* or sour-dough bread, lightly toasted
4 halves of sun-dried tomato, cut into strips
Salt and lots of freshly ground pepper

If you have time, salt the slices of aubergine lightly and leave for 30–60 minutes, to degorge. Wipe dry, and then brush with olive oil and grill under a thoroughly pre-heated grill, fairly close to the heat, until browned on both sides and tender through and through. Leave to cool until tepid. Spread the mascarpone on the cut sides of the ciabatta, or on each slice of bread. Season with salt and pepper. Sandwich the aubergine and the sun-dried tomatoes between the pieces of bread. Eat quickly, while still warm.

Opposite *Grilled Aubergine Sandwich with Mascarpone and Sun-dried Tomatoes*

Rich Mascarpone Custard Tart

SERVES 6–8

For the pastry:

125 g (4 oz) unsalted butter, softened

50 g (2 oz) caster sugar

1 large egg

250 g (8 oz) plain flour

A pinch of salt

For the filling:

300 ml (10 fl oz) single cream

1 vanilla pod, slit open

5 egg yolks

100 g (3½ oz) caster sugar

100 g (3½ oz) mascarpone

Finely grated zest of 1 lime

1 tablespoon lime juice

Ground cinnamon or icing sugar, to serve

To make the pastry, cream the butter with the sugar in a food processor, until light and fluffy. Add the egg and process until smoothly mixed. Sift the flour with a pinch of salt and add to the processor. Mix until smooth and then gather up into a ball. Wrap in cling film and let the pastry rest in the fridge for half an hour.

Pre-heat the oven to 180°C/350°F/Gas Mark 4. Line a deep 20 cm (8 inch) tart tin with the pastry and then leave it to relax again in the fridge for half an hour.

Prick the pastry base with a fork, line it with greaseproof paper or cooking foil, weight it down with baking beans and bake blind for 20 minutes.

Remove the beans and paper and return the pastry case to the oven for another 5–10 minutes to dry out, without letting it brown. Reduce the oven temperature to 170°C/325°F/Gas Mark 3.

To make the filling, put the cream into a pan, with the vanilla pod, and bring it gently up to the boil. Turn the heat down as low as possible, cover and leave to infuse for 15 minutes.

Beat the egg yolks with the caster sugar until pale and mousse-like. Gradually pour in the hot cream, stirring constantly. Strain a little of the mixture on to the mascarpone and beat it in, to slacken it. Now strain the remainder into the mascarpone, add the lime zest and juice and mix thoroughly but don't overwork. Pour the custard into the pastry case and bake for about 40–50 minutes, until the custard is virtually set but still has a hint of a wobble in the centre. This is best eaten warm but is good cold, too. Either way, dust it lightly with a little cinnamon or icing sugar before serving.

crème fraiche

When it comes to cream, there's a definite air of the grass being greener on the other side. In this case, the other side of the Channel and it's not so much the hue of the chlorophyll in the grass the cows eat, but what happens to the milk they produce. French cooks and chefs are deeply envious of our range of single, whipping and double creams while, on this side, we've taken a considerable fancy to their crème fraiche. As it happens, we are far luckier than the French. Though they do have their own *crème fleurette*, pouring cream, they are hard put to lay their hands on what we regard as commonplace creams. We, on the other hand, have only to walk into a decent sized big-name supermarket to find tubs of crème fraiche jostling for space on the shelves of the chill cabinet.

Crème fraiche is useless for whipping, but we have whipping and double cream for that, so who cares. Its superiority over other creams lies in its distinct, highly agreeable, slightly sharp taste – a joy compared with the blandness of your average tub of double cream – and its thick, voluptuous texture.

Both taste and texture are the gifts of a whole host of munificent bacteria. Like yoghurt, crème fraiche is not fresh in the strictest sense, but a substance created by introducing a bacterial culture to cream (or milk, in the case of yoghurt). The souring bacteria multiply and produce lactic acid and it is this acid, rather than the bacteria themselves, that makes the cream curdle and thicken so very deliciously. Though butterfat levels vary considerably most crème fraiche is about as rich as whipping cream – with around 35 per cent butterfat and has fewer calories than double cream or butter, which is always a consoling thought.

Buying and Storing Crème Fraiche:

Buying isn't a problem, here, now that crème fraiche has claimed its place on most decent-sized supermarket shelves. The commercial crème fraiche is fabulous stuff, but it can get better, and more over the top, still. Small producers in this country are just beginning to make their own crème fraiche and it is increasingly available from delicatessens. When it is good, it can be outrageously good, sometimes a little sharper than the French version, usually more characterful, and as rich as Croesus. Look out for it.

I am not so sure about the reduced-fat crème fraiche. I've never bought it. I can't see the point. Crème fraiche is all about spoiling yourself and indulgence. If the fat content or the calories scare you, ignore it altogether and stick with yoghurt. Besides, I suspect that it won't work as a substitute for full-fat crème fraiche in cooking, either. It certainly won't create the unctuous, silky sauce that you get from the original.

Kept in the fridge, crème fraiche has a longer shelf-life than ordinary cream but be guided by the use-by date.

Using Crème Fraiche

Spooned straight from the pot, crème fraiche is the most brilliant accompaniment to an endless number of puddings – I can think of nothing nicer with a slice of sticky *tarte Tatin*, or a sweet fruit compote. Decked out with a few chopped chives, it works just as well on many savoury dishes – with blinis or golden corncakes, as a floater on soups, or even spooned on to baked potatoes.

To transform into a dressing for salads, add a slurp of wine vinegar or lemon juice, thin with a little milk or oil if you wish, and add salt, pepper and lots of chopped fresh herbs. This is excellent with globe artichokes or as a dressing for a potato salad.

Crème fraiche is the French cook's not-so-secret weapon when it comes to making sauces. It liquefies as it heats up but never separates because of the super-high butterfat content. There's nothing like it for jazzing up simple ingredients to turn them into dishes for fancier occasions. You might, for instance, fry slices of chicken breast and then de-glaze the pan with a slug of white wine or vermouth and finish with a few dollops of cream. Pop a sprig of tarragon or rosemary in with it, then boil the sauce down to a fetching consistency, and you have an elegant last-minute dish for dinner.

Salade Cauchoise

From the chalky hills and valleys of the Pays de Caux in northern France comes this salad of ham, potatoes and celery, traditionally bound together with crème fraiche. It would usually be served as a first course though, in fact, it is sturdy enough to make an excellent main course for a light lunch or summer supper, or as part of a buffet. Mix all the ingredients together shortly before eating. Left sitting around, the salad can become claggy.

SERVES 4

500 g (1 lb 2 oz) waxy salad potatoes or new potatoes
1 tablespoon tarragon or white wine vinegar
5 celery sticks, trimmed and thinly sliced (reserve a few of the leaves, if available, to garnish)
100 g (4oz) high quality cooked ham, cut into small strips
7–8 tablespoons crème fraiche
2 tablespoons chopped fresh tarragon leaves
Salt and pepper

Cook the potatoes in their skins, until just tender. Drain, cool slightly, and then slice and peel as well as you can. Place in a bowl while still warm and drizzle over the vinegar. Season with salt and pepper, then turn the potatoes gently to mix. Leave to cool.

Add the celery and ham and then carefully stir in the crème fraiche – enough to coat well but not so much that it is overwhelming – and the tarragon. Taste and adjust the seasonings, then pile the salad in a shallow dish and garnish with reserved celery leaves, or a sprig of tarragon.

Ragout of Veal with Fennel and Shallots

Veal, fennel and lemon are happy companions and here they meet in a light ragout bound with a sauce of crème fraiche. Instead of using a purpose-made stock for the base of the sauce, the cooking water from the vegetables is boiled down to concentrate the flavour. This results in a lovely, pure-tasting sauce. When buying veal, do look out for pink meat that has been raised in Britain. Then you can rest assured that it has not been cruelly crated.

SERVES 4

12 small shallots
2 fennel bulbs
60 g (2 oz) butter
1 tablespoon sunflower oil
650 g (1 lb 6 oz) fillet, rump or loin of veal, cut into 2–3 cm (1–1 1/4 inch) cubes
6 tablespoons crème fraiche
Finely grated zest of 1 lemon
Salt and pepper
A squeeze of lemon juice

Leave the shallots in their skins, merely topping and tailing them. Trim the fennel, saving a few of the feathery green fronds. Cut each bulb into six or eight wedges, depending on size. Blanch the shallots, in their skins, in a pan of boiling water, for 4 minutes. Scoop out and drain thoroughly and then slip off their skins. Blanch the fennel wedges in the same water until half cooked – about 5 minutes but this will depend on their size. Scoop out and drain thoroughly. Don't throw out the cooking water but let it boil down to concentrate the flavours, while you get on with the rest of the preparation.

Make sure that the shallots and fennel are dry. Heat half the butter, with the oil. Fry the shallots and the fennel over a brisk heat until patched with brown. Set aside. Add the remaining butter to the pan, dry the pieces of veal and then brown them in the butter. Pour off excess fat and return the vegetables to the pan, along with about 300 ml (10 fl oz) of their reduced cooking water. Simmer for 5 minutes, until the veal is just cooked and then boil the sauce for a little longer to reduce the liquid to a few tablespoonfuls. Now add the cream and lemon zest, bring up to the boil and simmer for a few final minutes, until it has reduced to a satisfying consistency. Season with salt, pepper and a squeeze or two of lemon juice.

Tomates à la Crème

Fried tomatoes with a touch of indulgence. With their rich cream sauce, they make a marvellous accompaniment to plainly cooked meat. You could also serve them as a first course on slices of toast or, better still, fried bread.

SERVES 4

500 g (1 lb 2 oz) medium-sized tomatoes
Sunflower oil
150 ml (5 fl oz) crème fraiche
Chopped fresh parsley
Salt and pepper

Cut the tomatoes in half horizontally (that is, through the middle, rather than from stalk to stem end). Oil a heavy-based frying-pan lightly and set it over a high heat. Leave until searingly hot. Lay the tomatoes in it, cut-sides down, and cook for 30–60 seconds until browned underneath. Turn the other way up and reduce the heat. Cook for another minute or so and then spoon in the cream, parsley, salt and pepper. Simmer for a further 3–4 minutes, until the cream is reduced to a rich sauce. Taste and adjust the seasonings and serve.

Mango and Cardamom Gratin

This gratin was inspired by a dish from the south-west of France. Replacing the original peaches with mango and cardamom turns it into a most exotic pudding, best eaten warm from the oven.

SERVES 4–6

2 medium-sized mangoes
4 green cardamom pods
75 g (2½ oz) caster sugar
250 ml (8 fl oz) crème fraiche
1 egg, lightly beaten

Pre-heat the oven to 180°C/350°F/Gas Mark 4. Using a sharp knife, slice the unpeeled mangoes, cutting down towards the stones and easing the slices off, gradually working your way along and around the stones. Trim the skin off the slices and put them into a bowl. Slit open the cardamom pods and extract the black seeds. Crush to a powder with a little of the sugar. Sprinkle over the mango slices, together with about two-thirds of the remaining sugar. Leave to marinate for a few minutes, or up to an hour.

Lay the slices snugly in an oval gratin dish. Beat the cream with the egg and pour over. Let it settle and sprinkle with the rest of the sugar. Bake for 30–40 minutes, until lightly browned.

mozzarella

We wanted to treat ourselves to a long weekend on Italy's Amalfi coast, but flights to Naples were fully booked so we flew into Rome and drove down the coastal road to the south. As we neared Naples, the small shops on either side of the road were festooned with clusters of wooden *mozzarelle*, white paint blistered and flaking in the salt air. The reclaimed coastland was so flat and dull, the buildings so square and charmless, often in a sorry state of disrepair, the temperature so hot and the air so arid, that the area began to take on its own romance. We felt like we were in a black-and-white Italian road movie. We were driving through Mozzarella Country and, instead of cowboys and cattle, the fields were dotted with water buffalo. Eventually, we stopped at one of the shacks that lined the monotonous road for a drink and something to eat. Minutes later, we emerged with two bottles of ice-cold beer and a couple of rolls filled with the freshest mozzarella I have ever eaten. Mild, milky, tender and moist, this was the real McCoy.

Indian water buffalo were brought to Italy in the sixteenth century and are still bred and raised in a few areas for their milk. The mozzarella made from their rich milk looks like cows' milk mozzarella, is stored like cows' milk mozzarella in whey and pulls out into strings like cows' milk mozzarella when heated, but its texture and taste (and yes, it really does have a taste) are quite different and infinitely superior. As it happens, I do like cows' milk mozzarella but it is just not in the same league.

Both cheeses are made in much the same way. The pale curds are broken up and heated until they stretch like knicker elastic, at which point they are known as *pasta filata*. The threads are wound back up, small rounds of cheese are lopped off (*mozzare* means 'to cut off') and finally packaged, afloat in their own whey, in factories or sent out in tubs of whey.

Buying and Storing Mozzarella

Commercial mozzarella, made from cows' milk, is a strange cheese, bland-tasting and not unpleasantly rubbery. Let me make it clear that here I'm talking about Italian mozzarella and not the rectangular blocks of bleached tyre-substitute from other countries which wings its way into our shops masquerading as mozzarella. I wouldn't touch that stuff with a bargepole.

Cows' milk mozzarella is widely available now and *mozzarella di bufala* (buffalo-milk mozzarella) is moving out of the delicatessens and into smarter supermarkets. It is inevitably more expensive, but worth it every now and then. In delicatessens, you may also come across *bocconcini*, mini-*mozzarelle*, perfect for serving as part of a mixed *antipasto*.

Mozzarella is meant to be eaten fresh. Once the packet has been opened, unused mozzarella and its bath of cloudy whey should be transferred to a bowl. Add enough lightly salted water to cover the cheese and store in the fridge for up to four days.

Using Mozzarella

Save *mozzarella di bufala* for eating uncooked. It is too delicious and refreshing to melt into a medley of other ingredients, unless you are feeling flush. I love it eaten just as it is, seasoned with a little salt and pepper or perhaps accompanied with a thin slice of Parmesan. The overworked mozzarella and tomato salad (and avocado, if you want to go for the full *tricolore* Italian flag effect) that has become a staple of bistros takes on a whole new lease of life when it is made with high summer, sweet tomatoes, buffalo-milk mozzarella, fresh basil and the best olive oil.

Cows' milk mozzarella is pleasant enough eaten raw or in salads, though it doesn't make much of a mark. Far better to enjoy it cooked, on a pizza, in baked dishes of vegetables or lasagne, with pasta, or wherever the teasingly stretchy threads of molten cheese will be welcome. Don't expect to get much flavour out of it – for that you'll need to add some parmesan, or other lively seasonings – but just enjoy the texture.

Pasta with Three Cheeses

A simple pasta dish but one that always pleases and is very quick to cook. The sweetness of the fried onion balances the cheesiness of all those cheeses. For some reason, I have particularly taken to *orechiette*, 'ear-shaped' pasta, recently. I enjoy the feel of its curves against my tongue but any pasta shape will do perfectly well in its place.

SERVES 4

400–500 g (14–18 oz) *orechiette* or other pasta shapes
2 onions, sliced
5 tablespoons olive oil
140 g (5 oz) mozzarella, diced
110 g (4 oz) dolcelatte, diced
60 g (2 oz) Parmesan, freshly grated
2 tablespoons chopped fresh parsley
Salt and pepper

Tip the *orechiette* into salted, boiling water and cook until *al dente*.

Meanwhile, fry the onions in 3 tablespoons of the olive oil, until nicely browned. Set aside, with their oil. Re-heat as soon as the pasta is cooked. Drain the pasta and, while it's still piping hot, tip it into a bowl and toss with the cheeses, fried onions, pepper and a little bit of salt. Sprinkle with parsley and serve.

Aubergine Baked with Pesto and Mozzarella

This dish of aubergine layered with mozzarella and pesto and baked in the oven makes a good main course, or can be served as a rich side dish, accompanying plainly barbecued meat. It tastes best if you make the time to whizz up your own pesto, but you can always substitute bought pesto.

SERVES 6–8

2 large aubergines, sliced about 1 cm (1/2 inch) thick
Salt
Olive oil
5–6 tablespoons pesto (see page 30)
2 x 140 g (5 oz) mozzarella cheeses, diced
60 g (2 oz) Parmesan, freshly grated
Pepper

For the tomato sauce:

675 g (1 lb 8 oz) ripest red tomatoes
2 garlic cloves, chopped
2 tablespoons olive oil
Fresh thyme sprig
Salt and pepper
Sugar (optional)

Pre-heat the oven to 190°C/375°F/Gas Mark 5. Lay the slices of aubergine out and sprinkle with salt. Leave for half and hour or so to degorge their juices.

Wipe the aubergine slices clean and lay on oiled baking sheets. Brush lightly with olive oil. Bake in the oven for about 20 minutes, until golden brown and tender.

Meanwhile, make the tomato sauce. Cover the tomatoes with boiling water, leave for a minute and then drain and skin. De-seed and chop roughly. Put the garlic and olive oil into a frying-pan and heat over a moderate heat, until the garlic begins to sizzle and colour. Now add the tomatoes and thyme, and boil fiercely for 5–10 minutes, until the tomatoes have collapsed and the sauce is fairly thick. Season to taste with salt, pepper and a little sugar if it is on the sharp side.Discard the thyme stalk.

Down to the final stage. Oil a 30 cm (12 inch) gratin dish and make a bed of about one-third of the aubergine slices in it. Smear with half the pesto, add a thin coat of tomato sauce and then scatter with half the diced mozzarella. Season with pepper. Repeat the layers once more. Now finish with the last of the aubergine, and cover with the last of the tomato sauce. Sprinkle with Parmesan and drizzle over a little oil. Bake for 30–40 minutes, until browned and bubbling. Serve hot or warm.

Neapolitan Crostini

Anchovies, mozzarella and blood-red tomatoes are all part and parcel of southern Italian cooking. Essential flavours for the hot sun, and well met on these baked *crostini*. They could be served as a first course, as a pre-dinner taste-tickler with drinks or even as the focus of a light lunch, accompanied by salads. It's very difficult to be precise about the amount of bread you will need, as this is dictated more by the size of the loaf than anything else: you need as many slices as will allow you to to cut 16 broad fingers.

Although I've suggested cutting the bread into fingers, there's absolutely no reason why you shouldn't take liberties and make your *crostini* whatever shape takes your fancy.

SERVES 4–8

4–8 thick slices of good bread, crusts removed
Butter, softened
8 anchovy fillets
2 × 140 g (5 oz) mozzarella cheeses, sliced
3 ripe tomatoes, skinned, de-seeded and cut into long strips
Dried oregano
Salt and pepper

Pre-heat the oven to 180°C/350°F/Gas Mark 4. Butter the bread slices generously on one side and cut them into 16 fingers. Butter a baking tray and lay the bread, butter-side up, on it. Cut the anchovy fillets in half lengthways. Now lay slices of mozzarella, trimmed to fit, on each piece of bread, and put a couple of strips of tomato and a strip of anchovy across the mozzarella. Season with a little salt and pepper and a pinch or two of oregano. Bake for 20–30 minutes, until the mozzarella is melting and the bread crisp. Eat while the *crostini* are as hot as is bearable.

fromage frais

F*romage frais* is the French for 'fresh cheese' and that about sums it up. Not that fromage frais is at all cheesy in taste or consistency. This is cheese at its very earliest stage, the milk thickened with rennet and drained of whey, as fresh and milky and tender as can be. When I was a child, I used to go with my mother to buy fromage frais from the farm at the top of the village in France where we stayed every year. It was an unnerving expedition that I relished. The unnerving part was the big farm dogs that yapped and barked and rattled their chains. I knew they were securely tethered, which made them comfortably scary. The bit that I relished was walking into the small dairy room to collect the soft curds in their pierced container – the *faisselle* – knowing there would be fromage frais and apricot jam for pudding that night.

What we get here now, brought over in the main from France, is really, I believe, *fromage frais battu*, in other words, fromage frais beaten to smooth it out. The *battu* seems to have been lost along the way. Not only has commercial fromage frais been smoothed out but it has been enriched with cream to take it up to 4 per cent, or better still 8 per cent, butterfat. There is also a very low-fat fromage frais, with just a negligible 0.1 per cent fat. It is a real treat when you are watching calories (far nicer than most low-fat plain yoghurts, I find), though it inevitably has a drier feel in the mouth than its more voluptuous siblings.

Fromage frais, sprinkled with sugar or, better still, eaten with a generous spoonful of high-quality jam and maybe a crisp biscuit of some sort, is the kind of quick pudding that I love. It is also the perfect base for dips – spiced up with garlic and herbs, perhaps – or it can be used to make Indian raitas. In terms of cooking, it is remarkably similar to Greek yoghurt and should be treated in much the same way, with equal care and consideration.

Greek yoghurt

I can distinctly remember my first encounters with Greek yoghurt, when I was 14 and on a working holiday (for my father, at least) in Greece. One happy meeting came after a long, hot trail around some notable ruin. I haven't the faintest idea which one but I do remember the yoghurt. The site café has probably been modernized by now but I hope the yoghurt hasn't been displaced. It came in its own, small, rough earthenware pot (so much nicer than a plastic tub) and was sealed in with its own thick crust of cream. The yoghurt itself was a revelation, so smooth, slippery and rich after the thin yoghurts we were used to. On that same holiday, we lunched at a dairy on Omonia square in Athens, finishing our meal with wedges of yoghurt, cut this time from a larger bowl but still crusted, and sweetened with Hymettus honey.

The Greek or Greek-style yoghurt that we get here never seems quite so remarkable and sensuous but perhaps that is more to do with romantic memory than reality. I'm not really complaining; I love it anyway and our fridge is always equipped with at least one big tub of Greek yoghurt. It is still the next best thing to cream and better in some instances, neither as cloying nor as sickly. Of course, it also makes you feel that little bit more virtuous: yoghurt has such a healthy image and always tastes fresh, even when the calories are not insignificant.

A hint of yoghurty sourness goes supremely well with very sticky, sugary puddings of all kinds, and there are few better simple desserts than a bowl of yoghurt, mixed with fresh fruit or nuts and raisins and drizzled with really good, fragrant honey. In the summer, Greek yoghurt is a worthy substitute for cream in fruit fools. I use it in mousses, too, and in set creams. It is brilliant for all those Indian yoghurt-based curries but should be treated respectfully when cooking other dishes. Like most yoghurts, it will curdle if overheated, creating a mass of tough, unsightly, polystyrene-like globules. If you want to use Greek yoghurt to enrich a sauce, let the liquid stop bubbling and cool slightly, then stir in the yoghurt a tablespoonful at a time. Even if the first one or two do suffer from heat stroke, they will cool the sauce sufficiently to prevent the remainder from curdling and no one will be any the wiser.

Greek yoghurt can be used in quiche fillings and other cooked dishes where eggs and/or flour will help to stabilize it; cook them at a relatively low temperature to prevent separation.

ricotta

Italian ricotta is a light, cool cheese, with a delicate milky flavour verging on the bland. Quite how bland depends on the milk it is made from and how it is made. The best ricotta I've ever tasted was made from unpasteurized sheeps' milk and cooked up over smoking fires in huge open vats in a Sicilian shepherd's dairy – the kind of place and process that would give a British health inspector a heart attack. Most ricotta, however, is made from pasteurized cows' milk, under suitably hygienic conditions that ensure a uniform product but diminish its gentle character.

The word *ricotta* means 'recooked' and the cheese is made from milk that has been, literally, twice heated. The first time round it is warmed through to make a firm cheese that will age. The whey that is drained off is then heated again, until white clots of ricotta rise to the surface to form a thick white crust. The crust is scooped off and then drained in curved baskets (these days usually made of pierced plastic), which lightly mould the curds into a pure, snowy white dome. A true case of waste not want not, ricotta is the reward for thriftiness.

From time to time, you may come across two, more pungent, forms of ricotta that take it into the realms of more cheesey cheeses. Whole domes of soft ricotta may sometimes be smoked and salted to a more enduring firmness and pronounced flavour. *Ricotta salata*, salted ricotta, is as hard as fresh ricotta is soft. It is made by extracting the curds at a high temperature and then salting and drying them slowly.

Buying and Storing Ricotta

Many supermarkets now sell tubs of long-life ricotta in their chill cabinets, but I can't say that I like the stuff very much, since it has a cloying density that does not belong to proper ricotta. It's an expensive way of buying ricotta, too. When it comes down to it, convenience is its only selling point.

Fresh ricotta has a very short shelf-life, lasting no more than a couple of days before it starts to develop an unpleasant bitterness. The best place to buy ricotta, then, is in an Italian delicatessen frequented by Italians, where they stock freshly made ricotta that is sold quickly and replaced several times a week. Usually, it will have been made in this country, rather than in romantic Italy, but the shorter travelling time should mean that it is fresher.

Some places sell vacuum-packed ricotta that has a prolonged shelf-life though, once the pack has been opened, it must be used just as swiftly as the fresh version. I think it suffers slightly from such treatment, but vacuum-packed ricotta is still a far better bet than the mean little long-life tubs.

Store fresh ricotta in the fridge and use it within 24 hours of purchase. The same applies to vacuum-packed ricotta and long-life ricotta, once opened.

Using Ricotta

Ricotta's mildness or blandness, however you care to look at it, is also its chief virtue, making it an ideal vehicle for both subtle and bold flavours. Vanilla, chocolate, dried and candied fruit, honey and lemon regularly step out with ricotta in Italian puddings. Frequent savoury companions are Parmesan (a diametric opposite in cheese terms), spinach, chard, ham and nutmeg.

Ricotta is often used as a filling for pasta of one sort or another, and in pies and *strüdels*. In puddings, it can form the basis of a cheesecake, such as the *Almond, Honey and Ricotta Cheesecake* (see page 300), or be used as a filling. Italian ricotta tends to be softer than much of the ricotta I've bought here and, when sieved, it can be beaten to a creamy purée. If I'm following an Italian recipe, I often find that I need to add a dash of milk to ricotta, to loosen the texture. Sieved and beaten with a little single cream, sweetened with vanilla sugar or caster sugar and a few drops of vanilla essence, ricotta makes an excellent accompaniment to soft summer fruit.

Frittata con Ricotta e Basilico

A mild, thick ricotta 'omelette', flavoured with Parmesan and basil and served with a brassy, uncooked tomato sauce.

SERVES 4
350 g (12 oz) ricotta
6 eggs
5 tablespoons freshly grated Parmesan
A small handful of fresh basil leaves, roughly torn up
2 tablespoons finely chopped fresh parsley
1 tablespoon olive oil
Salt and pepper

For the sauce:
500 g (1 lb 2 oz) best, ripest tomatoes, skinned, de-seeded and finely diced
1–2 tablespoons balsamic vinegar
1/2 red onion, very finely diced
4 tablespoons olive oil
1–2 garlic cloves, crushed
Salt, pepper and sugar

Make the sauce first. Mix all the ingredients, cover and leave for at least an hour before using. Taste and adjust the seasoning, adding a pinch of sugar if needed.

Beat the ricotta with the eggs and then beat in the Parmesan, basil, parsley, salt and a generous dose of black pepper.

Heat the oil in a 25 cm (10 inch) frying-pan over a moderate heat. Add the ricotta mixture. Fry until the eggs are just set underneath and the omelette comes away freely from the base of the pan. As it cooks, push the set egg up with a spatula, so that the runny mixture can trickle down to the bottom. When the fritatta is just set, run the spatula or a knife around the edge to loosen it and then invert it on to a plate. Return the pan to the heat, and slide the frittata back into it, uncooked side down. Give it a minute or two to colour and then slide the whole thing out on to a serving plate. Cut into wedges and serve piping hot, with the cool tomato sauce.

Sweet Baked Ricotta

An Australian recipe, though I imagine inspired by Italian ricotta desserts, this comes from the Bather's Pavilion Restaurant, which overlooks the beach at Balmoral, near Sydney. There they serve it with grilled peach halves, though I like it with all manner of fruit. Try quartering some figs, without cutting them right through, dusting them with icing sugar and popping them under the grill for a few minutes and then serving them hot, with the cool baked ricotta. In the autumn, the ricotta goes well with a compote of blackberries, or poached pears or quinces. In winter and early spring, try it with lightly cooked forced or garden rhubarb or with the Prunes Cooked in Marsala and Orange on page 308.

Whatever you choose to serve it with, bake the ricotta a day in advance, so that it has time to firm up in the fridge. If the dimensions of the tin you use are different from mine, you may need to vary the cooking time a little accordingly, so allow plenty of time and judge whether it is done by eye.

SERVES 8
800 g (1 3/4 lb) ricotta
2 eggs
1 vanilla pod
200 g (7 oz) icing sugar

Pre-heat the oven to 170°C/325°F/Gas Mark 3. You will need a non-stick loaf tin about 22 cm (9 inches) long by 12 cm (5 inches) wide by 6 cm (2½ inches) deep. If you don't have a non-stick tin, line the one you have with cooking foil and brush the foil with almond or groundnut oil.

Sieve the ricotta and then beat it with the eggs (or process the two together). Slit open the vanilla pod and scrape the seeds out into the ricotta mixture. Sift in the icing sugar and mix thoroughly. Spoon into the loaf tin, smooth down, and cover with foil. Place the tin in a slightly larger baking tin and pour in enough hot water to come about halfway up the sides of the loaf tin. Carefully place in the oven and bake for an hour or so, or until barely firm.

Lift the tin out of its water bath and remove the foil. Leave to cool and then cover with cling film and refrigerate. When it is thoroughly chilled, you can turn it out of the tin and slice as required. Let it come back to room temperature before you serve it.

Parmesan

The making of Parmesan is a serious business, as well it might be. This isn't just any old cheese that has done well out of clever marketing. Parmigiano Reggiano, to give it its proper name, is about the most perfect cheese that any cook will ever come across. Not just modern cooks, either. As far back as the mid-fourteenth century, people were raving about it.

Six hundred years later, in 1951, the law stepped in to protect Parmesan's good name, laying down strict regulations about production and terminology to guard this king of cheeses from shoddy imitations (it's a pity our own Cheddar was never protected in the same way). Parmigiano Reggiano is the ultimate *Grana Padano* cheese. *Grana* is the name given to a whole collection of Italian cheeses that have a grainy, crystalline consistency, firm enough to be grated. *Padano* refers to the area it is made in, around the Po valley. Parmesan proper is made only in the provinces of Parma, Modena, Bologna, Reggio Emilia and Mantova. Anything made outside the legally defined border cannot bear the famous name.

When I visited the area, I was surprised by the lack of livestock in the fields. No cows in sight (and no pigs for the Parma ham, either). Diet, it turns out, is the first consideration. In order to prevent cows from eating the wrong things they are not allowed to graze willy-nilly but are fed a carefully controlled menu that will not taint the milk.

The cheeses themselves are still made in small factories by traditional methods. It takes around 16 litres (28 pints) of milk to make 1 kg (a generous 2 lb) of finished Parmesan. Each *forma di Parmigiano* weighs in at around 35 kg (70 lb). That's a phenomenal lake of milk per cheese, which can measure up to 45 cm (18 inches) across. As the cheeses mature, they are regularly tested and sampled by highly trained inspectors. Any that do not come up to scratch will not get the prized Parmesan seal of approval. In the local market, I noticed second-grade and young, immature cheeses being sold for a snip, relatively speaking.

Every cheese is matured for at least a year, at which point it is known as *Parmigiano giovane*, 'young Parmesan', a cheese that is primarily eaten as a table cheese. *Vecchio*, 'old', cheese is one and a half to two years old, while the very best, *stravecchio*, 'extra old', will have been matured for at least two years and probably longer.

The result of all this tender, loving care (and a lot of hard slog) is a cheese with an unparalleled depth of flavour, mellow but powerful at the same time, piquant and quite delicious. Hard enough to grate, it will still melt in the mouth. Even mature cheeses, assuming they have been stored properly, particularly after cutting, are ideal for eating, but they remain unchallenged, above all, as the perfect cheese for cooks.

Buying and Storing Parmesan

Even in Italy, Parmesan is expensive, but the compensation is that a little goes a long way. It should always be bought in a lump and grated only when needed, as the flavour diminishes rapidly once grated (that awful sawdust sold in plastic tubs bears no resemblance to the real thing). Supermarket plastic-wrapped pieces of Parmesan are fine, but store the piece in the fridge, wrapped in foil. Be sure to open the foil up at least every couple of days so that the cheese can breathe. If you come back from Italy clutching a colossal wedge of finest Parmesan, the best way to keep it for the long term is to freeze it, broken up first into more useful-sized bits. In emergencies, it can be grated straight from frozen.

Using Parmesan

Don't relegate Parmesan to nothing but pasta and cooked dishes. If it is in good condition it makes a great table cheese. Try serving it, thinly sliced, with

Opposite *Marinated Parmesan and Mozzarella with Garlic, Capers and Lemon*

mozzarella di bufala (see page 233). A bite of the two together is a joy. It is excellent, too, with pears or apples or, in the old Italian style, with thinly sliced fennel (rather as we eat celery with cheese).

The true glory of Parmesan, though, is as a cooking cheese. The great depth of flavour means that it takes only a relatively small amount of cheese to make a considerable impact on something like a béchamel or white sauce, without overloading it with heavy fat and making it greasy. Added to stuffings and dumplings, it helps to fuse the elements together as they cook, melting imperceptibly into the whole. It is essential in risotti, always stirred in at the end to thicken and enrich. Naturally, Parmesan and pasta go together hand in glove (though Italians frown on sprinkling it over many seafood pasta dishes). There's nothing quite like it for finishing off gratins, especially vegetable gratins, either sprinkled generously on the top on its own or mixed with breadcrumbs for a thicker, crisper layer.

Although Parmesan is usually grated for cooking, it has become very fashionable to scatter paper-thin shavings of the cheese over dishes as an appealing and appetising finishing touch. To shave Parmesan, use an ordinary vegetable peeler as your razor.

Sautéed Squash with Parmesan

We liked this a lot. Even the baby gobbled it down and, even more surprisingly, my fussy three-year-old loved it. Parents had to guard the remains for themselves. The sweet mealiness of butternut squash fried in butter is enhanced by the saltiness of the Parmesan. Together, they make a side dish that is good enough to eat as a course on its own.

SERVES 4

1 medium-sized butternut squash or about 675 g (1 1/2 lb) chunk of kabocha, onion or other winter squash, de-seeded and peeled
30 g (1 oz) butter
2 tablespoons olive oil
2 tablespoons finely chopped fresh parsley
45g (1 1/2 oz) Parmesan, finely shaved
Salt and pepper

Cut the squash into 1.5 cm (1/2 inch) cubes. Heat the butter with the oil in a heavy, wide frying-pan. Add the cubes of squash in a single layer. If there are too many to fit comfortably, take the excess out and save for some other dish or discard: you want the squash to fry and not stew in its own juices in an overcrowded pan. Sauté over a moderate heat until evenly browned and tender. Season with salt and pepper. Draw off the heat, stir in the parsley and tip into a serving dish. Scatter over the parmesan and serve immediately.

Marinated Parmesan and Mozzarella with Garlic, Capers and Lemon

Parmesan and mozzarella marinated together in a green dressing make a sensational first course served with ciabatta bread.

SERVES 4–6
1 buffalo-milk mozzarella
150–200 g (5–7 oz) Parmesan
For the dressing:
5 tablespoons olive oil
1 tablespoon lemon juice
Finely grated zest of 1 lemon
1 garlic clove, crushed
2 tablespoons small capers
2 tablespoons finely chopped fresh parsley
Salt and pepper

Slice the mozzarella and Parmesan and arrange alternately on a serving dish.

To make the dressing, whisk the oil into the lemon juice slowly, then stir in all the remaining ingredients. Or put the whole lot into a screw-topped jar, seal and shake to mix. Taste and adjust the seasoning. Spoon over the cheeses, cover and leave for at least an hour before serving.

Parmesan and Polenta Biscuits

These biscuits have a crisp, grainy texture. Eat warm from the oven, with pre-prandial drinks.

MAKES ABOUT 20
100 g (4 oz) fine polenta or cornmeal, plus a little extra for rolling out
50 g (2 oz) plain flour
60 g (2 oz) Parmesan, grated
80 g (3 oz) chilled butter, diced
1 egg, lightly beaten
1 egg yolk
Extra grated Parmesan, or sesame or caraway seeds, to decorate

Pre-heat the oven to 190°C/375°F/Gas Mark 5. Put the polenta or cornmeal, flour and Parmesan in the processor, then add the butter. Process to breadcrumbs, then add enough beaten egg to form a soft, but rollable, dough. Wrap in cling film and chill in the fridge for half an hour.

Roll out thinly to a thickness of about 5 mm (1/4 inch), on a board sprinkled with polenta or cornmeal (or flour if you prefer). Stamp out circles of dough (I use a 6 cm (2 1/2 inch) cutter) and lay them on a baking tray lined with non-stick baking parchment. Mix the egg yolk with 1 tablespoon of cold water, to make an egg wash. Brush the wash over the biscuits and sprinkle them with the Parmesan or seeds. Bake for 10 minutes, until golden brown.

Lift on to a wire rack to cool. Store in an airtight tin if not using immediately.

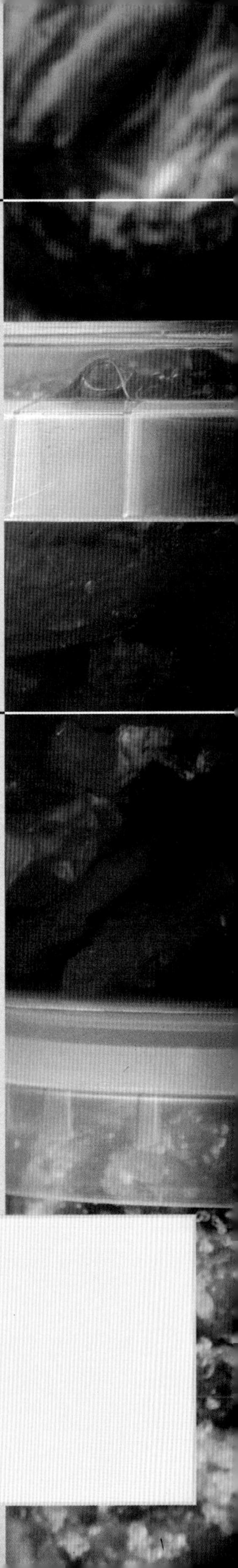

sun-dried
tomatoes

sun-dried
tomatoes in oil

savoury preserves

olives
capers
salted
capers
caper
berries

sun-dried tomatoes

The Italians aren't half so smitten with sun-dried tomatoes as we are. Strange, but true. To a northerner from, say, Milan or Turin, sun-dried tomatoes are a curiosity from the poor south, but not much more than that. It's taken proper cold climate northerners, i.e. us, to show a real fancy for them.

My first glimpse of sun-dried tomatoes was from the window of a rattling train, chugging its way to Sicily through Calabria, the toe of Italy. They weren't actually dried, but drying, spread out on sheets of black polythene on the tarmac of little-used roads. At least, I assume those roads were pretty much traffic-free – the squashed-flat appearance of a piece of sun-dried tomato should be created by natural dehydration, not by grimy tyres! In coastal towns, I saw skeins of dried tomatoes threaded on string and hung up for sale in dark groceries (along with dried aubergines and peppers), and many a repast began with a selection of local salamis and air-dried meats, spiced up with chilli, a few slices of cheese and a bowl of salty, supple sun-dried tomatoes soaked in herb-scented oil. Good enough to make a meal of, which, being an impoverished student, I did whenever possible.

To me, sun-dried tomatoes capture some of the essence of southern Italy. They hold memories of hot sun and have the intense, rich, deep, gutsy flavour that characterizes the local cooking. There's nothing fancy about them, even though they have become so fashionable as to be almost commonplace in British bistro-land. They are plain, simple and honest fare – just fully flavoured tomatoes, salt and, possibly, a few herbs and some olive oil (or cheaper oils for lowlier versions).

Sun is essential. It is necessary first to ripen the tomatoes on the vine to their utmost, tomatoiest, sweetest flavour. Glasshouse tomatoes won't do nearly as well. Then, when the tomatoes are at the height of their sun-blessed season in August, the sun beats down like nature's furnace, sucking out the moisture of the split-open tomatoes, all day long, day after day, concentrating the flavours that it gave in the first place to produce the deep, caramelized, fruity tones that make sun-dried tomatoes what they are. The saltiness, nicely balanced in a high quality product, is introduced when the tomatoes are halved; to get them off to a head start they are salted, to draw out the first wave of watery juice, before the sun gets to work.

Some smarty pants chefs and cooks are getting rather snooty about sun-dried tomatoes – they are becoming a bit too well known and common, you see – but I don't care. I love them, I love using them, and I love eating them and shall continue to do both for a long time yet.

Buying and Storing Sun-Dried Tomatoes

Sun-dried tomatoes come in several different forms. You can buy them fully dried, in packets, unadorned and plain – they will need to be rehydrated to some degree (see below), which means that you can imprint your own personal stamp on them. However, it is probably easier to buy them ready to use in jars of oil. The best are always stored in olive oil (though the calibre of the oil can vary considerably) and will often be animated with sprigs of herbs and maybe some garlic. Most brands are pretty good but you do get what you pay for. A higher price tag generally indicates a classier sun-dried tomato.

Look out, too, for sun-dried tomato purées and creams, which, again, usually come in glass jars but are also sold, rather conveniently, in tubes just like ordinary tomato purée.

As long as the sun-dried tomatoes are completely submerged in their oil, they will keep for months in a cool, dark cupboard. I usually store the puréed versions in the fridge once opened, covering the surface with a thin layer of olive oil to keep the purée fresh.

Using Sun-Dried Tomatoes

If nothing else, serve them straight from the jar as an accompaniment to an Italian *antipasto*, a first course of salamis, cured and cooked hams and, possibly, cheeses, together with some Italian bread, such as warm focaccia or ciabatta.

Once you develop a taste for sun-dried tomatoes, there are endless other options. Cut into strips, they can be scattered over salads (use some of the oil from the jar in the dressing) or tossed into hot pasta, together with fresh, skinned, diced tomato, crushed garlic, basil and olive oil or just with grated Parmesan and butter or olive oil (again, from the jar). I add them to sandwiches (or spread a little of the purée on the buttered bread); they are particularly nice with rocket and mozzarella, or watercress and cream cheese, or with air-dried ham. To make your own sun-dried tomato bread (most of the bought stuff is very disappointing), work them plentifully into white bread dough at the second kneading stage. They are excellent, finely chopped, in stuffings, and give a whole new lease of life to a plain tomato sauce. I often stir a couple of spoonfuls of sun-dried tomato purée into a tomatoey sauce, soup or stew, to give it an extra lift. This is very good in mince dishes, too. When you are making a savoury tart, a thin smear of the purée on the base of the pastry case can be very welcome.

To Rehydrate Fully Sun-Dried Tomatoes

Rinse the tomatoes in a sieve and drain them. Spread them out in a shallow bowl and cover with hot water. Leave for 3–5 minutes and then drain them and take a nibble to see if they are soft, supple and juicy enough. They should still be a little chewy. Don't leave them for too long or too much of their flavour will leach out, leaving a muted, pappy shell. They can be used as they are now but I prefer their flavour when marinated in olive oil with a few aromatics.

To do this, you must first dry the soaked tomatoes *thoroughly* on kitchen paper or a clean tea-towel. Then pack them into jam jars, tucking in sprigs of rosemary and/or thyme, and a few peeled cloves of garlic, as the fancy takes you. You might like to tuck a couple of dried chillies into one jar, for a bit of a kick. Fill the jars to the top with olive oil (or a mixture of half and half olive oil and sunflower oil, if you prefer). Leave to stand for a few hours. Now top up with more oil, making sure that the tomatoes and aromatics are fully covered. Seal tightly and store in the cupboard for a few days before using.

Sun-Dried Tomato and Toasted Walnut Pesto

You can buy red pestos galore in jars from big supermarkets these days, but it is very easy to make your own. This version, held together with toasted walnuts, is superb, though I say it myself. Stir it plentifully into hot pasta for a quick supper – you might like to scatter a few torn-up basil leaves over the top as well – and use any left-over pesto to boost the flavours of tomatoey sauces or stews. I sometimes stir it into mince for something like a cottage pie, or a bastardized version of a bolognese sauce.

You don't have to use the chilli but I reckon it's a good idea. A medium-hot red chilli won't turn it into a fire-raising sauce but it does give an extra lift.

SERVES 4–6 ON PASTA

60 g (2 oz) walnuts

100 g (3½ oz) drained sun-dried tomatoes in oil

3 garlic cloves, roughly chopped

60 g (2 oz) Parmesan, broken into chunks

1 fresh red chilli, de-seeded and roughly chopped (optional)

Oil from the jar of tomatoes

Olive oil

Pre-heat the oven to 200°C/400°F/Gas Mark 6. Spread the walnuts out on a tray and toast them in the oven for 3–4 minutes, shaking once or twice, until browned. Keep an eye on them, as they burn quite easily and then they will be good for nothing but the bin. Tip the browned nuts into a wire sieve and shake the sieve over a sheet of newspaper, to remove loose flakes of papery skin. Leave to cool.

Once cooled, tip the nuts into a food processor and add the sun-dried tomatoes, garlic, Parmesan and chilli, if using. Process until smooth and then, with the motor still running, trickle in enough oil (I use a mixture of tomato oil and olive oil) to give a creamy sauce.

If you want to store the pesto, spoon it into a screw-topped jar, smooth down and cover with a thin layer of olive oil. Screw the lid on tightly and keep in the fridge, where it will last for at least two weeks as long as you remember to cover it anew with olive oil every time you dip into it. It will probably last a good deal longer, in fact, but I can't be sure, because we always eat it up pretty quickly.

Sun-Dried Tomato Bread

MAKES A 450 G (1 LB) LOAF

450 g (1 lb) strong white flour
1 1/2 teaspoons salt
1 sachet easy-blend yeast
1 teaspoon sugar
2 tablespoons olive oil, from the jar of tomatoes
1/2 jar sun-dried tomatoes in olive oil, drained and chopped

Mix the flour with the salt, yeast and sugar. Add the olive oil and enough water to form a soft dough. It is better to err marginally on the damp side, as the flour absorbs a good deal of water as you knead. If the worst comes to the worst, dust overly sticky dough with extra flour as you knead.

Knead the bread energetically for a good 5 minutes, until it is satin-smooth and elastic. Return to the bowl and cover with a damp tea-towel. Leave in a warm place until it has doubled in bulk, which will take around an hour depending on the room temperature.

Punch the dough down, knead briefly and then spread it out as best you can. Dot with half the sun-dried tomatoes, roll up, knead again briefly and then repeat. Give it another quick kneading, to distribute the pieces of sun-dried tomato evenly. Place in a greased, 500 g (1 lb) loaf tin. Cover with a damp tea-towel and again leave to rise in a warm place, until the dough has risen to fill the tin. Pre-heat the oven to 220°C/425°F/Gas Mark 7.

Bake the loaf for about 25–30 minutes, until it is cooked through. To test, turn the tin upside-down and shake the bread out – it should slide out fairly easily. Tap the bottom: if it sounds hollow, the bread is done. If the loaf sticks mercilessly to the tin, or all you get is a dull thud when you tap it, return to the oven for another 5 minutes or so, to finish cooking. Leave the loaf to cool on a wire rack.

Variation

Instead of using pieces of sun-dried tomato, use sun-dried tomato purée and replace the tomato oil in the dough with olive oil. After the dough has had its first rising, knead it for about 3 minutes, to smooth it out. Using the palms of your hands, flatten out the dough and then smear it thickly with the purée. Roll up like a Swiss roll and then settle it as neatly as you can in its tin. Bake as above.

Panzanella with Sun-Dried Tomatoes and Rocket

Panzanella is an Italian salad, made with bread and tomatoes or sometimes, celery and carrots. This is my version of the original, made with rocket and sun-dried tomatoes. It is essential that you use high quality, sturdy bread for this salad. Sliced white will definitely not do.

SERVES 6

2 thick slices of stale sour-dough bread or other good-quality, country-style bread, weighing about 200 g/7 oz, crusts removed, cut into 1 cm (1/2 inch) cubes
12 sun-dried tomatoes in olive oil, drained and cut into ribbons
1/2 red onion, finely chopped
450 g (1 lb) tomatoes, skinned, de-seeded and diced
1/2 teaspoon dried oregano
1 tablespoon red wine vinegar
4 tablespoons olive oil
60 g (2 oz) rocket, roughly torn up
Salt and pepper

Put the bread into a large salad bowl and sprinkle with water – enough to soften it a little, so that it doesn't absorb too much of the dressing, but not so much that it drowns and disintegrates. Leave for 10 minutes.

Now add all the remaining ingredients, except the rocket and seasoning. Turn to mix evenly and then leave for about 1/2–1 hour.

Shortly before serving, add the rocket. Turn with your hands to mix evenly and then taste and add a little salt and lots of freshly ground pepper. Serve immediately.

olives

Have you ever eaten an olive straight from the tree? No? Well, don't. They are unutterably vile. It's a mystery how anyone ever imagined that they might be made palatable, let alone chanced upon the method. Luckily, they did, and so one of the quintessential flavours of the Mediterranean came into being. It is said that olives are an acquired taste but I can't remember a time when I didn't love them. I suspect that some people never do acquire the taste, because they've suffered cheap, nasty, soapy olives. What a shame this is, because a first-rate olive, suffused with herbs and good olive oil, is one of life's great little pleasures.

The method, or rather methods, that transform the raw horrors into pleasures are not so very complicated. They vary in detail from place to place, from home-curing to commercial curing, but generally involve prolonged soaking, rinsing and salting, the use of soda solutions in commercial set-ups, sacks and vats, brine and oil, herbs and aromatics, and plenty of other quirks. Add to that all the different varieties of olive and what you end up with is a seemingly infinite range of olives, with amazingly wide differences in taste, texture, look and smell.

The major division, naturally, is between green olives which are picked unripe and immature, usually in the autumn, and black olives, which are fully ripened and harvested in January or February. Green olives tend to have a firmer, waxier texture and a lighter, greener flavour and their flesh clings stubbornly to the stone. Black olives are usually softer and juicier, with a deeper, more complex flavour, which is tempered with a hint of ripe sweetness. That is where generalizations end and the fun begins.

Every olive-producing country has its own styles of olives, changing from one region to another, influenced by tradition, soil, climate and the other agricultural products that grow around and with the olives. Go to any market around the Mediterranean and you are bound to come across a stall selling a startling choice of olives, many of them grown and cured locally.

In Nice, for instance, you will find characteristic small, black, wrinkled olives, with a low ratio of flesh to stone but imbued with such an intense flavour that no one will complain. France also produces neat, slender, green *picholene* olives. From Kalamata, in the south of Greece, come big, juicy purple-black olives, taut-skinned and plump, often preserved in vinegar, which gives them a pleasing sharpness, making them so radically different from the Niçoise olive. In rural Spain, I've enjoyed rougher, green-purple olives, cracked open, home-cured and with a refreshing edge of bitterness, while from Greece come similar-looking, green cracked olives, scented with lemon zest and coriander. Morocco sends out barrels of garlicky and chillied black olives, while in Sicily the olives may well be scented with orange zest and fennel seeds. All these treasures and more, from the most unpromising of beginnings.

Buying and Storing Olives

'Taste before you buy' is the golden rule here. Olives vary so enormously in flavour and in amongst the very fine specimens there are some terrible, rank little things that don't deserve any shop space at all but get it all the same. If you can, go to a shop where olives are sold loose and enjoy yourself while you chew out an olive that you really like. For cooking, you may want to play safe and opt for a plainly preserved variety with a fine, true flavour. On the other hand, one of the delights of cooking with olives is that you can use the same recipe ten different times, using a different kind of olive each time, and end up with ten different dishes.

The trouble with tinned or bottled olives is that you can't taste before you buy. A few brands are excellent (Kalamata olives tend to come through the process well and I've eaten some superb Spanish bottled olives lately) but many of the ones on the supermarket shelves are decidedly second-rate. Experience has to be your guide here, and that can entail several costly mistakes. On the whole, I would advise that you steer clear of stoned olives. They may save time but are rarely as tasty as olives on the stone. The only stoned olives that I really like are the green ones stuffed with anchovies, garlic or almonds (but not those little horrors filled with chirpy strips of reconstituted red pepper), but they are definitely pre-dinner nibble candidates and not for cooking with.

Store olives in airtight jars, covered completely in olive oil or a heavy brine (salt and water solution). Brine-covered olives are best kept in the fridge but oil-covered olives will last happily for months in a cool, dark cupboard, so long as they are not exposed to the air. If you want to jazz up a jar of disappointing olives, empty out any liquid, replace with good olive oil and slip a couple of halved cloves of garlic into the jar, along with a sprig or two of rosemary or thyme, or a teaspoonful or two of dried oregano, or some bruised coriander or fennel seeds, or strips of lemon or orange zest, and so on. A mixture of aromatics can be good but don't overdo it.

Using Olives

One of the cook's most tedious jobs is stoning olives but, however onerous, it really does pay dividends in terms of flavour. Turn on the radio or your favourite CD, take a deep breath and settle down to it. You can use a cherry-stoner but I find that an awful lot of flesh gets left behind on the olive stone. A sharp knife and fingernails are more effective. The flesh of green olives nearly always clings tightly, so I usually, lazily, buy large ones to minimize fiddling about. Black olives vary considerably but the riper and softer they are, the more easy they should be to stone. My favourite method is to bash each one firmly with a wooden spoon, splitting it open to reveal the stone which should then slip out neatly. This takes a bit of practice – at first, you may find a disconcerting number shooting across the kitchen – but it works admirably once you master the knack.

In most instances, it's best to add olives to a stew or sauce only in the final stages of cooking. Prolonged simmering spoils their texture, while the sauce may sup up too powerful a whiff of olive. This is particularly important when olives are extremely salty (be cautious with the salt, anyway, as any olive is bound to contribute more) or have been stored in vinegar. To dampen salt content without ruining taste, the olives can be briefly blanched first. Cover with water, bring up to the boil and then drain and run under cold water. Taste and repeat if necessary.

Tapenade

Olive pastes, patés and purées abound in delis and supermarkets these days but Provençal tapenade is the granddaddy of them all. It has many uses, the simplest being as a relish spread thinly on slices of toasted bread, or as a dip with crudités. It can be dolloped on grilled fish or chicken, or smeared thinly over a whole fish to be baked in the oven. For a softer flavour, mash hard-boiled egg yolks with an equal quantity of tapenade and pile back into the halved egg whites to make *oeufs à la tapenade* or use tapenade to flavour mayonnaise or butter.

There are innumerable variations on the basic idea, though all of them include black olives and capers (from which the purée takes its name). Brandy goes into some but not others. Odder ingredients include dried figs, or roasted tomatoes. Adding the tuna mutes the flavour slightly but it is by no means essential. Ideally, small, black, wrinkled Niçoise olives should be used but be warned: they are a pig to pit. Note that '220 g (8 oz) black olives, pitted' means 220 g black olives weighed with their pits or stones still *in situ, not* weighed after you have removed the pits.

SERVES 8

220 g (8 oz) black olives, pitted
1–2 garlic cloves, roughly chopped
30 g (1 oz) drained and rinsed capers
45 g (1 1/2 oz) tinned or salted anchovy fillets, or salted pilchard fillets, roughly chopped
60 g (2 oz) tinned tuna fish (optional)
1 tablespoon lemon juice
1 tablespoon brandy (optional)
8 tablespoons olive oil
Pepper

To make in a processor, blend all the ingredients together, gradually trickling in the olive oil as the blades whirr.

Without a processor, chop all the solid ingredients together and then pound to a paste in a mortar, with a pestle, gradually incorporating the lemon juice, brandy and finally the olive oil. Either way, be generous with the pepper.

Chicken and Pork Paté Studded with Olives

Chicken and pork form the basis of this paté, which is studded with green olives and flavoured with brandy and orange. Like all patés, its flavour improves with keeping for a day or two; in any case, you need to begin at least two days before you want to eat it, to allow for overnight marinating and then pressing. Serve sliced, with hot toast and a fruity chutney or pickled caper berries or *cornichons* (baby gherkins).

SERVES 8–10

1 boned, skined chicken breast
Juice of 1 orange
1 tablespoon brandy
3 strips of orange zest
1 bay leaf
2 tablespoons olive oil
340 g (12 oz) de-rinded belly of pork, small bones removed
6 boned, skined chicken thighs
3 tablespoons chopped fresh parsley
1 1/2 tablespoons finely chopped fresh chives
1 teaspoon fresh thyme leaves
1 tablespoon plain flour
100 g (3 1/2 oz) green olives, stoned and sliced
Salt and pepper

Cut the chicken breast into two long, fat strips. Marinate overnight with the orange juice, brandy, orange zest, bay leaf and olive oil.

Pre-heat the oven to 170°C/325°F/Gas Mark 3. If you buy your meat from a friendly butcher, ask him to mince the belly of pork with the chicken thighs for you. If he can't or won't do that, mince them yourself, if you have a mincer. If you don't, either chop the two meats together very, very finely, which is laborious but gives an excellent texture, or chop them roughly and then process in brief bursts in a processor, scraping the mixture down frequently and trying your best not to reduce it to a totally smooth mush.

Take the chicken breast out of the marinade. Discard the orange zest and bay leaf and then mix about half the marinade into the minced meats, along with the parsley, chives, thyme, flour, salt and pepper. Use your hands to get it all thoroughly and evenly mixed and then break off a small knob and fry quickly. Taste it to assess the seasoning situation – add more salt and pepper to the mixture if it seems a bit bland. Finally, work in the olives.

Smooth half the mixture in a china terrine, or 500–750 g (1–1 1/2 lb) loaf tin. Nestle the strips of chicken breast down the centre and then cover with the remaining mixture, pressing it down firmly. Cover the terrine with its lid or foil and stand it in a roasting tin. Pour in enough hot water to come about halfway up. Bake for 1 1/2–2 hours, until the paté has pulled away from the sides of the tin and the fat runs clear. Give it a final test by plunging a skewer into the centre: if the juices run clear, it is done. Let the paté cool.

Cover the paté with a clean piece of foil and weight it down with tins or weights. Leave overnight in the fridge. Serve in thick slices.

Roast Fillet of Beef with Quick Tomato, Red Wine and Olive Sauce

This is the perfect dish for a mid-week dinner party. Fillet of beef is expensive but it cooks quickly with no waste. The meat is as tender as butter but has a tendency to be on the bland side, and that's where the sauce comes into play, pepping up the whole ensemble.

SERVES 4, GENEROUSLY

600–700 g (1 1/4–1 1/2 lb) piece of finest beef fillet
1 garlic clove, halved
Olive oil
1 onion, sliced
Salt and pepper
For the sauce:
2 garlic cloves, crushed
500 g (1 lb 2 oz) fresh tomatoes, skinned, de-seeded and chopped, or 14 oz (400 g) tin chopped tomatoes
110 ml (4 fl oz) red wine
1/2 teaspoon sugar
2 tablespoons tomato purée
1 teaspoon Worcestershire sauce
3 tablespoons chopped parsley
12 black or green olives, stoned and halved
2 tablespoons capers
Salt and pepper

Pre-heat the oven to 220°C/425°F/Gas Mark 7. Rub the beef all over with the cut sides of the halved clove of garlic and then season with salt and pepper. Oil a small roasting tin generously, spread out the onion in it and toss in the halved garlic, too. Place the fillet on top and drizzle over 2 tablespoons of olive oil. Roast for 20 minutes, until cooked medium-rare. Transfer the fillet to a warmed serving dish and keep it warm while you make the sauce.

Lift the onion and garlic halves out of the roasting tin with a slotted spoon, letting the oil and juices drip back into the tin. Place the tin over a moderate heat. Add all the sauce ingredients, except the parsley, olives and capers. Stir to mix and then turn up the heat and cook the sauce at a furious pace, stirring frequently to prevent it from catching, until well reduced, thick and not at all watery. Aim for about 5 minutes' cooking time, at most. Now stir in the parsley, olives and capers. Give them a few seconds to heat through and then taste and adjust the seasoning.

Slice the fillet and serve with the sauce.

Cuban Picadillo

From Cuba comes this unusual minced beef hash, cooked with tomatoes, raisins, capers and olives. It's an odd idea but a real winner for all that. Serve it over boiled rice (or sautéed potatoes, as they sometimes do in Cuba), along with slices of avocado, or guacamole (mashed avocados mixed with finely diced tomato, onion, garlic, a hint of chilli, lime juice and chopped fresh coriander). It also makes a very good filling for tortillas, or taco shells, along with a tomatoey salsa (such as *Salsa Mexicana*, see page 53), avocado again and generous dollops of soured cream.

SERVES 4–6

1 onion, chopped
1 green pepper, de-seeded and finely chopped
2 tablespoons sunflower oil
4 garlic cloves, chopped
450 g (1 lb) minced beef
150 ml (5 fl oz) passata
12 green olives, stoned and roughly chopped
60 g (2 oz) raisins
1 tablespoon capers
150 ml (5 fl oz) dry white wine
1 teaspoon caster sugar
Salt and pepper

Fry the onion and green pepper gently in the oil until tender, without browning. Add the garlic and cook for about a minute more, then add the minced beef. Fry, breaking up the lumps, for about 5 minutes. Now add all the remaining ingredients, reduce the heat, cover and simmer for a further 25–30 minutes, stirring occasionally. By the time the hash is cooked, it should be reduced and thick but still quite wet. Taste and adjust the seasoning and then serve.

capers

Capotes, *capucines* and *nonpareilles* are extravagant names that define nothing more romantic than piquant capers. But hold on a minute ... capers not romantic? Don't you believe it. Those little khaki spheres swilling in vinegar in a forgotten jar at the back of your cupboard are the culmination of a story of thwarted beauty and unexpected gastronomic delight.

The caper plant grows wild all around the Mediterranean, thriving on rocky outcrops and ancient stony ruins. The tenacious roots burrow deep down, to suck up moisture that other plants would never find, anchoring rubble and rocks in place. I saw them growing on the rugged coast of Gozo, spreading out long, spined stems and blue-green leaves to bask against the rock. It was in early July, already so hot that by 10.30 in the morning I could hardly bear to sit down in the direct sun. The ethereal flowers of the caper plant are barely any hardier. In the early morning they unfurl their delicate white or pale pink petals, letting fall a startling cascade of purple stamens. They smell of jasmine and honeysuckle and caper all blended harmoniously together. A short-lived perfection for, by early afternoon they have wilted and drooped away, one step nearer to becoming a caper pod or berry (see page 263). The caper, as we know it in our little jars, is actually the bud of the flower, an ugly duckling that never got its chance to mature into a swan. Its destiny, though, is a longer, preserved and pickled life.

Capers can be cultivated, indeed they often are, but experts reckon that the wild ones are the best. Spain is the biggest producer of cultivated capers, which are mostly grown in the south, in Andalucia and the Balearic islands. Wild or not, harvesting is exacting, back-breaking work. Every morning, each plant must be checked and perfect buds snipped off before they become too fat and blowsy, threatening to burst open. The fresh capers are fermented to produce the characteristic flavour and then packed either in salt or vinegar. A good caper is a tiny capsule of unique piquancy, underlined by its preservation medium but retaining something of the sun-drenched climate that witnessed its birth.

Buying and Storing Capers

Most people reckon that the smallest *nonpareilles* are the choicest – the tiny wild ones from the Italian island of Pantellaria get superstar billing. The bulk of the capers sold in Britain are medium-sized *capucines*, while the cheapest tend to be the *capotes* and *gruesas*, big and loose and coarser than the rest.

Vinegar-packed capers have a natural sharpness that I rather like, though it can overwhelm the natural flavour of the bud. Look out, though, for the excellent tiny capers preserved in sherry vinegar from Spain and the even better tiddlers in balsamic vinegar from Italy. These really are capers at their very best. Many people have a passion for the salted capers and these are beginning to make fairly regular appearances over here. If you find them (look out for them in Mediterranean markets when you are on holiday, if you can't get them in your area), be sure to give them a try, in order to discover what a clean, pure addition to a dish a caper can be.

Kept under salt, or under their vinegar, capers will keep for months in a cool, dark cupboard.

Using Capers

Before you cook with any type of caper, taste first. They vary enormously in flavour, mainly due to their preservation medium. Some vinegar-preserved capers will be incredibly vinegary, others less so. Either way, they may well be improved by rinsing before using. Salted capers nearly always need rinsing. You may even need to soak them for 10–20 minutes, changing the water once or twice, to reveal the true caper taste, unsullied by heavy salt. Even so, go easy on the salt in the finished dish and be prepared to add an extra dash of vinegar or lemon juice, as the majority of recipes tested in this country will have been tried out with vinegar-preserved capers.

In some recipes, larger capers should be roughly chopped so that they are not too dominant (in stuffings, say), whereas cute little *nonpareilles* can go in whole.

Tiny capers ginger up all manner of dishes with great aplomb. The classic caper butter for fish is a fine example – really nothing more than butter cooked until brown and then sharpened with lemon juice and dotted with capers, it is one of the purest, most ideal sauces, not only for skate but for other fish as well. Capers are always welcome scattered lightly over salads; they marry well, too, with many meat dishes, and indeed with eggs as well. One nifty garnish that has swung into fashion lately is fried capers. Make sure that the capers are thoroughly rinsed and dried and then fry them briefly in hot oil until they begin to crisp. Drain and use immediately.

Tomatoes with Tarragon Butter and Capers

Adapted from one of Elizabeth David's recipes (from her *Spices, Salts and Aromatics in the English Kitchen*, a book that is often ignored in the shadow of her French and Italian works), this is a sublime and beautiful dish of whole plum tomatoes, cooked gently in butter and finished with lots of tarragon and a sprinkling of capers. Though it is meant as a side dish (excellent with red meats), it is really too good to play second fiddle. I serve the tomatoes as a course on their own, with thick slices of sturdy bread to mop up the juices.

SERVES 4

30 g (1 oz) butter
500 g (1 lb 2 oz) firm plum tomatoes
1–2 tablespoons small capers
Salt and sugar

For the tarragon butter:

85 g (3 oz) butter, softened
1 1/2 tablespoons very finely chopped fresh tarragon
A dash of lemon or lime juice and black pepper

To make the butter, mash the butter and tarragon together well and season with pepper and a dash of lemon or lime juice. Wrap in foil and chill in the fridge. You won't need all the tarragon butter for this recipe but it keeps quite well, and can be used on vegetables or fish.

Opposite *Tomatoes with Tarragon Butter and Capers*

Keep the tomatoes whole. Melt the ordinary butter in a frying-pan. Add the tomatoes and season with salt and a pinch or two of sugar. Cook over a very low heat for about 10 minutes, turning the tomatoes once or twice, very gently.

When they are soft (but not collapsing) and the juice is running a little, add a tablespoon of the tarragon butter and the capers. Turn up the heat for a few seconds, to melt the butter. Spoon the pan juices over the tomatoes and then serve them quickly, before they lose their shape and turn to sauce.

Cold Roast Swordfish with Caper, Tuna and Sun-Dried Tomato Mayonnaise

Inspired by that magnificent Italian dish of veal with tuna mayonnaise, this takes the fishy theme one step further, by replacing veal with a great hunk of swordfish. Roast swordfish is far nicer cold than hot and better still with this zesty mayonnaise. An excellent cold dish for a summer party.

SERVES 4–6

1 kg (2 1/4 lb) piece of swordfish
2 garlic cloves, cut into long, thin slivers
110 ml (4 fl oz) dry white wine
2 tablespoons olive oil
Salt and pepper
Chopped fresh parsley, to garnish

For the mayonnaise:

1 1/2 tablespoons capers
3 anchovy fillets, roughly chopped
100 g (3 1/2 oz) tinned tuna, drained
2 tablespoons sun-dried tomato purée
8 tablespoons mayonnaise
Salt and pepper
A dash of lemon juice

Pre-heat the oven to 190°C/375°F/Gas Mark 5. Don't muck around with the swordfish: leave it in one big chunk with the skin on. The one thing you should do is to make small slits here and there through the skin and push in slivers of garlic. Place the joint of swordfish, skin-side up, in a shallow, lightly oiled baking dish. Pour over the white wine, drizzle with olive oil and season with salt and pepper. Roast, basting frequently, for 40–45 minutes, until just cooked through but no more than that. Leave to cool, basting occasionally with its own juices.

Meanwhile, make the mayonnaise by processing all the ingredients except the seasoning together until smooth. Taste and adjust the seasoning with salt, pepper and a dash of lemon juice.

To serve, slice the swordfish fairly thinly, discarding the skin, and arrange the slices on a dish. Serve straight away, with the mayonnaise in a separate bowl. Alternatively, spread the mayonnaise over the fish before serving and scatter with a little chopped parsley.

Cucumber, Caper and Horseradish Salad

A finely diced, cool salad to serve with summer fish – grilled or poached – or on its own as a first course with bread, or as part of a buffet. We ate the left-overs piled on to steaming hot, baked potatoes. Very nice, too.

SERVES 6

1 cucumber, peeled, de-seeded and finely diced
1 1/2 tablespoons creamed horseradish
3 tablespoons capers, roughly chopped if large
1 shallot, very finely chopped
2 tablespoons finely chopped fresh parsley
250 g (9 oz) Greek yoghurt
1/4 teaspoon sugar
Salt and pepper and lemon juice

Spread the cucumber out in a colander and sprinkle it with 2 teaspoons of salt. Leave to drain for at least half an hour and, if time allows, a full hour.

Rinse and dry thoroughly and then mix with all the remaining ingredients except the seasoning. Taste and adjust the balance of flavours, adding a little salt, if needed, freshly ground pepper and a dash of lemon juice. Pile into a pretty bowl and serve at room temperature.

caper berries

Caper berries are actually the seed pods of the caper plant. For many years, they have been ignored outside the local communities that harvest the capers themselves. The tender seed pods were a secret perk, picked and pickled at leisure after the flowers had faded. They taste something like capers but are larger, a little sweeter, more like a little khaki lollipop (you bite off the round pod but leave behind the stalk), filled with tiny soft seeds. They are usually served with sliced salamis, chorizos and air-dried hams as part of a mixed *antipasto*, though I tend to associate them more with Spain than Italy. They also make a very good accompaniment to a slice of paté, be it the rougher-cut *paté de campagne*, or a more refined terrine of veal, chicken or rabbit. And, on a more patriotic note, they're terrific with a wedge of traditional mature British farmhouse Cheddar.

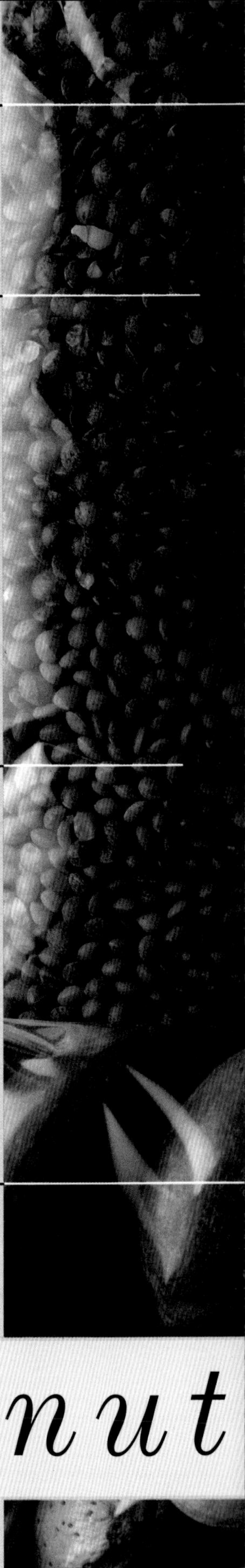

chickpeas

Puy lentils

brown lentils

pecans

pulses and nut

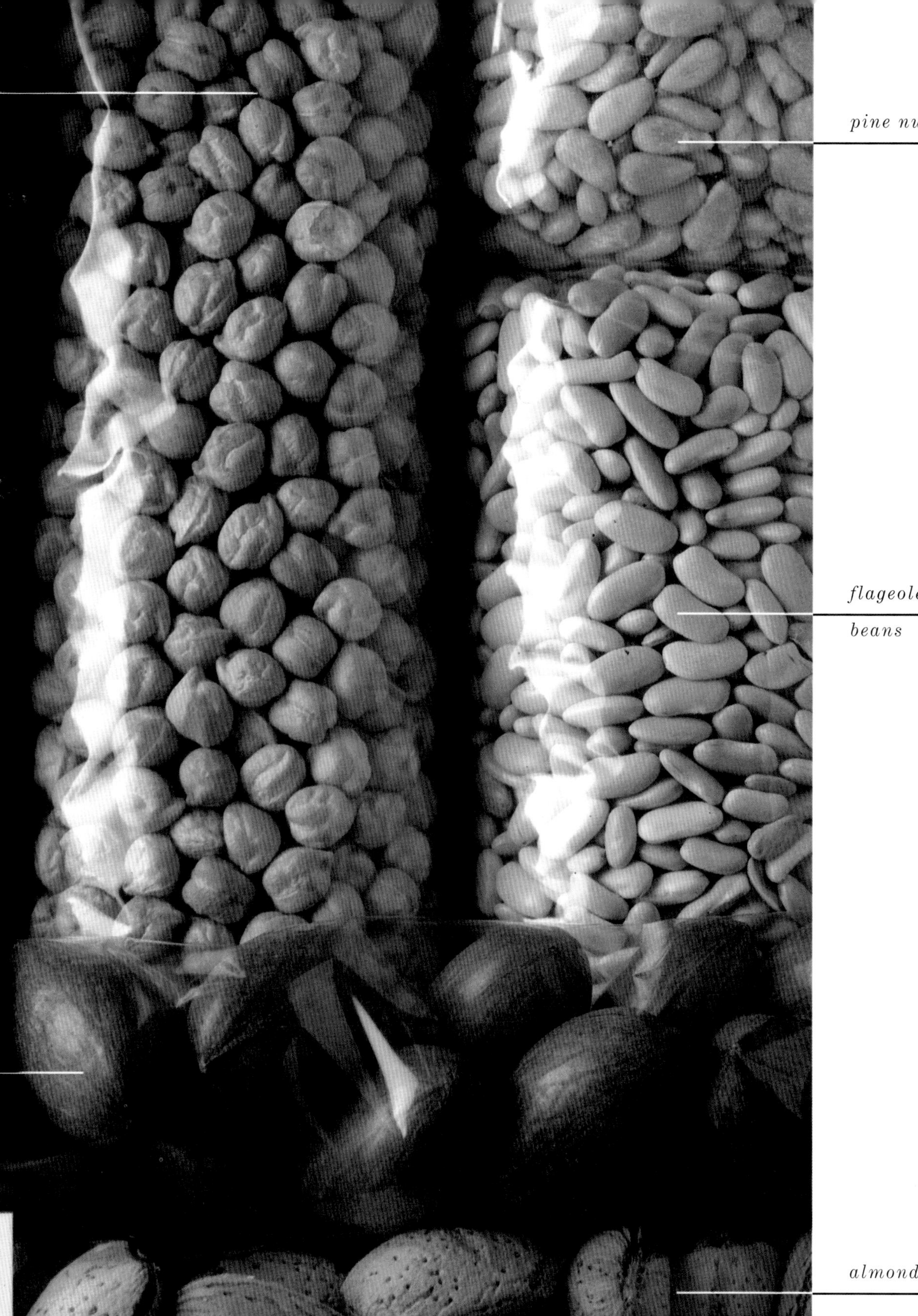
pine nuts
flageolet beans
almonds

pine nuts

When she was 18, a colleague of mine stayed for a while with an Italian family in Fregeni, near Rome. One afternoon, she and the children trooped down to a pine grove by the sea-shore to gather pine cones. She was amazed to discover that the cones were filled with small, hard-shelled nuts, a secret treasure-trove that her hosts gathered in every year. In fact, all pine cones conceal a hoard of nuts but, in most varieties, they are either so small that they are barely noticeable, or too strongly resinous to be palatable. Her cones came, I imagine, from the magnificent Mediterranean stone pine or umbrella pine, *Pinus pinea*, which grows all around the Mediterranean, wild in some parts, planted deliberately in others.

The Lebanese food writer Anissa Helou also remembers the pleasure of shaking the pine kernels out of the cones as a child: 'We sat by a flat stone and with another small stone, we started cracking the hard kernels open. The secret was how to scale the strength of the hit so that we broke the shell without crushing the nut ... ' She says, too, that pine nuts can be eaten fresh and green, in a similar style to green almonds: ' ... the fresh, ripe cone is cut with a knife into wedges and the soft, fleshy pine kernels are taken out, dipped into salt and eaten whole' (Anissa Helou: *Lebanese Cuisine*, Grub Street).

My colleague's family and Anissa Helou let nature do some of the work for them, gathering their pine cones in high summer, after they had been lying on the ground for some time. For commerce, the cones are brought in in mid-winter, to protect them from the ravages of weather and insects and the appetites of wild animals. They are stored until summer, when the force of the hot sun is enough to open them up. Dry as a bone, the individual pine nuts or kernels can be shaken out, still encased in a brittle, protective shell. Each little nut then has to be cracked (luckily, there are machines to do this now) to extract the nut meat. Apparently, one ton of pine cones yields a mere 38 kg (84 lb) of nuts. All in all, a lengthy process for small returns, which accounts for the phenomenal price. Not only are pine nuts more expensive than any other type of nut, they are also amongst the most expensive of all agricultural products, falling into third place behind saffron and truffles.

Buying and Storing Pine Nuts

Most of the pine nuts sold here come, not from the Mediterranean, but from much farther afield: the north-east of China. Small and tear-drop shaped, they're the nuts of the *Pinus koraiensis*, the Korean pine. These have the characteristic buttery, soft texture and sweetness that is so very appealing, but they can be bettered. Look out for long, slender pine nuts from the Lebanon in Middle Eastern groceries. They cost an arm and a leg but have a distinct pine flavour that will transform your notions of what a pine nut should be.

When buying pine nuts make sure that they are fresh, if you can. In small shops, where they are sold loose, the best thing is to taste a few before buying. These little golden morsels are extremely rich, being made up of almost 70 per cent fat, most of it unsaturated. This is partly what makes them so very good but the drawback is that they will turn rancid if stored for too long in a warm place. You can freeze them but I think it is better to buy them in small quantities, store them in the fridge (and definitely not in a metal canister) and use them up quickly.

Using Pine Nuts

As with most nuts, the flavour of pine nuts is improved and heightened by heat. Dry-frying or roasting them in the oven takes only a couple of minutes but they must be watched over carefully as they burn in the twinkling of an eye. Toasted, pine nuts are one of the nicest nuts to add to a salad (green, mixed or even sweet and fruity) or use them in stuffings, since they will add plenty of texture and taste without distracting from the impact of the whole. Some recipes call for pine nuts to be fried in butter or oil, an excellent last-minute garnish for rice, amongst other things. You will also find pine nuts appearing in pilaffs and other rice dishes. Untoasted, their most famous use is probably in the Genoese sauce, *Pesto* (see page 30).

Spinaci alla Genovese

This dish of spinach (or sometimes chard) cooked with pine nuts and raisins is popular in Genoa but resurfaces in Catalonia and the Balearics. It is a surprisingly good combination and an easy way to dress up plain spinach.

SERVES 4

650 g (1 lb 6 oz) fresh spinach leaves
3 tablespoons olive oil
3 anchovy fillets, finely chopped
2 tablespoons finely chopped fresh parsley
60 g (2 oz) raisins or currants
60 g (2 oz) pine nuts
Salt and pepper
Freshly grated nutmeg

Pick over the spinach and discard any damaged leaves or tough, thick stalks. Rinse thoroughly in several changes of water and then drain but do not dry. Cram into a pan, cover and cook over a moderate heat, stirring once or twice, until the spinach has collapsed. Drain thoroughly, squeezing out excess moisture, and then chop roughly.

Warm the oil in a saucepan over a moderate heat and add the chopped anchovies and the parsley. Stir for a minute or two and then add the spinach, raisins or currants, pine nuts, salt, pepper and nutmeg. Mix and cook gently for 5 minutes or so, half-covered. Serve piping hot.

Tarte aux Pignons

There are many versions of the Provençal *tarte aux pignons*, some made with shortcrust pastry, some filled with custard. This particular one has to be amongst the best. It is quite my favourite pine nut dessert, with a soft, gooey, scented filling, studded with browned pine nuts. It comes from an American book by Antoine Bouterin, a Provençal chef who now cooks at New York's Le Périgord restaurant, called *Cooking Provence.*

SERVES 6

250 g (9 oz) puff pastry

For the filling:

130 g (4½ oz) ground almonds

Finely grated zest of 1 orange

220 g (8 oz) caster sugar

1 tablespoon orange-flower water

2 tablespoons honey

2 large eggs, beaten

2 tablespoons extra virgin olive oil

115 g (4 oz) pine nuts

Pre-heat the oven to 200°C/400°F/Gas Mark 6. Roll the pastry out very thinly and use it to line a 20–23 cm (8–9 inch) tart tin, doubling the pastry over the rim, to make a double-thickness rim, and crimping it securely. Prick the base with a fork and leave it to rest for half an hour in the fridge. Cover the pastry base with a square of buttered cooking foil (butter-side down!), fill the case with baking beans and bake blind for about 10 minutes. Remove the foil and return the pastry case to the oven, for about another 10 minutes to dry out , without colouring. Leave to cool.

For the filling, put the ground almonds in a bowl and add the orange zest and sugar. Mix, make a well in the centre and then add the orange-flower water, honey, eggs and oil. Mix thoroughly, to give a thick, smooth batter. Tip in two-thirds of the pine nuts, pour the mixture into the pastry case and sprinkle evenly with the remaining pine nuts. Bake until browned and almost, but not quite, firm in the centre: about 20–25 minutes.

Opposite *Tarte aux Pignons*

Asparagus, Poached Egg and Pine Nut Salad

A fresh-tasting spring salad to serve as a first course or a light lunch.

SERVES 2

250 g (9 oz) medium-sized asparagus spears

45 g (1 1/2 oz) pine nuts

2 eggs

A handful of rocket leaves

2 slices of air-dried ham, e.g. Parma, Jamon serrano or Cumbrian

30 g (1 oz) Parmesan

Salt

For the dressing:

2–3 tablespoons olive oil

1/2 tablespoon balsamic or sherry vinegar

Salt and pepper

Trim off the tough, woody ends of the asparagus and, if necessary, peel the lower parts. Cut off the top 3 cm (1 inch) of the tips. Cut the rest into 2.5 cm (1 inch) lengths. Drop these into a pan of salted, boiling water, simmer for 2 minutes and then add the tips. Cook for a further 2–3 minutes. Drain, run under the cold tap and drain again thoroughly.

Dry-fry the pine nuts in a heavy frying-pan over a medium heat, until browned. Tip into a bowl before they burn.

For the dressing, whisk the oil into the vinegar and season with salt and pepper.

Use a vegetable peeler to make thin shavings or flakes or Parmesan.

Shortly before serving, poach the eggs. Toss the rocket and asparagus in just enough of the dressing to coat them evenly. Arrange on two plates. Drape a slice of air-dried ham over each one, scatter with pine nuts, nestle a poached egg on top and, finally, strew with Parmesan. Serve immediately.

Pine Nut and Saffron Pilaf

A lovely, golden pilaf perfumed with saffron and dotted with buttery pine nuts. Serve as a side dish to grilled fish or chicken, or even on its own, in which case the garlicky yoghurt becomes a key player.

SERVES 4–6

A generous pinch saffron threads
600 ml (a generous pint) hot chicken or vegetable stock
1 large onion, chopped
1 clove garlic, chopped
85g (3oz) butter
250g (9oz) Basmati rice, rinsed and thoroughly drained
1 bay leaf
4 green cardamom pods
85g (3oz) pine nuts
3 tablespoons chopped parsley
Salt and pepper
To serve: (optional)
200g (8oz) Greek yoghurt
3 cloves garlic, crushed

Mix the yoghurt with the crushed garlic if using. Pre-heat the oven to around 150°C/300°F/Gas Mark 2. To make the pilaf, put the saffron into a small bowl and spoon over 2 tablespoons hot stock. Leave to steep until needed. Fry the onion and garlic gently in 30g (1oz) of the butter in a heavy based saucepan, without browning, until tender. Add the rice, bay leaf and cardamom pods and stir for about 30 seconds. Pour in the remaining stock and season with salt and pepper. Bring up to a lazy simmer, cover tightly, reduce heat as low as possible and leave to cook, undisturbed, for 10 minutes.

Meanwhile, sauté the pine nuts in half the remaining butter until lightly browned. Check the rice – by now it should be just nicely cooked and all the liquid should have been absorbed. If not, uncover and let it boil off for a few minutes. Stir in the parsley and saffron. Turn the rice into a shallow dish, spoon over the pinenuts and dot with the last of the butter. Cover with foil and pop into a warm oven to steam and keep warm – it can stay there happily for half an hour or so. Serve with the garlicky yoghurt, if using.

almonds

Just as the Japanese have their cherry blossom, so the Sicilians have their almond blossom. It blooms in February, with a spectacular show of white and pink spread right across the island. The Valley of the Temples, stretching down towards the sea below the town of Agrigento, must be one of the most beautiful sites. Here lie and stand the remains of seven magnificent Greek and Roman temples, surrounded on all sides by crowds of almond trees. In that early spring, the masonry seems to float on a sea of scented flowers flowing away as far as the eye can see.

Almonds are native to the eastern Mediterranean but they grow well wherever the climate is warm enough to safeguard the early spring fruits, though they've never taken to the tropics. The Sicilian fondness for almonds stems from the two hundred years the Arabs occupied the island (from the middle of the ninth century), bringing with them orange and lemon trees and irrigation to make the island bloom and prosper more than it had ever done before. They introduced sugar cane, too. Almonds and sugar – what a combination! Praline, sugared almonds, marzipan and a whole host of other European confectionery, right down to our own Bakewell tarts, all offspring of this happy conjunction.

Almonds have become perhaps the most important European nut. Their sweet, subtle, quiet flavour and their abundance has made them welcome everywhere, and they appear time and again, with little fanfare, in recipes both sweet and savoury. Salted and spiced, toasted or fried, whole, ground, nibbed, flaked and slivered, blanched or unblanched, they are about the most useful and under-rated nuts around.

Buying and Storing Almonds

If you truly want to get the fullest flavour from almonds, buy them unblanched, still wrapped snugly in their soft, papery brown skins. You could go the whole hog, of course, and buy them in their shells, but that's pushing matters a little too far. Save all that cracking for Christmas, when you want nothing more than a relaxed nibble as you sip on coffee or the last of the dessert wine.

When you do have at least a small amount of time on your hands, though, it does pay to blanch almonds yourself. They taste sweeter, more almondy and less dry than ready-blanched almonds. I can only guess that this is because the skins work like natural cling film, sealing in the goodness but letting the nut breathe at the same time. No plastic sachet can do quite such an efficient job. Finding almonds in their skins is not so easy these days; you'll probably have to repair to a wholefood shop or a Middle Eastern food store (always a good source of nuts of all kinds).

Otherwise, you'll have to put up with the almonds that come in those plastic sachets. They're fine and far more practical in reality. Once the packet has been opened, store the nuts in an airtight container (not a metal one) in the fridge for up to a month.

To blanch unskinned almonds, cover with boiling water and leave for about 2 minutes. Drain well. Using the tip of a knife or your fingernail, nick the skin open on each almond and squeeze out the ivory nut. For some dishes (for instance, if you want to grind the almonds to a powder), you will then need to dry them out a little, spread out on a baking sheet in a low to moderate oven for 5 minutes or so.

The light, delicate flavour of the plain almond is often the reason that this nut, above others, is right for a dish; where a more powerful almondy flavour is required, toasting heightens and changes the flavour dramatically. I usually spread the almonds out on a baking sheet and toast them in a hot oven, shaking once or twice, until they are a shade or two darker; it takes a matter of minutes, so keep checking.

The uses of almonds are legion, mostly sweet but by no means exclusively so. *Truite aux amandes* and Indian kormas are two of the savoury uses that spring to mind. For more ideas, one must turn to the cooking of almond-growing countries. In Spain, for instance, they use almonds to make ghostly-pale soups.

Almond Milk

My first encounter with almond milk was in Italy when I was a student. The taste was fine but the texture reminded me too much of the chalkiness of old-fashioned milk of magnesia and, for years afterwards, I avoided it. When I finally did try it again, I realized that I had been missing out on one of summer's most refreshing, cooling drinks. I must have been unlucky all those years before, for good almond milk is smooth and velvety.

MAKES 570 ML (1 PINT)

250 g (9 oz) home-blanched almonds

Finely grated zest of 1 lemon or 1 orange

Icing sugar, to taste

Put the almonds into a food processor, with the zest and a couple of tablespoons of water. Whizz the almonds to a powder and gradually work in 300 ml (10 fl oz) of water. Transfer the mixture to a bowl and add another 300 ml (10 fl oz) of water. Stir, then cover and leave in a cool place for at least 4 hours, or longer.

Line a sieve with muslin and strain the mixture through it. Gather up the ends of the muslin and squeeze out every last drop of almond milk. Add enough water to make up to 570 ml (1 pint) and then sweeten the milk to taste. Even if you don't have a sweet tooth, you will find that it benefits enormously from a few spoonfuls of sugar. Serve the almond milk well chilled.

Paris-Brest

This must be the only cake to be named after a bicycle race. A wheel of almond-studded choux pastry is filled with praline-flavoured buttercream (if you are really pushed for time, you can substitute 300 ml (10 fl oz) of double cream, whipped, for the plain buttercream). Sumptuous.

SERVES 8

For the buttercream:

100 g (3½ oz) caster sugar or vanilla sugar

3 egg yolks, lightly beaten

180 g (6 oz) unsalted butter, softened

200 g (7 oz) *Almond Praline* powder **(see page 275)**

For the choux pastry:

100 g (3½ oz) butter

150 g (5¼ oz) strong white bread flour

4 eggs

A pinch of salt

To decorate:

1 egg, lightly beaten, to glaze

45 g (1½ oz) flaked almonds

Icing sugar

The buttercream can be made 24 hours in advance. Stir the sugar with 4 tablespoons of water over a medium heat until the sugar has completely dissolved. Brush down any sugar crystals stuck to the side of the pan, with a brush dipped in cold water. Bring up to the boil and boil until the syrup reaches the soft-ball stage, that is 115°C/240°F. To test, drip a little into a glass or bowl of iced water: if it forms a soft, but not sticky, ball, it is done.

Pour the hot syrup slowly into the egg yolks, beating constantly. Keep beating (an electric whisk is a great help) until the mixture is cool and very thick. Cream the butter until it is light and fluffy and then beat in the egg mousse. Fold in the praline powder.

Make the ring of choux pastry only on the day it is to be eaten. Pre-heat the oven to 220°C/425°F/Gas Mark 7. Put the butter and 225 ml (8 fl oz) of water into a pan and bring up to the boil. As soon as it boils, draw off the heat, tip in the flour and salt and beat until thoroughly mixed. Return to a low heat, stirring constantly, until the mixture pulls away from the sides of the pan and spoon. Draw off the heat and beat in the first three eggs, one by one. Beat the last egg lightly in a separate bowl and beat it into the dough gradually, until the dough is smooth and glossy and just slides off the spoon. You may not need all of the last egg.

Line a baking tray with non-stick baking parchment and mark out a 25 cm (10 inch) circle. Pipe or dot the mixture all around the circle, smoothing it, if necessary, to form a wheel about 4 cm (1½ inches) wide. Brush with egg glaze and sprinkle with flaked almonds. Bake for 15 minutes.

Reduce the oven heat to 180°C/350°F/Gas Mark 4 for a further 20 minutes, until the pastry is puffed and pleasingly golden brown.

Carefully slice the ring in half horizontally and open it up, so that steam can escape while it cools. Don't worry if you have a few breaks; once the whole lot is reassembled they will hardly show at all.

The last part, best left until the last possible moment, is to pipe or spoon the buttercream into the bottom of the ring. Replace the top carefully, nestle it down, dust lightly with icing sugar and it's ready to go!

Almond Brittle and Almond Praline

From one recipe, two outcomes. Almond brittle makes a lovely sweet. Ground to a powder it becomes praline, mainstay of patisserie and chocolate-making. In Sicily, they use the cut-side of a halved lemon to smooth and flatten down the cooked brittle. It's a clever trick, obvious when you have lots of lemons to hand, as they do in Sicily, but still worth borrowing here, where we don't.

MAKES 200 G (7 OZ)

100 g (4 oz) whole blanched almonds

100 g (4 oz) caster sugar

Pre-heat the oven to 190°C/375°F/Gas Mark 5. Oil a cool marble surface, if you have one, or a baking tray if you haven't. Spread the almonds out on another baking tray and toast them in the oven, until they are a fairly light golden brown, shaking them every couple of minutes. This should take around 6 minutes but check frequently.

Put the sugar into a pan with 4 tablespoons of water. Stir over a moderate heat until the sugar has completely dissolved, brushing down the sides with a brush dipped in water, to remove any sugar crystals that adhere to the pan. Raise the heat and let the syrup boil, without stirring. Swirl the pan now and then to even out the effects of odd hot spots. As soon as the syrup has caramelized to a rich brown, draw the pan off the heat and instantly add the almonds. Pour on to the prepared surface, smooth down with a cut lemon, if you have one to spare (see above), and leave to cool. Break up into bits, and you have a delicious heap of almond brittle.

Grind the bits to a powder, either in a food processor or with a pestle in a mortar, and you have equally delicious praline powder. Either will keep as long as they are stored in an airtight container, well away from moisture.

pecans

This is the American nut *par excellence*. Indigenous to the Mississippi valley and south down into Mexico, it was known and used appreciatively by Native Americans, long before Old World colonists intruded into their land. Its very name comes from the Algonquin word *paccan*. Now, of course, the pecan has achieved worldwide fame in sticky pecan pie, which we all think of as a quintessential American tart. However, when you look a little closer, you realize that pecans belong to the Deep South. The pecan tree, a type of hickory, will not grow north of the 40th Parallel and thrives in the states where cotton grows in balmy warmth. During my one, all-too-brief visit to New Orleans, I came across pecans in all sorts of dishes – with fish and meat, as well as in stuffings, ice creams and puddings. Best of all, and far nicer than the famous pie, were the fabulous pecan pralines of Louisiana. Not praline as in our European sugary almond confection, but whole nuts embedded in a thin, solid disc of smooth, melt-on-the-tongue, velvety, firm fudge. Don't miss them if you ever go there.

Pecan kernels look something like walnuts, though there are obvious differences. The outer shell is a smooth, burnished, red-brown, shaped something like an elongated olive. Being thin, it is easy to crack, and generously filled. Inside, the meat has the double-lobed form of a walnut but stretched out, flattened and with kinks ironed out. The skin has a golden colour when the nuts are 'wet' and newly harvested, but darkens to a rusty rich brown as they are dried for storage. They taste sweeter and softer than walnuts, without the hint of bitterness that gives walnuts their edge. The kernel is oilier than that of the walnut (70 per cent oil, beaten in richness only by the Australian macadamia nut) but comparatively low in protein.

Buying and Storing Pecans

Pecans are widely available, particularly around Christmas when they glow confidently amongst the crowd of more familiar European nuts. It used to be common practice to dye the shells an unnaturally pinkish red, which always put me off, though it didn't seem to affect the kernel at all. Recently I've noticed that most imported, shell-on pecans are as nature intended and far more attractive for it. Shelled pecans are usually to be found, right through the year, stashed away amongst the other shelled nuts.

Whether you buy pecans in or out of their shells, it is important to get the new season's pecans and not older ones. The high oil content means that pecans turn rancid more quickly than many others if not stored properly. Vacuum-packed, or sealed under gas in clear plastic bags, they will last well; sold loose, they have a relatively short shelf-life. Use up whole pecans in their shells quickly. Once a pack has been opened, shelled pecans are best stored in an air-

Opposite *Roast Rack of Lamb with a Pecan, Lemon and Parsley Crust*

tight container (not a metal one, as that hastens deterioration) in the fridge; even so, eat them up within a week or two.

Using Pecans

Rich, sweet and tender, pecans are heaven-sent for puddings of all sorts and can be used like walnuts in pies and tarts. Little nuggets of chopped pecan are lovely in stuffings for chicken or turkey and they even go rather well with fish.

Like all nuts, their flavour is enhanced by toasting: spread them out on a tray and pop into a moderate to hot oven for a few minutes, until they turn a shade darker. Check every 2–3 minutes to see how they are doing and give them a quick shake, so that they brown evenly. Remember that, with their high oil content, they will burn easily. Toasting also seems to release the oils, and toasted pecans make a brilliant nut butter. Just process, adding a little salt and nothing more.

Instead of toasting pecans in the oven, try them fried in a little oil or butter. They make an excellent spiced nut for parties. Fry for a few minutes, drain briefly on kitchen paper and then toss in freshly toasted ground cumin, mixed with a hint of cayenne pepper and some salt. Eat warm from the pan.

Pecans and maple syrup are not only compatriots, but also soul mates. If you want an instant lift for a plain pastry or ice cream, warm up some maple syrup with a knob of butter stirred into it, add plenty of chopped pecans, and your maple pecan sauce is ready to serve.

Roast Rack of Lamb with a Pecan, Lemon and Parsley Crust

The nuts in the crust toast in the oven's heat, making a sweet, rich, crisp contrast to the tender lamb. The same mixture can be used on thick pieces of fish fillet (cod, for example, if it is very fresh), which, again, can be roasted in a hot oven.

SERVES 4

2 racks of lamb, French trimmed (see method)

For the crust:

60 g (2 oz) shelled pecans

30 g (1 oz) fine, slightly stale white breadcrumbs

Finely grated zest of 1 lemon

2 tablespoons chopped fresh parsley

45 g (1 1/2 oz) butter, melted

Salt and pepper

A butcher will prepare the racks of lamb for you (and they are sold ready-prepared in some supermarkets) but, if you have to do it yourself, here's how to proceed. Carefully cut off the skin from each rack, leaving a thin layer of fat. Trim the tips of the cutlets, scraping away the scraps of meat and fat and exposing the top 4 cm (1 1/2 inches).

Pre-heat the oven to 230°C/450°F/Gas Mark 8. To make the crust, chop the pecans very finely in a food processor or by hand. Mix with all the remaining ingredients, working in the butter with your hands until it is all evenly distributed.

Lay the racks of lamb, curved up, in a lightly oiled, ovenproof dish or roasting tin. Pat the crust mixture evenly and firmly on to the racks. Roast for 20–30 minutes, depending on how well cooked you like your lamb. I usually opt for around 23 minutes, for nice pink lamb. If necessary, cover the crust loosely with foil towards the end of the cooking time, to prevent it from burning.

Let the meat rest for 5 minutes in a warm place. Bring it to the table uncut since, unless your knife is supremely sharp and you are very deft, the crust is bound to crumble as you carve. To serve, slice down between the cutlets, dividing each rack in half.

Grilled Figs with Orange, Honey and Pecan Sauce

This is a pretty, light pudding for early autumn, when purple or green figs are at their plumpest and most succulent. Blanch the zest and prepare the sauce in advance; then there is precious little to do when it comes to finishing the pudding for serving.

SERVES 4
1 orange
2 tablespoons honey
60 g (2 oz) butter
1 tablespoon icing sugar
5 cm (2 inch) fresh rosemary sprig
8 figs, halved
60 g (2 oz) shelled pecans
Single cream, to serve

Pare the zest from the orange and cut it into fine shreds (or use a zester). Blanch the shreds in boiling water for a minute, drain and repeat. Reserve. Squeeze the juice from the orange and place it in a pan with the honey, butter, icing sugar and rosemary. Stir over a low heat for 5 minutes, until smoothly mixed. Set aside until needed.

Shortly before you wish to serve, pre-heat the grill thoroughly. Brush the cut sides of the figs with a little of the sauce and grill until sizzling and lightly browned. Meanwhile, remove the rosemary sprig from the sauce, add the pecans and re-heat. Arrange the figs on individual plates, spoon some of the sauce around them and garnish with the blanched orange zest. Serve immediately, with single cream.

Pecan Tuiles

Pecans give these thin, lacy biscuits a subtle, buttery sweetness. Crisp and brittle, they are lovely served with creamy puddings or munched with coffee. Either way, they disappear very quickly.

MAKES ABOUT 12
120 g (4 oz) unsalted butter
120 g (4 oz) caster sugar
30 ml (1 fl oz) double cream
1/4 teaspoon vanilla essence
90 g (3 oz) shelled pecans, finely ground
60 g (2 oz) plain flour
A pinch of salt

Pre-heat the oven to 180°C/350°F/Gas Mark 4. Line several baking trays with non-stick baking parchment. Put the butter, sugar, cream, vanilla essence and ground pecans into a pan, with a pinch of salt, and place over a gentle heat. Stir continuously, until the mixture begins to boil. Immediately tip in the flour, mix in evenly and cook for 4 minutes, stirring continuously. Draw off the heat and leave to cool slightly. Drop teaspoonfuls on to the baking trays, leaving a good 7 cm (3 inch) gap between dollops, to allow for spreading.

Bake for 9–12 minutes, in relays, leaving a couple of minutes between each tray, until the edges are browned and the centre is a light golden tan. Now you have a choice. The easy route is just to leave the biscuits on the trays for about 3 minutes, until firm, and then lift them on to a wire rack to cool. If you want to be fancy, you can curve them into *tuiles* (the French for curved roof tiles). This second option looks good but demands split-second timing and is bound to leave a few broken biscuits in its wake – cook's perk. If you are aiming at curvaceous *tuiles*, cook only four biscuits on each tray. Once they're out of the oven leave to cool for 1 1/2 minutes. Then, while they are still soft enough to bend without cracking, drape each one over a rolling pin and curve it round. They'll harden up very quickly and can be removed after a minute or two. This is easy, once you get the knack and the right timing. The biscuits can be made in advance and stored in an airtight container.

flageolet beans

Flageolets are a small, elegant, pale green type of haricot bean. They bear the freshest, subtlest flavour of all the dried pulses and are very highly prized in France. Keep an eye out for the new season's haricot beans, only partially dried, if you are holidaying in France in August or September. They are the nicest of all. Otherwise, rely on dried flageolets or tinned ones, which I have a sneaking preference for. It goes back a long way. I can remember hiding an opened tin in a cupboard in my room when I was a child, to dip into secretly. Looking back, I'm sure that my mother would have been delighted to know that I longed for beans rather than sweets, but no doubt the secrecy was all part of the pleasure.

Buying and Storing Flageolets

Tinned flageolets are fairly widely available from supermarkets and delicatessens, and they make an excellent storecupboard stand-by for feeding unexpected guests, when you need a comforting treat, or just in case you get snowed in.

Dried flageolets also keep well stored in an airtight container and, like all dried pulses, they work out cheaper than the tinned ones. The younger they are, the better, since they will require less cooking. Look for a use-by date on any packet – the further it is away, the better.

Using Flageolet Beans

Ignore anyone who tells you that they don't need soaking. They do, and a full 8 hours or overnight is required. Drain them and cook them in plenty of fresh water adding, if you wish, a quartered onion and a few herbs, but no salt. Salt toughens up any dried pulse and flageolets are no exception. Don't slip in tomatoes or lemon juice, either, at this stage, since anything acidic also delays softening. Bring the unsalted flageolets to the boil, boil hard for 10 minutes and then reduce the heat and leave them to simmer until tender. Depending on the age of the beans, they will take 1–2 hours to become soft, mealy and perfectly cooked. Don't undercook them – too worthy tasting – and don't overcook them – too mushy. As they take rather a long time to cook, it is no bad idea to do double quantities. Unused beans freeze well and it's much quicker to defrost a batch than to cook them from scratch. If you want to replace dried beans with tinned or pre-cooked frozen ones in a recipe, you'll need about double the weight.

Flageolets are generally considered rather aristocratic beans, and the French pamper them with lots of butter or cream. You can serve flageolets just as they are, well drained and glossed with butter, or dress them up with cream sauces, garlic or tomato, or all three! They are delicious as a salad, either solo or mixed with other beans. Dress them while still hot, so that they absorb some of the dressing. Embellished with fresh tomato, grilled peppers, hard-boiled eggs and fresh herbs, the plain salad is transformed into a summery lunch dish.

Flageolets Maitre d'Hotel

A fancy name for flageolets dressed with butter, parsley and lemon. This is a lovely combination that brings a touch of class to, say, a few grilled lamb chops. Use the same *maitre d'hotel* butter to upgrade tinned flageolets.

SERVES 6

300 g (10 oz) dried flageolet beans, soaked overnight and drained
4 fresh parsley sprigs
1 fresh thyme sprig
2 garlic cloves, halved
Salt and pepper

For the maitre d'hotel butter:

75 g (2½ oz) butter
3 tablespoons finely chopped fresh parsley
½ tablespoon finely grated lemon zest
A generous dash of lemon juice

Put the flageolets into a pan with the parsley and thyme sprigs tied together with a piece of string, and the garlic. Add enough water to cover by about 5 cm (2 inches). Do not add any salt. Bring up to the boil, half-cover and simmer for 1–2 hours, or until very tender but not collapsing.

Drain the beans, reserving some of the cooking water, and discard the bundle of herbs and the garlic. If not using immediately, tip the beans into a bowl, add a little of their cooking water to moisten them, leave to cool and cover with cling film.

While the beans cook, mash the butter with the chopped parsley, lemon zest and lemon juice. Pile into a bowl and chill until needed.

Shortly before serving, put the beans into a wide shallow pan (a frying-pan is fine for this) and place over a moderate heat, with 2 tablespoons of their cooking water. Season with salt and pepper. Let them re-heat for a few minutes, tilting and shaking the pan so that they are evenly heated through. Dot the butter on to the beans in small pieces. Keep swirling and tilting and shaking the pan so that the butter melts into the beans appetizingly. Taste and adjust the seasoning and serve immediately.

Flageolet Beans in Tomato and Cream Sauce

A recipe that I unashamedly reprint (it appeared first in my *Ingredients Book*), because it is so very, very good. The cooked beans are re-heated in a rich tomato and cream sauce flavoured with rosemary, a combination that's hard to beat.

SERVES 8

340 g (12 oz) dried flageolet beans, soaked overnight and drained
1 bay leaf
2 fresh parsley sprigs
1 fresh rosemary sprig
5 garlic cloves, unpeeled
For the sauce:
½ onion, chopped
1 tablespoon butter
400 g (14 oz) tin of tomatoes or 500 g (1 lb 2 oz) fresh tomatoes, skinned and chopped
1 tablespoon tomato purée
1 large fresh rosemary sprig
½ teaspoon sugar
150 ml (5 fl oz) double cream
Salt and pepper

Cook the flageolets in fresh water with the herbs tied in a bundle with string, and the garlic, until tender. Drain and pick out the garlic and herbs. Reserve the garlic but discard the herbs.

To make the sauce, cook the onion gently in the butter. Add the tomatoes, tomato purée, rosemary, sugar, salt and pepper. Simmer for 10 minutes. Discard the rosemary.

Squeeze the reserved garlic cloves out of their skins and add to the sauce. Liquidize and sieve, or pass through the fine blade of a *mouli-légumes* (vegetable mill). Return to the pan and stir in the cream and the flageolets. Simmer gently for a few minutes, to heat through. Taste and adjust the seasoning and serve immediately.

green and brown lentils

Forget the cheerful yellow and red lentils that cook down to a soothing slush. The lentils of the moment are the drab green and brown types. Drab is not entirely fair. Some are indeed a muddy brown or a dull dark khaki, but others are blessed with deep tones of slatey blue, olive green or honeyed tan, quite beautiful in their dusky way. These are the lentils that hold their shape when cooked, swelling but not bursting (unless you boil them to death, that is) to a plump, earthy, soft deliciousness that anchors any dish firmly to real food.

Three specific varieties of green and brown lentil have taken pride of place on the shelves. Puy lentils reign like gods over the world of pulses. They are grown, indeed can only be grown because their name is protected by law, in the Auvergne around the town of le Puy, where they are cultivated and graded according to stringent standards. Unfortunately, a fair number of companies who should know better are passing off lentils grown elsewhere, particularly in Canada, as Puy lentils. I've cooked and compared so-called Puy lentils from around the world and, although they all tasted perfectly good, there genuinely was a difference and the finest were undoubtedly the real French ones.

Proper Puy lentils are, technically, green lentils but are actually tiny, slate-coloured speckled discs. They have a very fine skin (some cheaper lentils are thicker skinned) and a distinguished flavour. More obscure are the excellent lentils from Norcia in the Sibylline mountains of Italy. These are brown and small and, again, have a superior flavour. Finally, from Spain come larger, brown Salamanca lentils, highly favoured by the Spanish, though I have to say that I didn't find the taste justified the extortionate price.

Buying and Storing Lentils

Once you had to make your way to a wholefood store to find lentils. Now you can buy them at any supermarket worth its salt.

If you want to find out what all the fuss over Puy lentils is about, you'll have to track down the genuine article, which probably means a trip to a classy delicatessen (where you may also be lucky enough to happen across Salamanca lentils) unless you are lucky enough to come across them in a supermarket. Be suspicious. Search the packet for the country of origin and, if it isn't France, you will know you are not getting what you are paying for. Look again in chic general, or good Italian, delicatessens for the brown lentils from Norcia. If you can't find them near you, you'll probably have to wait until you can take a holiday in Italy, where they are far easier to find. Otherwise, ordinary brown or green lentils are still a good buy.

Store all lentils, once the packet has been opened, in an airtight container.

Using Lentils

These days, lentils have usually been thoroughly cleaned and picked over before packaging. If you buy them loose, though, give them a good rinse and hunt for small stones, grit and bits of stick. Lentils do not need to be soaked, though I suppose there's no harm in it and it may reduce the cooking time by a couple of minutes.

Cook them in plenty of water or stock if you prefer. Never add salt or anything acidic (lemon juice, vinegar or even tomatoes, for instance) to the pan, until the lentils are cooked to just the degree that you want. Other aromatics – onion, garlic and herbs in particular – are fine. Bring the lentils up to the boil, give them 5 minutes at a rolling boil and then continue cooking at a slower pace. It only takes some 15–20 minutes for them to simmer to a nutty firmness that suits some dishes, particularly salads. Give them another 10–15 minutes or so to render them soft and mealy, which transforms them into serious comfort food.

For a salad, lentils should be dressed while still warm and the dressing needs to be fairly assertive. Make the vinaigrette sharper than you would normally; the starchiness of the lentils will dampen it down. Add plenty of parsley or other herbs and lighten the salad, if you wish, with finely diced shallots, cubes of fresh tomato, or the sweetness of skinned, grilled red peppers.

Hot lentils love bacon, butter and parsley and need generous seasoning. Keep them moist, with a sprinkling of their cooking liquid, but don't let them drown. In the depths of winter, a steaming mound of lentils with grilled sausages and French mustard is to be relished. *Lentilles aux tomates* is simply cooked lentils re-heated with home-made tomato sauce (not too much of it – the lentils should predominate) until piping hot. It's another great winter warmer and, when it comes to winter warmers, lentils make a brilliant soup, too.

Lentilles aux Lardons et Saucisson à l'Ail

This is my kind of food. I love this sort of filling, solid, comforting fodder that is the mainstay of the French brasserie in the winter months. Here, the lentils are simmered slowly with a piece of bacon and a garlic sausage, absorbing their flavours. The salt of the meats and the wine slow down the cooking process, so that the lentils take longer to cook than they would normally. It's worth the wait.

SERVES 4, HEARTILY

300 g (11 oz) Puy lentils or other small, green lentils, rinsed
150 g (5 oz) meaty streaky bacon, in a single chunk, with rind
45 g (1 1/2 oz) butter
1 onion, chopped
2 garlic cloves, chopped
1 garlic sausage or rich pork boiling sausage
1 generous wine glass (200 ml/7 fl oz) red wine
1 bay leaf
2 fresh thyme sprigs
1 fresh parsley sprig
2 tablespoons chopped fresh parsley
Salt and pepper
French mustard, to serve

Rinse and drain the lentils. Carefully cut the rind off the bacon in a single piece and reserve it. Melt 30 g (1 oz) of the butter in a moderately large saucepan and fry the onion in it gently, until translucent. Add the garlic and the lentils and stir them about in the butter for a minute or so. Push the chunk of bacon, its rind and the sausage (pricked here and there with a fork and cut in half, if necessary) down into the lentils. Pour in the red wine and let it simmer for about 3 minutes. Add the herbs, tied in a bundle with string, pepper and enough water to cover by about 3 cm (1 inch). Bring up to the boil, reduce the heat, half-cover and leave to simmer for 50–60 minutes, or until the lentils and bacon are tender.

Discard the bacon rind. Lift out the bacon and sausage and keep them warm. Drain off most of the cooking liquid, leaving just enough to keep the lentils moist. Stir in the remaining butter and the chopped parsley. Taste and adjust the seasonings. Spoon the lentils into a serving dish. Slice the bacon and sausage and arrange them on top and serve with lots of French mustard.

Lentil Purée with Roast Carrots, Red Onions and Mint

'Baby food', my husband said, when he saw this, but that didn't stop him tucking in keenly. The smooth, earthy lentil purée, enriched with butter and a slug of cream, makes a brilliant backdrop for the sweetness of roast carrots and onions, finished with a breath of fresh mint. A good dish for vegetarians and any obdurate carnivores can be soothed with a grilled or fried sausage on the side.

SERVES 4

For the roast vegetables:

2 red onions, cut into 8 wedges each, slicing from stalk to root end
600 g (1 1/4 lb) carrots, halved (or quartered, if large) lengthways
3 tablespoons olive oil
2 teaspoons balsamic vinegar
1 1/2 tablespoons chopped fresh mint
Coarse salt and freshly ground black pepper

For the lentils:

220 g (8 oz) green or brown lentils
2 shallots, peeled and halved
1 large carrot, quartered
2 garlic cloves
1 bay leaf
2 fresh thyme sprigs
1 fresh rosemary sprig
1 fresh parsley sprig
30 g (1 oz) butter
2 tablespoons double cream
Salt and pepper
Fresh mint sprigs, to garnish

Pre-heat the oven to 190°C/375°F/Gas Mark 5. Put the onions and carrots in a shallow oven-proof dish, large enough to take them in a single, snug layer. Spoon over the oil and then turn the vegetables, so that they are coated in oil. Add 2 tablespoons of water and season with salt and a little pepper. Roast for 1–1 1/4 hours, basting from time to time, until the carrots and onions are tender and patched with brown. Drizzle over the vinegar and then stir in the mint. Taste and adjust the seasoning.

While the vegetables are cooking, put the lentils in a pan with the shallots, quartered carrot, garlic and 1.2 litres (2 pints) of water. Tie the herbs in a bundle with a length of string and pop those into the pan, too. Do not add any salt. Bring to the boil and simmer gently for about 45 minutes, until the lentils are very, very tender. Reserve a tablespoon of cooked lentils. Discard the herbs, and tip the rest of the contents of the pan into a food processor. Season with salt and pepper, add the butter, and process until smooth. Stir in the cream. Taste and adjust the seasoning.

Serve in shallow dishes, ladling some lentil purée into each dish, topping with carrots, onions and their juices and then scattering a few of the reserved lentils over and around the whole lot. Garnish with sprigs of mint.

chickpeas

All of a sudden, the two most fashionable styles of cooking in the capital's quicksand restaurant scene are 'Retro' (back to the seventies dinner party) and Middle Eastern. What bizarre bedfellows! Quite enough to raise a hollow laugh amongst those who have never given up on prawn cocktail or have long been influenced by the magic of the Levant's spicy, irresistible food. If Middle Eastern cuisine takes root as strongly as Thai has done, then sales of chickpeas will rocket sky-high. There isn't much call for them in Retro cuisine, but that's another story altogether. Until lately, chickpeas in this country have been stuck fairly firmly in the vegetarian-wholefood lodge, making only the occasional excursion, usually in the guise of hummus.

Chickpeas are widely cultivated, not only in the Middle East, but also in Mexico, India, North Africa and China, and have been known and grown for over seven thousand years. According to the late Tom Stobart, author of *The Cook's Encyclopaedia*, chickpea plants are 'sticky and secrete so much oxalic acid that walking through the crop can spoil your shoes'. A salutary warning.

Buying and Storing Chickpeas

The same rules apply to chickpeas as to other dried pulses, except more so. Since they take such a dismayingly long time to cook at the best of times, it is doubly important to buy new season chickpeas. Chickpeas that have been hanging around in a warehouse for a year or more will be quite edible, but they'll take even more simmering to pound them into tenderness. If nothing on the packet or bag indicates when they were harvested and dried, check the sell-by or use-by date, and make sure that it is as far distant as possible. And if there's no sell-by date, or you are buying them loose, ask when they came in. The finest chickpeas are the smallest ones, with the added bonus that they should be a little quicker to cook.

Chickpeas can be stored ad infinitum in an airtight jar or canister, as long as they are kept away from damp. Buy them in relatively small quantities and use up relatively quickly (i.e. within a couple of months, but don't let them drag into years).

Tinned chickpeas vary in quality, so it's worth shopping around and trying out different brands. They will, of course, keep for ages in the cupboard or larder.

Using Chickpeas

Dried chickpeas need to be properly soaked before use (at least 8 hours) and then they usually take around 2–3 hours to cook to a good tenderness. Some cooks like to add a little bicarbonate of soda to the water, but I've never found that this makes a significant difference either to cooking time or the degree of flatulence incurred. Never salt the water, or add anything acidic like tomatoes or vinegar to the pan, as all of these delay softening.

Tinned chickpeas are very welcome, but they honestly don't have the same flavour as dried ones and they do tend to be too soft and soapy. While they may be fine as an occasional shortcut, it does pay, just once in a while, to cook chickpeas from scratch. Always cook more than you need and freeze the rest for another occasion.

Chickpeas are used whole in soups and stews from many parts of the Mediterranean, and of course in Indian vegetarian curries, but my favourite chickpea dish has to be the Middle Eastern falafel, fritters of ground chickpeas, served with tahina (ground sesame seed paste) dip or hummus and salad packed into a hot pitta bread. This is one of the few dishes where you absolutely have to use dried chickpeas, and where they are cooked in a matter of minutes.

Chickpea flour is used in the South of France to make *socca*, a thin wide pancake, and again in Genoa to make *panissa*, chickpea chips. It resurfaces in India as *besan*, where it gives flavour and holds together deep-fried vegetable bhajis and pakoras.

Hummus bi Tahina

Is it worth making your own hummus? Now if you were to ask about taramasalata instead, the answer is an unhesitant, loud 'yes'. When it comes to hummus, I think that these days I have to admit to a rather quieter 'just about'. Commercial hummus is so good, for the most part, that there is no great impetus to cook up your own, but if you do have the time and you remember to put the chickpeas to soak the day before, you will end up with something even more delectable and more-ish than the best bought hummus.

SERVES 6–8

150g (5oz) chickpeas, soaked overnight
Juice of 2 lemons
2 cloves garlic, roughly chopped
4 tablespoons light tahina paste
A pinch of salt

To serve:

A little olive oil
Paprika or cayenne pepper
Ground cumin

Drain the chickpeas and put into a pan with enough water to cover by about 3 inches. Bring up to the boil and simmer gently until they are very tender, adding extra hot water if the level drops too low. Drain, reserving a little of the cooking water.

Put the chickpeas into the processor with 2 tablespoons of their cooking water, the garlic, lemon juice, tahina and salt. Process to a smooth cream, adding a little more of the cooking water if necessary. Don't leave it too heavy and claggy like damp clay – all too often the problem with home-made hummus. Taste and add more lemon juice or salt as needed.

Spoon into a bowl. Shortly before serving, drizzle a little olive oil over the top and dust lightly with a little paprika or cayenne and ground cumin. Serve with warm pitta bread or crudités, spoon over salads or serve with grilled fish, meat or vegetables. Thin down the hummus a little, if necessary, and use as a particularly wonderful dressing-cum-sauce.

Falafel

There's a street in Tel Aviv which is home to a clutch of falafel stalls, all vying to take the falafel makers' crown, all with their own courtiers and admirers. Were the falafel that I tasted here the best ever? I'm inclined to think so, though it may have been partly the fun of the occasion, and the enthusiasm of the hordes of falafel snackers around me that added an extra dose of deliciousness.

Falafel are deep-fried balls of ground chickpeas flavoured with garlic and parsley. Cheap snack food in the Middle East, they're now becoming rather fashionable in this country. Unfortunately, they are all too often rather poorly made – too large and stodgy, or cooked far too early and reheated in the microwave, which makes them soggy and greasy. They should be crisp on the outside, soft on the inside. Piled hot from frying into a warm pitta bread, with simple fresh salad and oodles of tahina dressing to smooth the whole lot together, they are quite sensational. If you want a rather more refined presentation, dispense with the pitta bread (or serve this on the side), and arrange the falafel on a bed of salad, drizzling the tahina dressing over the top. Perch a sprig or two of coriander on top, and tuck a wedge of lemon in, too.

If you must cook the falafel themselves in advance, re-heat them in hot oil to restore the crisp exterior.

SERVES 4–8 DEPENDING ON HUNGER AND GREED

8 pitta bread, warmed through in the oven or under the grill
4 tomatoes, deseeded and roughly chopped
1/2 cucumber, peeled and diced
6 cos or webb's or other firm lettuce leaves, shredded
Salt and pepper

For the tahina dressing:

180g (6oz) light tahina paste
3 cloves garlic, crushed
juice of 1 1/2–2 lemons

For the falafel themselves:

220g (8oz) chickpeas, soaked for 24 hours in cold water
1 tablespoon cumin seeds
2 teaspoons coriander seeds
1 small onion, chopped
2 cloves garlic, chopped
3 heaped tablespoons chopped fresh coriander
1 tablespoon flour
1/4 teaspoon baking powder
Salt and pepper
Sunflower oil for deep frying

To make the falafel, begin by draining the chickpeas and tipping them into the bowl of a processor. Dry-fry the cumin and coriander seeds in a small heavy frying pan over a high heat until they turn a little darker and their scent wafts through the kitchen. Cool and grind to a fine powder. Process together until smooth. To test for seasoning, break off a small knob of the mixture and shallow fry in a little oil. Taste and add more spices or salt if needed. Wet your hands and roll the remaining mixture into small balls – no bigger than a walnut, and even smaller for a higher ratio of crisp exterior to soft interior. Set aside until you are ready to fry them.

To make the tahina dressing, put the tahina into a bowl with the crushed garlic and lemon juice. Start to mix, gradually beating in enough water to make a creamy mixture with the consistency of double cream (90–150ml or 3–5 fl oz should be about right). Don't worry that the tahina seizes up like cement at first. Keep adding water and beating and it will smooth out. Season with salt, and add a little more lemon juice if needed. Cover and set aside until required.

Put the pitta in a low oven to warm through and place tomato, cucumber and lettuce in individual bowls on the table so that everyone can help themselves. Heat up a panful of sunflower oil (I actually use my wok for most deep frying) over a moderate heat, until a small cube of bread dropped into the oil sizzles immediately, but doesn't start to brown straight away. Fry the falafel a few at a time, taking care not to overcrowd the pan. When they are richly browned (they should take about 8 minutes – any quicker and the interior won't be properly cooked), drain briefly on kitchen paper. Season with a little salt and take to the table for everyone to start making up their pittas, while you cook the remaining falafel.

The rough order to fill pitta breads is this: slit open the pitta bread along one of the long curved sides, first put a little of the diced tomato in and maybe a shred or three of lettuce. Now drop in four or five falafel, then drizzle over some tahina. Then add some more tomato and cucumber and stuff in more lettuce and finish with more tahina dressing if you can!

dried cherries

prunes

Hunza apricots

sweet things

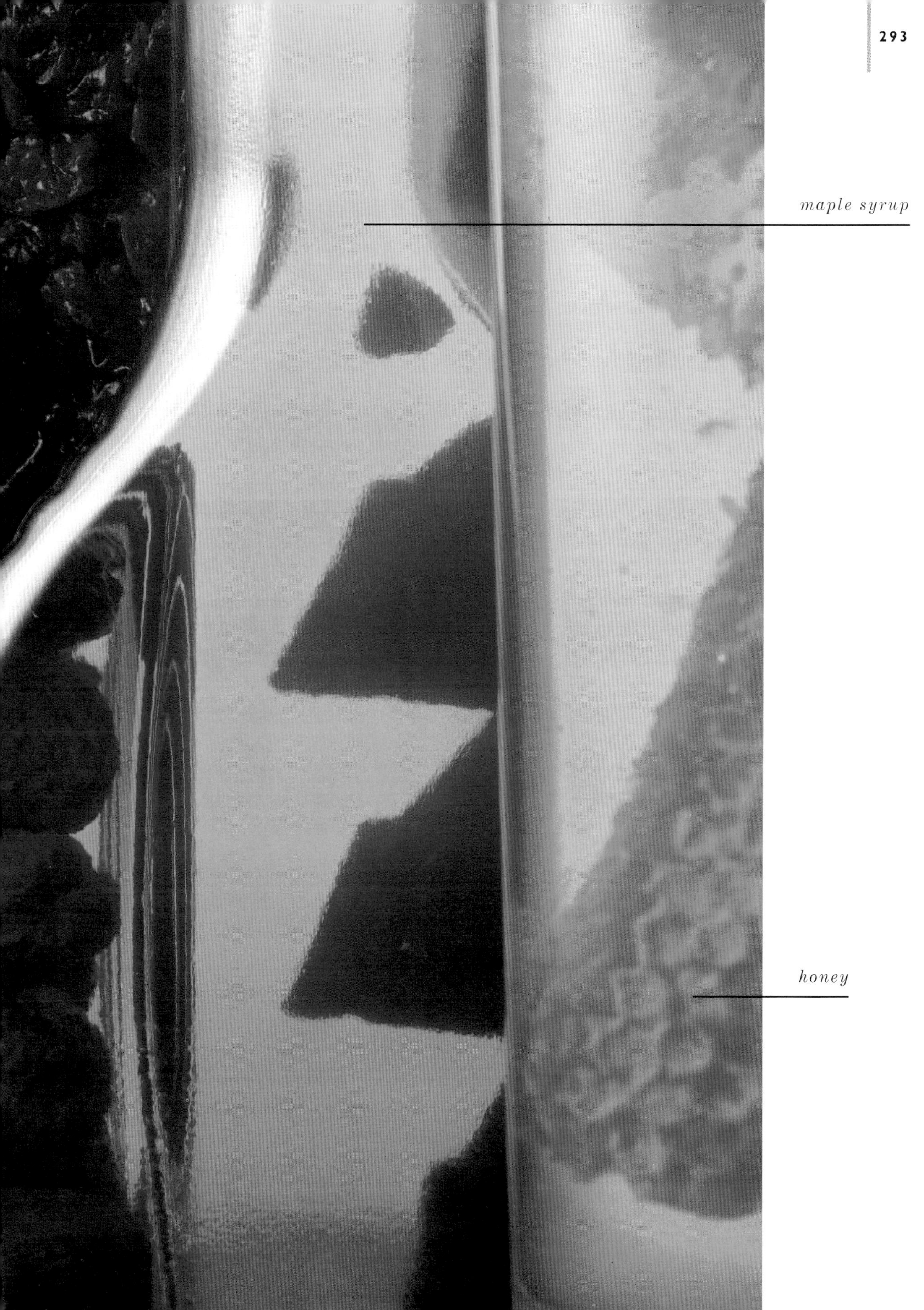
maple syrup
honey

maple syrup

Maple syrup is a product that has barely changed since time immemorial. When the first European settlers arrived in North America, they described the way that the Native Americans around the Great Lakes and the St Lawrence River drew 'sweet water' from the trees and boiled it down to a syrup over wood fires. And that's about it. Still. To this day. Simple technology has brought more certainty to the method and greater yields per tree but, when it comes down to it, maple syrup is nothing more than evaporated sap.

You wouldn't want anything else, anyway. Fake maple syrups, sometimes sneakily called 'maple-flavoured syrups' with the word 'flavoured' in small print tucked discreetly between the maple and the syrup, are not worth buying. They have a distinctly unpleasant undertaste and you would do far better with a jar of runny honey. Real, 100 per cent pure maple syrup is like nothing else, one of the all-time great, voluptuous, sticky, sophisticated, rich, finely scented sweeteners you can lay your lucky hands on. It doesn't come cheap, but pour it over a tower of hot buttermilk pancakes oozing melted butter, fill your mouth with a heavenly syrupy forkful and I bet you'll reckon that it is worth every last penny.

The states of Vermont and New York are America's main producers of maple syrup but Canada, in particular Quebec, could wash them away with its tidal wave of the stuff. The sapping season comes towards the end of winter, when the first signs of spring are in the air. Nights are still bitterly cold but the days are noticeably warmer and the sap begins to flow through the trees in preparation for the new season. Sugar maples and black maples produce the most sap. The Norway maple comes hot on their heels in third place. The larger the diameter of the trunk and the greater the spread of the foliage, the more sap the tree will yield.

It is collected, traditionally, by drilling holes into the trunk 5–8 cm (2–3 inches) deep and no more, so that the tree is not damaged – and pushing spiles (spouts made of wood or metal) into the holes. A bucket is slung underneath and regularly emptied as the level of clear liquid rises towards the brim. A healthy tree can produce around 12–16 gallons of sap, which sounds a lot until you realize that it takes a good 35 gallons or more to make one lone gallon of maple syrup.

In the sugarhouse, the sap is boiled down in great big open vats until it reaches the required density. Nothing remains now but to filter and bottle it. And with the syrup all in the can, comes the 'sugaring-off party': a celebration not only of a successful harvest but also of the end of winter. In the past, the *pièce de résistance* of the party was 'sugar on snow': '... Grandma stood by the brass kettle and with the big wooden spoon she poured hot syrup on each plate of snow. It cooled into soft candy, and as fast as it cooled they ate it ... there was plenty of syrup in the kettle and plenty of snow outdoors' (Laura Ingalls Wilder, *The Little House in the Big Woods*). To make 'sugar on snow', or maple taffy, boil maple syrup to 22–40 degrees above the boiling point of water, in other words to 235–250°F, somewhere between the soft-ball and hard-ball stages. To judge this, drip a little syrup into a cup of cold water; it should form a coherent ball which can be rolled between your fingers and feels soft or hard, whichever you prefer. Then ladle it out on to pans of clean, fresh snow. As they say in the Ontario Maple Syrup Producers Association (OMSPA) booklet, 'When this chewy, ice cold concoction is eaten with a spoon or a clean stick, its flavour is unsurpassed in the way of sweet treats.'

Buying Maple Syrup

Always double-check the lable. If there is an ingredients list then it isn't pure maple syrup. Once you've established that there is nothing unwanted in the bottle or can, you may have come to the end of the road. It is rare to come across much of a choice of syrups in this country but, if you can see the syrup itself, you will be able to tell a little more about it. The lighter the colour, the more delicate the flavour, and it is these 'light amber' or 'fancy' syrups that are recommended for pouring on pancakes or waffles, or over ice creams. Darker, glowing, hazelnut-coloured syrup – if it is Canadian it will be graded as Canada No. 2 Amber – has a stronger flavour, which makes it a better bet for cooking.

Storing and Using Maple Syrup

Unopened maple syrup will keep almost indefinitely in a dark cupboard (don't worry about any crystals that may form) but, once opened, it should always be stored in the fridge.

The simplest way to use maple syrup is as a pouring sauce over ice creams, pancakes, French toast, rice pudding or whatever you fancy. For a fancier touch, warm it gently and add a shake or two of rum. Go cautiously when you use it in cooking. Too much maple syrup can overwhelm. Regard it first and foremost as a flavouring. The Ontario Maple Syrup Producers Association gives this advice on substituting maple syrup for ordinary sugar: 1 1/2 cups of maple syrup is the equivalent of 1 cup of ordinary sugar, that is 1 1/2 times the volume provides the same degree of sweetness. When used in baking, you should also add 1/4 teaspoon of bicarbonate of soda for every 250 ml (9 fl oz) of maple syrup. When substituting maple syrup for half the sugar (more might be too much), reduce other liquids by one-quarter. All very mathematical, but easier in practice than it sounds in theory.

Maple and Walnut Parfait

This is a spectacularly good, light, frozen mousse. Maple syrup and walnuts go very well together but for an all-American parfait, you could substitute pecans.

SERVES 6
60 g (2 oz) walnuts
200 ml (7 fl oz) maple syrup
1 egg white
240 ml (9 fl oz) double cream
Salt

Pre-heat the oven to 200°C/400°F/Gas Mark 6. Spread the walnuts out on a baking sheet and toast them in the oven for around 5 minutes or so, until browned, checking once or twice to make sure they don't burn. Tip into a wire sieve and shake off all the loosened, papery skin. Cool and chop roughly.

Heat the maple syrup to boiling point. Meanwhile, whisk the egg white with a pinch of salt until it forms soft peaks. Gradually pour in the very hot syrup, whisking constantly. Continue whisking until you have a thick, stiff meringue. Use an electric whisk, if you have one, as this doesn't happen instantly by any means. Leave to cool.

Whip the cream until just stiff and then fold it into the maple meringue. Finally, fold in the nuts. Spoon into a dish and freeze; there's no need to pay it any attention while it freezes because all that whisking and cream guarantees a smooth, creamy ice cream. Transfer to the fridge to soften half an hour before serving.

Buttermilk Pancakes with Maple Syrup

To be frank, there is no better way to enjoy maple syrup than poured straight over hot pancakes, like these American buttermilk ones. They are good plain and possibly even nicer with blueberries. For breakfast, serve sausages as well (that's right – as well as the syrup, though you might be wise to dispense with the blueberries). A brilliant combination.

SERVES 4–6
220 g (8 oz) plain flour
1 teaspoon baking powder
1 teaspoon bicarbonate of soda
1/4 teaspoon salt
1 tablespoon caster sugar
450 ml (16 fl oz) buttermilk
2 eggs
2 tablespoons melted butter
100 ml (3 1/2 fl oz) milk
200 g (8 oz) blueberries (optional)
Oil or clarified butter, for greasing
Butter and lots of maple syrup, to serve

Sift the flour with the baking powder, bicarbonate of soda and salt. Mix in the sugar. Mix the buttermilk with the eggs and butter. Add the dry ingredients and stir until more or less smooth (don't worry about the odd small lump). Stir in the milk and then the blueberries, if using.

Heat a heavy cast-iron frying-pan or griddle over a medium heat. Brush with a little oil or clarified butter. Ladle about 2 tablespoons of the batter per pancake on to the griddle. Turn when the bubbles are all rising to the surface and bursting and the underneath is nicely browned. Cook briefly on the other side until hazelnut brown. If the pancakes seem a bit flabby and the bubbles are having trouble rising, thin the mixture down with a little water or extra milk. Serve the pancakes piping hot, smeared with butter and smothered in maple syrup.

Maple Beans with Smoked Ham Knuckle

Based on a recipe from the Ontario Maple Syrup Producers' booklet of maple syrup recipes, this is an unusual take on slow-cooked beans, sweetened with the syrup, salted with the juices of the ham and spiced up with Tabasco sauce. The fruity apple slices bring all the elements of the dish together, so don't be tempted to leave them out.

SERVES 6

500 g (1 lb 2 oz) dried *cannellini* beans, soaked overnight
1 large onion, chopped
4 garlic cloves, sliced
2 fresh thyme sprigs
1 large fresh rosemary sprig
1 bay leaf
4 strips of lemon zest
1 ham knuckle, soaked overnight
150 ml (5 fl oz) maple syrup
1–1 1/2 tablespoons Tabasco or other chilli sauce
1 tablespoon Dijon mustard
Salt and pepper

For the topping:

3–4 eating apples, cored and cut into 8
30 g (1 oz) butter, softened

Drain the beans, put them into a pan and cover them with fresh water. Bring up to the boil and boil hard for 10 minutes. Reduce the heat and simmer until properly tender – about 45–60 minutes. Drain, reserving the cooking water. Pre-heat the oven to 150°C/300°F/Gas Mark 2.

Put half the beans, together with half the onion and garlic into a large, ovenproof casserole. Tie the herbs together with a piece of string and tuck them in, too. Bury two of the strips of lemon zest in the beans. Lay the ham knuckle on top and then cover with remaining beans, onions, garlic and lemon zest. Mix the syrup, Tabasco or chilli sauce and mustard and pour them over. Season lightly with salt and pepper and then pour over enough of the reserved cooking water to barely cover. Cover the casserole tightly and bake for 3 hours.

Arrange the apple pieces decoratively over the beans; you may not need them all. If there is rather too much liquid left in the dish, just scoop a little out so that the apples can perch more comfortably. Dot with butter and return to the oven for a final hour until the apples are tender. Serve piping hot.

Maple-Glazed Shallots

These sweet, buttery shallots serve as a kind of relish, rather in the style of fashionable onion marmalades and go well with dark game meats, such as venison or grouse, or with boiled gammon or ham.

SERVES 4–6
600 g (1 1/4 lb) small, round shallots, peeled
60 g (2 oz) butter
3 tablespoons maple syrup
2 tablespoons lemon juice
Salt and pepper

Leave the shallots whole. If some of them are much larger than others, remove the outer layers to reveal twin inner shallots of a more equal girth. Melt the butter in a heavy pan, large enough to take the shallots in a single, snug layer. Fry the shallots in the butter, until patched with brown – about 5 minutes. Drizzle over the maple syrup and stir for around 1 minute. Now add the lemon juice, salt and pepper and enough water just to cover. Bring up to the boil, then reduce the heat and leave to simmer gently, stirring every now and then, until the shallots are very tender (add a little more water if necessary) and there is only a thin layer of syrupy liquid left in the pan. This will take around 30–40 minutes. Re-heat when needed (they will keep in the fridge, covered, for two or three days).

Canadiana Sauce

An almost instant sauce from the OMSPA booklet.

SERVES 6
300 ml (10 fl oz) whipping cream
130 ml (4 1/2 fl oz) maple syrup
85 ml (3 fl oz) rye whiskey

Whip the cream and slowly fold in the maple syrup and rye whiskey. Serve over hot puddings.

honey

When I was 18, I moved to London and my first bedsit. As bedsits go, it was rather a fancy one – pleasant, airy and bright, with huge windows looking out over the trees and flowers of a private square. I remember only two drawbacks. The major one was the sordid state of the shared bathroom. The second was my landlady's bees, which all too frequently forsook the pleasures of the great outdoors for a lengthy and fruitless buzz around my territory.

Beehives and their occupants, it seemed to me at the time, belonged firmly in some pastoral idyll, far away from the bedlam of the city. After all, that's part and parcel of the romance and allure of honey – a nostalgic picture of happy little honey bees busily working their way through flower-strewn meadows. That landlady, and more recently James Hamill, bee-keeper *extraordinaire*, have shown me the error of my ways. Urban honey is in no way inferior to rural. In fact, those busy little town bees are having a ball. There they are, surrounded by hundreds of small and occasionally large gardens all jam-packed together, not to mention the parks and tree-lined avenues. A paradise with endless blossom, from early spring right through to the late autumn.

It wasn't until I met James, however, that I began to understand my landlady's fondness for her bees. His erstwhile hobby has taken over his life and he now runs The Hive, in south London, a shop dedicated to honey and bee-keeping. Togged up like a soft-shell astronaut, covered reassuringly from head to foot, I strode quietly but confidently (at least that's how I hoped it looked) towards a half-dozen of his hundred or so urban hives, clustered together in the middle of a stretch of south London allotments. Within minutes, I found myself holding a wooden frame, packed with honeycomb but almost invisible through the mass of bees crawling over its surface. James talked me straight into the magic of bees. The social structure of each hive is phenomenal, the way it conducts its business truly remarkable. The details are riveting and copious, but suffice it to say that, within a couple of hours, I was on the verge of laying down a deposit on a hive and the full bee-keeper's rig. I didn't quite make it that time but, one day, I think I might well take the plunge.

One single fact struck me with more force than any other. The bees do not sip nectar at random from just any flower. Oh no, far too undisciplined. Forager bees fly out from the hive to reconnoitre the area, spreading their search for up to three miles. On their return, they perform a special dance to tell their co-workers which flowers are the best bet. A democratic decision is taken and, from then until they have worked them to the limit, the bees from that hive all concentrate single-mindedly on one type of flower and one only. That is how we get single-flower honeys – perhaps apple blossom in the spring in this country, or orange blossom in warmer climates. Each type of honey is uniquely flavoured and readily distinguishable.

Buying and Storing Honey

Cheaper, commercially blended honeys are absolutely reliable, tasting exactly the same from one jar to another, but there is always the risk that they have been heated during the blending process, and heat destroys the finer aspects of any honey, leaving it duller and more commonplace. More expensive and more rewarding are the regional and single-flower honeys. Just as wine depends on grape variety, so the main characteristics of honey – flavour, colour and consistency – are dictated by the type of flower the bees sup on. Mother Nature ensures that these characteristics vary from terrain to terrain and year to year.

Specified area honeys, such as Jura, Gatinais or Schwarzwälder, depend on the unique local flora for their individuality. Naturally, this allows for a fair amount of variation from one producer to another, but the wild, herb-strewn *maquis* of Provence will yield up a honey that is very different to that of a northern European forest.

When it comes to single-flower honeys, I have a preference for the strongly flavoured. I love the almost burnt, deep richness of chestnut flower honey, or the aromatic scent of lavender honey, perfectly balanced with a shot of acidity, or the resinous clarity of lime flower (*tilleul*) honey. Apple flower honey is more fragrant, perfect for toast and crumpets.

Honey can be stored anywhere that is neither damp nor in direct sunlight. Indirect light doesn't hurt it, nor does warmth. It is only humidity that can do lasting damage, as it allows the honey to ferment and bubble and deteriorate. So keep the jar tightly sealed and don't let stray drops of breakfast tea or orange juice anywhere near.

All honeys, by the way, begin life runny and clear and gradually crystallize to a firm set, cloudy state. It is easy to reverse the process, though not so easy to speed it up. To restore set honey to its runny state, bring a pan of water to the boil, draw it off the heat and sit the jar in the water. Leave for half an hour or so (renewing the hot water, if necessary) until the honey flows clear.

Using Honey

Honey and butter soaking down into thick slices of toasted bread, dripping stickily down chins and fingers ... doesn't that take you back? Honey for tea is a must, but don't leave it at that. For quick puddings, drizzle honey – Greek Hymettus honey in particular – over thick Greek yoghurt and scatter with raisins and pine nuts, walnuts or pistachios. Even better, hide a sliced banana underneath the yoghurt.

No reason, though, not to get more out of that jar of honey. After all, honey was once the only sweetener, used in cooking right around the world before sugar became readily available.

Sadly, high heat destroys the subtler, distinctive nuances of fine honey, so where it has to undergo prolonged heating there's no point in wasting your very best, delicate honey. One with a strong flavour will stand the heat far better. The favourite option, though, is to add the honey right at the very end of the cooking time, wherever possible, so that it stays true.

In terms of sweetness, four parts honey is roughly equivalent to five parts sugar. Theoretically, if you replaced the full 100 g or 5 oz of sugar in a cake recipe with 80 g or 4 oz honey, reducing the liquid content a touch to compensate for the extra moisture, the cake would end up equally sweet. In practice, however, the flavour would probably be too intense for most people's taste. Keep enthusiasm for honey in check, using it modestly and with restraint.

Sweetening cakes and breads partially with honey will make the finished item more moist and a moist cake or bread keeps longer.

Honey Fudge Sauce

The best honey fudge sauce in the world is made by James Hamill's wife, Ute, and is sold in small jars from their shop, The Hive. They guard the recipe jealously and couldn't be persuaded to part with it. I hope they'll forgive me for imitating it. This may not be quite as wicked as Ute's but it is still outrageously silky, rich and gooey. Try it over ice cream or sliced bananas, with a slick of cream to cap it all.

Small jars of honey fudge sauce make very welcome presents.

SERVES 6–8

110 g (4 oz) raisins
4 tablespoons rum
60 g (2 oz) butter
85 g (3 oz) caster sugar
60 g (2 oz) light muscovado sugar
110 g (4 oz) honey
100 ml (3½ fl oz) evaporated milk

Soak the raisins in the rum for at least 24 hours – if you have time, soak them in enough rum to cover in a sealed jar for a month or two.

Put the butter into a heavy-bottomed pan with the caster sugar, muscovado sugar and honey. Stir over a low heat, until the butter has melted and the sugar has dissolved and everything is evenly mixed. Stir for about 4 minutes, always over a low heat. Stir in the evaporated milk, a little at a time, and then stir in the drained raisins. Bring back to the boil, still stirring, and then draw off the heat and stir for a minute or two more. If not using immediately, spoon into a hot, sterilized jam jar (see page 124), seal tightly and leave to cool. Once opened, store in the fridge where it will keep for up to 2 weeks (or possibly longer, but I couldn't tell you because we couldn't keep our hands off it any longer).

Almond, Honey and Ricotta Cheesecake

A virginal white cheesecake with a hint of lime sharpness, a delicate waft of honey and finely chopped almonds to give it some texture. The crème fraiche topping is one of those easy touches that worries many people as they can't see how it could possibly set solidly. Don't let it worry you – it does set as it cools and gives a silky, rich finish.

SERVES 8

200 g (7 oz) digestive biscuits, finely crushed
110 g (4 oz) butter, melted
For the filling:
85 g (3 oz) almonds, toasted
450 g (1 lb) ricotta
3 eggs, separated
5 tablespoons runny honey
2 tablespoons caster sugar
finely grated zest and juice of 1 lime
½ teaspoon vanilla essence
A pinch of salt
For the topping:
300 ml (10 fl oz) crème fraiche
1 tablespoon vanilla sugar
Toasted flaked almonds
A few fine strands of lime zest

Pre-heat the oven to 190°C/375°F/Gas Mark 5. Mix the crushed digestives thoroughly with the butter and press them evenly into the base of a 5 cm (2 inch) deep, 20–22 cm (8–8½ inch) tart tin or cake tin with a removable base, spreading them slightly up the sides. Bake for 10 minutes and then leave to cool.

Grind the almonds to a coarse powder in a food processor until finely chopped. Beat the ricotta until smooth and then beat in the egg yolks, honey, sugar, lime zest and juice, vanilla essence, salt and, finally, the almonds. Whisk the egg whites until they form stiff peaks, then fold into the ricotta mixture. Spoon into the crushed digestive case. Bake the cheesecake for 25–35 minutes, until almost set but with a very minor wobble in the centre. Take out of the oven and let it stand for 5 minutes.

Mix the crème fraiche with the vanilla sugar, then pour over the cheesecake and spread out evenly. Return to the oven for 10 minutes. Leave to cool in the tin and then chill for 4 hours. Run the blade of a knife, dipped first into hot water, around the edge, then unmould. Decorate with flaked almonds and lime zest, and serve.

Grilled Lamb Chops in a Honey and Ginger Marinade

Unlike prawns (see recipe below), lamb with honey sounds like quite a reasonable proposition – and indeed it is. Serve these with noodles tossed in a little sesame oil.

SERVES 4

4 lamb chops

Oil

For the marinade:

2 tablespoons honey

1 teaspoon finely grated fresh ginger

1 garlic clove, crushed

2 tablespoons soy sauce

1 fresh red chilli, de-seeded and finely chopped

3 fresh thyme sprigs, bruised

3 tablespoons sunflower oil

Mix all the marinade ingredients and pour over the lamb chops. Turn the chops so that they are nicely coated and then leave to marinate for at least an hour, turning occasionally.

Pre-heat the grill thoroughly, and line the grill pan with foil. Brush the rack with a little oil. Grill the chops for about 4–5 minutes on each side, until browned and crusty outside but still pink and juicy inside. Serve immediately.

Stir-Fried Prawns With Honey and Spices

This is a marvellous treat of a first course or light main course for a special occasion. I can see that you might have doubts. I quite agree that honey and prawns don't sound too promising together but, believe me, in this instance, it is a combination that works. The honey plays a relatively quiet, but not unimportant, role tempered by the saltiness of soy sauce, garlic and spices. This is definitely not breakfast with prawns on top.

For a starter, serve the prawns just as they are, with some good bread to mop up the juices. For a main course, serve them with rice and maybe some stir-fried mangetout or broccoli.

SERVES 4

16 large, raw, shell-on prawns (tiger prawns or king prawns)

1 1/2 tablespoons sunflower oil

For the marinade:

2 generous tablespoons honey

4 tablespoons dry sherry

2 tablespoons dark soy sauce

1/2 teaspoon Chinese five-spice powder

2 garlic cloves, finely chopped

2.5 cm (1 inch) piece of fresh ginger, grated

Mix together the marinade ingredients and pour them over the prawns. Turn to coat evenly, then cover and marinate for at least an hour, or longer, in which case, be sure to put them in the fridge. If necessary, bring back to room temperature before cooking. Turn the prawns once in a while as they marinate.

Take the prawns out of the marinade. Heat a wok or a wide frying-pan over a high heat until it smokes and then add the oil. Give it a couple of seconds, then add the prawns and stir-fry for about 1 minute, until they have all turned pink. Pour in the marinade and 2 tablespoons of water. Let the liquids bubble down until they are well reduced and syrupy, stirring constantly – a matter of a few minutes – and serve immediately.

Don't forget to pass round plenty of napkins for all those sticky fingers.

Hunza apricots

From far away in the Hunza valley in Pakistan come some of the most unprepossessing-looking of dried fruits. They also happen to be one of the most delicious, guarding their secret well inside a pale tan, wrinkled and utterly unremarkable exterior. Hunza apricots are all too easy to overlook but don't be fooled. Buy them when you see them in healthfood and wholefood shops, soak them in just enough water to cover for a couple of hours and then simmer gently in their soaking water for just long enough to soften them. Scoop the apricots out of the cooking water into a dish, boil down the liquid until reduced and slightly syrupy, then pour back over the apricots and leave to cool. Your faith and patience will be rewarded tenfold. With no need for any added sugar, the apricots will taste so scented and heavenly sweet that you will be quite bowled over. All in all, a brilliantly easy pudding, lovely with Greek yoghurt or crème fraiche. Next morning, invert the proportions and spoon any left-overs over larger helpings of yoghurt, or eat with cereal. And, if patience is your virtue, there's one more well-guarded secret. Crack open the stones and the inner kernel is as sweet and nutty as an almond.

If you want to go one step further along the creative pudding road, sieve the cooked apricots and mix the purée with a little whipped cream, to make a fool; for an ice cream, mix with an equal quantity of whipped double cream and freeze.

Opposite *Stir-fried Prawns with Honey and Spices*

prunes

I've always harboured a fondness for prunes and I've never understood what others held against them, though I have profited from their dislike: at primary school, I bartered my roast potatoes for stewed prunes and I reckon I got the best of the bargain. I suppose I was lucky, for my early introduction to prunes came in France, where they rate them highly as one of life's rare affordable and unsinful pleasures. The highlight of my prune education was the annual outing to a glamorous patisserie in Tours, to buy their most exquisite *pruneaux fourrés de Tours* – plump, jet-black prunes stuffed with apricot and almond pastes, glazed to a high gloss with apricot gel. They were mightily expensive and worth every last centime.

Those prunes were a hangover from the days when Tours lay at the centre of a prosperous prune-making area (other prune dishes remain as evidence, including a strange-sounding but excellent stew of eel, bacon and prunes). Now it is the district around Agen, in the south-west of France, which reigns supreme. The extra summer warmth produces a plum that is gorged with sweetness, balanced with a dose of tartness, which is exactly what is called for whether it is to be eaten fresh or dried.

The plum in question is the *prune d'Ente*, a purple-skinned fruit said to have been brought to France by crusaders returning from Syria. In 1856, this same variety was taken over to California by a Frenchman, Pierre Pellier, for his brother Louis, who had abandoned the search for gold but found his fortune as a nurseryman. Within 50 years, some 90,000 acres of plums were being grown for drying. Now California produces 70 per cent of the world's prunes.

A few years ago, a French prune producer admitted to me, ruefully, that he didn't think you could tell the difference between a first-class *pruneau d'Agen* and a first-class American prune. You may come across prunes from other countries, but they are unlikely to have undergone the rigorous quality controls that are implemented by both Californian and French producers.

Buying and Storing Prunes

The very choicest of all French prunes are sometimes sold like handmade chocolates, arranged plumply in pretty boxes, perfectly wrapped to preserve their moisture and with a price tag to make you shudder. These are luxury grade prunes, to be eaten, just like chocolates, one by voluptuous one.

Even for more everyday purposes, though, I like my prunes big. I like them to look glossy and sleek and pampered and I like to be able to dip into the bag or box and eat them as I cook. This means the top grade, ready-to-eat prunes, which have a residual moisture of around 29–35 per cent.

Having said that, I recently bought a packet of old-fashioned, almost totally dehydrated prunes. Soaked for 24 hours in brandy and a sugar syrup, they tasted sensational, quite good enough to serve up as a sophisticated pudding on their own. I usually buy prunes with the stone in but I suspect that this is a personal foible. I don't think there can really be much to be gained from it, if the prunes are to be stoned anyway. Possibly the stones may impart a modicum of flavour when the prunes are cooked whole, but I'm not entirely convinced of that. The one thing that can be said for them is that they hold their shape better over prolonged cooking.

Once the bag or wrapping has been breached, the prunes should be kept in an airtight container. As most prunes these days have a relatively high moisture content, they will not keep indefinitely. It's probably best to eat them up within a week or so, or to expose them to the air and let them dry out naturally.

Using Prunes

Most modern prunes will not need soaking but that doesn't mean that you should never soak them. The old fashioned habit of soaking dried fruit in tea is worth retaining, as long as you use good tea. Prunes soaked overnight in Earl Grey, for instance, will take on some of the bergamot fragrance of the tea and will swell to a melting plumpness. Come September or October, I occasionally fill a Kilner jar loosely with prunes and then cover with two-thirds brandy and one-third sugar syrup. By Christmas, they are absurdly, beautifully boozy and make a tremendous grown-ups-only pudding, spooned over vanilla ice cream or with a scoop of mascarpone.

Prunes, like fresh plums, are very good with all kinds of meat. In France, they bring their sweetness to rabbit, chicken and pork stews; in Scotland, they are essential to that great soup, *Cock-a-Leekie* (see page 307). Delicious, too, cooked in patés (replace the olives with stoned prunes in the recipe for *Chicken and Pork Paté Studded with Olives* on page 255–6 and you have a completely different, and equally good, dish) or made into a compote (stewed prunes with a little wine vinegar added to the cooking liquid to sharpen slightly) to serve alongside a bought paté.

When stewing prunes for puddings, do it with care and thought. Badly stewed or, worse still, slimy, tinned school prunes have put so many people off for life. Simmer them briefly, perhaps in a light sugar syrup flavoured with a cinnamon stick or a vanilla pod; or go for something grander by using a sweet wine like the very reasonable, raisin-scented Moscatel de Valencia. The alcohol will evaporate as it is boiled, so even children can eat the prunes if they like the taste. And, memories of school again notwithstanding, properly stewed prunes served over a bowlful of creamy, properly made rice pudding, are a dream.

It has been discovered (by the Californian Prune Growers' marketing people, not surprisingly) that puréed prunes can replace fat in baking. I've tried this with chocolate brownies; it worked and they tasted marvellous (prunes and chocolate are great together). I can't vouch for it in other baked goods but, if you are on a low-fat diet, you might want to give it a try one day.

Prune and Chocolate Tart

This is a tart to dazzle and delight, a grand finale to a dinner party and proof positive, if it is needed, that prunes are no joking matter. On a base of crisp *paté sablée* pastry, runs a layer of dark prune purée, covered discreetly with a baked mousse of dark chocolate. Serve it warm or chilled, with whipped cream, crème fraiche or mascarpone.

SERVES 10–12

For the pastry:

210 g (7½ oz) plain flour

75 g (3 oz) icing sugar

150 g (6 oz) unsalted butter

2 small egg yolks

A pinch of salt

For the prune purée:

280 g (10 oz) stoned, ready-to-eat prunes

2 tablespoons brandy

For the chocolate filling:

100 g (3½ oz) plain chocolate, broken into squares

3 eggs, separated

300 ml (10 fl oz) double cream, lightly whipped

90 g (3 oz) caster sugar

Icing sugar, to decorate

To make the pastry, sift the flour with a the salt and the icing sugar. Process the dry ingredients, with the butter and egg yolks, to form a soft dough. Scrape the dough out on to a floured work surface and knead it very briefly, to smooth out. Then roll it into a ball, wrap in cling film and chill in the fridge for at least half an hour.

Put a baking sheet in the oven and pre-heat it to 180°C/350°F/Gas Mark 4. Roll out the dough on a well-floured surface and use to line a 25–28 cm (10–11 inch) tart tin. Don't worry if the pastry tears; just patch up holes or splits with the trimmings and no one will be any the wiser. Prick the pastry base and leave it to rest again in the fridge for half an hour.

Line the pastry case with greaseproof paper or foil, weight it down with baking beans and bake blind, on the hot baking sheet, for 20 minutes. Remove the paper and beans and return to the oven for about 10 minutes to dry out, without browning.

Meanwhile, make the prune purée by putting the prunes into a pan with barely enough water to cover. Bring to the boil and simmer for 5–10 minutes, until the prunes are very tender. Lift out with a slotted spoon and process the prunes with the brandy and just enough of their cooking liquid to make a thick purée (some 2–3 tablespoons). Spread over the base of the pastry case.

To make the chocolate layer, chop the chocolate roughly and put it in a bowl, set over a pan of gently simmering water, making sure that the base of the bowl does not come into contact with the water. Lift the bowl off the pan as soon as the chocolate has melted. Cool slightly and then beat the egg yolks in, one by one. Fold in the cream. Whisk the egg whites until they form soft peaks. Sprinkle over the sugar and then whisk until pale and glossy. Fold into the chocolate mixture. Pour into the pastry case and smooth down lightly. Bake at the same temperature for about 40 minutes, until puffed, and set around the edges but still very slightly wobbly in the centre. Take out of the oven and serve warm or cold, lightly dusted with icing sugar.

Cock-a-Leekie

Once of Scotland's finest culinary creations and more than a match for the haggis, even if it does sound the most unlikely collection of ingredients. *Cock-a-Leekie* requires long simmering but very little effort. You must use whole prunes, with stones in. Stoned prunes will go mushy at best and may well collapse. *Cock-a-Leekie* actually tastes much better if re-heated the day after it is made though, inevitably, you lose some of the freshness of the sliced leeks.

SERVES 8

1 kg (2¼ lb) piece of shin of beef
2 bay leaves
2 fresh thyme sprigs
4 fresh parsley sprigs
1 kg (2¼ lb) leeks
1 large free-range chicken
675 g (1 lb 8 oz) prunes with stones in
Salt and pepper
Chopped fresh parsley, to garnish

Put the shin of beef into a large pan and add enough water to cover it generously (at least 3.5 litres/6 pints and probably more, depending on the shape of your pan). Tie the herbs together with a piece of string and drop those in, too. Trim and clean half the leeks, leaving them whole. Tie them together with a piece of string and tuck them into the pot alongside the beef. Bring up to the boil, skim off any scum, season with salt and pepper and then leave to simmer for 2 hours. If the water level drops, exposing the beef and leeks too much, top up with hot water. Skim again, if necessary.

Now add the chicken and continue simmering for another hour or so, until the chicken and beef are very tender. Lift out and discard the bundles of herbs and leeks.

While the meats are cooking, trim and clean the remaining leeks and slice them into rings about 1.5 cm (½ inch) thick. Add these and the prunes to the broth, once you have discarded the tired bundle of whole leeks. Leave to simmer for another 30 minutes.

Some 5 minutes or so before the soup has finished simmering, lift out the chicken and beef and cut the meat into small pieces discarding the bones and carcass. Return to the pan of simmering soup (or to a warmed tureen, if you are dishing this up smartly). To serve, ladle the soup into big soup plates, making sure everyone gets a good share of meats, prunes and leeks. Scatter with a little chopped parsley and serve.

Prunes Cooked in Marsala and Orange

Most of the alcohol is cooked off but the taste remains in this upmarket version of stewed prunes. Stewed really is quite the wrong word in this case, since the prunes are cooked very briefly and then left to absorb the scent of their syrup over a period of time.

SERVES 4
2 oranges
300 ml (10 fl oz) Marsala
140 g (5 oz) demerara sugar
1 cinnamon stick
450 g (1 lb) prunes, weighed with stones in, soaked if necessary
300 ml (10 fl oz) whipping cream, to serve

Pare four strips of orange zest from one of the oranges, then squeeze the juice from both fruit and place in a pan, with the strips of zest, Marsala, sugar and cinnamon stick. Bring up to the boil, stirring until the sugar has dissolved. Leave to simmer for 5 minutes and then add the prunes. Simmer for another 5 minutes and then draw off the heat, tip into a deep serving bowl and leave to cool.

When cold, cover and chill in the fridge for at least 24 hours (the prunes will keep, and improve, for at least 6 days and perhaps longer).

Shortly before serving, whip the cream with 2 tablespoons of the syrup from the prunes, until it just holds its shape. Spoon the prunes into individual glasses or pretty bowls and top with a swirl of whipped cream. Serve at once.

chocolate

I am an out-and-out chocolate snob but I am also a chocolate slob. For cooking, I refuse to use anything but the classiest, darkest, most expensive, highest-quality chocolate but, when I'm feeling tired or lacking in energy and in need of a boost, it is cheap milk chocolate bars that I crave. When I met Nicola Porter, the founder of the Chocolate Society, I didn't dare admit that only the day before, after long hours of filming, I'd fallen upon the spoils from a stop at a motorway service station and made a lunge for a bar of what she would dismiss as mere confectionery and not real chocolate at all.

Before you get the wrong idea, let me assure you that this ambassadress for fine chocolate is not remotely intimidating. I joined her at a primary school, where she was teaching a class of enthralled seven-year-olds the ins and outs of chocolate, from the cocoa pod itself to the finished article, and beyond to the sticky world of truffle-making. She had them literally and metaphorically eating out of her hand. She explained why cheap chocolate leaves a greasy feeling in the mouth (because it is made with low-cost vegetable fats instead of pure cocoa butter) and gave them samples to try. Even those young children could tell which was which.

She drew them into the sheer heaven of rolling and coating truffles in chocolate, without batting an eyelid as more and more of the chocolate spread its way over hands and table, working its way into little mouths as the truffles became ever stickier and more uneven. By the end of the day, the little mites were thoroughly gorged with chocolate and chocolate know-how, but mercifully – amazingly – none of them had been sick, or at least not in school grounds.

I hadn't realized that chocolate is as absorbent of strong smells as a dry sponge is of water. You should never start making truffles or chocolate mousse straight after breakfast if you've just burnt the toast or if you've slapped on an over-generous measure of perfume or, worse still, if someone is smoking or has just stubbed out a fag. All of these smells will work their way into the chocolate, lingering on to taint the finished product. Nor had I known that the way to be sure that an unwrapped square of chocolate contains cocoa butter instead of vegetable fats is to clasp it firmly between finger and thumb for a few seconds and then look to see if a fingerprint lingers – a sure sign of high quality.

Buying and Storing Chocolate

There is no real difference between cooking chocolate and eating chocolate. What is sometimes sold as 'cooking chocolate' is just plain, bitter chocolate, usually of high quality, with relatively little sugar in it, which connoisseurs would consider a prerequisite for any fine chocolate. There is a big difference between chocolate and such things as 'chocolate-flavoured coating'. Anything with the word 'flavoured' in it is bound to be a second-rate imitation and is best left well alone.

For cooking, always buy chocolate with a high percentage of cocoa solids. Cocoa solids include both the dark cocoa mass and the pale cocoa butter. The more there are of the pair, the less room there is for extraneous matter. As you cook, you'll be adding lots of other ingredients that will soften and dampen the flavour, so you must start with a powerfully strong, pure chocolate which can hold its own. The percentage of cocoa solids is marked clearly somewhere on the wrapper of every bar of chocolate and most supermarkets sell their own brands of 'de luxe cooking chocolate', which contain around 70 per cent cocoa solids. Check, too, that the chocolate is flavoured with real vanilla and not the synthetic vanillin. Spanish or Latin American chocolate may be scented with cinnamon instead of vanilla.

The really grand chocolates may even specify the type of cocoa bean they are made from. Criollo is reckoned to be the *grand cru* and comes with a correspondingly high price tag.

Unopened, chocolate will keep well for weeks, if not months, as long as it is stored in a cool spot away from humidity. If you have some left over after cooking, eat it. If restraint is your forte, wrap it in foil and return it to the cupboard, but use it up within a week or two.

Using Chocolate

Melting chocolate is easy but has its pitfalls. Begin by breaking it up into squares, or, better still, chopping it in a food processor, which will speed up the melting considerably. Put the squares or chopped chocolate in a bowl and set it over a pan of gently simmering water, making sure that the base of the bowl does not come into contact with the water. Stir every now and then and lift the bowl off the heat the moment the chocolate has all melted. If the chocolate overheats, it will seize up like cement and the whole lot will have to be binned. A safer method still is to microwave it in a bowl covered tightly with cling film. Heat it in short bursts on half power, giving it a stir between bursts, until runny.

Guard fiercely against water once the chocolate has melted. One drop can be enough to curdle the chocolate to a useless graininess. If you want to incorporate a liqueur, say, put it into the bowl *before* melting the chocolate and stir occasionally as it heats. Once the chocolate has melted, you must incorporate something fatty, like butter or egg yolks, to stabilize the mixture before trying to mix in liquids.

Chocolate Meringue Cake with Cherries and Mascarpone

It is a shame that Black Forest gateau has been so bastardized and ruined by commerce, since cherries and chocolate are a natural partnership. Raspberries, too, go blissfully well with chocolate. This chocolate cake, slathered with rich mascarpone and fruit, is even more indulgent than a proper Black Forest gateau. The cake is crisp and meringue-like on the outside and fudgey with chocolate on the inside. All in all, this makes an indecently rich and wicked pudding. For an even fudgier interior, but a slightly less crisp top, leave the cake to stand overnight covered with a clean tea-towel. If you don't like mascarpone, just serve with whipped cream alone.

SERVES 8

For the cake:

110 g (4 oz) plain chocolate
110 g (4 oz) unsalted butter, softened
3 eggs, separated
30 g (1 oz) plain flour
110 g (4 oz) caster sugar

To serve:

150 ml (5 fl oz) whipping cream, whipped
220 g (8 oz) mascarpone
450 g (1 lb) cherries, stoned, or raspberries

Opposite *Chocolate Meringue Cake with Cherries and Mascarpone*

Pre-heat the oven to 170°C/325°F/Gas Mark 3. Line the base of a 19–20 cm (7½–8 inch) cake tin with a circle of non-stick baking parchment and butter the sides generously.

For the cake, break the chocolate into squares or chop it in a food processor and melt it (see page 310). As soon as it has melted, take the bowl off the heat. Beat in half the butter, a little at a time, and then the egg yolks.

Blend the flour with the remaining butter until soft and evenly mixed and stir into the chocolate mixture, until completely amalgamated. Whisk the egg whites until stiff, add half the sugar and whisk again, until shiny and thick. Fold in the remaining sugar. Lightly fold the meringue into the chocolate mixture and pour into the cake tin. Stand the tin in a roasting tin half-filled with hot water and bake for 1¼ hours. Remove from the oven and leave to cool. Turn out just before serving.

Fold the whipped cream into the mascarpone. Either pile high on the cake and top with a tumble of cherries or raspberries, or arrange slices of cake on individual plates, with a large dollop of mascarpone cream and a generous mound of fruit scattered over. Devour.

Chocolate-Chilli Glazed Pork

Before you throw up your hands in horror at the title, read the rest of this paragraph. This recipe was invented by that truly original chef, Paul Gayler, for his book *Great Value Gourmet (Meals and Menus for £1)* published by Weidenfeld & Nicolson. It sounded so weird that I had to try it. It's fabulous, as it turns out. Everyone in our house pooh-poohed the idea as I was cooking (we suffered a lot of jokes about puddings and pigs) but the ribbing (get it?) stopped once it was cooked. In fact, an appreciative silence descended and, within a remarkably short time, the dish was empty. Be bold and give it a try. You'll be amazed.

SERVES 4

675 g (1 lb 7 oz) pork belly, cut into 3 cm (1¼ inch) strips
4 fresh red chillies, de-seeded
2 tablespoons clear honey, warmed
50 g (2 oz) plain chocolate, melted (see page 310)
Salt and pepper

Pre-heat the oven to 200°C/400°F/Gas Mark 6. Season the pork, lay on a rack in a roasting tin, and then roast it in the hot oven for 30–35 minutes, until golden brown.

Meanwhile, in a liquidizer, blend the chillies and the honey. Add the melted chocolate and process again to mix.

Remove the pork from the oven and drain off the fat. Brush the meat generously all over with the chocolate glaze and return to the oven for 10 minutes. Serve on a bed of crisp vegetables, stir-fried with a little ginger.

dried cherries

Fresh cherries can be sweet or sour, so it's only logical that the same goes for dried cherries. For once, logic works smoothly. Drying accentuates many of the keynotes of any fruit and dried sweet cherries can be as sweet as any raisin. The sour ones, though, have more character by far; they are pleasingly tart with a glorious concentrated cherry flavour that is brilliant in savoury dishes, particularly with fatty meats such as lamb, pork, duck or goose, or with game, particularly grouse and venison. Sweet or sour, dried cherries can also be chewed straight from the packet and, these days, you can even get them ready-stoned, so no one can complain that the ratio of flesh to stone seems mean.

Dried cherries used to be almost impossible to find. They were a treat to be sought out while travelling in the Middle East or in America. I once hauled back two years' supply of dried sour cherries from the fabulous market in Tel Aviv. These days, you don't have to trek halfway round the world to find them. Good general delicatessens may well stock them and they are sold by several of the larger supermarket chains. Modern dried cherries retain a greater degree of residual moisture than traditionally dried fruit but they still benefit from a good soaking, to swell them up before use. The soaking liquid should be incorporated into the sauce or stew, so as not to waste an iota of flavour. To make a compote of dried cherries (sour ones to go with meat; sweet to serve over rice pudding, ice cream or Greek yoghurt), simmer the cherries in their soaking liquid for 5 minutes and then stir in sugar to taste and simmer for another 5 minutes, until syrupy. You might like to sharpen a compote for meat with a dash of balsamic or sherry vinegar, or to flavour a sweet one with a cinnamon stick.

suppliers

This is just a small selection of the many suppliers of high-class ingredients that now abound in this country. It is highly selective, but may be of use when you are trying to track down a special ingredient (most of the suppliers will send goods by post), or if you just happen to be passing close by.

BLUEBERRIES

TREHANE CAMELLIA NURSERY
Stapehill Road
Hampreston
Wimborne
Dorset BH21 7NE
Tel: 01202 873490
Contact: Jeremy Trehane
Pick your own blueberries. Will send blueberry bushes by post, with instructions on how to grow them.

CHILLIES

PEPPERS BY POST
Sea Spring Farm
West Bexington
Dorchester
Dorset DT2 9DD
Tel/Fax: 01308 897892
Contact: Joy and Michael Michaud
Mail-order fresh chillies in season.

COOL CHILE CO.
PO Box 5702
London W10 6WE
Tel: 0171 229 9360
Dried Mexican chillies and other hard-to-find Mexican ingredients by post.

COUSCOUS

LE MAROC
94 Goldborne Road
London W10
Tel: 0181 968 9783
An Aladdin's cave of a Moroccan grocery, selling all kinds of couscous, olives, *smen*, tagines and *couscoussiéres*.

HONEY

THE HIVE
53 Webb's Road
London SW11 6RX
Tel: 0171 924 6233
Contact: James Hamill
Honey, honey, honey everywhere. Plenty to eat, wicked Honey Fudge Sauce and Chocolate Honey Fudge, honey soaps and literature, cards, bee-keeping equipment, and even a full working beehive behind glass!

INDIAN CHUTNEYS

MRS BASSA'S INDIAN KITCHEN
Unit 133
Wandsworth Workshops
86–96 Garrett Lane
London SW18
Tel: 0181 871 4460
A small mother-and-daughter business, making some of the best Indian chutneys available. The coriander chutney is sensational, but it was the lime pickles that sent me into ecstasy. They will send any of their chutneys by post.

SALT COD AND SALTED PILCHARDS

THE PILCHARD WORKS
Tolcarne
Newlyn
Cornwall TR18 5QH
Tel: 01736 332112
The last surviving Cornish pilchard factory and a fascinating working museum – here Nick Howell makes his superior wet-cured salt cod (and ling and pollack, too) but to buy any of his products by post, get in touch with Cornish Fish Direct.

CORNISH FISH DIRECT
The Pilchard Works
Tolcarne
Newlyn
Cornwall TR18 5QH
Orders: Tel/Fax: 01327 263438
Mail-order fish company, specializing in high quality, amazingly fresh, Cornish inshore fish. Can also supply wet-cured salt cod and salted pilchards. I will come clean and admit a family interest – my husband is Nick Howell's partner in CFD.

GOATS' CHEESE

NEAL'S YARD DAIRY
17 Shorts Gardens
London WC2H 9AT
Tel: 0171 379 7646
Fax: 0171 240 2442
Neal's Yard Dairy has long been a beacon amongst cheese shops, pioneering our own fine home-produced farm cheeses, including many good goats' cheeses. The cream of the crop, if you'll excuse the pun. They will deliver by mail order.

MANGOES

LEON'S FOOD STORE
78 Soho Road
Handsworth
Birmingham B21 9BN
A tiny Afro-Caribbean grocery which always has a good selection of mangoes.

AIR-DRIED HAM

RICHARD WOODALL
Lane End
Waberthwaite
Nr. Millom
Cumbria LA19 5YJ
Tel: 01229 717237
Long-time curers of traditional York-style hams, Woodall's also make fine air-dried Parma-style hams. Since they also run the village post office, mail order is no problem.

CHOCOLATE

THE CHOCOLATE SOCIETY
Clay Pit Lane
Roecliffe
Nr. Boroughbridge
N. Yorks YO5 9LS
Tel: 01423 322230
Fax: 01423 322253
Contact: Nicola Porter
For the finest chocolate, plus a regular chocolate bulletin and chocolate events, look no further than the Chocolate Society.

SPICES

THE SPICE SHOP
1 Blenheim Crescent
London W11 2EE
Tel: 0171 221 4448
A tiny shop, jam-packed full of spices from floor to ceiling. Conveniently situated opposite Books for Cooks if you need a few recipe ideas.

OLIVE OILS AND VINEGARS

THE OIL MERCHANT
47 Ashchurch Grove
London W12 9BU
Tel: 0181 740 1335
Some of the finest olive oils (including Granverde Colonna lemon olive oil) and vinegars (including balsamic and sherry vinegar), all available by post.

FRESH OLIVES DIRECT
PO Box 25
Goring
Reading RG8 0YU
Tel/Fax: 01865 201046
As well as the most addictive range of olives, this company also mails out excellent olive oils and balsamic vinegars.

WILD MUSHROOMS

TASTE OF THE WILD
31 London Stone Business Estate
Broughton Street
London SW8 3QJ
Tel: 0171 498 5654
This is the retail and mail-order branch of Wild Harvest, specializing in fresh and dried wild mushrooms.

index